Professional ADO RDS Programming with ASP

John Papa, Matt Brown, Charles Caison, Peter DeBetta and Eric Wilson

Wrox Press Ltd. ®

Professional ADO RDS Programming with ASP

wrox

Published by Wrox Press Ltd.
se, 1102 Warwick Road, Acock's Green, Birmingham, B27 9BH, UK
Printed in Canada
ISBN 1-861001-64-9

Trademark Acknowledgements

Wrox has endeavored to provide trademark information about all the companies and products mentioned in this book by the appropriate use of capitals. However, Wrox cannot guarantee the accuracy of this information.

Credits

Authors
John Papa
Matt Brown
Charles Caison
Peter DeBetta
Eric Wilson

Development Editor
Anthea Elston

Editors
Joanna Mason
Ian Nutt

Technical Reviewers
Robert Chang
Jason Cropley
Alex Homer
Robert MacDonald
Craig McQueen
John Mendler
Boyd Nolan
David Sussman
Andrew Zack

Cover
Andrew Guillaume
Concept by Third Wave

Design/Layout
Tony Berry

Index
Diane Brenner

About the Authors

Johnny Papa (a MCP, MCT and MCSD) is a trainer and a developer with Blue Sand Software, Inc in Raleigh, NC where he specializes in DNA architecture developing in VB, ASP, ADO, MTS, RDS, SQL Server and DHTML technologies. Johnny has co-authored several books including Sam's SQL Server 6.5 Programming Unleashed and the upcoming 7.0 release of the same title. In addition, he often contributes articles to Visual Basic Programmer's Journal (VBPJ) and Microsoft Internet Developer (MIND) and speaks at various industry technical events.

Johnny prides himself on his close knit family and attributes all that he has become and all that he will achieve to God, his parents John and Peggy, and his loving wife, Colleen. You can contact him at **johnp@bluesand.com** or through **http://www.bluesand.com** on the Internet.

Matt Brown is a technical consultant and trainer for DBBasics in Raleigh North Carolina. He lives with his vivacious wife Karen and his children: Matthew, Erin, and Dominic. In his spare time he enjoys sleeping, reading, eating large quantities of meat, long walks and sunsets. In his spare time he resents having to shave and bathe, but does so on a regular basis. Among Matt's favorite authors are Robert Silverberg, Ayn Rand, and Guy Gavriel Kay. Matt wishes to make mention of and thank: Gary Kohan, Tim Waters, and his father Al Brown. You can send email to Matt at **Mattbr@hotmail.com.**

Charles Caison is an instructor with DBBasics Corporation (**http://www.dbbasics.com**). He has been involved in Windows development since 1992. He is a contributing author to Visual Basic Programmer's Journal, Windows NT magazine, Microsoft Interactive Developer and other industry publications. He also speaks at Microsoft Developer Days and other industry events. You can reach him at **charlesc@dbbasics.com**.

Eric Wilson is an MCSD and an MCT. He is also the President and founder of Web Basix, Inc (**http://www.webbasix.com**) specializing in business applications for the Internet/Intranet. Eric himself specializes in Client/Server Development for LAN/WAN and Internet applications. He also teaches Visual Basic, Visual InterDev and SQL Server. You can reach him at **ericw@webbasix.com.**

Peter DeBetta has been programming for 19 years, exploring a variety of languages, and has now come to work primarily with Visual Basic, VBScript, JavaScript, and Microsoft SQL Server. He has been published in "Microsoft Internet Developer", "Visual Basic Programmer Journal", and has even been the lead author on the "SQL Server 6.5 Programming Unleashed" book. Peter is a consultant, developer, and teacher with Blue Sand Software, Inc. out of Raleigh, NC. If you would like to reach Peter, just send him an email at **peterd@bluesand.com.**

Acknowledgements

Foremost, I would like to thank my family. To my wife, Colleen, thank you for supporting me through long nights and endless weekends of preparing this book. You are my rock, which without, I would certainly fall. To my mother, Peggy, thanks for everything you've inspired me to become and especially for the support and the enduring love you've freely given. Although it may seem otherwise at times, I'll always love you. To my father, John, I can only hope to become half of the man you are. You are my best friend and I am very proud to be your son. To my sisters Julie, Sandy, Laurie and Debbie, thank you for staying so close. Our family is the source from which I have always drawn my strength. And to my Kadi girl, for keeping me company on long nights of writing. Without you all, I could never have come so far.

I'd like to thank Carole Bohn for supporting my dreams and visions. You've been a good friend to me. I'd also like to thank Erik Johnson, Brian Sokolowski, Byer Hill, Saju Joshua and Bruce Suitt; good friends who inspired ideas for contributions to this book through our conversations. To Charlotte Taber, Jim Matthews and Timoth Lederman at Siena College, thanks for preparing me for my future - you are not forgotten. And to all of the students who sparked my mind in new avenues, thank you all.

When Peter, Eric, Matt and Charles and I started this venture, we didn't realize how many people it takes to make a book get on the shelves and into your hands. And we'd like to thank Anthea Elston and her staff at Wrox for putting the personal touch, even across the seas, into this hectic business. We'd also like to thank the editors who helped make our vision a reality. Without them, we couldn't have made this book the successful tool that it has become.

To Peter DeBetta, a wonderful friend, partner, colleague and fellow Robert Frost fanatic; a special thank you for getting me involved in my first book. I would also like to thank Eric, Matt and Charles. These guys spent countless hours of effort to bring this work together and to your desk.

And to those who I have not mentioned here but have made a lasting impression on this book, thank you for your contributions. The fact that you're reading this book is a testament to the people who inspired us, the authors, to reach out and write this book.

Without the publishers, editors, reviewers and all of the family, friends and colleagues who inspired us, this book simply wouldn't have existed. Thank you all.

--Johnny Papa

"Two roads diverged in a wood, and I --
I took the one less travelled by,
And that has made all of the difference."
--Robert Frost

Dedication

This book is dedicated to my wife Colleen, who taught me how to live and love and is expecting our first child. Thank you for being my partner in this world. --Johnny Papa

Table of Contents

Table of Contents

Table of Contents

Introduction

What is this Book About?

ActiveX Data Objects (ADO) 2.0 is the latest data manipulation toolset for the development of enterprise business solutions. ADO 2.0 is an integral component in enterprise business solutions, including Internet/intranet applications, as it combines high-speed data access and flexible data structure with its simple interface. **Remote Data Services (RDS)** is a high-performance client-side data-caching technology that transports data in intranet/Internet solutions. The real power of RDS is derived from its foundation: ADO. Using RDS and ADO in ASP yields powerful Web-based solutions that can be built upon a multitude of data resources.

This book exploits the real world experiences of expert ADO/RDS trainers and developers who know how to squeeze the most out of these hot topics. It helps to jump-start development by assuming that the reader has a basic knowledge of ASP, VBScript and SQL. As a result, the examples will start off short, tight and to the point to express the ADO/RDS techniques. Then the topics will expand into real world scenarios to show how flexible and powerful ADO and RDS can be, using screenshots accompanied by code samples.

The implementation of ADO sometimes differs slightly, depending on the data provider. This book concentrates on using ADO with ASP to access data in a SQL Server database. There are also two chapters that focus on data access with an Oracle database, including sample code and descriptions.

The book offers a straightforward explanation of the ADO/RDS toolsets, including all details of properties, methods and events of the object models. The material includes discussion of each tool's features and the practicalities and pitfalls of using them in real Web-based scenarios. You can try the examples out for yourselves, by downloading the reusable code samples from the Wrox Press website (more on that below).

Why Should I Read This Book?

One of the most powerful features of web technology is that we can create web pages dynamically using data from a database. If you're a web developer, the chances are that you're being asked – increasingly – to tie more data from databases to your web pages. ASP and ADO are the most popular tools that are being used to achieve this task. ADO is the premier data access technology – in version 2.0, it has been greatly enhanced.

RDS is a little known feature that is growing in popularity. Because it allows us to pass recordsets over a network or the Internet (using DCOM or HTTP, respectively), developers are beginning to realize its potential.

This book looks at using the features of ADO and RDS to handle real world issues. Of course, we'll show you the syntax – we must, or we wouldn't be giving you a complete ADO book. But most importantly, we will show you how to make these features an integral part of your web applications.

The background to the book is this. My fellow authors and I have been working on web projects involving these technologies since the advent of ADO and ASP. As you'd expect, we were often (*too often!*) asking questions to which no book, magazine article or web site documentation could provide the answer. The available ADO reference materials were virtually useless when it came to solving complex programming issues – especially when they involved Oracle! The only solution was to gain expertise by researching these problems for ourselves.

Now, questions like 'How do you create a client-side pick list in RDS?' and 'How do we create disconnected recordsets that persist?' are common questions that are posed to us by our students and colleagues. Thus, we decided to gather all of the practical knowledge we've learned from our programming experiences into this book.

You can see that this book came from a real world Web programming environment combined with the ideas from training numerous developers in these topics. You know the topics in this book are useful, because they all came from real problems in real applications that we've all hit.

So why should you read this book? Because we've got the answers to some of the tough ADO and RDS questions that you're puzzling over right now.

What Will I Learn from This Book?

This book contains practical examples that are intended to jump-start you in the areas you need. You can skip right to a specific chapter and reap its benefits. We have also included reference material in the appendices, so that the book serves as a complete solution.

You'll find real insight into the problems facing programmers today. I find that the majority of my students don't only want to hear about the theory – they want to know how they can program what they need to accomplish their "real-world" scenarios. So, while most books give you the definition of what a tool or technology is, we'll take that idea one step further – by providing you with insight on *why* you should care about these technologies and *how* you can use them to implement your solutions.

Chapter 1 is an introductory chapter that briefly discusses ADO's basic features, and goes on to give you a glimpse and a map to the focus of this book. In Chapters 3 and 4 we move on to lay the foundation of ADO, by describing the Connection and Command objects. We lay the groundwork for the Recordset object in Chapter 5. In Chapters 6–9 we go into extensive detail on the features of the Recordset object, and we use code samples and syntax to see how we can reap its benefits. We'll look at types and locations of cursors, locking strategies and batch updating. We also add to these basic features by including real world uses for custom recordsets that you can create without a database connection, the hierarchical recordset feature (introduced in ADO 2.0) and disconnected recordsets.

In Chapters 10–13 we move on to the RDS features and how we can use them to implement business solutions. We'll do the groundwork first, before focusing in on remote instantiation of objects, the Tabular Data Control, and how RDS and DHTML can work together.

And we don't stop there! In Chapters 14 and 15, we've included coverage on using Oracle with ADO. From an ADO point of view, Oracle has always worked slightly differently than SQL Server. Now, with the embrace of OLE DB providers, it is more important than ever to know the key points of how to code against an Oracle database and its stored procedures. We've also included a quick reference to Oracle in Appendix F.

Who is this book for?

The book is not intended as a quick reference, or a beginner's introduction to RDS and ADO. Rather, we go straight to intermediate and advanced web programming topics. The book is designed to be a hardcore concentrated programming book for anyone who programs using ADO/RDS 2.0 with ASP.

Because of the advanced nature of some of the topics, we do assume a basic knowledge of SQL and ASP.

What this book doesn't cover

For the purposes of this book, we will cover how to program ADO from a scripting language on the server (such as in ASP), or on the client (in a browser). However, this book doesn't cover how to program ADO from within languages such as Visual Basic. We propose to cover the syntax and implementation of ADO in VBScript in ASP for the main chapters of the book, without detailing any other language implementation. Because we will also be concentrating on RDS, which is entirely supported by Microsoft's IE browser, we will be consistent by only covering VBScript on the client. This provides a smooth and consistent way of demonstrating the features of ADO and RDS in ASP.

ADO 2.0 fully integrates several events into its arsenal. However, events are of limited usefulness in a stateless environment such as ASP; therefore the discussion of these events will be kept to a minimum (Appendix A).

Samples and Updates

We provide the source code for the samples you'll see in this book on our web site; and if you don't fancy installing them on your own server, you can also run most of them directly from our site. To access the main samples menu page for this book, you have two choices. You can navigate to `http://www.wrox.com`, follow the **Source Code** link and select **ADO RDS Programming with ASP**, or you can navigate directly to `http://webdev.wrox.co.uk/books/1649/`. This second option also contains a range of other resources and reference material that you might find useful – articles, links to useful websites, and information on other books that demonstrate how to apply ASP in different settings.

If you plan to run the samples yourself, download the `.zip` file and extract all the files to a virtual directory set up on your web server.

Conventions

We have used a number of different styles of text and layout in the book to help differentiate between the different kinds of information. Here are examples of the styles we use and an explanation of what they mean:

Advice, hints and background information comes in this type of font.

Important pieces of information come in boxes like this.

Bullets appear indented, with each new bullet marked as follows:

- ❏ **Important Words** are in a bold type font
- ❏ Words that appear on the screen, in menus like the <u>F</u>ile or <u>W</u>indow, are in a similar font to that which you see on screen
- ❏ Keys that you press on the keyboard, like *Ctrl* and *Enter*, are in italics

Code has several fonts. If it's a word that we're talking about in the text – for example, when discussing the **For...Next** loop – it's in a bold font. If it's a block of code that you can type in as a program and run, then it's also in a gray box:

```
Response.Write("Hello World")
```

Sometimes you'll see code in a mixture of styles, like this:

```
<%
   Dim strLastName
   strLastName = Request.Form("LastName")
   Response.Write("Your surname is " & strLastName)
%>
```

The code with a white background is code we've already looked at and that we don't wish to examine further.

Naming Conventions

We have outlined the variation of the Hungarian naming convention that we used for this book in the table below. Yeah, I know, there is only one datatype in ASP's VBScript, and it's variant! But we feel it is important to use these conventions to clarify what type of data the variables are intended to represent.

Constant	Description	Constant	Description
ary	Arrays	int	Integer
bit	Bit data (1 or 0)	lng	Long Integer
boo	Boolean data (True or False)	obj	Object
cur	Currency/money	str	Character data (String)
dat	Date/time	vnt	Variant data

You have probably seen alternative variations of this naming convention. But the important point to keep in mind is that no matter what naming conventions you use, be consistent throughout your project.

Tell Us What You Think

We've worked hard on this book to make it useful. We've tried to understand what you're willing to exchange your hard-earned money for, and we've tried to make the book live up to your expectations.

Please let us know what you think about this book. Tell us what we did wrong, and what we did right. We take your feedback seriously – if you don't believe us, then send us a note. We'll answer, and we'll take on board whatever you say for future editions. The easiest way is to use email:

feedback@wrox.com

You can also find more details about Wrox Press on our web site. There, you'll find the code from our latest books, sneak previews of forthcoming titles, and information about the authors and editors. You can order Wrox titles directly from the site, or find out where your nearest bookstore with Wrox titles is located.

Customer Support

If you find a mistake, please have a look at the errata page for this book on our web site first. Appendix J gives more details of how to submit an errata, if you are unsure. You'll find the errata page on our main web site, at

http://www.wrox.com

If you can't find an answer there, tell us about the problem and we'll do everything we can to answer promptly!

Just send us an email to support@wrox.com or follow the advice given on our website:

http://www.wrox.com/contacts.asp

ADO and RDS Defined

Microsoft have refined their data access landscape quite dramatically in recent years. Data Access Objects (DAO) and Remote Data Objects (RDO) have both had their 15 minutes in the sun. Today, ActiveX Data Objects (ADO) is the technology in the spotlight. As we'll see in this chapter, ADO is much simpler to use, it's more flexible, and it lends itself much more readily to scalability.

With so much attention focused on ADO, it seems appropriate to give not only an introduction to it, but to also show how things have changed. As we explore, we will center our focus on ADO technology, and we will dive into such topics as the ADO object model, benefits of ADO and Remote Data Services (RDS).

So, in this chapter we will examine the following:

- ❑ Universal Data Access
- ❑ A history and comparison of data access methods (DAO, RDO and ADO)
- ❑ OLE DB
- ❑ The ADO object model – a first look
- ❑ ADO in the Web environment
- ❑ Client-side data access with RDS

Universal Data Access

The computer world is changing. That's probably no great surprise to anyone, but you might be interested in how Microsoft sees one part of this change taking place. For a few years the concept of data access has really revolved around relational databases, with a few technologies plugging the gaps between the PC world and the mainframe world.

Then along came the Internet and the Web, and now we not only have databases in the machine room along the hall, but on the other side of the world. And now we have to deal with database via HTTP, and that brings a whole new ball game into the picture because of its stateless nature. That means that as programmers, we have to build in extra functionality to cope with the transparent nature of our clients – that is, we might not know (or care) whether they are local or remote, or for how long they will remain connected. And if we're using web technologies, then we need to keep track of the data, and its state, as it flies around the world.

Universal Data Access (UDA) is Microsoft's way of dealing with these problems, and it's all based upon OLEDB, and in particular, the two types of data users: **Providers** and **Consumers**. A Provider is something that provides data – it interfaces with the holder of the data and supplies the data to whoever requests it. A Consumer is something that uses that data. There are other terms we'll look at in a moment, but the diagram below gives a clear idea of how OLEDB fits into this picture:

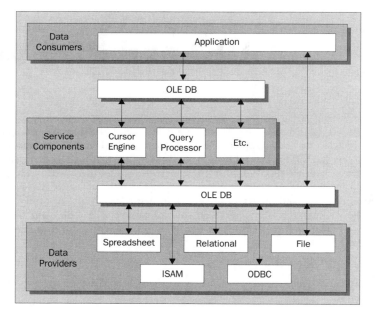

So, OLEDB is what interfaces between the actual data and us. As well as doing this, it provides some ancillary services, such as a cursor engine, query processors, etc., to ensure that standard facilities are always available. This saves the people who write OLEDB data providers from having to write these facilities into their own components.

Windows DNA

Distributed iNternet Applications (DNA) architecture is the big picture for how we can develop applications in the Internet world. It's not really an architecture, but more a set of fairly common, and sensible, suggestions about how to build n-tier client/server systems. Because it's not language or product dependent it works very well with the multifarious nature of the Web. DNA can be easily summed up by three logical layers:

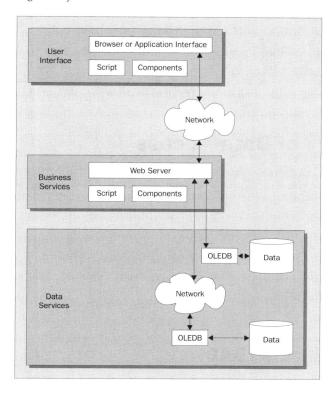

The User Interface is what the user sees and deals with. He or she should be completely unaware of what happens elsewhere. The Business Services layer is where the Web server (and possibly other services such as MTS or MSMQ) sit, conducting the business rules of the application. This middle tier fetches data from the Data Services via OLEDB.

This layered architecture is extremely flexible for several reasons:

❑ Breaking the services into smaller, more manageable components brings greater freedom, not only in development, but in component re-use.

❑ Abstracting the business rules means that it's very easy to build clients of different natures, such as web clients or Visual Basic clients.

❑ Using OLEDB allows data from a myriad of sources to be obtained.

When it comes down to it, DNA is really just like a jigsaw – the plugging of various components together.

ADO and RDS

ADO and RDS are two sides of the same coin. ADO is intended for general data access, where the connection to the data source is permanent, or semi-permanent. RDS provides many of the same facilities as ADO, but is intended to work in situations where there may be no connection to the data source. In the disconnected (and unpredictable) nature of the Web, this gives a great degree of flexibility.

Making RDS work in disconnected situations allowed it to sit at the User Interface level. This doesn't really break the idea of the DNA architecture, because the data is still sourced from the appropriate place. It just gives us the ability to provide a better user interface, allowing data manipulation on the client, thus avoiding some of the long delays that can occur when obtaining data from Web servers.

A Brief History of Data Access

Before we look at ADO in more detail it's useful to see the history of Microsoft as a Data Access provider. This will give you a clear picture of what's been tried before, and why we've arrived at the OLEDB solution.

ODBC

In 1991 Microsoft presented a new method of data access, called ODBC (Open DataBase Connectivity). ODBC gives developers the ability to access a number of different types of data sources. It became a familiar thing among C and C++ programmers, and was in fact adopted as an international standard. However, for Visual Basic developers implementing ODBC required a great deal more work.

Data Access Objects (DAO)

For early Visual Basic developers, the only integrated way of accessing data was via Data Access Objects (DAO). Of course, third party vendors offered us alternative (and in some cases more efficient) solutions. But Microsoft stuck to their guns and we used DAO to get to our databases.

ODBC, DAO and JET Engines

DAO is based on the JET Engine – a native data engine for the Microsoft Access database. DAO initially offered a set of objects that allowed us to get to data, and even data definitions. These objects were a logical representation of the various parts of a database to which we would need access – things like tables, queries, and so on. By design, DAO gave us the fastest and simplest means of manipulating Access databases – because the objects of the DAO object model are direct reflections of the objects found in an Access database.

However, many of these objects have reduced functionality (or no functionality at all) when used in conjunction with non-Access databases. If your database *wasn't* an Access database, the JET Engine was required to translate the commands before they were sent. Thus, if you wanted to use DAO to access an Oracle database (via ODBC), or a FoxPro database (via ISAM), or any database other than Access, the necessary translation compromised performance.

DAO also left a lot to be desired when it came to accessing remote data sources (such as Oracle or SQL Server database servers). Connecting via ODBC to a client-server database such as Microsoft SQL Server was handled in a very non-client-server manner. For example: in client-server data access, data retrieved from the database is parsed on the *server*, and then the client only receives the data that was originally requested. However, when DAO retrieves data from SQL Server, JET pulls *all* of the data and then parses it all on the client machine.

ODBCDirect and RDO

So Microsoft provided us with Remote Data Objects (RDO), which allowed us to access database servers (Microsoft's SQL Server, Oracle, etc) without having to go through the JET Engine. RDO is a set of objects that encapsulates ODBC, rather than encapsulating the JET Engine. Since JET is not used, access to ODBC data sources does not require the additional translation – and that results in faster retrieval of data.

Subsequently, DAO introduced ODBCDirect, to help with ODBC database connectivity. ODBCDirect is a means of connecting to an ODBC database that bypasses the JET Engine – it actually used RDO rather than being routed to the ODBC API. ODBCDirect allowed for a more efficient communication mechanism when connecting to databases such as Oracle and Microsoft SQL Server.

In addition, now JET also included additional objects whose usability would depend upon the type of connectivity you chose.

RDO gave us the speed of making direct calls to the ODBC Application Programming Interface (API) while maintaining a COM-based object model that was simple to use. But still, RDO was limited to using ODBC (which only allows connectivity to relational database sources) and was less effective when accessing JET and ISAM data sources. Although much of the data that any organization deals with is relational, not all of the data is stored in a relational data system.

OLE DB and ADO

Then Microsoft introduced OLE DB. Like ODBC, it was more complicated to work with (from a Visual Basic developer's standpoint). However, it did lay a new foundation for data access. OLE DB expanded on the variety of types of data stores that could be accessed. It also provided the foundation for the arrival of ActiveX Data Objects (ADO). ADO took the basic concepts of data access, and presented them in an object model that was simpler than DAO and RDO, and which had the flexibility to access almost any type of data. Now, you could access almost any type of relational database – and you could also access non-relational data.

Although initially simple, giving us only the basics for accessing our data, ADO has grown over the past two years, maturing and expanding its capabilities. With ADO 2.0, data can now be accessed using a paging methodology (which is excellent for web-based application development). We can disconnect recordsets from the original data source, and continue to manipulate them on the client. We can nest data within data (known as data shaping), to allow for a hierarchical representation of data – for example using a recordset of customers with an associated recordset of customer orders.

We will be discussing these and other features of ADO in much greater detail in the following chapters.

DAO, RDO and ADO – a Comparison

All in all, these three data access technologies are built on the same conceptual level: each offers a means of connecting to a database, retrieving records from that database, executing SQL code against the database, and so on. In fact, both the DAO (with and without ODBCDirect) and RDO object models are nearly identical in their usage (although they operate quite differently behind the scenes). In the following table, we can compare the various data access models and their objects:

Object/ Collection	DAO	DAO ODBCDirect	RDO	ADO
Database Engine	DBEngine	DBEngine	rdoEngine	
Workspace	Workspace	Workspace	rdoEnvironment	
Database	Database			
Connection		Connection	rdoConnection	Connection
Table Definition	TableDef		rdoTable	
Query Definition	QueryDef	QueryDef	rdoQuery	Command
Parameter	Parameter	Parameter	rdoParameter	Parameter
Recordset	Recordset	Recordset	rdoResultset	Recordset
Field	Field	Field	rdoColumn	Field
Error	Error	Error	rdoError	Error

The RDO object model was made to mimic the DAO object model – and thus make the transition from DAO to RDO easier. Although the object names are different, their functionality is essentially the same. A workspace is created from the database engine. Using the workspace, we can open a connection, which in turn allows us to do things like access recordsets and query definitions.

The table shows that the TableDef object is not implemented via DAO with ODBCDirect – nor is it in ADO. And although there is an equivalent in RDO – rdoTable – its functionality is limited. As we mentioned above, DAO's model was intended for use specifically against a Microsoft Access database. Although the TableDefs are accessible when using a non-Access database, some functionality is lost.

The table does not show all of the objects from DAO or RDO. However, ADO is fully represented, save for its `Properties` collection. You can see that ADO has a far simpler set of objects – we'll return to this point later in this chapter. The ADO objects function in much the same way as their DAO and RDO counterparts – however, ADO objects (unlike DAO and RDO objects) can exist independently of one another. For example, consider the act of creating a `Recordset` object. In DAO, we must (at the very least) create a `Database` object and connect it to a data source – only then can we use the `Database` object's `OpenRecordset` method to create a `Recordset` object. In ADO, we can create a standalone `Recordset` object. This not only simplifies our coding, while maintaining the flexibility that exists in the other two models; it also makes for a lighter weight client application.

So it should come as no surprise that ADO is intended to be the replacement for both DAO and RDO. ADO can do everything its predecessors can do, but with greater ease and better performance. As the industry takes in ADO, more and more native connection mechanisms to data will appear. There are already native OLE DB providers for data from Oracle, SQL Server, Access, Exchange, Index Server and ODBC – and the future will only mean that more and more providers will appear on the market.

More about OLE DB

ADO is a high-level interface (that is, it has a simple object model) which is based on another interface – OLE DB. In essence, ADO is a wrapper around OLE DB – exposing its capabilities while hiding its complexities.

OLE DB is a COM-based, low-level programming interface that provides access to data from all parts of an organization. It provides for all of the abilities of ODBC, by making ODBC one of the providers of data (applications can use the OLE DB provider for ODBC). Indeed, OLE DB reaches beyond ODBC by providing high performance access to all kinds of data, relational and non-relational. (It should be noted that OLE DB isn't intended as a replacement for ODBC.)

As mentioned before, OLE DB exposes two main components for connectivity to data: **consumers** and **providers**. Consumers, such as a client-server or Web-based applications, use data. Providers are the components that talk to the data, translating the information and exposing a common interface for any type of consumer. The consumer does not need to know how the data is being accessed; this ability is encapsulated within OLE DB itself (via the providers).

For lists of available OLE DB providers see Appendix E

OLE DB is designed for all types of data stores, including relational databases and non-relational data sources, such as email or file system information. By providing access to such a myriad of information while maintaining a simple, standard means of retrieving and manipulating this information, OLE DB jumps beyond all the previous data access strategies of Microsoft.

OLE DB contains additional components that do not own data, but encapsulate some service by producing and consuming data. Service components are both consumers and providers. One such component, the query processor, allows for joins between heterogeneous sources of data, or between data from tables in two different types of data source. The query processor acts as a consumer by fetching rows from each of the tables. It acts as a provider by creating a set of data from both data sources and returning it to the consumer as a single recordset.

The Data Shaping provider (of which you'll see more later in the book) is another example of being both a consumer and a provider, using other providers to get the data, manipulating the data, and then serving the manipulated data up to the client. This flexibility and componentization, allows OLE DB to build upon itself to provide better services.

The ADO Object Model

So, one of the real beauties of the ADO object model is that it's simple in design. It consists of just four objects and two collections. ADO's interface is composed of the methods, properties and events of these objects. Here's the object model:

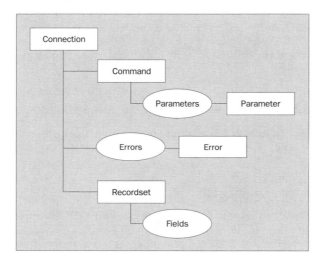

Note the two collections – the Fields collection of the Recordset object, and the Parameters collection of the Command object. Let's briefly introduce all of the objects and collections shown in the figure.

The Connection Object

The Connection object represents our link to the data source. It can directly execute statements against the data source, manage transactions, and even expose events that let us know when we have completed tasks – such as connecting or disconnecting from the data source. It also provides us with the Error object/collection, giving us access to the error information being returned from a data store.

As the diagram suggests, we need a Connection object if we are to use a Command object or Recordset object in conjunction with a data connection. However (as we mentioned earlier), ADO does not require us to declare the Connection object explicitly – if it's needed then ADO is capable of quietly creating one behind the scenes. The Connection object does provide us with some special functionality that is not available in any of the other objects – and can also provide performance benefits, for example when retrieving multiple recordsets from the same data source/connection string.

The Command Object

The Command object is, in essence, a query that can be issued against the data source. It provides a means to access and modify data. The Command object can contain a SQL statement, a table name, or the name of a stored procedure. The command can be executed directly against the data source, or it can be used in conjunction with a Recordset object to retrieve data. Since a Command object can be easily associated with a Connection object, the same query can be easily reused against different connections with very little effort. Command objects can also be used to execute batch operations or create or modify databases.

The Parameters Collection

The Parameters collection is a dependency of the Command object and can be used with most data stores. We can use the Parameters collection in conjunction with a parameterized query (such as a SQL statement) or stored procedure. Each of the query's (or procedure's) parameters is represented by a Parameter object – these objects are placed in the Parameters collection, either by appending them manually or by refreshing the Parameters collection of a Command object. A Parameter object holds the information needed by the query or procedure, which is then used internally to process the request made by the Command object.

The Recordset Object

The Recordset object lies at the very heart of data access, and is the most intricate of the ADO objects. ADO's excellent data manipulation abilities are reflected in the number of properties, methods and events that are exposed by the Recordset object. It supports features such as data paging, disconnected recordsets, filtering, sorting, and storing multiple data sets in a single Recordset object.

The Fields Collection

The Fields collection allows us to access the information contained within the individual columns of data. The Fields collection exists within the Recordset object, and represents a list of fields (the columns of the recordset). Each field is represented by a Field object (hence the name – the Fields collection). The Field object itself exposes several properties, that we can use to reveal the value for the row data, as well as the type, size, precision and scale of the data. The Field object also provides for retrieval of memo and image data.

The Errors Object

The Errors collection consists of individual Error objects – an Error object is created when an error occurs while accessing data. It allows us to see error information – not only from ADO, but also from the data provider. Consequently, it is a crucial and powerful tool in debugging and error tracking. The Errors collection is only accessible via the Connection object.

The Properties Collection

With the exception of the Error object, every ADO object features an interface called its Properties collection. The Properties collection is comprised of individual Property objects which represent the properties inherent to the object. Each Property consists of a name, type, and value (plus a set of attributes). The great advantage of the Properties collection is that it is dynamic, allowing OLEDB providers to supply their own properties. Not building them into OLEDB keeps the OLEDB model simple, while allowing provider writers to give the very best service they can without compromise.

ADO in the Web Environment

Because it is implemented as a set of COM-based objects, ADO can be used in many different programming environments. This book focuses on ADO development in a web environment. ADO is programmable via VBScript and JavaScript, and also supports specialized abilities that make it more web-friendly – and is therefore likely to the best choice for data-driven web applications. In order to better understand ADO's abilities in this arena, we will first examine the process involved when using the Web.

The Web is a stateless environment. This means that when you (as a web user) browse to a web site, you are only connected to the Web server for the duration that it takes to retrieve the information for the single request. Once the browser has received the information, the connection between client and server is broken.

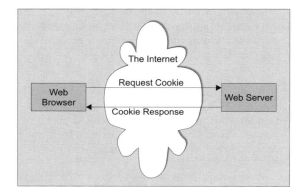

This disconnection is not a physical disconnection – you don't have to redial your internet provider each time you want to browse to a new location. Once the Web server sends out the requested information, it forgets about the requestor. The truth of the matter is that multiple client connections quickly become resource intensive for the Web server – so much so that it affects the server's ability to function efficiently.

So here's a question: when you're shopping on-line, how come the server appears to remember your order, from the first item that you add to the 'shopping cart', right until you navigate to the 'checkout'? The uncomplicated explanation is that the Web server sends additional nuggets of information in the form of cookies. A cookie is a small file provided by the server and stored on the client. It's a way for the Web server to maintain a match between what the server kept for a visiting client and the visiting client itself upon reconnection. When the client continues his order he does so by returning the cookie to the server – the server matches this information and continues the shopping service, without having to support a continuous connection.

So how can ADO help with this example? Well, ADO provides several facilities which allow us to perform the same task with greater efficiency, flexibility, functionality and scalability.

For example, ADO supports disconnected recordsets, which allow us as programmers to fetch data from a database and then disconnect from the database. The recordset is persisted locally in the client browser, where it can be sorted, filtered and manipulated without the need for a server connection – and with far greater functionality than is supported by (say) an array or a collection.

Moreoever, ADO's Remote Data Service (RDS) allows us to move data from a server to a client, modify data on the client, and then send the data back to the server without maintaining a constant connection. RDS also allows the browser to make calls to a COM component via DCOM and HTTP.

Client-side Data Access with RDS

Remote Data Services (RDS) provides us with a means of distributing data through the Web. RDS makes data-based web applications a reality by combining client-side caching of data along with the manipulation of that retrieved data.

RDS Brings Data Access to the Web

RDS expands data access through the Web by allowing the browser to download a set of data, update that retrieved data, and send it back to the web and database server. This reduces the number of requests needed to be made by the browser to the Web server, reducing the amount of bandwidth used and processing required by the server. RDS can also use ActiveX controls, such as grids, and list boxes, to allow us to create more sophisticated user interfaces for our end users, while minimizing our programming efforts. With RDS, we can alter, add, and delete data that we retrieved. The changes are buffered locally, and can be submitted to the Web server for processing and storage in the database. The ability to locally cache data prevents extra trips to and from the Web server, speeding up our data access and minimizing the performance hit against the web and database servers.

RDS can also invoke remote objects over HTTP and DCOM, giving us the ability to develop distributed Web applications. COM objects can expose services to client-side applications, while encapsulating the business logic.

RDS comes with several components to make web application development easier: the `DataControl`, `DataSpace` and `DataFactory` objects.

RDS handles all data in the same fashion when it is on the client, regardless of the source of the data. Since RDS is a part of ADO, it can take advantage of the full-featured data access abilities of ADO, including all ODBC data sources, all native OLE DB providers, and all non-relational sources of data. And since the recordset on the client is disconnected, it works in accordance with the stateless environment of the Web.

- ❑ The `DataControl` object is not a visual tool, but an embedded, client-side control used in web pages that acts as the source for the data, and acts a bit like the Data Control in Visual Basic. The `DataControl` actually stores the ADO recordset and allows HTML controls to be bound to columns in the data, as well as the ability to use scripting languages to manipulate the data.

- ❑ The `DataSpace` object is a client-side component that allows for automating objects via DCOM or HTTP. This means that business objects on a remote server can be instantiated and used as though they were local components.

- ❑ The `DataFactory` is a server-side object that performs data retrieval, either directly via SQL statements, or by instantiating components. In the latter case, it is the `DataFactory` that provides the interface between the component and the client-side `DataSpace` object.

Why choose ADO?

Why should we choose ADO over DAO or RDO? Let's summarize some of the reasons:

- ❑ **The ADO object model is similar to those of DAO and RDO, but simpler to use.** ADO provides for all of the core functionality inherent in DAO and RDO, leaving a "flattened", core set of objects. Unlike DAO and RDO, ADO's object model is not hierarchical – thus, with ADO there is no need to build up a chain of objects before finally getting to the set of data.

- ❑ **ADO has a simple yet scalable interface.** ADO's object model is simple in design, yet allows access to data from many different types of sources, both relational and non-relational – from Access database files to mainframe ISAM/VSAM and hierarchical databases.

- ❑ **ADO is usable in both traditional client–server application and web application development.** ADO has a COM-based interface. This makes it usable in traditional n-tier client–server applications using languages such as Visual Basic and Visual C++. Because ADO is implemented as COM objects, it also fits well into Microsoft's DNA (Distributed iNternet Applications architecture), and hence provides an easy and uniform means of providing data access from within all Microsoft's development environments (including server-side and client-side scripting).

  ADO also dramatically decreases the amount and complexity of the written code, which also contributes to its suitability for use in web-based applications. If there's less code running on the client, the middle-tier business object, or even the server, this translates to higher performance. Additionally, ADO gives us disconnected and remote-able recordsets, which in turn allows for better functionality in the stateless environment of the World Wide Web.

- ❑ **ADO is cross-language.** ADO's COM interface allows access from VB, C++, Java, VBScript, JavaScript ... in fact, any programming environment that supports COM.

- ❑ **ADO is independent of the data source and the programming environment.** ADO does not change its interface based on the type of data accessed or the language that employs it. The functionality of each of the ADO objects remains constant.

- ❑ **ADO has a long future**. OLEDB, and therefore ADO, is the cornerstone of many Microsoft projects, and both are actively being improved. DAO and RDO, whilst perfectly acceptable technologies, have had their day, and no future development will take place on them.

- ❑ Another consequence of ADO's COM roots is that it works in the same manner, whether you are building a simple data solution in a small office with Windows 95, or creating a large scale On Line Transaction Processing (OLTP) system, using Windows NT and SQL Server on a DEC Alpha that will support thousands of users.

Summary

This chapter only just begins to explore all of the features of ADO and RDS that make for powerful and flexible data-driven web applications. In the coming chapters we will learn more about these features, starting with the basics: connections, commands and recordsets. As we continue further through the book, we will expand on these topics and see how to apply data shaping, how to use disconnected recordset, and how to work with custom recordsets.

Next we will begin our discussion of RDS. We will delve into topics such as the `DataFactory` object and its use, how to bind data controls on a web browser, how to use RDS with DHTML, and how to use RDS to make remote calls to our business layer applications via a web browser.

And finally, since the examples in this book primarily focus on using ADO with SQL Server, we have also dedicated two chapters to using ADO with Oracle.

Highlights of ADO 2.0

Wondering why you should be interested in ADO 2.0? Or if you are already a seasoned ADO 1.x developer, are you wondering why you should switch to ADO 2.0? The plethora of new features introduced in ADO 2.0 makes it an exciting prospect to developers! If you have developed with previous versions of ADO, I am sure that you've caught yourself saying "I wish they'd include a sorting mechanism" or "I'd really love to have a `Find` method like in DAO". Usually, to our dismay, these types of requests seem to fall upon deaf ears. However, with ADO 2.0, the technicians at Microsoft certainly weren't asleep at the wheel! We not only received both sorting and finding mechanisms, we also received a slew of expanded and new features that are sure to make you rethink your position on ADO.

In chapter 1 we took a cursory look at what ADO is and how RDS is intermingled with it. In this chapter, we'll explore the highlights of ADO 2.0: its latest and greatest features. First, let me state that we won't be going into detail on each of these new features. That is not the purpose of this chapter. The purpose of this chapter is to give you an overview on the new features of ADO 2.0. Usually before developers adopt a new technology (or a new version of a great technology such as ADO 2.0 in this case), we first need a substantial reason to convert. We'll discuss these new features and why they warrant our attention. Finally we'll also see what we can look for in ADO 2.1. So without further delay, I have included a list of the topics we'll discuss in this chapter below:

❑ Non-Recordset-returning execution
❑ Data Shaping
❑ Expanded Filtering and State features
❑ Indexing
❑ Sorting
❑ Finding
❑ Appending/Deleting Fields
❑ Persistent Recordsets
❑ New events
❑ ADO 2.1

Non-Recordset-returning operation

There are several ways to execute action queries using ADO 2.0. For example, we can execute SQL using the `Command` object, or we could use the `AddNew` method of a recordset, or we can create a `Command` object to execute a stored procedure containing an action query. Most developers have tackled most of these options, if not all, at one time or another. However, sometimes we simply want to execute a SQL statement that updates, inserts or deletes records. Ideally, we would like to use stored procedures, but sometimes we do not have that choice. So that often leaves us with the next best choice: executing an action query SQL statement via the `Connection` object's `Execute` method.

Often we use this technique to execute SQL. We rarely use this technique for returning recordsets, because we know that we have little control over the type of recordset that is returned (forward-only, read-only). However, the `Execute` method is an ideal choice for issuing action queries such as:

```
objConn.Execute "DELETE authors WHERE au_lname = 'white'"
```

This code deletes all of the authors with the last name of "White". However, what you probably didn't know is that in previous versions of ADO this operation also generated a `Recordset` object. "What!? ", you say. That's right, the `Execute` method of the `Connection` object generates a `Recordset` object to be returned, whether or not you want it. It obviously makes no sense in this case. What would we possibly want to retrieve about this? Nothing. Whether you asked for a recordset back as a return value from the `Execute` method or not, ADO 1.x versions generated the recordset anyway. You may never have noticed because it occurred under the covers, but Microsoft corrected it in ADO 2.0.

I don't want to belabour this issue, but it is apparent that this is not an efficient means to execute action queries. I cannot tell you why it ever worked this way, but you can probably guess that I am going to tell you that it no longer does. Well, you are partly right. Now we have a choice. We can choose to have the `Connection` object's `Execute` method generate and return a recordset or not, by specifying the constant `adExecuteNoRecords`. The code below shows how we can do this:

```
dim objConn
const adExecuteNoRecords = 128

set objConn = Server.CreateObject("ADODB.Connection")
objConn.Open "Provider=SQLOLEDB.1;Persist Security Info=False;Initial
Catalog=pubs;Data Source=mycomputer;User ID=sa;Password=;"

objConn.Execute "DELETE authors WHERE au_lname = 'white'", ,adExecuteNoRecords
```

Notice that we specified the constant `adExecuteNoRecords` in our script. We could have included the `adovbs.inc` file, which contains all of the ADO enumerators for VBScript. (You can find the `adovbs.inc` file in the `\Program Files\Common Files\System\ADO` directory on your workstation). However, this would have been a waste of memory as we only needed the single enumerator.

You can find all of the ADO enumerators and their corresponding values in Appendix G, ADO and RDS Enumerators.

Data Shaping

Data shaping is another new feature introduced in ADO 2.0's specifications. Data shaping is a way to view hierarchical cursors with ADO 2.0. Before we get into the terminology, let's take a step back for a moment to try to understand what data shaping is all about. The most simple way to describe data shaping is to envision the Windows Explorer tree view. In the root of your C: drive you probably have files and subfolders such as Program Files and WinNT. Then within each subfolder you also have more subfolders and files.

What does this all have to do with Data Shaping? Well these folders and subfolders could be viewed as parent-child relationships. Your C: drive root is a parent that has many child folders (i.e. Program Files and WinNT). These child folders can also have children, and so on and so forth.

Now let's come back to the world of ADO and its terminology. We can translate this hierarchical folder structure to a structure containing sets of data that relate to one another in a parent-child manner. This figure depicts a structure where we can see the relationship between sets of data. The customer is a parent recordset which has a child recordset of orders, which in turn has a child recordset of line items.

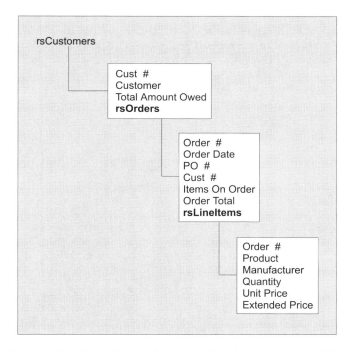

Just to give you an idea of what data shaping brings us, here's an example of its power. Let's take the hierarchical recordset of customers, orders and line items shown in the figure above. This recordset contains no duplicate data other than the foreign keys that define the relationships in the database. Now consider joining all of this data in SQL join syntax: the resulting recordset could contain duplicate values for customers and orders! In fact, any time a parent has more than a single child, a SQL join will have to duplicate the parent's information for each of those children. Hierarchical recordsets give us an edge here as they reduce data redundancy and network traffic. This also means that we can update each recordset within the data shape, whereas in a SQL join this would be impossible!

We won't reveal all of the hierarchical recordset's secrets here, but as you are beginning to see, they are a new way of looking at one to many data sets. Chapter 7, *Data Shaping*, goes into detail on what these recordsets are, how they can be utilized and when we should or should not use them. But for now, simply know that hierarchical recordsets (or Data Shaping as we refer to it in this book) allows us an alternative way to express SQL joins.

Expanded Filtering and State features

There are also some relatively hidden changes that were made to ADO 2.0 that can be easily overlooked, in particular the `Filter` property and the `State` property. We'll take a glance at each of these new features in this section.

The Filter Property

From ADO 1.5, we know that the `Filter` property of the `Recordset` object lets us reduce the number of records that we can see in a recordset based upon our filter criteria. (For a refresher and further details on the `Filter` property refer to Chapter 6, *Building on the Recordset Foundation*.) But there is now a new setting to the `Filter` property: `adFilterConflictingRecords`.

What does this do for us? Well, when issuing batch updates we run the risk of having one or more of our updated records causing all of the records in the batch not to commit. When this occurs, we can now set the `Filter` property to this setting to reveal the records that caused the conflict. (For more information on batch updating, also see Chapter 6, *Building on the Recordset Foundation*.) The code to employ this new setting is simple, as I have included it below:

```
objRS.Filter = adFilterConflictingRecords
```

This is a minor change that yields a great deal of functionality that was clearly missing from previous versions of ADO.

The State Property

The `State` property of the `Connection` and `Recordset` objects lets us examine the state that these objects are in. As this is a read-only property, we can now determine whether the connection or recordset is closed, still connecting, still executing an operation, still fetching records, is involved in an asynchronous operation or is open.

Indexing

We all know that placing indexes on fields in a database can greatly enhance the performance of our SQL queries and stored procedures' execution. But what about speeding up the recordset itself? Often I find myself wanting to sort a recordset, find a particular record or even filter a recordset on a particular field. Before ADO 2.0, sorting and finding were not implemented and filtering could be a slow process.

However, introduced with ADO 2.0 is the new indexing technique. We can now create an internal index for a `Field` object by setting its dynamic `Optimize` property to `True`. This dynamic property is added to the `Field` object's `Properties` collection when you set the `CursorLocation` property to `adUseClient`. (For more information on the dynamic `Properties` collection, refer to Appendix C, *Detailed Properties Collection*.) Keep in mind that this index is internal to ADO 2.0, so we are not placing an index in the database itself. The code example below shows how we can create an index on a `Field` object within a `Recordset` object.

```
objRS.Fields("au_lname").Properties("OPTIMIZE").Value = True
```

Likewise, we can remove an index from a `Field` object by setting the property to `False`. When creating an index on a `Field` object, the index only exists within the memory space of the ADO cursor engine. Therefore, we must have a client side recordset (`objRS.CursorLocation = adUseClient`). Indexing has speeded up the filtering process and has given birth to some new properties. So without further delay, let's take a look at some of the methods that are derived from ADO's new indexing feature, `Find` and `Sort`.

> *For a detailed discussion of these features, refer to Chapter 6, Building on the Recordset Foundation.*

Finding records

You can now find a record in an ADO recordset by passing criteria to the `Find` method. Once a record is found, that record becomes the current record in the recordset. The criteria resembles a SQL `WHERE` clause, without the `WHERE`, as the syntax below shows:

```
objRS.Find criteria, SkipRows, searchDirection, start
```

To implement this feature, let's look at an example that locates the first occurrence of the record with an author's last name of Ringer, starting at the next record after the current record.

```
objRS.Find "au_lname = 'Ringer'", 1
```

Sorting a Recordset

We can sort a recordset using its `Sort` property. The syntax for the `Sort` property is quite simple, as shown below:

```
objRS.Sort = FieldName1 [asc|desc] [[,FieldName2 [asc|desc]] ... , FieldNamen
[asc|desc]]
```

The `Sort` property specifies one or more field names on which the recordset is sorted, and whether each field is sorted in ascending or descending order. (The order is defaulted to ascending order if it is omitted.) To implement this feature, let's look at an example that sorts a recordset in ascending order by the author's last name and then by the author's first name.

```
objRS.Open "SELECT * FROM authors"
objRS.Sort = "au_lname asc, au_fname asc"
```

Keep in mind that the data is not physically rearranged within the `Recordset` object. Rather, the data is simply accessed in the sorted order using an indexing scheme that utilizes a type of "pointer". Getting back to the indexing topic, a temporary index will be created for each field specified in the `Sort` property if an index does not already exist. We can remove the sort order and the temporary index by simply setting the `Sort` property to an empty string.

Appending/Deleting Fields

If you have ever wanted to create a recordset on your own, without a database as its source, your wish has been granted! We can now use the `Append` method to add `Field` objects to the `Fields` collection. These are fields that you define to be used in your application. Here is an example of how we can use the `Append` method to create a new `Field` object and place it in the recordset's `Fields` collection:

```
objRS.Fields.Append "EmployeeNumber", adInteger
objRS.Fields.Append "FirstName", adVarChar, 30
objRS.Fields.Append "LastName", adVarChar, 30
```

Here is the complete syntax for the `Append` method:

```
Recordset.Fields.Append (Name, Type, [DefinedSize], [Attrib])
```

You might want to create a custom recordset to house some data that you read in from a text file or an Excel spreadsheet. You could also use a custom recordset to read values input by a user through a table on a data entry screen. You then have all the data the user entered in a recordset that you can loop through, sort, filter and find records in.

> *Chapter 9, Custom Recordsets, discusses the* `Append` *method in detail as the entire chapter is focused on creating your own custom recordsets and what you can do with them.*

Persistent Recordsets

There are some situations where we want to make our recordsets last beyond the scope of when a PC is powered off. Maybe we have a field engineer who needs to operate disconnected from any network or external application. The `Save` method will allow you to save data to a local file, in a proprietary format (Microsoft's ADTG or Advanced Data TableGram format), which you can then retrieve later using the `Open` method of a `Recordset` object. With version 2.1 of ADO (to be released with IE5 and Office 2000), we will be able to save the recordsets in an additional format, XML, but for now, we only have a single option of using the ADTG format.

> *The ADTG format is a Microsoft proprietary format that dematerializes a recordset on the server, sends its particles over the network/internet and then rematerializes them on the client.*

To save a recordset to a file you need to use the following syntax.:

```
Recordset.Save (FileName, [PersistFormat])
```

Asynchronous Operation and Events

ADO 2.0 introduces asynchronous operations on the `Command`, `Connection` and `Recordset` objects using the `options` parameters of these objects' execution methods. With asynchronous operations, we get faster perception of response times to user requests. This rarely has a useful application for ASP, as the user has to wait for the page to fully process anyway, but we can utilize this functionality with RDS and VB.

Asynchronous operations allow us to get control back to the program as soon as we issue the operation. Events are available so that if the operation has a problem, completes or is simply letting us know its status, we can be informed. The events will then be fired and break into the current operation to inform us of its cause. At this point, the programmer can intercept the event and take action as appropriate.

> *You can find all of the events in RDS and ADO in Appendices A and B.*

Introducing ADO 2.1

So far in this chapter we've looked at some of the major new features of ADO 2.0. AD0 2.1 is an update to ADO 2.0, available with IE5 and Office 2000. To round this chapter off, let's have a brief glance at what we can look forward to. ADO 2.1 builds on the solid foundation offered by ADO 2.0 to offer us some additional functionality. The principal features of the 2.1 release of ADO include:

- ❑ ADOX and Jet replication objects. This is a superset of the DDL and replication ability of DAO 3.5, now built into an ADO library, giving full Data Definition and security features.
- ❑ DAO 3.6 support, to support the new Jet 4.0 Unicode features when connecting to Access 2000 databases.
- ❑ A SQL Server 7.0 provider (and an ODBC driver), to support the latest release of MS SQL Server.
- ❑ Better remoting support, to enable resync and conflict resolution amongst n-tier clients.
- ❑ Introduction of client side indexes and the Seek facility, to improve client performance.
- ❑ Persistance to XML, allowing recordsets to be saved locally in XML format.

Of these ADOX is probably the most important since it brings several new commands to light, allowing creation of databases, tables, etc, without resorting to SQL statements. For those in the Windows DNA game, then the added facilities to the Resync section of ADO give better control for resolving data conflicts, and local persistence and indexing can add a great deal of usability to client applications. All in all, ADO 2.1 is not a major change, but shows the steady improvement in ADO technology.

Summary

With the multitude of new features that ADO 2.0 introduces and enhancements to its toolset, ADO 2.0 steps to the foreground of the development tools available. We have not discussed all of the new features as I have left that task for the remainder of this book. We are sure you will find many uses for the new features as well as new uses for the old features!

The Connection Object

Before we can access any part of a database, we need to establish a connection to it. Establishing the connection was also fundamental when using DAO (with ODBC – via its Connection object) and also when using RDO (via the rdoConnection object). However, ADO does things more flexibly. With ADO we can create a connection explicitly using the Connection object. Alternatively, we can create a connection indirectly via the Command object or the Recordset object, without the need for a Connection object at all. Further, we can opt to connect 'on the fly' when we use either the Command or Recordset object. In essence, we don't actually *need* a Connection object to execute commands or retrieve data from a data store.

I know what you're asking: "Why use Connection objects at all? And why dedicate a whole chapter to the Connection object?!"

The reason that we still use the Connection object is that it offers us some special capabilities when managing our data. For example, we can only explicitly create transactions via the Connection object, and the Errors collection is also only accessible through a Connection object. We are going to take an in-depth look at the Connection object while covering the following topics:

- ❑   What is a connection?
- ❑   Creating and managing a connection
- ❑   Using the Connection object to update a database or generate a recordset
- ❑   Executing stored procedures through a Connection object
- ❑   Connection pooling
- ❑   The Errors collection

What is a Connection?

A connection furnishes us with a means of accessing data, and we can use the `Connection` object to represent that connection. By creating an instance of the `Connection` object, and placing information in its properties, we can build a predefined link between the consumer and the data provider. Then when we establish a connection to the data store, we can use the `Connection` object again – to execute commands directly against the data store, to execute predefined stored procedures, and to retrieve and manipulate data. We can also control transaction scope via a `Connection` object.

The `Connection` object gives us access to the `Errors` collection. If errors occur during the execution of a command, or during data retrieval, we can iterate through the `Errors` collection in order to find out exactly what happened. Of course, we can also check the `Err` object in our ASP code – but the `Err` object only shows us the *first* item from the `Errors` collection (the remaining error messages are discarded, and we never get to see them). With the `Connection` object we get easy access to the *whole* `Errors` collection.

The `Connection` object also offers us the benefit of connection pooling – a method that keeps connections open even though we have explicitly closed them. Opening and closing connections can be resource-hungry for the Web server, so connection pooling can give us a great performance gain – when, for example, a Web server is regularly being accessed.

In order to better understand what a `Connection` object offers us, we'll explore its methods and properties in the following sections.

Creating a Connection

There's more than one way to connect to a data provider – indeed, as we mentioned in the introduction it's possible to connect implicitly using a `Recordset` object or `Command` object, without the need for a `Connection` object at all. But this chapter is all about the `Connection` object, and the advantages that it offers, so let's start off by using the VBScript `CreateObject` method to create an instance of the `Connection` object:

```
Dim objConn
Set objConn = CreateObject("ADODB.Connection")
```

Now we can use `objConn` to define our connection, to open it, to execute commands and retrieve data across it, and to close it. `objConn` will represent a unique session with the data provider. We can redefine the parameters of the connection and use it to connect and interact with a different data provider. In fact, it usually makes more sense to create multiple `Connection` objects – one for each different data provider.

Setting and Opening the Connection

How do we tell the `Connection` object the details of the connection that we want to open? Arguably the easiest way is through its `ConnectionString` property.

The ConnectionString Property

The ConnectionString property establishes all the necessary information that the Connection object needs to connect to a data store, including:

- ❑ The data provider (this is also accessible via the Provider property)
- ❑ The data source
- ❑ The initial database
- ❑ The username and password
- ❑ The ODBC data source name (if we are using a DSN)

Not all providers require all of these items in order to make a connection. To illustrate, let's look at a couple of examples. The connection string for a SQL Server database, using the native SQL Server OLE DB provider, might look like this:

```
Dim strConn                             ' Declare the connection string
strConn = "Provider=SQLOLEDB; "         ' Build the connection string
strConn = strConn & "Data Source=MyServer; "
strConn = strConn & "Initial Catalog=pubs; "
strConn = strConn & "User Id=" & Session("UserName") & "; "
strConn = strConn & "Password=" & Session("Password")

objConn.ConnectionString = strConn
```

In the next example, we see that the connection string for an Access database using the native Access OLE DB provider might look something like this:

```
Dim strConn
strConn = "Provider=Microsoft.Jet.OLEDB.3.51; "
strConn = strConn & "Data Source=C:\ProjectX\Data\ProjectX.mdb"

objConn.ConnectionString = strConn
```

So, what entries can we place into the connection string? The complete list is contained in the following table:

Attribute	Description
Provider	The driver for the data source (the provider's name)
Data Source	The name of the database server or the name of the data source file
Initial Catalog	The name of the database
User Id	The name of the user attempting to connect
Password	The password for the user
File Name	The name of the file that contains the provider connection information
Remote Provider	The name of the provider when using RDS
Remote Server	The name of the server when using RDS

Note that `File Name` and `Provider` are mutually exclusive. If you supply a provider name in the connection string, there's no need to supply the file name for provider information – and vice versa. `Remote Provider` and `Remote Server` are used in conjunction with RDS, and represent the server's provider and data source information.

> *There's a neat way of finding the correct syntax for a DSN-less connection: go to the ODBC (or ODBC32) control panel applet and create a File DSN for the database in question. This creates a file with the extension `.dsn` – its contents might look something like this:*

```
[ODBC]
DRIVER=SQL Server
UID=sa
PWD=secret
UseProcForPrepare=0
DATABASE=pubs
WSID=HOBBES
APP=Microsoft® Windows® Operating System
SERVER=ntsql7
```

> *You can view the contents of the `.dsn` file using a text editor such as Notepad. Now simply copy these contents and use them in your ADO code.*

There's more about `ConnectionString` settings in Appendix E. We'll talk a little about accessing and setting individual attributes later in this section.

The Open Method

OK, so we've set all our settings that the `Connection` object needs to open the connection. To establish a link to a data store, we use the `Connection` object's `Open` method. The full syntax of the Open method is as follows:

`objConn.Open [ConnectionString], [UserID], [Password], [Options]`

As you can see from the syntax, it allows four parameters. All of these four parameters are 'optional', although the `Connection` object needs a certain amount of basic information about the connection you want in order to open it. Perhaps the clearest way to open a connection for the first time is to feed the connection string into the `Open` method as its first parameter, like this:

```
objConn.Open "Provider=Microsoft.Jet.OLEDB.3.51; " & _
              "Data Source=C:\ProjectX\Data\ProjectX.mdb"
```

or this:

```
Dim strConn
strConn = "Provider=Microsoft.Jet.OLEDB.3.51; "
strConn = strConn & "Data Source=C:\ProjectX\Data\ProjectX.mdb"
objConn.Open strConn
```

Alternatively, you can assign the connection details to the `ConnectionString` property, and then you can call the `Open` method with no parameters at all:

```
Dim strConn
strConn = "Provider=Microsoft.Jet.OLEDB.3.51; "
strConn = strConn & "Data Source=C:\ProjectX\Data\ProjectX.mdb"
objConn.ConnectionString = strConn
objConn.Open
```

You can also supply a user name and a password, if needed, instead of supplying them as part of the connection string. In ADO, the the only valid value for the *Options* parameter is adAsyncConnect – this allows us to connect asynchronously.

The State Property

While we're on the subject of opening connections, it's worth a word or two about state. A connection is either *open* or it's *closed* – we refer to this as the **state** of the connection. So far we've created a Connection object (that represents a unique connection to a data store), and we've opened that connection – we'll take a look at how to close it later in this section.

The Connection object has a property called State, which indicates whether the connection is open or closed. The State property is read-only (fairly obviously), and will return one of the following two values:

- ❑ adStateOpen – indicating the connection is open
- ❑ adStateClosed – indicating the connection is closed

For example, we might use the State property to check the connection state of objConn, and call the ConnectToDatabase procedure *only* if the connection is currently closed:

```
If objConn.State = adStateClosed Then
   Call ConnectToDatabase
End If
```

More on Connection Settings

So far we've seen the raw ingredients we need to create a connection to a data store. The Connection object gives us a lot more functionality and options, and we'll look at some of them in the next part of the section.

Setting Default Database and Provider

We've already seen that we can pass connection details to the Connection object via a connection string. We've also seen that some of these details – like the username and password – can be passed as arguments of the Open method. The DefaultDatabase and Provider properties give us another way of specifying the database that we want to connect to, and the provider that we want to use for our connection.

The DefaultDatabase Property

The DefaultDatabase property specifies the default database to which we will be connected when the connection is opened. It is a read/write property – its value can be changed, even while the Connection object is supporting an open connection. (However, once set, it can never be set to an empty string.)

In this example we set the default database to the pubs database, which means that we don't need to specify it when we query the database:

```
objConn.DefaultDatabase = "pubs"
Set objRSAuthors = objConn.Execute("SELECT * FROM authors", ,adCmdText)
Set objRSTEmployees = _
   objConn.Execute("SELECT * FROM northwind.dbo.employees", ,adCmdText)
```

What's happening here? Since the `authors` table is in the `pubs` database, we only need to specify the name of the table. The `employees` table, however, is not part of the `pubs` database; rather, it is part of the `northwind` database, so we must qualify the database name if we want to select data from it.

The `DefaultDatabase` property is not usable with all OLE DB providers – for example, some OLE DB providers are providers of non-database type data, and some database vendors don't implement this feature fully.

The Provider Property

The `Provider` property determines the type of data store we will access. If a value is assigned to this property, there is no need to place a `Provider` entry into the `ConnectionString`. For example:

```
Dim strConn
objConn.Provider = "SQLOLEDB"

strConn = "Data Source=MyServer; "
strConn = strConn & "Initial Catalog=pubs;"
strConn = strConn & " User Id=" & Session("UserName") & "; "
strConn = strConn & " Password=" & Session("Password")

objConn.ConnectionString = strConn
objConn.Open
```

In this example, notice that our `ConnectionString` does not specify any provider information. When the connection is opened, the `ConnectionString` implies that the 'current' provider (contained in the `Provider` property) should be used.

Conversely, if the provider information were contained within the `ConnectionString` when the connection is Opened, the `Provider` property will (subsequently to the `Open` method call) reflect the current provider information supplied in the connection string.

Note that if *both* the `ConnectionString` and the `Provider` property specify a provider, then the `Provider` property value overrides the value set in the `ConnectionString`.

Some General Properties

Before we discuss closing the connection, we'll just quickly walk through some assorted properties.

The Mode Property

The `Connection` object's `Mode` property determines the read/write permissions for the connection. It can be set to one of the following values:

- ❑ `adModeUnknown` – permissions cannot be determined or have not been set as yet (default)
- ❑ `adModeRead` – read-only connection
- ❑ `adModeWrite` – write-only connection
- ❑ `adModeReadWrite` – read/write connection
- ❑ `adModeShareDenyWrite` – prevents others from opening a connection with write permissions
- ❑ `adModeShareDenyRead` – prevents others from opening a connection with read permissions
- ❑ `adModeShareExclusive` – prevents others from opening a connection
- ❑ `adModeShareDenyNone` – prevents others from opening a connection with any permission

While a connection is open, the Mode property is read-only. When the connection is closed, it is read/write – so we can specify the permission state for the connection. Setting the Mode property prior to opening a connection is *not* a mandatory requirement: the user's permissions that are assigned in the data source will be assigned to this property upon connection.

The ConnectionTimeout Property

As its name states, the ConnectionTimeout property determines the *maximum* length of time (in seconds) that the connection should wait while attempting to connect to a data store, before generating an error. Like the CommandTimeout property (see Chapter 4), assigning a 0 value will make the timeout an indefinite period. The default value for ConnectionTimeout is 15 seconds. To change the ConnectionTimeout to 20 seconds, we would code something similar to the following:

```
objConn.ConnectionTimeout = 20
```

This property is read-only once the connection has been opened.

The OpenSchema Method

The OpenSchema method gives us the ability to retrieve schema information from our data provider. For example, we can use the OpenSchema method to create a table information recordset from within our data store:

```
<% Set objRSTables = objConn.OpenSchema(adSchemaTables) %>
<FORM ACTION="Criteria.asp" METHOD="POST">
  <P ALIGN="center"><SELECT NAME="TableName" SIZE="1">
  <% Do While Not objRSTables.EOF%>
    <OPTION VALUE="<% =objRSTables("TABLE_NAME") %>">
    <% =objRSTables("TABLE_NAME") %></OPTION>
  <%Loop%>
```

This snippet of ASP code will create a drop list box containing all of the table names within our data store to which objConn is connected. Although this can be very useful, not all providers allow for the use of this method. You'll find more about the OpenSchema method in Appendices A and D.

The Version Property

This read-only property simply returns the ADO version number as a string.

Closing the Connection

To close up this section of Chapter 3, we'll cover how to close a connection!

The Close Method

This method closes an open connection. Once the connection is closed, you can reopen it again by calling the Open method.

Closing a connection releases the resources that were being used to support the connection on the server-side. If you want to remove the object from memory altogether, you must set the object variable to Nothing – as demonstrated in the following code:

```
If objConn.State = adStateOpen Then
   objConn.Close            ' Close connection; release server-side resources
End If
Set objConn = Nothing       ' Remove Connection object from memory
```

When you close a connection, any `Recordset` objects associated with the connection will be closed automatically. Note that the object variables of any such recordsets still exist in memory – to erase them from memory you need to set the variable to `Nothing`. (Before closing the connection, it's tidier to close any associated recordsets.)

Any `Command` objects associated with the connection will remain open, but the `Command` object's `ActiveConnection` property will be cleared. This action causes any recordsets that used the `Command` object to become disconnected.

If a transaction is in progress when we close the connection, an error will occur, and any pending transaction will be rolled back. There's more about transactions later in the chapter.

Cursors

A cursor is a pointer to a record in a database or recordset. Cursors are really the territory of the `Recordset` object, so we'll leave discussion of them until Chapter 5 and subsequent chapters. However, we will mention the `Connection` object's `CursorLocation` property.

The CursorLocation Property

This property determines the location of the cursor engine. It can be set to one of the following values:

- ❑ `adUseServer` – use a server-side cursor
- ❑ `adUseClient` – use a client-side cursor
- ❑ `adUseClientBatch` – same as `adUseClient` (provided for backward compatibility only)
- ❑ `adUseNone` – do not use any cursor library (not recommended; provided for backward compatibility)

Note that `adUseClientBatch` and `adUseNone` are available for backward compatibility only, and should not generally be used.

A recordset created through the connection uses the cursor location value in place at the time the recordset is opened. Re-setting the the `Connection` object's `CursorLocation` property doesn't affect the cursor location of existing recordsets. For example:

```
objConn.CursorLocation = adUseServer
Set objRSAuthors = objConn.Execute("SELECT * FROM authors", ,adCmdText)

objConn.CursorLocation = adUseClient
Set objRSTitles = objConn.Execute("SELECT * FROM titles", ,adCmdText)
```

Here, `objRSAuthors` uses a server-side cursor, and `objRSTitles` uses a client-side cursor. Any further `Recordset` objects opened with this connection will inherit this property value. Disconnected recordsets (Chapter 8) always require that we use a client-side cursor.

Commands and the Connection Object

One of the features of the `Connection` object is the ability to directly execute SQL code against the data provider (provided it does not return data), and to create recordsets, without the need to create an explicit `Command` object. We also have the `Cancel` method that we can use to cancel any existing asynchronous `Execute` or `Open` operations. Let's look these methods before examining a couple of examples.

The Execute Method

We can use the Execute method either to execute a command that does not return data, or to create a recordset. It's useful for firing stored procedures that are used for maintanence or periodic updates, or simply do not return data. Its syntax looks like this:

```
Set objRS = objConn.Execute (CommandText, [RecordsAffected], [Options])
```
or
```
objConn.Execute (CommandText, [RecordsAffected], [Options])
```

The Execute method has one mandatory parameter, *CommandText*, which specifies the command statement we wish to execute.

The *RecordsAffected* parameter can be used to find out how many rows were affected by the execution of the command. This works by passing a variable as the *RecordsAffected* parameter – that variable will be assigned a value indicating the number of affected rows. If the provider cannot determine the number of rows affected, or an asynchronous operation is performed, the RecordsAffected parameter will return a value of −1. Asynchronous operations do not return all records immediately, and this prevents us from knowing exactly how many records we will be dealing with until the operation has completed. If no variable is passed into the *RecordsAffected* parameter, or a literal is passed, the provider will have no means of indicating the number of affected rows.

Examine the following code using the *RecordsAffected* parameter.

```
Dim lngRows
objConn.Execute "DELETE stores WHERE state = 'CA'", lngRows, _
               adExecuteNoRecords
Response.Write "<B>" & lngRows & " stores</B> were deleted."
```

In this fragment, the number of deleted records is passed into the lngRows variable, which is then written to the client using the Response.Write.

The *Options* parameter allows us to specify the type of command that is to be executed. It also allow us to determine if we are going to perform the execution of the command asynchronously. Its value can be one or more of the following constants (use logical And for more than one, for example adCmdStoredProc And adAsyncExecute):

- ❏ adCmdText – execute a SQL string
- ❏ adCmdTable – opens the table specified in the CmdText property
- ❏ adCmdTableDirect – opens the table specified in the CmdText property
- ❏ adCmdStoredProc – execute a stored procedure
- ❏ adCmdFile – opens a recordset saved via the Recordset object's Save method
- ❏ adCmdUnknown – the command type is not known
- ❏ adAsyncExecute – executes the command asynchronously
- ❏ adAsyncFetch – fetches data asynchronously
- ❏ adAsyncFetchNonBlocking – fetches data asynchronously and does not block
- ❏ adExecuteNoRecords – used with commands that do not return rows

If no command type is specified in the *Options* parameter, adCmdText is assumed and no asynchronous processing will occur. Let's look at a few examples. This first code snippet opens a recordset in objRSPubs, that contains all the publishers. It also assigns to lngRows the number of rows in the recordset. This fragment uses a SQL statement to perform the task:

```
Dim strSQL
Dim lngRows
strSQL = "SELECT * FROM publishers"
Set objRSPubs = objConn.Execute(strSQL, lngRows, adCmdText)
```

This second snippet does the same thing, but opens the table directly instead of using a SQL statement:

```
Dim strSQL
Dim lngRows
strSQL = "publishers"
Set objRSPubs = objConn.Execute(strSQL, lngRows, adCmdTableDirect)
```

Let's take a look at another example. This code snippet finds the titles whose price is between 10 and 20, and increases those values by 25%. In this case we've decided that we don't need to know the number of rows affected by this command, so we have not specified a variable for the *RecordsAffected* parameter:

```
Dim strSQL
Dim lngRows
strSQL = "UPDATE titles SET price = price * 1.25 WHERE price BETWEEN 10 AND 20"
objConn.Execute strSQL, , adCmdText And adExecuteNoRecords
```

ADO does provide for asynchronous operations, but this is not a common practice when developing web applications via ASP. You still might execute multiple asychronous commands if you have created a COM component that accesses the data and you are calling that from ASP. In order to find out when an asynchronous operation has completed, you would need to use the ExecuteComplete event of the Connection object. And although it is also possible to capture events when developing web applications using ASP, it is rarely done, because ASP executes the entire script file in its entirety in one pass from top to bottom.

The CommandTimeout Property

The CommandTimeout property determines the timeout period (in seconds) for executing a command. The default value is 30. If you know that your commands are going to take more than 30 seconds to execute, you can change this value to reflect the maximum length of time you're prepared to allow the connection to wait for the data store to return information to us.

If the command does not complete within the specified period, the command is cancelled and an error is invoked. We can specify an indefinite timeout by setting the value of the CommandTimeout property to 0.

For example, to set the CommandTimeout property to 15 seconds, we would code the following:

```
objConn.CommandTimeout = 15
```

This setting applies *only* to execution directly via the `Connection` object. `Command` objects have their own `CommandTimeout` property, which overrides the value specified in the `Connection` object's timeout property. So, in the following code, although the `objCommand` is using `objConn` as its connection, it still has its own `CommandTimeout` property. When `objCommand` executes, it will timeout in 30 seconds (the `Command` object's timeout default), not 15 seconds:

```
objConn.CommandTimeout = 15
'...
Set objCommand.ActiveConnection = objConn
objCommand.Execute
```

The `Command` object does inherit its timeout value from its `ActiveConnection`. However, if the `Command` object's `CommandTimeout` property is changed subsequently, the `Command` will use the newly-assigned value for its timeout. In the example below, we override the initial timeout value of 15 seconds by changing it to 20 seconds for the `objCommand` object.

```
objConn.CommandTimeout = 15
Set objCommand.ActiveConnection = objConn
objCommand.CommandTimeout = 20
objCommand.Execute
```

The Cancel Method

The `Cancel` method cancels any pending asynchronous `Execute` or `Open` operations. If a connection is opened asynchronously, we can cancel the process by calling this method:

```
Connection.Cancel
```

If no asynchronous operations exist, this method call will invoke an error. There's more on asynchronous operations, in the sections on the `Execute` and `Open` methods in this chapter. Using the `Cancel` method has no effect on the current transaction state.

Executing SQL

So let's take a look at the `Connection` object executing SQL code directly against the data provider.

Updating the Data Store

The following example shows that we can insert, update or even delete data from our data store with fairly simple code:

```
Dim strSQL
Dim intCount
Dim strSSN
Dim strLastName
Dim strFirstName
Dim strPhone
Dim blnUnderContract

strSSN = Request("txtSSN")
strLastName = Request("txtLastName")
strFirstName = Request("txtFirstName")
strPhone = Request("txtPhone")
blnUnderContract = Request("chkUnderContract")
```

```
Set objConn = Session("Connection")

On Error Resume Next

strSQL = "INSERT authors (au_id, au_lname, au_fname, phone, contract) VALUES("
strSQL = strSQL & "'" & strSSN & "', "
strSQL = strSQL & "'" & strLastName & "', "
strSQL = strSQL & "'" & strFirstName & "', "
strSQL = strSQL & "'" & strPhone & "', "
strSQL = strSQL & blnUnderContract & ")"

objConn.Execute strSQL, , adExecuteNoRecords

If Err.Number <> 0 Then
  Response.Write "A problem occurred while adding the "
  Response.Write "new author '" & Request("FirstName") & " "
  Response.Write  Request("LastName") & "'.<BR>"
Else
  Response.Write "New author '" & Request("FirstName") & " "
  Response.Write  Request("LastName") & "' was added.<BR>"
End If
```

This code requests the new author's information from the previously-served web page. Each text box on that page is concatenated into an INSERT statement, which is then executed directly against the connection. The strSQL variable might contain an INSERT statement as follows:

```
INSERT authors VALUES('123-45-6789', 'Doe', 'Jane', '555-1212', 0)
```

This statement is then executed via the objConn object and the results are reported back to the browser indicating the success or failure of the statement. (We'll see the Errors collection in action later in this chapter.)

Notice that the *Option* parameter of the Connection object's Execute method specifies adExecuteNoRecords. This option, new to ADO 2.0, instructs the Connection object not to generate a recordset. Why would it? Well, in this case it shouldn't create a recordset because we haven't asked for any data to be returned. This was a glitch in previous versions of ADO that has been corrected in ADO 2.0. If you omit the adExecuteNoRecords in the execution of this statement, ADO will generate a recordset of no records – which takes up extra memory and time and is essentially a waste of resources.

The moral to this story is to always specify this option if you are executing an action query, otherwise you are going to have extraneous memory overhead.

Creating Recordsets

We can also use the Connection object's ability to create recordsets to generate data dynamically on our web pages. We'll cover recordsets in depth beginning at Chapter 5 – however it's useful to see this example in context.

The following code uses a select table name and dynamically generates a table of data from the selected table. It uses the Fields collection of the Recordset object to create the row header of the table; and then proceeds to process through the data and add it to a table on the web page.

```
<%
strSQL = "SELECT * FROM " & Request("TableName")
Set objConn = Session("Connection")
Set objRSData = objConn.Execute(strSQL)
%>
<TABLE border=1 CELPADDING="2" CELLSPACING="0" WIDTH=100%>
  <TR>
    <%For intCol = 0 To objRSData.Fields.Count - 1 %>
      <TD nowrap bgcolor="#000060" valign="top">
        <FONT FACE="helvetica,verdana,arial" SIZE=2 COLOR="#99cccc"><B>
        <% = objRSData.Fields(intCol).Name%></B></FONT>
      </TD>
    <%Next%>
  </TR>
  <%
  objRSData.MoveFirst
  Do Until objRSData.EOF
    %>
    <TR>
      <%For intCol = 0 To objRSData.Fields.Count - 1%>
        <TD nowrap bgcolor="<%=strColor%>">
          <FONT FACE="helvetica,verdana,arial" SIZE="1">
          <% If IsNull(objRSData.Fields(intCol).Value) Then
            Response.Write " "
          Else
            Response.Write objRSData.Fields(intCol).Value
          End If
          %></FONT>
        </TD>
      <%Next%>
    </TR>
    <%
    objRSData.MoveNext
  Loop
%>
</TABLE>
```

As you can see from the code, we create the recordset by using the `Connection` object's `Execute` method to execute the SQL statement. We then iterate through the field names to create the header row of the table. Next we move through the records and populate the table with the data from the recordset.

Executing Stored Procedures

Likewise, stored procedures can be called by the `Connection` object. Let's take a look at the definition of the following stored procedure in SQL Server.

```
CREATE PROC prAddAuthor
  @au_id char(11),
  @au_lname varchar(40),
  @au_fname varchar(20),
  @phone char(12),
 @contract bit
AS

INSERT authors (au_id, au_lname, au_fname, phone, contract)
VALUES (@au_id, @au_lname, @au_fname, @phone, @contract)

GO
```

And now let's examine the ASP code that calls this stored procedure via the `Connection` object's `Execute` method:

```
Dim strSQL
Dim intCount
Dim strSSN
Dim strLastName
Dim strFirstName
Dim strPhone
Dim booUnderContract

strSSN = Request("txtSSN")
strLastName = Request("txtLastName")
strFirstName = Request("txtFirstName")
strPhone = Request("txtPhone")
booUnderContract = Request("chkUnderContract")

Set objConn = Session("Connection")

On Error Resume Next

strSQL = "EXEC prAddAuthor "
strSQL = strSQL & "'" & strSSN & "', "
strSQL = strSQL & "'" & strLastName & "', "
strSQL = strSQL & "'" & strFirstName & "', "
strSQL = strSQL & "'" & strPhone & "', "
strSQL = strSQL & booUnderContract & ")"

objConn.Execute strSQL, , adExecuteNoRecords

If Err.Number <> 0 Then
  Response.Write "A problem occurred while adding the "
  Response.Write "new author '" & Request("FirstName") & " "
  Response.Write  Request("LastName") & "'.<BR>"
Else
  Response.Write "New author '" & Request("FirstName") & " "
  Response.Write  Request("LastName") & "' was added.<BR>"
End If
```

As you can see, this is largely similar to the code we saw in the previous section, and again, we are requesting the new author's information from the previous web page. This time, however, each text box from that page is concatenated into a call to a stored procedure, which is once again executed directly against the connection. The `strSQL` variable might contain the following:

```
EXEC prAddAuthor '123-45-6789', 'Doe', 'Jane', '555-1212', 0
```

Although the result is the same as the dynamically generated `INSERT` statement in the section above, this method produces better overall performance since the stored procedure is already compiled on the server. When a dynamic query is sent to the server it must be syntax-checked and compiled before it is executed; in contrast, a stored procedure could very well be in cache and all that need happen is the actual execution of the code.

We will further examine both of these abilities when looking at the `Command` *object in Chapter 4.*

Transactions

ADO has a number of methods and properties, belonging to the Connection object, to support transactions. You can start a transaction with the BeginTrans method. It is also possible to nest transactions, i.e. to start another transaction before concluding the previous one. Each transaction can be rolled back (the RollbackTrans method) or committed (the CommitTrans method). Depending on the value set in the Attributes property, another transaction may be started automatically when the previous transaction is completed with either of these two methods. Finally, you can also specify how transactions will interact with one another, using the IsolationLevel property.

In order to start a transaction for the Connection object, the data provider must support transactions. Keep in mind that some data providers do not support transactions, while others not only support them, but also support nested transactions (ODBC does not support nested transactions). In addition, some providers (such as SQL Server 6.5) support nested transaction syntax, but do not commit any transactions until the outermost one is called (known as fake nesting). Let's look at these transaction-related properties and methods.

The BeginTrans Method

The BeginTrans method starts a transaction for the Connection object. All changes to any data that uses this connection will be cached until the transaction is either committed or aborted. To determine if the provider supports transactions, we can examine the Transaction DDL property in the connection's Properties collection.

```
Dim blnTransactions
blnTransactions = objConn.Properties("Transaction DDL")
If blnTransactions <> DBPROPVAL_TC_NONE Then
  ' --Transactions are supported
  objConn.BeginTrans
End If
```

The Transaction DDL property will return one of five possible DBPROPVAL_TC constants, indicating whether transactions are supported, whether transactions can contain Data Definition Language (DDL) and Data Manipulation Language (DML) statements, and whether these statements will be ignored or cause errors.

> **You can find the complete listing of these constants, with their descriptions, values and where to find them, in the DBPROPVAL_TC table in Appendix I, *DB Schema Constants*.**

In the code example above, we are checking to see if any type of transaction is supported, and if so, we begin a transaction against the connection.

The RollbackTrans Method

The RollbackTrans method allows us to abort a transaction, causing any changes to data that occurred in the transaction to be abandoned. We'll see an example of this below.

The CommitTrans Method

Using the CommitTrans method causes any pending changes within the current transaction to be saved and ends the current transaction. If we have nested transactions, only the inner transaction will be completed.

```
objConn.BeginTrans                          ' -- Start Main Transaction A

  objConn.Execute "UPDATE authors SET au_lname = 'Black' " & _
                "WHERE au_lname = 'White'

  objConn.BeginTrans                        ' -- Start Sub-Transaction B
    objConn.Execute "UPDATE authors SET au_lname = 'Green' " & _
                "WHERE au_lname = 'Greene'
  objConn.CommitTrans                       ' -- Commit Sub-Transaction B

  objConn.BeginTrans                        ' -- Start Sub-Transaction C
  objConn.Execute "UPDATE authors SET au_lname = 'Smith' " & _
                "WHERE au_lname = 'Smyth'
  objConn.CommitTrans                       ' -- Commit Sub-Transaction C

objConn.CommitTrans                         ' -- Commit Main Transaction A
```

As we can see in the above code, for each `BeginTrans` there must be a matching `CommitTrans` or `RollbackTrans`. Although some providers offer this capability of nesting transactions, it is not a common practice. Additionally, if the `Attributes` property (see the next section) has been set to automatically start a new transaction after another was completed, you can get locked into a nested transaction. Examine the following code:

```
objConn.Attributes = adXactCommitRetaining
objConn.BeginTrans                          ' -- Start Main Transaction A

  objConn.Execute "UPDATE authors SET au_lname = 'Black' " & _
                "WHERE au_lname = 'White'

  objConn.BeginTrans                        ' -- Start Sub-Transaction B
    objConn.Execute "UPDATE authors SET au_lname = 'Green' " & _
                "WHERE au_lname = 'Greene'
  objConn.CommitTrans                       ' -- Commit Sub-Transaction B

              ' -- Another Sub-Transaction (C) will automatically start
    objConn.Execute "UPDATE authors SET au_lname = 'Smith' " & _
                "WHERE au_lname = 'Smyth'
  objConn.CommitTrans                       ' -- Commit Sub-Transaction C

              ' -- Another Sub-Transaction (D) will automatically start
  objConn.RollbackTrans                     ' -- Rollback Sub-Transaction D

objConn.CommitTrans                         ' -- Commit Main Transaction A

        ' -- Another Main Transaction (E) will automatically start
```

As we can see, every time we committed a transaction, a new one was started, keeping us in the nested transaction. Only after we performed a `RollbackTrans` (transaction D) are we able to get back to the main transaction (A) in order to commit it. When we commit transaction A, that commit causes another main transaction to commence. It is important to keep in mind the effect that the `Attributes` property and nested transactions can have.

The Attributes Property

This property controls the capability of automatically starting transactions after another transaction has been committed, aborted, or both. The default value for this property is 0. There are two enumeration constants as defined by the **adXactAttributeEnum**:

- ❑ `adXactCommitRetaining` – Automatically start a new transaction after one has been committed (with the `CommitTrans` method)
- ❑ `adXactAbortRetaining` – Automatically start a new transaction after one has been aborted (with the `RollbackTrans` method)

We can set the `Attributes` property to either value, or we can **AND** these values together to have a new transaction start after another transaction has either completed or been aborted. For example:

```
objConn.Attributes = adXactCommitRetaining And adXactAbortRetaining
```

We need to be aware that all providers do not necessarily support this ability. Also, some data providers (such as SQL Server) can have this type of automatic transaction capability already turned on at the back end. Changing this value overrides the settings pre-established on the server.

To clear this property (and prevent transactions from automatically starting), just set the value to 0.

The IsolationLevel Property

This property indicates the transaction isolation level for the connection, which determines how transactions interact with each other. Let's take a look at the settable values and then we will go through a more detailed explanation.

- ❑ `adXactUnspecified` – the isolation level cannot be determined or the level we specified is not available.
- ❑ `adXactChaos` – prevents us from overwriting pending changes from another user.
- ❑ `adXactBrowse` or `adXactReadUncommitted` – allows us to see uncommitted changes to data. In other words, data that is exclusively locked by one transaction is visible even while that transaction is still in effect. Reading uncommitted data is known as a *dirty read*.
- ❑ `adXactCursorStability` or `adXactReadCommitted` (default) – transactions that exclusively lock data will bar all other transactions from accessing that data until the lock is released.
- ❑ `adXactRepeatableRead` – prevents us from seeing changes made by other transactions until the data is requeried.
- ❑ `adXactIsolated` or `adXactSerializable` – transactions are completely isolated from one another. During the scope of a transaction, any type of lock will bar other transactions from accessing the data, no matter what type of lock the initial transaction used.

For example, let's say we want to be able to read data regardless of its current locking state. We would set the IsolationLevel as follows:

```
Dim strConn

strConn = "Provider=SQLOLEDB; Data Source=MyServer; Initial Catalog=pubs;"
strConn = strConn & " User Id=" & Session("UserName") & "; "
strConn = strConn & " Password=" & Session("Password")
objConn.ConnectionString = strConn

objConn.IsolationLevel = adXactReadUncommitted
```

```
objConn.Open

objConn.DefaultDatabase = "pubs"

Set objRSAuthors = objConn.Execute("SELECT * FROM authors", ,adCmdText)
```

Now, no matter what the state of the data that we are trying to read, we will retrieve its current values. If another user had been in the middle of changing the last name of one of the authors from 'Greene' to 'Green', we would retrieve the changed value of 'Green'. However, if that other user rolled back his/her transaction, we would have inaccurate data.

Some data providers allow for this setting to be overridden on an individual command basis. For example (using SQL Server):

```
Dim strConn

strConn = "Provider=SQLOLEDB; Data Source=MyServer; Initial Catalog=pubs;"
strConn = strConn & " User Id=" & Session("UserName") & "; "
strConn = strConn & " Password=" & Session("Password")
objConn.ConnectionString = strConn

objConn.IsolationLevel = adXactSerializable

objConn.Open

objConn.DefaultDatabase = "pubs"

Set objRSAuthors = _
               objConn.Execute("SELECT * FROM authors (nolock)", ,adCmdText)
```

The SQL Server (nolock) optimizer hint specified in the SELECT statement overrides the isolation level setting for the connection.

> *This is an explicit override that will be particular to the data store. The optimizer hint needs to be stated explicitly in order to override the existing transaction isolation level. Otherwise, the specified isolation level will be used. The isolation level is the implicit feature – for example, by choosing a transaction isolation level of "Serializable", we are implicitly using (without stating it in our SQl code) the "holdlock" optimizer hint.*

So in the example code above, even if a user was in the middle of changing an author's last name, we would still read the uncommitted data.

Connection Pooling

Connection pooling is a technique that ADO uses to maintain connections behind the scenes even after we close them in our code. The connection itself is only closed if it is not reused within a certain period of time. The connection will only be reused if the information about the newly-requested connection (including the user name and password) is *exactly* the same as the cached connection.

This process saves overhead by reducing the number of times we need to physically go through the connection process. When we make a request for a connection (using the Open method of the Connection object), the provider looks for an existing connection in the pool that matches the requested connection. If a match is found, we are handed this *existing* Connection object – thus avoiding the need to create a new one.

It does not matter who originally owned the connection; when anyone 'closes' a connection, the connection is placed in the connection pool and waits to be reused. Unused connections do not sit in the connection pool forever – after a predetermined period of time, unused connections are automatically discarded and their resources released.

If we do not want to use connection pooling, we can use the OLE DB Services property from the Properties collection of the Connection object. Take a look at the following code:

```
objConn.Properties("OLE DB Services") = DBPROPVAL_OS_ENABLEALL AND (NOT
DBPROPVAL_OS_RESOURCEPOOLING)
```

or

```
objConn.Properties("OLE DB Services") = -2
```

You can use either of these lines of code to specify that the Connection object, objConn should pool its connections. Thus, each time a connection is closed, it really is closed. Although you can turn off connection pooling, it is not a recommended practice.

> *More detailed information regarding the* Properties *collection can be found in the Detailed Properties Collection – Appendix C.*

When using ODBC providers, the connection pooling option can be configured through the ODBC applet in the Control Panel.

The Errors Collection

The Errors collection provides us with the ability to see all and any problems that are reported by the data provider when executing SQL statements and stored procedures, and retrieving recordsets. The Errors collection is dynamically populated with Error objects, whenever the provider has a problem and needs to report it back to the consumer. ADO errors are not included in the Errors collection; rather, those cause a run-time error in the application code. The Errors collection houses only those errors and warnings supplied by the data provider itself.

The Errors collection is a property of the Connection object. The Errors collection itself has the following methods and properties:

- ❑ The Clear method clears the Errors collection
- ❑ The Count property is the current number of Error objects in the Errors collection
- ❑ The Item property is the indexed Error object within the collection
- ❑ The Refresh method refreshes the Errors collection

The `Error` object also has the following properties:

- ❑ `Description` – the descriptive text of the error
- ❑ `HelpContext` – the help context identification for the error
- ❑ `HelpFile` – the name of the help file for the error
- ❑ `NativeError` – the provider's native error number
- ❑ `Number` – the error number
- ❑ `Source` – gives the source of the error (i.e. the name of the application or object that raised the error)
- ❑ `SQLState` – the SQL error number (the SQL state for a given error object returns a 5-character error string)

The following code demonstrates a call to a data store (SQL Server) that will cause an error. The error will then be returned to the browser.

```
Dim strSQL
Dim intCount

On Error Resume Next

strSQL = "INSERT authors (au_id, au_lname, au_fname, phone, contract) VALUES('"
strSQL = strSQL & Request("SSN") & "', '"
strSQL = strSQL & Request("LastName") & "', '"
strSQL = strSQL & Request("FirstName") & "', '"
strSQL = strSQL & Request("Phone") & "', "
strSQL = strSQL & Request("UnderContract") & ")"

objConn.Execute strSQL, , adExecuteNoRecords

If Err.Number <> 0 Then
  Response.Write "Error(s) occurred while adding new author.<BR><BR>"
  For intCount = 0 to objConn.Errors.Count - 1
    Response.Write objConn.Errors.Item(intCount).Description & "<BR>"
  Next
Else
  Response.Write "New author was added.<BR>"
End If
```

The code above attempts to insert a new author into the `authors` table. If the `INSERT` statement being executed fails, the description of each error in the `Errors` collection will be displayed in the browser. Otherwise, a message indicating a successful addition will be displayed.

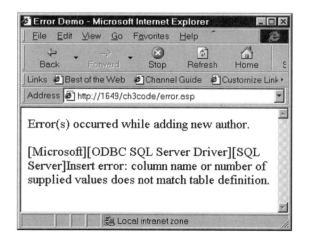

The Errors collection does not work properly when used with custom objects in Microsoft Transaction Server (MTS). MTS causes a generic "Automation Error" to be passed back. If we want to retrieve the ADO error information, we must send those errors via some other mechanism (for example, via a function that encapsulates iterating through the Errors collection, and returns an array containing the error information from within the custom object).

Summary

We've seen in this chapter how an instance of the ADO Connection object represents a unique connection to a datastore. Its methods and properties give us control over the connection. Among other things, the Connection object allows us to:

- ❑ Execute SQL directly against the connection, and even retrieve data into recordsets
- ❑ Manage data, transactions and isolation (locking) levels
- ❑ Retrieve schema information from our data provider
- ❑ Access the data provider's error information, via the Errors collection
- ❑ Control connection pooling

As we've seen, we can achieve some command and recordset functionality using the Connection object, without explicitly creating a Command or Recordset object.

Having had a taster of commands and recordsets in this chapter, let's now move on to the Command object itself.

The Command Object

The Command object, like the Connection object, allows us to execute commands against a data store. Looking at the available properties and methods (found in Appendix A), we can see that the Command object has fewer of both. Yet the Command object is designed to perform a single task: execute code against a data store, whether this is sending a dynamically generated SQL statement to the database server or executing a stored procedure.

Because of its specialized function, the Command object gives us further extensibility when executing code statements. The Connection object can indeed call stored procedures, even those with parameters; but the Command object can dynamically retrieve the parameters and send them to the client. The client can dynamically display these parameters (without having to know the number or type of the parameters), request values from the user, and then call the procedure while passing back the parameters' values.

We are going to delve into the intricacies of the Command object while exploring the following topics:

- ❑ What is a Command?
- ❑ Using Command Objects
- ❑ The Parameters Collection
- ❑ The Parameter Object
- ❑ Using Stored Procedures

For each broad area we'll look at the relevant methods and properties.

What is a Command Object?

The name of this object also provides a definition. As we stated above, a Command object provides us with a means of executing statements against a data store and optionally returning records back to a Recordset object – or in other words, it represents a command that can be issued to a data store.

In strict regards to executing code, a Command object can do all that a Connection object can do although it cannot manage transactions (which is considered a connection level feature). A Command object, however, also gives us some additional abilities not found in the Connection object, such as disconnected recordsets and use of the parameters collection.

Disconnected Recordsets

Command objects can also be used to create disconnected recordsets. To do this we first create a Command object and associate it with a connection. We can then create a recordset from the Command object via the Execute method. Finally, we disassociate the Command object from the connection. Although disconnected, the recordset can still be traversed and even sent back to the data store for updating. We will see more about disconnected recordsets in Chapter 8.

Parameters

As we will see in a later section of this chapter, the Parameters collection plays an important role when accessing stored procedures in the data store. If a stored procedure passes values back through its parameters, a Connection object cannot retrieve the values. However, a Command object can use its Parameters collection to both send and retrieve changed parameter values, and retrieve a stored procedure's return value.

So without further ado, let's jump into the heart of the matter by exploring the properties and methods of the Command object.

Using the Command Object

Under the heading *Executing Commands* below, we'll begin by looking at the command itself, and how it is executed. Following on from this, under the heading *Connecting to a DataSource*, we'll look at properties and methods relating to connections and other operations.

Executing Commands

In this section we'll cover the CommandText, CommandType, CommandTimeout and Prepared properties, and the Execute method.

CommandText Property

```
String = Command.CommandText
Command.CommandText = String
```

The `CommandText` property gives us a means of holding our command (as a string) for later execution. It can contain a SQL statement, a stored procedure name, a table name, or a command that is specific to the data provider. The type of command stored here is reflected in the `CommandType` property.

For example, we can assign a simple SQL statement to the `CommandText` property.

```
objCommand.CommandText = "SELECT * FROM authors"
```

Alternatively, perhaps we want to call a stored procedure. We place the name of the procedure into the `CommandText` property, and we tell the data store that the command is a stored procedure.

```
' Create the session instance of the command "AddAuthorCmd"
Set objCommand = CreateObject("ADODB.Command")
objCommand.CommandText = "prAddAuthor"
objCommand.CommandType = adCmdStoredProc

' Code to create and append parameters would be here
' We will see an example of this later in the chapter

Set Session("AddAuthorCmd") = objCommand
Set objCommand = Nothing


' Create the session instance of the command "UpdateAuthorCmd"
Set objCommand = CreateObject("ADODB.Command")
objCommand.CommandText = "prUpdateAuthor"
objCommand.CommandType = adCmdStoredProc

' Code to create and append parameters would be here
' We will see an example of this later in the chapter

Set Session("UpdateAuthorCmd") = objCommand
Set objCommand = Nothing
```

This code creates two session command instances: `AddAuthorCmd` and `UpdateAuthorCmd`. This code could be placed in the `Global.ASA` file so the two `Command` objects could be referenced throughout the session. Each one has a simple `CommandText` property that holds the name of the respective stored procedure.

As we have seen in the previous chapter, we can also dynamically create the statement that we want to send to the server and place it into the `CommandText` property. But by using a stored procedure, and appending some parameters beforehand, we make the process of modifying or adding authors simpler and we now have more modular, reusable code.

> *Depending on the* `CommandType` *property setting, ADO may alter the* `CommandText` *property. You can read the* `CommandText` *property at any time to see the actual command text that ADO will use during execution.*

CommandType Property

```
CommandTypeEnum = Command.CommandType
Command.CommandType = CommandTypeEnum
```

The CommandType property is used to clarify what type of command will be sent to the data store. You can override this value with the Options parameter of the Execute method – we'll see this a little further on. It can contain one of the following values:

- ❑ adCmdText – execute a statement against the data store (e.g. a SELECT statement in SQL Server)
- ❑ adCmdTable – opens a table (e.g. using "SELECT * FROM TableName")
- ❑ adCmdTableDirect –directly opens a table (not supported by all providers)
- ❑ adCmdStoredProc – execute a stored procedure
- ❑ adCmdFile – opens a recordset saved via the Recordset object's Save method (See Chapter 8, *Disconnected Recordsets*)
- ❑ adCmdUnknown – the command type is not known. This is the default.

This first example shows a simple SQL statement to retrieve the first and last names of all of the authors. Since it is an SQL statement, we assign adCmdText to the CommandType property:

```
objCommand.CommandType = adCmdText
objCommand.CommandText = "SELECT au_fname, au_lname FROM authors"
```

Or we can set up the command to make a call to a stored procedure, in which case we would code the following:

```
objCommand.CommandText = "prAddAuthor" ' The name of the stored procedure
objCommand.CommandType = adCmdStoredProc       ' Specify a stored procedure type
```

The next two code snippets show two different ways of accessing all the data from the authors table. The first one uses a command type of adCmdText to execute a query against the authors table:

```
objCommand.CommandType = adCmdText
objCommand.CommandText = "SELECT * FROM authors"
Set objCommand.ActiveConnection = objConn
Set objRSAuthors = objCommand.Execute
```

This second snippet uses a command type of adCmdTable to open the authors table:

```
objCommand.CommandType = adCmdTable
objCommand.CommandText = "authors"
Set objCommand.ActiveConnection = objConn
Set objRSAuthors = objCommand.Execute
```

Both will return all columns and all rows from the authors table.

Execute Method

```
Set Recordset = Command.Execute([RecordsAffected], [Parameters],
[Options])
Command.Execute([RecordsAffected], [Parameters], [Options])
```

Like its Connection counterpart, the Command object's execute method provides us with the means to actually execute the command and retrieve data from the data store. Unlike the Connection object, however, the Command object allows parameters to be passed to the data store. The Execute method has three optional arguments: RecordsAffected, Parameters and Options. Let's take a closer look at these items.

RecordsAffected

When a variable is supplied as this argument, the provider updates the variable's value to be equal to the number of rows that were affected by the execution of the Command object. In the following example, lngRows will contain the number of authors whose contract field was updated:

```
strSQL = "UPDATE authors SET contract = 1 WHERE state = '"
strSQL = strSQL & Request("txtState") & "'"
objCommand.CommandText = strSQL
objCommand.CommandType = adCmdText

' Now execute the procedure and put the number of rows affected
' by the update into the variable lngRows
objCommand.Execute lngRows, , adExecuteNoRecords
```

We can now take this value of how many records in the authors' table were updated and report it back to the client who made the request for the update.

Parameters

If we need to supply a set of parameters in order for the command to execute, we can either use the Parameters collection, or pass the set of parameters in as this Parameters argument. The argument requires that the array (or a variable if there is only one parameter) that is passed in, has the same number of parameters used in the procedure. If this argument is supplied, it overrides the values of the items in the Parameters collection. As we can see in the following code, although the @phone and @contract parameters were assigned in the Parameters collection, their values never get sent to the data store, since we supplied an array for this argument.

```
' Assign the parameter values
objCommand.Parameters("@au_id").Value = strSSN
objCommand.Parameters("@au_lname").Value = strLastName
objCommand.Parameters("@au_fname").Value = strFirstName
objCommand.Parameters("@phone").Value = strPhone
objCommand.Parameters("@contract").Value = booUnderContract

' Assign the parameter values to an array
arrParams = Array(strSSN, strLastName, strFirstName, "UNKNOWN", 0)

' Now execute the procedure
objCommand.Execute , arrParams, adExecuteNoRecords
```

We would never write code as we see here, but it demonstrates the overriding capability of this argument. The phone and contract fields will be sent as UNKNOWN and 0 respectively, regardless of our previous assignment of those values in the Parameters collection.

Options

One feature of the Options argument is that it lets us override the CommandType of the Command object. Like the CommandType property, we can specify adCmdText, adCmdStoredProc, etc.... We can also tell the command to run asynchronously by supplying one of the following items: adAsyncExecute, adAsyncFetch or adAsyncFetchNonBlocking. If we want to supply more than one of these options, we need to Or them together, like so.

```
objCommand.Execute , , adCmdText Or adAsyncExecute
```

The full list of available values for the Options parameter can be found in Appendix A.

CommandTimeout Property

```
Long = Command.CommandTimeout
Command.CommandTimeout = Long
```

Just like the same property of the Connection object, it establishes the timeout value for the execution of a command sent to the data store. The default timeout value is 30 seconds – we could set it to 25 seconds like this:

```
objCommand.CommandTimeout = 25
```

This value is not inherited from the associated connection, nor does the associated connection's CommandTimeout value override the Command object. The CommandTimeout for a connection only applies to when we call the Execute method of the connection itself. The CommandTimeout for a command applies only to the command itself. And one last note, assigning a value of 0 causes the command to run indefinitely.

Prepared Property

```
Boolean = Command.Prepared
Command.Prepared = Boolean
```

The Prepared property tells the data store whether or not to create a temporary compiled version of the command on the data store before it is actually executed. This is useful for commands with a CommandType that is not adCmdStoredProc. The first time the command is executed, we take a performance hit, since the code must be compiled on the data store, but any execution after the first will run faster, since there is no need to check syntax or compile the code again. This is useful if we need to execute the same command multiple times.

Connecting to a Data Source

In this section we'll cover the ActiveConnection, State and Name properties, and the Cancel method.

ActiveConnection

```
Set Connection = Command.ActiveConnection
Set Command.ActiveConnection = Connection
String = Command.ActiveConnection
Command.ActiveConnection = String
```

The `ActiveConnection` property is used to establish a connection to a data store for the `Command` object. We can supply either a valid `Connection` object or a connection string (like that of the `Connection` object), depending on whether or not we had a `Connection` object already created. If we use a connection string, a new connection is created anyway. This is, of course, if a connection is not found in the connection pool (see Chapter 3).

> *If a connection string is assigned to the* `ActiveConnection` *property, a connection is created to the data store (through a* `Connection` *object that is created in the background). The connection pool applies to all connections that are instantiated, whether through a connection object directly or another object indirectly.*

Here's how we set the `ActiveConnection` property with a connection string:

```
Dim strConn

strConn = "Provider=SQLOLEDB; Data Source=MyServer; Initial Catalog=pubs;"
strConn = strConn & " User Id=" & Session("UserName") & "; "
strConn = strConn & " Password=" & Session("Password") & ";"
objCommand.ActiveConnection = strConn
```

Alternatively we can use a `Connection` object:

```
Set objCommand.ActiveConnection = objConn
```

Either of these will establish a connection for the `Command` object. In order to disassociate a command with a connection, we must set the `ActiveConnection` property to `Nothing`, as shown here.

```
Set objCommand.ActiveConnection = Nothing
```

When the `Command` object is reconnected to a data store, it will retain all of its properties with one exception. If we generated a collection of parameters by using the `Parameters` collection's `Refresh` method (covered later in the chapter), the collection will be emptied. This does not apply to situations where parameters were manually appended to the `Parameters` collection using the `Append` method. These manually-appended parameters will remain. Appending parameters offers us the ability to maintain a command and its parameters, while allowing us to disconnect and reconnect as needed. The process of manually appending parameters also offers us not only the ability to use parameters with a wider range of data providers, but it is more efficient than refreshing the parameters.

Let's put some of what we have seen together in a more concrete example. In this following example we are responding to a request for either an update of author information or the addition of a new author. The form object `CommandType` determines which, as we will see in the following.

```
<INPUT TYPE="SUBMIT" NAME="CommandType" VALUE="ADD">
<INPUT TYPE="SUBMIT" NAME="CommandType" VALUE="INSERT">
```

If the user clicks the ADD button, then the `Command` object for adding an author, which is already established in the session, is used and associated with the existing connection (also held in the session). The same holds true for modifying an author, where an existing command for updating author information is used.

```
<%@ LANGUAGE="VBSCRIPT" %>
<HTML>
<HEAD>
<META HTTP-EQUIV="Content-Type" content="text/html; charset=iso-8859-1">
<TITLE>Results Page</TITLE>
</HEAD>
<BODY BGCOLOR="#FFFFFF">
<P ALIGN="CENTER"><IMG SRC="images/Results.gif" WIDTH="219" HEIGHT="108"></P>
<P ALIGN="CENTER"><FONT COLOR="#400080" SIZE="5"><STRONG>Report Selection
</STRONG></FONT></P>
<P ALIGN="CENTER"><FONT COLOR="#400080" SIZE="3">
<%
Dim strSSN
Dim strLastName
Dim strFirstName
Dim strPhone
Dim booUnderContract

strSSN = Request("txtSSN")
strLastName = Request("txtLastName")
strFirstName = Request("txtFirstName")
strPhone = Request("txtPhone")
booUnderContract = Request("chkUnderContract")

Set objConn = Session("Connection")

If Request("CommandType") = "ADD" Then
     Set objCommand = Session("AddAuthorCmd")
Else
     Set objCommand = Session("UpdateAuthorCmd")
End If

Set objCommand.ActiveConnection = objConn

' Assign the parameter values
objCommand.Parameters("@au_id").Value = strSSN
objCommand.Parameters("@au_lname").Value = strLastName
objCommand.Parameters("@au_fname").Value = strFirstName
objCommand.Parameters("@phone").Value = strPhone
objCommand.Parameters("@contract").Value = booUnderContract
```

```
objCommand.Execute , , adExecuteNoRecords     ' Now execute the procedure

If Request("CommandType") = "ADD" Then
     Response.Write "New author '" & Request("FirstName") & " "
     Response.Write  Request("LastName") & "' was added.<BR>"
Else
     Response.Write "Author '" & Request("FirstName") & " "
     Response.Write  Request("LastName") & "' was updated.<BR>"
End If
%>
</P>
<P ALIGN="CENTER"><FONT COLOR="#400080" SIZE="3">
<A HREF="MainMenu.asp">Click here to continue</A></FONT></P>
</BODY>
</HTML>
```

By using pre-existing `Command` objects with pre-existing parameters, we save ourselves the trouble of recreating them each time we need to make a call with either command. Keep in mind, however, that we incur additional overhead by maintaining these objects on the server. We are going to see several variations on this same theme throughout the chapter.

State Property

Long = Command.State

The read-only `State` property indicates the current condition of the `Command` object and can return one of the following values:

- ❑ `adStateClosed` – the command is closed (disconnected from a data store)
- ❑ `adStateOpen` – the command is open (connected to a data store)
- ❑ `adStateExecuting` – the command is in the middle of executing
- ❑ `adStateFetching` – the command is in the middle of fetching data

The last two items can only be returned if we are in the middle of running an asynchronous command. For example, we may need to check if a `Command` object is still connected to the data store. If not, we can reassign its `ActiveConnection` property and continue working.

Cancel Method

Command.Cancel

The `Cancel` method is used in conjunction with asynchronous operations of the `Command` object. Although ADO supports asynchronous operations, they are not typically implemented in web-based applications. If an asynchronous operation is not in effect, executing this method will cause a run-time error in our code. In general, asynchronous operations are used in middle-tier (business layer) applications that provide business rules to a 3-tier client-server application. Since we are concentrating on writing ADO code within Active Server Pages and not in a middle-tier, we will find very little use for asynchronous operations against a data store.

Name Property

```
String = Command.Name
Command.Name = String
```

Name is really quite an interesting property. It allows us to create a new "method" for a Connection object. If the Name property of a Command object has been set and it is associated to a Connection object (via the ActiveConnection property), that Connection object inherits the name as a new method, which executes the CommandText of the associated Command object. Let's take a look at the following example to help clarify:

```
' Code to create the connection objConn should go here

' Create the session instance of the command "AddAuthorCmd"
Set objCommand = CreateObject("ADODB.Command")
objCommand.CommandText = "prAddAuthor"
objCommand.CommandType = adCmdStoredProc

' Code to create and append parameters would be here
' We will see an example of this later in the chapter

objCommand.Name = "AddAuthor"
Set objCommand.ActiveConnection = objConn
' Assign the command to the session and clear the local variable
Set Session("AddAuthorCmd") = objCommand
Set objCommand = Nothing

' Create the session instance of the command "UpdateAuthorCmd"
Set objCommand = CreateObject("ADODB.Command")
objCommand.CommandText = "prUpdateAuthor"
objCommand.CommandType = adCmdStoredProc

' Code to create and append parameters would be here
' We will see an example of this later in the chapter

objCommand.Name = "UpdateAuthor"
Set objCommand.ActiveConnection = objConn
Set Session("UpdateAuthorCmd") = objCommand
Set objCommand = Nothing

Set Session("Connection") = objConn
```

We have created two Command objects with the following names: AddAuthor and UpdateAuthor. Each is associated with objConn, which is then stored back in the session. Now that connection has two new methods based on the names of the two Command objects. If we change some of the code we saw earlier, we can still opt to insert or update an author, but via these two new methods.

```
<%@ LANGUAGE="VBSCRIPT" %>
<HTML>
<HEAD>
<META HTTP-EQUIV="Content-Type" content="text/html; charset=iso-8859-1">
<TITLE>Results Page</TITLE>
</HEAD>
<BODY BGCOLOR="#FFFFFF">
<P ALIGN="CENTER"><IMG SRC="images/Results.gif" WIDTH="219" HEIGHT="108"></P>
<P ALIGN="CENTER"><FONT COLOR="#400080" SIZE="5"><STRONG>Report Selection
```

```
</STRONG></FONT></P>
<P ALIGN="CENTER"><FONT COLOR="#400080" SIZE="3">
<%
Dim strSSN
Dim strLastName
Dim strFirstName
Dim strPhone
Dim booUnderContract

strSSN = Request("txtSSN")
strLastName = Request("txtLastName")
strFirstName = Request("txtFirstName")
strPhone = Request("txtPhone")
booUnderContract = Request("chkUnderContract")

Set objConn = Session("Connection")

If Request("CommandType") = "ADD" Then
   objConn.AddAuthor strSSN, strLastName, strFirstName, _
     strPhone, booUnderContract
   Response.Write "New author '" & Request("FirstName") & " "
   Response.Write  Request("LastName") & "' was added.<BR>"
Else
   objConn.UpdateAuthor strSSN, strLastName, strFirstName, _
     strPhone, booUnderContract
   Response.Write "Author '" & Request("FirstName") & " "
   Response.Write  Request("LastName") & "' was updated.<BR>"
End If
%>
</P>
<P ALIGN="CENTER"><FONT COLOR="#400080" SIZE="3">
<A HREF="MainMenu.asp">Click here to continue</A></FONT></P>
</BODY>
</HTML>
```

Notice how we do not need to reference the commands, but rather, the new methods of the connection itself. We pass in the author's information as parameters of the two new methods.

Parameters

The `Parameters` collection holds the individual parameters that are used by the `Command` object. The collection itself allows us to find a count of items, address the individual items, append new items and delete existing items.

The Parameters CollectionCount Property (Parameters Collection)

Long = Command.Parameters.Count

This property will return the number of `Parameter` objects in the `Parameters` collection.

Item Property (Parameters Collection)

Parameter = Command.Parameters.Item(Index|Name)
Parameter = Command.Parameters(Index|Name)

The `Item` property is the default property of the `Parameters` collection; thus it need not be used when referencing items in the collection. This is a consistency we see in many object models, so much so that we often forget that these collections even have an `Item` property. When referencing an item, we may use either the index number (zero-based) or the name of the parameter itself. If the name is not unique within the collection, the referenced parameter will be the first item in the collection with that name value.

Append Method (Parameters Collection)

`Command.Parameters.Append Parameter`

The `Append` method is used to add a `Parameter` object to the end of the `Parameters` collection. There are two reasons why we append parameters rather than retrieve the list of parameters from the data store by using the `Refresh` method. First is the issue of performance. Using the `Refresh` method requires a call to the data store, which means extra processing by the database, and extra network flow. This extra flow over the network causes an even greater performance hit when the network is the Internet itself. The second and more compelling reason is that certain providers do not support the `Refresh` method. In these cases it is necessary to manually create and append parameters, since there is no way to request the list from the data store. And as we have mentioned before, if we want to be able to disconnect from the data store and maintain the parameters in the `Command` object, we must append the parameters, since a set of parameters that were generated using the `Refresh` method will not be maintained when the connection is released from the `Command` object.

In its defense, unless we are making frequent calls to the `Refresh` method, it does not make our ASP code run extremely slow. Yes, we might see the barely noticeable change in performance, but, overall, it would be invisible to the users of our web application. The best thing to do is to try each methodology and see if there is a significant enough performance difference. Processor speed, type of data store and other factors may have a more profound effect on the performance for the `Refresh` method.

We can create a parameter and then append it to the `Parameters` collection as such.

```
Set objParam = objCommand.CreateParameter("@qty", adInteger, adParamInput)
objCommand.Parameters.Append objParam
```

Or we can create and append the parameter in one step.

```
objCommand.Parameters.Append objCommand.CreateParameter("@qty", adInteger,
adParamInput)
```

The only difference between these two code snippets is the extra creation and destruction of the `objParam` object variable. It is more efficient to create the parameter and use it directly with the `Append` method.

> *Whereas the performance issue with* `Refresh` *is one of a call to the data store, the issue here is one of object instantiation (and multiple objects – one per parameter). In a table with a large number of parameters, the single line of code is more efficient, although the difference in performance will probably be minimal.*

In addition, using the intermediate object `objParam` may make the code easier to read. We are going to see this method in more detail later in this chapter in the *Using Parameters* section.

Delete Method (Parameters Collection)

```
Command.Parameters.Delete {Index|Name}
```

The nice feature about the `Delete` method is that it will accept both the index number of the parameter or the name of the parameter as the determining factor for deletion. Under normal operating conditions, we would never put more than one parameter with the same name into the `Parameters` collection. And under these conditions, either the index or the name of the parameter will suffice for removing the item from the collection. We should keep in mind that once a parameter is removed, the other parameters will shift to fill its place in the index order: if we delete the parameters with an index of 2, all parameters with an index of 3 or higher will shift to fill the empty slot, making the one with index of 3 become 2, with index of 4 become 3, etc....

> Since the order of the parameters corresponds to the order of the arguments in the procedure, it is important that if we delete any parameter but the last, we change the order of the parameters in the collection. This can adversely affect the execution of the command if the parameters in the collection do not correspond correctly to the arguments in the procedure. The results can be anything from incorrect records being returned to an error being generated because of mismatched datatypes.

If the name of a parameter is not unique within the `Parameters` collection, it is not advisable to use the name as the basis for the deletion of a parameter. It seems that the last parameter with the given name is the one that is deleted, but we cannot guarantee this fact.

The Parameter Object

We will now take a closer look at the parameters themselves.

Refresh Method (Parameters Collection)

The `Refresh` method makes a request to the data store for the list of parameters used by the command. We can use this list to create a set of text boxes on the browser dynamically. The following code snippet shows how this is done.

```
Set objCommand = CreateObject("ADODB.Command")
objCommand.CommandText = "prAddAuthor"
objCommand.CommandType = adCmdStoredProc
Set objCommand.ActiveConnection = Session("Connection")

Set Session("Command") = objCommand

objCommand.Parameters.Refresh

<%
For i = 0 to objCommand.Parameters.Count - 1
%>
```

```
        <P ALIGN="CENTER">
        <%=objCommand.Parameters(i).Name %>
        <INPUT TYPE="text" NAME="<%=objCommand.Parameters(i).Name %>">
        </P>
<%
Next
%>
```

The user would type in the values, and when the form was submitted, we could retrieve those values like so.

```
Set objCommand = Session("Command")

For i = 0 to objCommand.Parameters.Count - 1
    objCommand.Parameters(i).Value = Request(objCommand.Parameters(i).Name)
Next

objCommand.Execute , , adExecuteNoRecords
```

The `Refresh` method is useful when we do not know the parameters of the procedure which we are calling. Again, we should keep in mind that if we are planning to disconnect the `Command` object from its connection, the parameters will be removed automatically.

> Not all data providers support the **Refresh** method. A key example is the SQL Server OLE DB provider (SQLOLEDB). If we are using SQL Server as our data store and we want to be able to refresh parameters, then we must use the ODBC provider (MSDASQL) with an SQL Server ODBC driver. Although, if we want to use the Data Shaping abilities of ADO with SQL Server, then we must use the SQL Server OLE DB provider. One last note: SQL Server 7.0 does support the use of the **Refresh** method when using the SQL Server OLE DB provider. The issue here lies only with SQL Server 6.5.

CreateParameter Method (Command Object)

```
Set Parameter = Command.CreateParameter([Name], [Type], [Direction],
[Size], [Value])
```

The `CreateParameter` method is a very powerful tool of the `Command` object. It allows us to create parameters that are used within stored procedures or parameterized queries and have them maintained, even when the command has been disassociated from a connection.

This step is not essential in order to maintain the association between parameters and the stored procedure in a disconnected connection; however, it is better coding and self-documentation to use the Parameters *collection and address* Parameter *objects, than to use an array of parameters.*

The Name argument is the name of the parameter in the stored procedure. The Type is the type of data that the parameter will hold. A list and description of this DataTypeEnum can be found in Appendix G, *ADO 2.0 and RDS 2.0 Enumerations*. The Direction argument determines which way the value for the parameter will flow. The accepted values are:

- ❑ adParamUnknown – the direction is not known
- ❑ adParamInput – the parameter is assigned by the consumer and used by the provider
- ❑ adParamOutput – the parameter is assigned by the provider and used by the consumer
- ❑ adParamInputOutput – the parameter can be assigned or used by either the consumer or provider
- ❑ adParamReturnValue – the parameter is the return value from the procedure on the provider

The Size argument is used when specifying character and binary data types. It is the number of characters (in the case of character type) that the Value property can hold. The Value property itself is the data that is sent to the provider to be evaluated. In the next few sections we will examine each of these items in the context of the Parameter object itself.

Name Property (Parameter Object)

```
String = Parameter.Name
Parameter.Name = String
```

This property represents the name of the parameter. Although the name value assigned here is not required to match the actual name within the procedure, it is wise to use the same name, making the code easier to decipher in the future. The position in the Parameters collection determines how the parameter is used by the procedure. Also, for Parameter objects not yet appended to the Parameters collection, the Name property is read/write. For appended Parameter objects and all other objects, the Name property is read-only. And while the names do not have to be unique within the collection, it is good practice to keep them unique.

Type Property (Parameter Object)

```
DataTypeEnum = Parameter.Type
Parameter.Type = DataTypeEnum
```

The Type property lets us determine the data type of the parameter. We can either assign this value when creating a parameter, or we can assign the property the value after the initial creation of the parameter. The following table shows an abridged version of the items found in the DataTypeEnum that are pertinent to SQL Server. For a complete list, refer to the ADO 2.0 online documentation, or refer to Wrox Press, ADO 2.0 Programmer's Reference, ISBN:1861001835.

Enumeration	Description	SQL Server Datatype
adBoolean	a boolean value	bit
adCurrency	a currency value	money
		smallmoney
adDBDate	a date value (yyyymmdd)	datetime

Table Continued on Following Page

Enumeration	Description	SQL Server Datatype
		smalldatetime
adDecimal	a decimal value	decimal
		numeric
adInteger	a long integer value	int
adSingle	a single-precision floating point value	float
		real
adSmallInt	a short integer value	smallint
adUnsignedTinyInt	a byte value	tinyint
adVarBinary	a binary value	binary
		image
		timestamp
		varbinary
adVarChar	a character value	char
		text
		varchar

We will discuss the coding aspects of the Type property in the section on creating parameters.

Direction Property (Parameter Object)

ParameterDirectionEnum = Parameter.Direction
Parameter.Direction = ParameterDirectionEnum

The Direction property determines if we are sending values to and/or receiving values from the procedure in the data store. We saw the enumerated types when we looked at CreateParameter method. If the parameter direction is not known, the Direction property will return a value equal to the adParamUnknown enumeration.

If a parameter is for input only (adParamInput), we assign the Value property before executing the command. That value is sent to the provider and used by the procedure. If the parameter is for output only (adParamOutput), we retrieve the value from the parameter after executing the command. The provider assigns a value to the parameter in its procedure code. If a parameter is for input and output (adParamInputOutput), we can assign a value to it before command execution, and also retrieve a value from it after the execution.

Stored procedures also have the ability to yield a return value back to the consumer. Take a look at the following stored procedure.

```
CREATE PROC prUpdateAuthorContractsByState
     @state char(2),
     @contract bit
AS

UPDATE authors
SET contract = @contract
WHERE state = @state

RETURN @@ROWCOUNT
```

There are three parameters in this procedure. The two parameters that are clearly evident are @state and @contract. The third is the return value from the procedure. In this case, it will contain a value equal to the number of rows that the UPDATE statement affected. After executing the Command object, we can request the return value by referencing the parameter with a name of RETURN_VALUE. Take a look at the following code snippet.

```
objCommand.CommandText = "prUpdateAuthorContractsByState"
objCommand.CommandType = adCmdStoredProc
Set objCommand.ActiveConnection = objConn
objCommand.Parameters.Refresh

objCommand.Parameters("@state") = Request("txtState")
objCommand.Parameters("@contract") = Cint(Request("chkContract"))

objCommand.Execute , , adExecuteNoRecords

lngRows = objCommand.Parameters("RETURN_VALUE").Value
If lngRows = 0 Then
     Response.Write "No authors were updated in '" & Request("txtState") & "'"
Else
     If lngRows = 1 Then
          Response.Write Cstr(lngRows) & " author was updated in '"
          Response.Write Request("txtState") & "'"
     Else
          Response.Write Cstr(lngRows) & " authors were updated in '"
          Response.Write Request("txtState") & "'"
     End If
End If
```

Using the return value, we can inform the user about what actually happened when the procedure was executed.

> Once again, it is important to note that not all providers support this feature. When using an Access database as the data store, only input parameters are supported. When using SQL Server, however, all direction types are supported.

Size Property (Parameter Object)

```
Long = Parameter.Size
Parameter.Size = Long
```

This property can represent either the storage size (e.g. 4 bytes for a long integer) or the physical size (the number of characters for character types, the number of bytes for binary types, etc.). Although not important for most datatypes, it is imperative that when we create parameters with character or binary datatypes, that we assign the `Size` property a value. We need to match the number of bytes in the parameter to the number defined in the parameter in the stored procedure.

Value Property (Parameter Object)

```
Variant = Parameter.Value
Parameter.Value = Variant
```

The `Value` property is used to assign and retrieve values from the parameter. If the parameter is for input only, we assign the value prior to executing the command. On the other hand, if the parameter is either a return value or only an output parameter, we retrieve the value after the execution of the command has completed. If the parameter is for both input and output, we assign a value prior to the command execution and can retrieve the potentially changed value after the execution of the command.

> Although the Value property is the default property of the Parameter object, it is advisable to always explicitly state it when writing code. Even though
>
> lngRows = objCommand.Parameters("RETURN_VALUE")
>
> and
>
> lngRows = objCommand.Parameters("RETURN_VALUE").Value
>
> are evaluated in the same manner in most development environments, in ASP code this is not a guarantee. Much time has been spent debugging code where the fix was to just explicitly state the property name, such as Value. And on top of it all, perfomance is more efficient when explicitly stating properties and methods.

NumericScale Property (Parameter Object)

```
Byte = Parameter.NumericScale
Parameter.NumericScale = Byte
```

`NumericScale` indicates how many decimal places are supported for the parameter. Both `NumericScale` and `Precision` are used in conjunction with numeric and decimal data types in the data store.

Precision Property (Parameter Object)

```
Byte = Parameter.Precision
Parameter.Precision = Byte
```

`Precision` represents the maximum number of digits that could be used to display the numeric value of the parameter. Since the `CreateParameter` method does not include either `NumericScale` or `Precision` as one of its arguments, we must first create the parameter, and then set these two properties accordingly.

```
set objParam = objCommand.CreateParameter("@HoursWorked",adDecimal )
objParam.NumericScale = 2
objParam.Precision = 4
```

Attributes Property (Parameter Object)

```
ParameterAttributesEnum = Parameter.Attributes
Parameter.Attributes = ParameterAttributesEnum
```

The `Attributes` property lets us assign or retrieve certain characteristics about the parameter. It can be hold one or more of the following values:

❑ `adParamNullable` – the parameter accepts null values
❑ `adParamSigned` – the parameter accepts signed values (default)
❑ `adParamLong` – the parameter accepts long data (i.e. binary data)

When assigning this property, we can specify one of the enumerated values, or we can `Or` the values together to specify more than one, like so:

```
objParam.Attributes = adParamNullable Or adParamSigned
```

If we want to know if a parameter accepts null values (perhaps after we call the `Parameters` collection's `Refresh` method), we can code as follows.

```
Set objParam = objCommand.Parameters(1)
If objParam.Attributes And adParamNullable Then
     ' The parameter accepts nulls
Else
     ' The parameter does not accept nulls
End If
```

Using Parameters

First and foremost, we are going to discuss the creation of parameters using the `Command` object's `CreateParameter` method. Let's re-examine a stored procedure that we saw earlier in the chapter:

```
CREATE PROC prUpdateAuthorContractsByState
     @state char(2),
     @contract bit
AS

UPDATE authors
SET contract = @contract
WHERE state = @state

RETURN @@ROWCOUNT
```

Now, if we wanted to create a command and append parameters to it, we would code as follows:

```
Set objCommand = CreateObject("ADODB.Command")
objCommand.CommandText = "prupdateAuthorContractByState"
objCommand.CommandType = adCmdStoredProc
Set objCommand.ActiveConnection = objConn

' Here, we'll create a parameter and then append it to the collection
Set objParam = CreateObject("ADODB.Parameter")
Set objParam = objCommand.CreateParameter ("RETURN_VALUE", _
  adInteger, adParamReturnValue)
objCommand.Parameters.Append objParam
Set objParam = Nothing
```

The code above demonstrates one of the many features of utilizing parameters. It shows the creation of a `Command` object and its association with a connection. This section uses the `CreateParameter` method of the `Command` object to create a `Parameter` object, which is then appended to the `Parameters` collection of the `Command` object. The first parameter will be used to retrieve the return value from the stored procedure, so its direction is set to `adParamReturnValue`. It needs to be the first parameter in the collection.

```
' For a different approach, we'll create a parameter object
' No need to recreate the parameter since we have one already...

objParam.Direction = adParamInput
objParam.Name = "@state"
objParam.Type = adVarChar
objParam.Size = 2
objParam.Value = Request("txtState")
' and then append the parameter to the collection
objCommand.Parameters.Append objParam
' and remove the parameter object
' (we no longer need it since it is now in the parameters collection
Set objParam = Nothing

' Again, we'll create and append the parameter in one statement
objCommand.Parameters.Append objCommand.CreateParameter("@contract", _
  adBoolean, adParamInput, , Cint(Request("chkContract")))
```

The next two parameters are the input values for the `@state` and `@contract` arguments of the stored procedure. We create the first parameter and manually assign its properties. After all the appropriate property values have been set, we append it to the `Parameters` collection. Next, we create and append the last parameter all in one step by using the `CreateParameter` method of the `Command` object in conjunction with the `Append` method of the `Parameters` collection.

```
objCommand.Execute , , adExecuteNoRecords

lngRows = objCommand.Parameters("RETURN_VALUE").Value
If lngRows = 0 Then
    Response.Write "No authors were updated in '" & Request("txtState") & "'"
Else
    If lngRows = 1 Then
        Response.Write Cstr(lngRows) & " author was updated in '"
        Response.Write Request("txtState") & "'"
    Else
```

```
                Response.Write Cstr(lngRows) & " authors were updated in '"
                Response.Write Request("txtState") & "'"
        End If
    End If
```

After setting up all of the parameters needed to call the procedure, we execute the command (returning no records); and then we retrieve the return value from the RETURN_VALUE parameter. The final portion of the code outputs the results of the command execution to the browser.

Using Stored Procedures

The command type adCmdStoredProc is not just used for accessing stored procedures in data stores such as Oracle or SQL Server. For example, an Access query can be used as a stored procedure, and even its parameters can be retrieved via the Refresh method. Take a look at the following code.

```
Set objConn = CreateObject("ADODB.Connection")
objConn.Provider = "MSDASQL"
objConn.ConnectionString = "DSN=MyAccessDB"
objConn.Open

Set objCommand = CreateObject("ADODB.Command")
objCommand.CommandType = adCmdStoredProc
objCommand.CommandText = "qryOrdersByDate"
Set objCommand.ActiveConnection = objConn
objCommand.Parameters.Refresh
```

A few restrictions apply when using an Access query as a stored procedure type and wanting to refresh its parameters as shown above. First, we must use the ODBC provider for Access (MSDASQL) as opposed to the Access OLE DB provider (Microsoft.Jet.OLEDB.3.51). Second, we must explicitly create the parameters in the query, as shown here:

```
PARAMETERS [Enter the Start Date] DateTime, [Enter the End Date] DateTime;
SELECT Orders.OrderID, Orders.EmployeeID, Orders.CustomerID, Orders.OrderDate
FROM Orders
WHERE Orders.OrderDate Between [Enter the Start Date] And [Enter the End Date];
```

Although the next query works essentially the same in the Access environment, we would not be able to use the Refresh method to retrieve the parameters. We would have to manually append them to the Parameters collection in order to get the results from this query.

```
SELECT Orders.OrderID, Orders.EmployeeID, Orders.CustomerID, Orders.OrderDate
FROM Orders
WHERE Orders.OrderDate Between [Enter the Start Date] And [Enter the End Date];
```

The main difference between them is that Access can resolve and prompt for unknown items when internally executing the SQL statement itself, but external (non-Access) sources cannot. Since the parameters are not defined as any particular data type, no type checking occurs and can lead to potential errors if the supplied values are not of a DateTime type. This second query would appear to work fine in Access, but it is really incomplete without the declaration of the parameters.

Now if we were to create an equivalent procedure in SQL Server, the procedure definition would look something like this:

```
CREATE PROCEDURE prOrdersByDate
     @dtmStartDate     Date,
     @dtmEndDate       Date

AS

SELECT OrderID, EmployeeID, CustomerID, OrderDate
FROM Orders
WHERE OrderDate Between @StartDate And @EndDate
```

Although the object in each of these data stores is very different, their implementations in ADO are nearly identical. The only difference lies in the connection string and the name of the query/procedure. All other aspects of the ADO code are the same.

```
Set objConn = CreateObject("ADODB.Connection")
objConn.Provider = "MSDASQL"
objConn.ConnectionString = "DSN=MySQLDB; User Id=peter; Password=peter"
objConn.Open

Set objCommand = CreateObject("ADODB.Command")
objCommand.CommandType = adCmdStoredProc
objCommand.CommandText = "prOrdersByDate"
Set objCommand.ActiveConnection = objConn
objCommand.Parameters.Refresh
```

Advanced Command Object and Stored Procedures

Another issue that we mentioned earlier in this chapter was the use of the Refresh method and compatibility with the SQL Server OLE DB provider (SQLOLEDB). If we want to use features such as Data Shaping, we need to use this provider, but it will not allow us to refresh parameters dynamically from the stored procedure in SQL Server. To resolve this, we can create a stored procedure that returns to us all the pertinent information about the parameters. Let's take a look at the following stored procedure.

```
CREATE PROC prStoredProcParams
     @strProcedureName varchar(30)
AS

SELECT     0 AS ColIndex,
     'RETURN_VALUE' AS Name,
     3 AS Type,
     0 AS Size,
     0 AS NumericScale,
     10 AS Prec,
     4 AS Direction

UNION

SELECT     sc.colid AS ColIndex,
     sc.name AS Name,
     CASE sc.usertype
          WHEN 16 THEN 11   --adBoolean, bit
          WHEN 21 THEN 6    --adCurrency, smallmoney
```

```
                WHEN 11 THEN 6     --adCurrency, money
                WHEN 22 THEN 133   --adDBDate, smalldatetime
                WHEN 12 THEN 133   --adDBDate, datetime
                WHEN 24 THEN 14    --adDecimal, decimal
                WHEN 10 THEN 14    --adDecimal, numeric
                WHEN 7 THEN 3      --adInteger, int
                WHEN 23 THEN 4     --adSingle, real
                WHEN 8 THEN 4      --adSingle, float
                WHEN 6 THEN 2      --adSmallInt, smallint
                WHEN 5 THEN 17     --adUnsignedTinyInt, tinyint
                WHEN 3 THEN 204    --adVarBinary, binary
                WHEN 4 THEN 204    --adVarBinary, varbinary
                WHEN 80 THEN 204   --adVarBinary, timestamp
                WHEN 20 THEN 204   --adVarBinary, image
                WHEN 1 THEN 200    --adVarChar, char
                WHEN 2 THEN 200    --adVarChar, varchar
                WHEN 19 THEN 200   --adVarChar, text
        END AS Type,
        sc.length AS Length,
        sc.scale AS NumericScale,
        sc.prec AS Prec,
        CASE sc.status & 64
                WHEN 64 THEN 3     --adParamOuput
                ELSE 1             --adParamInputOutput
        END AS Direction
FROM  syscolumns sc
        INNER JOIN sysobjects so ON sc.id = so.id
WHERE       so.name = @strProcedureName

ORDER BY ColIndex
```

We designed this procedure to be used with ADO parameters. It returns back a recordset of the parameter information (including the RETURN_VALUE parameter) and all the ADO equivalent values for the enumerations of data type and direction.

```
Sub RefreshParams (objCmdObject)
        Set objCommand = CreateObject("ADODB.Command")
        objCommand.Commandtext = "prStoredProcParams"
        objCommand.Commandtype = adCmdStoredProc
        Set objCommand.ActiveConnection = objCmdObject.ActiveConnection
        Set objParam = objCommand.CreateParameter("@strProcedureName")
        objParam.Type = adVarChar
        objParam.Size = 30
        objParam.Direction = adParamInput
        objParam.Value = objCmdObject.Name

        Set objRSParams = objCommand.Execute

        Do Until objRSParams.EOF
                Set objParam2 = objCmdObject.CreateParameter(objRSParams("Name"))
                objParam2.Type = objRSParams("Type")
                objParam2.Size = objRSParams("Size")
                objParam2.Precision = objRSParams("Prec")
                objParam2.NumericScale = objRSParams("NumericScale")
                objParam2.Direction = objRSParams("Direction")
                objCmdObject.Parameters.Append objParam2
```

```
        Set objParam2 = Nothing
    Loop

    Set objRSParams = Nothing
    Set objCommand = Nothing
End Sub
```

In our ASP code, we would set up the Command object as usual. But then, we would call the RefreshParams subroutine and pass in the Command object. The RefreshParams procedure uses the existing information stored in the Command object to find the parameters for the stored procedure, and automatically appends them.

```
Set objCommand = CreateObject("ADODB.Command")
objCommand.Commandtext = "prAddAuthor"
objCommand.Commandtype = adCmdStoredProc
objCommand.ActiveConnection = objConn

RefreshParams objCommand, objConn
' This equivacates to objCommand.Parameters.Refresh
```

Now we can refresh the Parameters collection, and still get the extra functionality of using the SQL Server OLE DB provider and Data Shaping.

Summary

The Command object offers us some enhanced capabilities that we cannot get from using the Connection object alone. Features such as disconnected recordsets and dynamic parameter retrieval, and support for output and return value parameters, are all part of the Command object and all but disconnected recordsets are unique to it. Using Command objects allows us to create multiple commands that can be executed at any moment, whereas a Connection object must redefine its command text for each different command it will execute. And since the Command object still uses a connection in order to perform its task, connection pooling is still utilized.

The Recordset Foundation

All hail the `Recordset` object! That's what we, as coders, should be saying to this magnificent object! OK, maybe that's a little overboard. But understanding the `Recordset` object is perhaps the best thing you can do, if you want to become 'as one' with your data... As you will see, this chapter is going to lay down the framework for the next five chapters, and perhaps the rest of the book.

Don't worry if you've never used the `Recordset` object with ADO, or with any of Microsoft's previous data objects, such as DAO and RDO (actually RDO called it the `rdoResultset`, but it was just the same thing). We'll start from the ground and move our way up. We will be hitting all major features of the `Recordset` object, as well as those minor features that we believe to be important. In this chapter, we will be covering the following:

- ❑ What a `Recordset` object is, and how to create an instance of it
- ❑ Retrieving data from the database
- ❑ Editing data – adding, deleting and amending
- ❑ Moving around the recordset
- ❑ The basics of the Fields collection
- ❑ The Underlying Value and Original Value – and how they relate to database updates
- ❑ Cursor types, cursor location and locking types

What is a Recordset Object?

The Recordset object, part of the ADO object model, is a creatable object (which means that we can instantiate our own copies of the object, just like the Connection and the Command objects). It is your interface to retrieving and manipulating data. The Recordset object gives you a nicely organized package that contains all your data, and allows you to perform various actions – all in a simple and logical format. You can use the available actions to manipulate your data – inserting, editing (i.e. updating), deleting, finding, sorting, etc. In this chapter, we will be covering how we do these things, and why we do them in this way.

Creating a Recordset Object

Before we can use the Recordset object, we have to create it. This doesn't mean that we have to write custom code defining the object – that's already been taken care of in the ADO object model. All we need to do is instantiate the Recordset object:

```
' Use the 'set' key word when assigning an object to a variable
Set objRS = Server.CreateObject("ADODB.Recordset")
```

This VBScript code creates an instance of the ADODB.Recordset object called objRS.

> ADODB.Recordset is the object's ProgID – ADODB is the object container and Recordset is the class name.

Retrieving Data

One of the most fundamental things you will do with the Recordset object is retrieve your data. When you're retrieving data from a database, you can control just exactly how much data (and which data) you receive. You can open an entire table directly, and retrieve all the data from every row and column; or you can open the table (or multiple tables via JOINs, of course) with a SQL statement. You can also use a SQL statement to retrieve all the data from one or more specified rows or columns, and you can conserve resources by just retrieving the columns you need.

Getting Ready to Retrieve Your Data

To retrieve your data from the database, you need to connect to it. (We'll discuss alternative data sources in Chapter 9.) You could use an existing active connection to the database, or you could pass the connection in as one of the arguments of the Recordset.Open method. We'll look at both of these in this section, but for a moment let's focus on the latter. The Recordset.Open method has the following syntax:

objRS.Open Source, ActiveConnection, [CursorType], [LockType], [Options]

The Source and ActiveConnection parameters are mandatory – in the sense that if you don't specify them you'll receive a nasty little error message and your code won't work. So we often specify the connection like this:

```
objRS.Open strSQL, objConn          ' Open the Recordset
```

However, if we set the *Source* and *ActiveConnection* parameters before we call the `Open` method, then there's no need to specify them again when we call the `Open` method. So we can also specify the connection like this:

```
objRS.ActiveConnection = objConn    ' Set the ActiveConnection Property
objRS.Source = strSQL               ' Set the Source Property
objRS.Open                          ' Open the Recordset
```

So which of these should you choose? It's really a matter of preference. If you want to be picky, you can get more out of your system by setting up your objects using parameters instead of properties. This is because you're marshalling data across the network or process space everytime you set a property – whereas, with a method call, you are sending all the parameters at once.

> *Since we are using in-process DLLs when using ADO with the ASP examples in this book, you'll find that the performance difference between property and method calls is negligible.*

Let's have a closer look at these.

Opening a Recordset using Parameters

In this first example, we will pass all the mandatory arguments in the appropriate parameters. We will not do the optional parameters yet (that would be getting ahead of ourselves).

In Chapter 3 we talked about the `Connection` object. Here we will build on that discussion and use the `Connection` object and/or the connection string to tell the `Recordset` object how to connect to the database to retrieve our information. We will use Microsoft SQL Server as the database server and the `pubs` database for our examples.

...Using the Recordset Object's Open Method

We start by declaring `Option Explicit`, which forces us to declare all the variables you will be using – apart from helping to catch any misspelt variables, it also allows me to use the code completion enhancements made available in Visual InterDev 6. We declare the `objRS` variable, which will represent the `Recordset` object. We also declare our other variables: in this case, a string that holds the necessary information for the connection, and a string containing the SQL command:

```
<%@ Language=VBScript%>
<% Option Explicit %>
<%
' Declare all objects to be used
Dim objRS        ' The ADO Recordset Object

' Declare all variables to be used
Dim strConn      ' The Connection String
Dim strSQL       ' The SQL statement
```

Now we use the `Server.CreateObject` method to instantiate a new ADO `Recordset` object:

```
' Create the Objects
set objRS = Server.CreateObject("ADODB.Recordset")
```

Now let's create the connection string, strConn:

```
' Create the Connection string we will be connecting to MS SQL Server
strConn = ""
strConn = strConn & "Provider=SQLOLEDB;"       ' Provider Name
strConn = strConn & "Data Source=winbook;"     ' Data source (SQL Server Name)
strConn = strConn & "Initial Catalog=pubs;"    ' Defaut Database
strConn = strConn & "User Id=sa;"              ' User id
strConn = strConn & "Password="                ' Password
```

Since we're using the strConn variable for the first time we can fairly safely assume that it's already clear; but it's just good practice to clear it anyway. Then we build up the string using concatenation. Note that the Data Source is the name of the server on which our SQL Server resides – my data server's name is winbook. If you changed the default password of sa, then you will need to supply that as well.

Now we need to figure out what data we want to get from the pubs database. In this example, we'll just build a simple SQL statement (although we could build more complex SQL statements, to make a more refined or specific query):

```
' Define the Records we want to return
strSQL = ""
strSQL = strSQL & "SELECT * "
strSQL = strSQL & "FROM publishers "
```

This simple SELECT * statement will retrieve all the columns FROM the publishers table of the database.

Since we're asking for the entire table (and it's only *one* table that we're interested in), we could have opened the publishers table by simply defining strSQL as follows:

```
strSQL = ""
strSQL = strSQL & "publishers"
```

*Opening a table directly, in this way, is just an alternative to using a SQL statement; however this method is not recommended with large tables. Also, remember that once your application has gone live, you should only request the information that you need. Therefore, you shouldn't use a SELECT * unless you really do need all the columns – and you should always have a WHERE clause (unless you absolutely need all the rows).*

To complete opening the recordset, we call the Open method. We just pass in the SQL string (strSQL) and the connection string (strConn) that we've just defined. The Open method will use those parameters to open the connection to the database and retrieve the data from the table:

```
' Open the Recordset
objRS.Open strSQL, strConn
%>
```

...Using the Connection Object's Open Method

Alternatively, if we had previously opened a connection using the Connection object's method (i.e. objConn.Open strConn), we could use that connection to open the recordset. Instead of passing in the connection string, strConn, as a parameter of objRS.Open, we simply pass in the Connection object itself:

```
Dim objConn      ' The ADO Connection Object

' Create the Connection Object
Set objConn = Server.CreateObject("ADODB.Connection")

' Open the Connection
objConn.Open strConn

' Open the Recordset Using the connection Object
objRS.Open strSQL, objConn
```

Of these two techniques, we recommend the second. By creating a Connection object, you can utilize its full feature set.

Setting the Source and Active Connection Properties First

Instead of passing the Connection object and source (i.e. the SQL statement) to the Recordset's Open method, we can set the Source and ActiveConnection properties separately – and *then* issue the Open method without passing in any arguments.

To do this, only minor modifications need to be made to the code we wrote previously. We build strConn and strSQL as before; then we replace the line objRS.Open strSQL, strConn with the following lines:

```
' Set the ActiveConnection Property
objRS.ActiveConnection = strConn

' Set the Source Property
objRS.Source = strSQL

' Open the Recordset
objRS.Open
```

This is the only difference in the two code examples. It really comes down to preference. If we had an existing connection to the database, we could make this functionally better by using that connection (instead of creating a new one). If a connection has already been opened – say in a previous section of code or if one was being passed around in a session variable (see below) – we could use that connection instead. Assuming that a connection object called objConn was already created and opened we could use the following:

```
objRS.ActiveConnection = objConn
```

By setting the ActiveConnection property to a Connection object, you'll be able to manage transactions for the Recordset through the Connection object's transaction methods: BeginTrans, CommitTrans and RollbackTrans.

Incidentally, as a rule we don't recommend passing a connection in a session variable. It should only be done if you need to maintain a transaction with the object.

> **Again, I suggest creating a `Connection` object explicitly in lieu of using a connection string. Otherwise, you can't take advantage of the `Errors` collection and reuse of a `Connection` object.**

Updating Data

Now that we can get data out of a database, let's look at how we can change that data. Updating the data is a simple matter of assigning a value to the correct field (while you are on the correct row, of course) and issuing the Recordset's `Update` method. The `Update` method has the following syntax:

```
objRS.Update [Fields], [Values]
```

Here, both *Fields* and *Values* are variants, and both are optional parameters. If *Fields* is a single field name (or ordinal position), then *Values* is a single value. Alternatively, *Fields* may be a variant array of field names (or their ordinal positions) – and in this case *Values* is a variant array of values.

*The **ordinal position** of a field is the numeric position by which it can be referenced in the Recordset object (note that the Recordset object is zero-based). For example, consider the following SQL statement: SELECT pub_name, city FROM publishers. In this case, the ordinal index of pub_name would be 0, and the ordinal index of city would be 1. They could be referenced by objRS(0) and objRS(1) respectively.*

The fact that the `Update` method's parameters are optional means that this method is just as flexible as the `Recordset` object's `Open` method. In the remainder of this section we'll show three different ways to update a record using the `Update` method. These examples will use the `pubs` database and the `publishers` table).

To open the connection and recordset, you can use the syntax we showed earlier in the chapter. However, you must change the recordset's LockType property from its default (adLockReadOnly, which evaluates to 1) before opening the recordset. We will cover lock types later in this chapter; to follow this example you set the LockType property to adLockOptimistic, which evaluates to 3 before you open the recordset:

```
Dim adLockOptimistic
adLockOptimistic = 3
objRS.LockType = adLockOptimistic
...
objRS.Open strSQL, strConn
```

Change the LockType before you open the Recordset. (For a list of all of the ADO enumerators, refer to Appendix G).

Using the Value Property

First we will assign values directly to the fields, and then we'll call the Update method:

```
objRS("pub_name").Value = "Wilson Publishing Company"
objRS("city").Value = "Durham"
objRS.Update
```

In fact, you don't need to specify the .Value part when assigning the value in this way – because Value is the default property of the Field object. However, it can make your code clearer for others reading it, and Microsoft claim that your code is significantly more efficient if you do specify .Value.

Passing a Value Direct to the Update Method

Alternatively, we can pass each value into the method. We issue an Update for each field that we intend to change:

```
objRS.Update "pub_name", "Wilson Publishing Company"
objRS.Update "city", "Durham"
```

As you may have guessed, this technique requires two hits to the database – one for each update. Of course, the more updates you program, the more process-intensive your application becomes. This is not really the best technique, but it's included here for completeness.

Passing an Array Direct to the Update Method

Tha final technique is to update the fields by passing an array into the Update method:

```
objRS.Update Array("pub_name", "city"), _
             Array("Wilson Publishing Company", "Durham")
```

So as you can see, using the Update method gives you a number of options on exactly how to perform the update. The one you choose is proabaly a matter of preference or habit. However, as we mentioned earlier, setting is less efficient – the array technique is probably the most efficient technique because it makes just one call to the Recordset object. (Curiously, in my experience I've found the first technique to be the most common...)

Inserting Data

Now we'll move on to inserting data into our tables. When inserting data using the Recordset object we use the AddNew method. Using the AddNew method resembles what we've just seen using the Update method; the only notable difference is that AddNew will create a *new record* in the database. The syntax for this method is also very flexible:

objRS.AddNew [*FieldList*], [*Values*]

You can think of *FieldList* and *Values* parameters in the same way we described the Fields and *Values* parameters of the Update method above – in particular, they are optional parameters. Here we will see three different examples of using the AddNew method.

In the first, we issue the `Update` method after assigning new values to the appropriate fields. The assignment does not take place until either an `Update` is issued, or the cursor is moved away from the current row (e.g. a `MoveNext` occurs).

Adding a new Record with Multiple Field Values

```
objRS.AddNew
   objRS("pub_id") = "9901"
   objRS("pub_name") = "My Publishing Company"
   objRS("city") = "Durham"
   objRS("state") = "NC"
   objRS("country") = "USA"
objRS.Update
```

What's happening behind the scenes? By calling the `AddNew` method, you implicitly change the `EditMode` property to `adEditAdd` (which evaluates to 2). When the `Update` method is called, or some sort of move occurs, the `EditMode` property is changed to `adEditNone` (which evaluates to 0). If *another* `AddNew` is called, first the current added record is saved – causing the `EditMode` to change to `adEditNone`, and then quickly to `adEditAdd`. Thus, as you can see, explicitly calling the `Update` is not actually necessary – however it is *much* clearer when it's explicitly called in your code.

Adding a new Record with a Single Field Value

This next example shows how to use the `AddNew` method when adding one value. For this to work you must either have only one column in the table, or the rest of your fields must accept nulls (as in the case of the `publishers` table):

```
objRS.AddNew "pub_id", "9903"
```

Adding an Entire Row of Values in a SIngle Statement

The final example shows how to insert an entire row of data using just one line of code (well OK, there are actually *two* lines in the example – but that's only because it doesn't fit on one line of the page. I used the line continuation character to break it up into two lines):

```
objRS.AddNew Array("pub_id", "pub_name", "city", "state", "country"), _
             Array("9904", "My Publishing Company", "Durham", "NC", "USA")
```

The 'less is more' rule applies here as well. One call to the `Recordset` object is probably going to be the most efficient means of passing the new data.

Deleting Data

To delete records from the `Recordset` object, we use the `Delete` method. To delete data with the `Recordset` object, you first locate the row that you need to delete (using `Find`, `MoveFirst`, `MoveNext` etc.) – then call the `Delete` method directly. If your cursor is not on a current valid record (e.g. it's pointing at an already-deleted record), then a runtime error will occur. The `Delete` method has the following syntax:

```
objRS.Delete [AffectRecords]
```

Here, *AffectRecords* is an enumerator value (of type AffectEnum – see Appendix G) that determines what records are affected. To delete the 'current' record, issue the following command:

```
objRS.Delete
```

You can delete a *group* of records. First, filter the recordset to select the group – for this you can use the Recordset's Filter property. Then call the Delete method, passing in the adAffectGroup enumerator (= 2). For example, this will filter all records in the Recordset that have the value NC in their state field, and then delete them:

```
objRS.Filter "state = 'NC'"
objRS.Delete adAffectGroup
```

Note that if you're in batch update mode, the Delete *method only* marks *the records for deletion – they're not removed from the data store until you call* BatchUpdate. *We'll see more about batch updates later in this chapter, and we'll look at the* Filter *property in more detail in Chapter 6.*

Navigating the Recordset

As you work with your recordset, you'll need to find your way around it. The Recordset object gives us five methods with which to navigate the Recordset: MoveFirst, MoveLast, MoveNext, MovePrevious and Move. The first four of these do not accept any arguments, and we'll mention those all together in a moment. First, we'll focus on the Move method.

The Move Method

The Move method will move the cursor forwards from the current row, through the number of rows specified by the first parameter. If the provider supports backward movement, the Move method will also allow you to do that. The Move method also allows us to specify the position from which to start moving – via any valid bookmark, as we'll see. The Move method has the following syntax:

objRS.Move *NumRecords*, [*Start*]

We have to specify a value for the *NumRecords* parameter, indicating how far (i.e. how many records forward or back) we wish to move. If we specify a positive number, then the movement will be forward. If we specify a negative number – and the provider supports backward movement – then the cursor is moved backward.

If you request backward movement from a provider that doesn't support it, you'll get a runtime error. You can avoid error messages by using the Recordset's Supports method to check if the provider supports backward movement. The following code tests for support of backward movement before attempting the move:

```
If objRS.Supports(adMovePrevious) Then
   objRS.Move -2
Else
   ' ... specify another way of finding the record
End If
```

The next code fragment moves the cursor five rows forward. We don't specify the second parameter, so the cursor counts five rows from its *current* location:

```
objRS.Move 5
```

If we want the cursor to start counting from a different starting point, we specify the starting point using the *Start* parameter (which takes the value of a valid bookmark – we'll see an example of this in the *Bookmarks* section of this chapter).

One final thing here: as you're moving round the recordset, you should watch out that you don't fall off the beginning or end of the recordset. If you go out of the bounds of the Recordset (i.e. past BOF or EOF), you'll get a 3021 error. In fact, if you use any of these Move... methods to access data when both EOF and BOF are true, you'll generate a runtime error. To prevent an error in this latter situation, you can wrap these methods up as follows:

```
If Not (objRS.EOF And objRS.BOF) Then
   objRS.MoveFirst
End If
```

If objRS.BOF and objRS.EOF are simultaneously true, then the beginning and end of the recordset file are the same – so the recordset is empty. (Note that EOF doesn't point at the last record, but *after* it. Thus, in a recordset with one record, BOF and EOF are different.)

The MoveFirst, MoveLast, MoveNext and MovePrevious Methods

These four methods provide the standard way of moving through your recordset. No parameters are available with these methods. MoveFirst and MoveLast will position the cursor on the first and the last records respectively. MoveNext and MovePrevious will move the position of the cursor one step forward or backward, per call of that method.

The RecordCount Property

The RecordCount property returns the number of records in the current Recordset object. This property is read-only, and it's not dynamic. This means that if you retrieve the RecordCount property, and then someone enters data in the database behind you, your RecordCount property does not update automatically. In order to refresh the RecordCount property, you'll have to re-query the database (in fact, it's also updated when you amend the database yourself).

To get the current value of RecordCount your code should look something this:

```
lngRecordCount = objRS.RecordCount
```

Here I am assigning the value of the RecordCount property to the variable lngRecordCount. Note that some cursor types don't support the RecordCount property. If the RecordCount property can't be determined, the 'return' value of RecordCount is –1.

Bookmarks

The `Bookmark` property is probably one of the most under-used properties of the `Recordset` object. It seems that nobody takes the time to understand this property. In fact, it's a very easy concept to grasp. Every time you create a new `Recordset` object, the `Bookmark` property is automatically filled with a variant data type that allows each row to be uniquely identified. This allows you to save your current position and return to it later – without the hassle of performing a `Find`, or `Move`-ing around the rows until you've found the record you're looking for. Moreover, bookmarks are more robust than using row numbers or row offsets, because they don't change when rows are added, deleted, filtered or sorted.

Here's a simple example using the bookmark property. First we move round in the recordset, write out the record, and set a variable called `varMyBookMark` to the `Bookmark` property of the `Recordset` object. Next, we move away from the bookmarked record, to the last record in the recordset. Then we use the `Bookmark` property to return to the record we bookmarked a moment ago. To prove that it worked, we simply write out the values again:

```
objRS.Move 3                          ' Move Forward Three Records
Response.Write objRS("pub_id") & _    ' Write out the value of the record
            objRS("pub_name")
varMyBookMark = objRS.Bookmark        ' Get a book mark
objRS.MoveLast                        ' Move to the end of the recordset
objRS.Bookmark = varMyBookMark        ' Set the Bookmark property
                                      '    to the saved bookmark
Response.Write objRS("pub_id") & _    ' Write out the Bookmarked values
            objRS("pub_name")
```

Note that the `Bookmark` property is generated when you create the new `Recordset` object – and it dies when you destroy the recordset. And because bookmarks are not persistent – they exist only within the scope of an open recordset – you can't use them across different recordsets. And again, you should be aware that some recordsets don't support bookmarks – you can use the `adBookMark` parameter of the `Supports` method to find out.

The Fields Collection – the Basics

Now that you have created a `Recordset` object you need to understand its `Fields` collection. Every recordset that you create will have a collection of fields – each field in the collection corresponds to a column of your recordset.

It is worth noting that the `Fields` collection is the default collection of the `Recordset` object, which means that you don't have to reference it explicitly. For example, if you want to refer to the `ID` field of the `Fields` collection, you can use either `objRS.Fields("ID")` or `objRS("ID")`. I'd recommend using the former – your code will be clearer for it.

We can step through the entire collection, one field at a time, using a `For Each` statement. The following code will loop through a recordset, and display the name and value of each field in the recordset:

```
Dim objField
If Not (objRS.BOF And objRS.EOF) Then
  objRS.MoveFirst
  Do Until objRS.EOF
    For Each objField In objRS.Fields
      Response.Write objField.Name & " " & objField.Value
    Next
  objRS.MoveNext
  Loop
End If
```

The Item Method

The Item method is the default method of the Fields collection, and returns a specific member of the Fields collection – a Field object. Because it's the default method, it is often not specified in code. We'll look at some examples of this in a moment.

The Value Property

Value is the default property of the Field object in the Fields collection. You'll often find that the Value property is not specified, simply because it is usually not mandatory to do so. In Chapter 7, however, we'll see that we need to tread more carefully when working in the context of Data Shaping.

Let's look at an example. The following line of code will assign the value 1 to the ID field:

```
objRS.Fields.Item("ID").Value = 1
```

However, we know that Value is the default property of the Field object (and Item("ID") is a Field object), and that Item is the default method of the Fields collection, and that the Fields collection is the default property of the Recordset object. Therefore, any of the following lines could be used to perform exactly the same action:

```
objRS.Fields.Item("ID") = 1
objRS.Fields("ID") = 1
objRS("ID") = 1
```

You can also specify the position of the field within the Fields collection, instead of the field's name. For example, any of the following:

```
objRS(0) = 1
objRS.Fields(0) =1
objRS.Fields.Item(0) = 1
```

If you're using IntelliSense, don't be confused if the value property does not show up – it's still there. It's just that ASP has a hard time employing IntelliSense when it comes to collections.

The UnderlyingValue and OriginalValue Properties

The OriginalValue property holds the value that was *originally* contained in that field when the Recordset object first fetched the records. This value will change only when the Update (or UpdateBatch for disconnected recordsets) is issued.

The `Underlying` property value of the `Field` object grabs the current (or most recently available) value for that field in the database. Let's expand on that a little. If your recordset is *not* disconnected, the `Underlying` property does a `Resync` to get the latest value from the database, but only for that field. If your recordset *is* disconnected, the `Underlying` property contains the value contained in the database the last time we updated the recordset.

These properties are central to the process of resolving conflicts. We'll look at an example of this at the end of this chapter – once we've covered the necessary groundwork in cursors. And in Chapter 8 we'll look at how they relate to conflicts between disconnected recordsets and databases.

The Type Property

The `Type` property returns the OLE DB data type (i.e. `adVarChar`, `adInteger`, or whatever) of the field. Basically, it tells you the underlying data type of the data.

The `Type` property can be a very useful property. For example, if you've ever had to create SQL statements dynamically, the `Type` property could quickly become your best buddy. In order to update a specific field, you need to generate the appropriate type of SQL string, depending on the data type of the field: a string needs single quotes, a numeric needs to have no quotes, and perhaps you need to add pound (#) signs if the value is a date type. You can use the `Type` property on the fly to determine the type of SQL string you need.

Here's a simple example:

```
Response.Write "The data type for pub_id is: " & _
               objRS("pub_id").Type & "<BR>"
Response.Write "The data type for pub_name is: " & _
               objRS("pub_name").Type & "<BR>"
```

If you run this code against our `pubs` database, you should get the following result:

The data type for pub_id is: 129
The data type for pub_name is: 200

We can compare the integer values returned against the DataTypeEnum enumerator type; see Appendix G. In this case, we get two different values for the two data types, even though they are both character formats: `pub_id` is of data type `char` (129), and `pub_name` is of data type `varChar` (200).

The Count Property

Here's one final property that's useful to know about at this stage. This property is simple enough – it indicates the number of `Field` objects in the `Fields` collection and returns a long data type:

```
lngCount = objRS.Fields.Count
```

Here, `lngCount` is assigned the number of `Field` objects in the `Fields` collection.

Things that Make the World Go Round

When you're developing your ADO application, there are three Recordset properties whose settings will help to determine whether your code runs smoothly, or whether you spend all evening pulling your hair out. These properties are the cursor type, cursor location and the locking type. When talking to a database, it's very important that these properties have the appropriate settings. In this section we'll take a close look at each of these settings, to see what they allow us to do and prevent us from doing.

Cursor Types

The Recordset's `CursorType` property determines what type of cursor we would like to use when opening a recordset. You can only set this property when the recordset is closed (or as an argument to the `Execute` method), or you'll get a runtime error. The following is a list of CursorTypeEnum enumeration values, which are the valid types available for this property:

Name	Value	Description
adOpenForwardOnly	0	Forward-only cursor. You can only move forward through the recordset and only one row at a time. This cursor will improve performance if you are only making a single pass through a recordset. This is the default.
adOpenKeySet	1	Keyset cursor. The data you receive is fixed, you do not see additions or deletions. However, the data in the fixed set is up-to-date. All types of movement are supported.
adOpenDynamic	2	Dynamic cursor. The data is not fixed – the data you see is up-to-date. All types of movement are supported. Note: some providers do not support bookmarks.
adOpenStatic	3	Static cursor. The data is fixed – so this is like a snapshot. All types of movement are supported.

It is worth noting that providers can extend this list, and that they do not have to support all cursor types. If a provider does not support a particular cursor type, then ADO will downgrade to the closest match available. (Appendix H contains information that indicates which `CursorType` you will get, based upon the data provider, `CursorType`, `CursorLocation` and `LockType` you specify.)

You can set the cursor type using the third parameter of the Recordset object's `Open` method. For example:

```
objRS.Open strSQL, strConn, adOpenKeySet
```

Alternatively, you can specify it as a property setting:

```
objRS.Source = strSQL
objRS.ActiveConnection = strConn
objRS.CursorType = adOpenKeySet
objRS.Open
```

Cursor Location

Quite simply, the cursor location specifies whether we use a client-side cursor or a server-side cursor. You can set the cursor location at the Recordset object level or at the Connection object level. If the Connection object has set the cursor location, the Recordset object will inherit this setting – unless another cursor location is specified at the Recordset object level. This can be specified only before the recordset is opened. Setting the CursorLocation property might look like this:

```
objRS.CursorLocation = AdUseServer
```

The CursorLocation property takes a value of type CursorLocationEnum:

Name	Value	Description
AdUseNone	1	Indicates no cursor location.
AdUseServer	2	Use server-side cursor (assuming the server will support it). This is the default.
AdUseClient	3	Use the Microsoft client-side cursor.
AdUseClientBatch	3	Use the Microsoft client-side cursor (exists for backward compatibility).

A server-side cursor (when available) handles data concurrency issues better than client-side cursors. Client-side cursors must be used when creating disconnected recordsets and custom recordsets.

> *If you get a message indicating that "the provider does not support this type of method or action", you should try switching the cursor location. Often, if a data provider can't support the features you're trying to implement, the ADO cursor engine can. You can use the Supports method to determine which features the data provider supports – see Chapter 6.*

Relating Cursor Type to Cursor Location

The cursor type and cursor location have a direct relationship. If the CursorLocation property is set to adUseClient or adUseClientBatch then only adOpenStatic cursor type is supported. So, even if you specify another CursorType, once you set the location to either adUseClient or adUseClientBatch ADO will downgrade the cursor type to adOpenStatic.

Locking types

Your data modifications can be dramatically impacted by the type of locking (or concurrency) you choose. The LockType property sets or returns the type of locking that the provider should use when opening a recordset. The LockType property can be set only when the recordset is closed (or as an argument of the Connection object's Execute method), and becomes read-only once open. If we set the LockType property via the recordset's Open method, we do it via the fourth parameter. For example:

```
objRS.Open strSQL, strConn, adOpenKeySet, adLockReadOnly
```

Alternatively, you can specify it as a property setting. For example:

```
objRS.Source = strSQL
objRS.ActiveConnection = strConn
objRS.CursorType = adOpenKeySet
objRS.LockType = adLockReadOnly
objRS.Open
```

The LockType property takes a value of type LockTypeEnum:

Name	Value	Description
AdLockReadOnly	1	A read-only recordset, no locking is provided since the recordset cannot be updated. This is the default.
AdLockPessimistic	2	Pessimistic locking is used. The provider attempts to lock the record once editing starts.
AdLockOptimistic	3	Optimistic locking is used. The provider locks the record only when the Update method is used.
AdLockBatchOptimistic	4	Optimistic locking for batch updates. Locks are issued when the UpdateBatch method is used, and not during field assignments.

Your choice of locking method will depend on the business rules applied to your application. You may have an application that needs pessimistic locking – this will lock the records as soon as you start selecting records. Pessimistic locking is mostly used in situations where you cannot afford to have a 'dirty read'. For example, consider making an airline reservation. You want to be sure that the unreserved seat that the salesperson sees is the seat you're going to get. If 'dirty reads' were allowed, that unreserved seat could be reserved simultaneously by two or more salespeople. Pessimistic locking ensures that the records you are sitting on *cannot* be updated by anyone else, until you release them. However, pessimistic locking does require that you maintain a connection to the database, which can often be impractical where the web is concerned.

Optimistic locking is much more forgiving in allowing multiple users to simultaneously access the same records – but you can run into 'dirty reads' conflicts. For example, two users select the same data from a database at the same time, and then start editing it. The first user to submit his changes will complete successfully. However, when the second user updates the database, the update will fail – because the second user's changes are based on the assumption that the database hasn't changed since he started editing his recordset. This error is trappable, and using the OriginalValue and UnderlyingValue properties we can find compare original and updated values and provide code that resolves the conflict accordingly. There's more about this in the next section, and in Chapter 8.

An Example – Resolving a Conflict

We'll end this chapter with an example that uses some of the material that we've seen in this chapter. We can use the Value, OriginalValue and UnderlyingValue properties to resolve conflicts that occur when using batch updates. Using a lock type of adLockBatchOptimistic allows your recordset to act differently than a normal recordset. In this case you can make changes to the records locally without actually changing them on the server. This is great when using disconnected recordsets, which is discussed in Chapter 8.

Imagine if you will, a recordset using batch updates. We'll walk through this recordset making changes. At the same time, someone else has accessed that recordset and has modified a value that we are also planning to modify. When we issue the update, an error occurs. Instead, we can avoid the error by checking to see whether the database's values have changed, detecting the conflict and resolving it.

In this code sample, we'll first add the constant values that we will be needing. Of course, you could include the adovbs.inc file instead, but I'm going to save on memory by typing out just the constants I need. We'll also declare the objects and other variables we will be using and instantiate the objects. We will set the boolean value to false, indicating that we believe no conflicts will occur. This value will be changed if conflicts do arise:

```
<%@ Language=VBScript %>
<%Option Explicit
' Declare ADO Constants
Const adOpenKeyset = 1           ' Keyset Cursor
Const adLockBatchOptimistic = 4  ' Batch Lock

' Declare all Objects
Dim objConn         ' ADO Connection Object
Dim objRSTitles     ' ADO Recordset Object

' Declare all other Variables
Dim strConn         ' OLE DB String Connection
Dim booConflict     ' boolean Conflict Value

' Assume no conflicts will occur
booConflict = false

' Create the ADO Objects
Set objConn = Server.CreateObject("ADODB.Connection")
Set objRSTitles = Server.CreateObject("ADODB.Recordset")
```

Now create the connection string, as we described earlier in the chapter. We're going to use SQL Server again here. The Data Source refers to the name of your Server or WorkStation that has SQL Server running on it, and in this case the system administrator's password is null. Then we open the connection to the database:

```
' Create the Connection String
strConn = ""
strConn = strConn & "Provider=sqloledb;"
strConn = strConn & "Data Source=winbook;"
strConn = strConn & "Initial Catalog=pubs;"
strConn = strConn & "User Id=sa;Password=;"

' Open the Connection
objConn.Open strConn
```

Now we'll set the properties of the recordset. As we explained above, we'll choose the adOpenKeyset cursor type and the adLockBatchOptimistic lock type. Then we'll use the recordset to open the titles table of the pubs database:

```
' Set the Recordset Properties
objRSTitles.ActiveConnection = objConn
objRSTitles.CursorType = adOpenKeyset
objRSTitles.LockType = adLockBatchOptimistic

' Opend the Titles table
objRSTitles.Open "titles"
```

With the open recordset we will start making changes to the recordset – i.e. assigning values to the Value properties of the recordset using the equal (=) sign. (These changes are not made on the database until we issue the BatchUpdate method. And we use BatchUpdate, instead of Update, since we opened this recordset with a Batch lock.) So let's make some changes: we'll loop through the recordset and change the Type field from business to big business:

```
' Change all the title types from "business" to "big business"
Do Until objRSTitles.EOF
  If Trim(objRSTitles("Type")) = "business" Then
    objRSTitles("Type") = "big business"
  End If
  objRSTitles.MoveNext
Loop
```

This is where it gets interesting. We're going to simulate another user. Our simulated user is going to make some changes to the database behind our back – so that, when we update the database, a conflict will occur. We'll do this by using the Connection object to execute some code:

```
' Simulate another user changing the same data
objConn.Execute "UPDATE titles SET type = 'small biz' " & _
            "WHERE type = 'business'"
```

Here, we are actually hitting the database and making changes directly to it. Remember that the Recordset object that we've used in the code so far – objRSTitles – is in Batch mode, so it's not making changes to the database directly.

OK, that's the end of the simulated user's part in proceedings – back to our own `objRSTitles` recordset. Because `objRSTitles` is operating in Batch mode, we will be nice and make sure that no one has changed the data. In the real world, there are real users – not simulated users – so we'd really need to check that nobody has changed the state of the database while we've been working on our recordset.

We check the `OriginalValue` and see if it still matches the `UnderlyingValue`:

```
' Now let's check for the changes
objRSTitles.MoveFirst
Do Until objRSTitles.EOF
  ' Check the Original value - try to match it to the Underlying value
  If objRSTitles("Type").OriginalValue <> _
                      objRSTitles("Type").UnderlyingValue Then
    ' They don't match - so let's inform the user
    Response.Write "<B>The Underlying data has changed! </B>" & "<BR>"
    Response.Write "Title ID " & objRSTitles("title_id") & "<BR>"
    Response.Write "Current Value = "  & objRSTitles("Type") & "<BR>"
    Response.Write "Original Value = " & objRSTitles("Type").OriginalValue
    Response.Write "<BR>"
    Response.Write "Underlying Value = " & objRSTitles("Type").UnderlyingValue
    Response.Write "<BR>" & "<BR>"
```

If a conflict arises, we not only notify the user, but we also change the `booConflict` flag to `true`, indicating that there was indeed a conflict:

```
    ' Since we have a conflict we change the flag
    booConflict = true
  End if
  objRSTitles.MoveNext
Loop
```

Now we check the flag. If there's a conflict, we cancel the batch update. If there's no conflict, we'd update the batch to the database (of course, in this example we know that the simulated user has already been round and laid the foundations for a conflict...):

```
' Check to see if we have conflicts
If booConflict Then
  ' Conflicts exist - abort the update
  objRSTitles.CancelBatch
Else
  ' Everying is ok continue with the update
  objRSTitles.UpdateBatch
End if
```

It's at this point that you can add code that resolves any conflicts that do occur – you can compare the `Value`, `OriginalValue` and `UnderlyingValue` values as part of this resolution. This code is likely to be dependent on your own business rules – but the mechanism is there for resolution. There's more on this in Chapter 8.

Finally, we set the database back the way we found it – so that you can do the demo all over again and get the same results:

```
' Close the Recordset
objRSTitles.Close

' Undo the changes we made since this only a demo
objConn.Execute "UPDATE titles SET type = 'business' " & _
                "WHERE type = 'small biz'"

' Close the Connection
objConn.Close
%>
```

The outcome of this ASP page should get four blocks of output like this:

The Underlying data has changed!
Title ID BU1032
Current Value = big business
Original Value = business
Underlying Value = small biz

Summary

This chapter covered the fundamentals of the Recordset object. You now have a firm base to stand on while you navigate through the rest of this book. Opening, inserting, updating and navigating with the Move... methods are the fundamentals of using the Recordset object. If you have these down then you are well on your way to mastering the Recordset object. We haven't gone through every property and method of the Recordset object in this chapter – we'll be covering further details on recordsets in the next few chapters, and you can find a complete reference in Appendix A. Always remember that the online help is your friend, and if you not sure how something works, try it out and see what happens. The best way to learn is to experiment.

In the next chapter, we'll look at more of the Recordset's functionality – including filtering, cloning and capturing multiple recordsets.

Building on the Recordset Foundation

In this chapter we will build on the foundation laid down in Chapter 5, by looking at some of the cool advanced features of the `Recordset` object. The `Recordset` object offers many features – some help our programs to handle data more efficiently, while the others (e.g. Supports and Transactional ASPs) help us to manage our data. In this chapter, we will look at:

- ❑ Cloning recordsets
- ❑ Paging through data
- ❑ How to tell what a recordset supports
- ❑ Applying filters to data after it is retrieved
- ❑ Indexing, searching and sorting
- ❑ Updating data in batches
- ❑ Capturing multiple recordsets in one trip to the server

Cloning Recordsets

Suppose you want to create an exact copy of a recordset. How would you do it? You *could*:

- ❑ Create and open a second `Recordset` object using the same SQL statement as the original – but it's not the most efficient way to do it, and changes to one recordset would not be reflected in the other.
- ❑ Set a newly-dimensioned recordset pointer to the existing recordset – but then you wouldn't be working with a *copy* of the original recordset.

The good news is that ADO gives you an easier way to copy a `Recordset` object: it's called **cloning**. The `Clone` method allows you to create an exact, synchronized copy of an existing `Recordset` object. It is the most efficient way you can use to get a copy of an existing recordset.

How to Create a Clone

There are a number of ways to clone a recordset. This first example creates a clone, called `objMyClone`, whose lock type is the same as the clone's progenitor, `objRS`:

```
set objMyClone = objRS.Clone
```

This second example also creates a clone with the same lock type as its progenitor:

```
set objMyClone = objRS.Clone adLockUnspecified
```

This third example creates a read-only clone:

```
set objMyClone = objRS.Clone adLockReadOnly
```

What Types of Recordsets are Cloneable?

It's worth noting that you can only clone bookmarkable recordsets. You can find out whether your recordset supports bookmarks by using the recordset's `Supports` method (covered later in this chapter). For example, a recordset with a forward-only cursor type is not a candidate for cloning – as we'll see in our first code sample.

The listing below demonstrates a common error that many of us run into when we try to clone for the first time. That is, we take the ADO default values – or worse, in our quest for efficiency, our own settings betray us. The code example below begins normally: we open an ADO connection to the `pubs` database (one of the sample databases provided with SQL Server) using our SQL Server OLE DB provider, and then we select a recordset from the `authors` table:

```
<%@ LANGUAGE="VBSCRIPT" %>
<HTML><HEAD><TITLE>Bad Clone</TITLE></HEAD>
<BODY>
<H1>Example of Illegal Cloning-- Forward Only Cursor</H1>
<%
  Dim objConn      ' as ADO conection
  Set objConn = CreateObject("ADODB.Connection")
  Dim objRS        ' as ADO Recordset
  Dim objClone     ' as ADO Recordset
  Dim strSQL       ' as string

  strSQL = "SELECT * FROM authors"              'Initialize the string
  objConn.Open "Provider=MSDASQL;" & _
               "User ID=sa;" & _
               "Data Source=winbook;" & _
               "Initial Catalog=pubs"           'Connect to database

  Set objRS = CreateObject("ADODB.Recordset")   'Create the recordset object
  Set objRS.ActiveConnection = objConn
  objRS.Open strSQL                              'Open the recordset
```

The code for this sample – and all the samples in the book – is available for download from http://webdev.wrox.co.uk/books/1649.

So far so good. Now we'll call the `Clone` method on our recordset. As I'll explain in a moment, it's this call that will cause a run-time error:

```
'Attempt to perform Cloning of a record set with forward only cursor
'Ah, but remember that the defualt cursor type is forward only:
'This statement will result in a confusing and ambiguous error message
   set objClone = objRS.Clone
%>
</BODY></HTML>
```

Here's the error message that we will receive when the code sample above is executed:

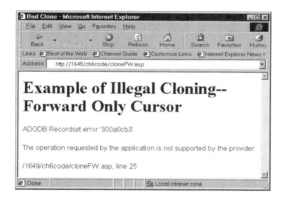

The error message suggests that we've got the wrong provider; but that's not the case. Remember that a clone inherits the cursor type of its creator. Since we've tried to clone a non-bookmarkable recordset (the original recordset, `objRS`, has the default cursor type, forward-only), we receive a runtime error.

The forward-only cursor is the default cursor type of any recordset (and in many cases is the most desirable and fastest). However, since we can't clone a recordset that's opened with the forward-only cursor, you will need to specifically request an alternate cursor type when you create the clone. In the next code listing, we'll see an example of cloning that works!

Creating our first Clone

We'll refine the sample above, explicitly specifying a static cursor for the original recordset. The static cursor, like the keyset and dynamic cursors, is a bookmarkable scrolling cursor and therefore a legal type for cloning:

```
Set objRS = CreateObject("ADODB.Recordset")   'Create the recordset object
'Use the static cursor type to clone with this provider
'You could also use a keyset cursor
objRS.CursorType = 3 'adOpenStatic
Set objRS.ActiveConnection = objConn
objRS.Open strSQL                              'Open the recordset
```

Once the recordset is open, we can clone it and see that it does provide some output:

```
Set objClone = objRS.Clone                    'Perform the legal clone
Do While Not objClone.EOF                      'Display the data to prove it
  Response.Write objClone(1).Value & "<br>"
  objClone.MoveNext
Loop
%>
</BODY></HTML>
```

The second field of the cloned recordset (i.e. objClone(1)) contains the surnames of the authors in the authors table, as shown in the screenshot:

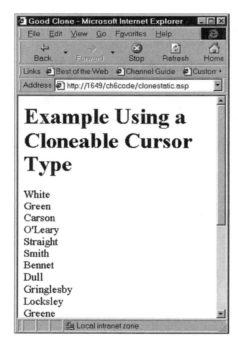

The Record Pointer of the Cloned Recordset

It's fair to ask how the cloned recordset's record pointer (i.e. the internal mechanism that points to the 'current row' of the recordset) behaves in relation to the original recordset's record pointer. We know that the cloned recordset is synchronized with its progenitor (and we'll get into the nitty-gritty of synchronized recordsets shortly) – but does that mean that the clone's record pointer follows the record pointer of the master recordset?

In fact, 'synchronized' does not mean 'in-step'. That is, the two record pointers move independently of one another. The example below shows this. After declaring all our variables, we set the query string to query the authors table; we open a data connection to the pubs database; and then open the recordset:

```
strSQL = "SELECT * FROM authors"              'Initialize the string
objConn.Open "Provider=MSDASQL;" & _
             "User ID=sa;" & _
             "Data Source=winbook;" & _
             "Initial Catalog=pubs"           'Connect to database

Set objRS = CreateObject("ADODB.Recordset")  'Create the recordset object
  'Use the static cursor type to clone with this provider
  'You could also use a keyset cursor
  objRS.CursorType = 3                         'adOpenStatic
  Set objRS.ActiveConnection = objConn
  objRS.Open strSQL                           'Open the recordset
```

Notice that we're using a static cursor again. Then we create the clone, just as we did in the previous example:

```
Set objClone = objRS.Clone                    'Perform the legal clone
```

Now we'll loop through the cloned recordset, displaying the fact that when we move the clone's record pointer, the original recordset's pointer remains firmly on the first record:

```
Response.Write "I don't follow my clone<BR>"  'Display the data to prove it
  Response.Write "<TABLE BORDER=1>"
  Do While Not objClone.EOF
    Response.Write "<TR>"
    Response.Write "<TD>My Clone is on record:" & objClone(0).Value & "</TD>"
    Response.Write "<TD>I am on record:" & objRS(0).Value & "</TD>"
    Response.Write "</TR>"
    objClone.MoveNext
  Loop
  Response.Write "</TABLE>"

  objClone.MoveFirst
  Response.Write "<P>My Clone does not follow me<BR>"
  Response.Write "<TABLE BORDER=1>"
  Do While Not objRS.EOF
    Response.Write "<TR>"
    Response.Write "<TD>I am on record:" & objRS(1).Value & "</TD>"
    Response.Write "<TD>My clone is on record:" & objClone(1).Value & "</TD>"
    Response.Write "</TR>"
    objRS.MoveNext
  Loop
  Response.write "</TABLE>"
%>
</BODY></HTML>
```

Here, we've compared the first field of each the recordset (objRS(0) and objClone(0)) as we move the record pointer through the cloned recordset – to show that objRS's record pointer doesn't follow objClone's record pointer. Then we do a similar comparison – but the other way round – to show that objClone's pointer doesn't follow objRS's pointer either:

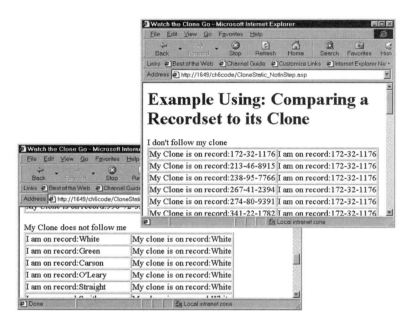

What are Synchronized Recordsets?

What exactly does it mean to say that a recordset and its clone are synchronized? We'll look more closely at that now. In this next example, we'll clone a recordset and then make some changes in an attempt to watch the synchronization at work.

We'll specify the SQL string (to query the authors table of the pubs database), and open the connection to the pubs database, in just the way that we've done in previous examples. Then we'll open a recordset against the authors table of the pubs database in SQL Server, and set the clone:

```
strSQL = "SELECT * FROM authors"            'Initialize the string
   objConn.CursorLocation = 3                  'adUseClient
   objConn.Open "Provider=MSDASQL;" & _
            "User ID=sa;" & _
            "Data Source=winbook;" & _
            "Initial Catalog=pubs"             'Connect to database

   objConn.BeginTrans    ' Use a transaction  – you'd need to call the
                         ' CommitTrans method in order to set changes
                         ' to the database
   Set objRS = CreateObject("ADODB.Recordset")   'Create the recordset object
   'Use the static cursor type to clone with this provider
   'You could also use a keyset cursor
   objRS.CursorType = 3                           'adOpenStatic
   objRS.LockType = 4                             'adLockBatchOptimistic
   Set objRS.ActiveConnection = objConn
   objRS.Open strSQL                             'Open the recordset
   Set objClone = objRS.Clone                    'Perform the legal clone
```

Note that we've used the BeginTrans method to start a transaction. I'll explain why in a moment.

Now we'll compare a couple of corresponding entries in the original and cloned recordsets (the au_fname and au_lname fields of the first record in the recordset):

```
Response.Write "<P>Compare data in the two recordsets:<BR>"
Response.Write "The clone is looking at: " & objClone("au_fname").Value & _
               " " & objClone("au_lname").Value & "<BR>"
Response.Write "The original is looking at: " & objRS("au_fname").Value & _
               " " & objRS("au_lname").Value & "<BR>"
```

Now let's edit these data items – but *only* in the original recordset, objRS:

```
Response.Write "<P>Make a change to the original recordset... "
objRS("au_lname").Value = "Waters"
objRS("au_fname").Value = "Tim"
objRS.Update
```

We call the Update method to update the changes to the database. This also has the effect of forcing the cloned recordset to follow the same changes as the original – as we'll see in the next part of the code. Now we'll compare those corresponding values again:

```
Response.Write "Now the clone has changed too!<P>"
Response.Write "<P>Compare data in the two recordsets:<BR>"
Response.Write "The clone is looking at: " & objClone("au_fname").Value & _
               " " & objClone("au_lname").Value & "<BR>"
Response.Write "The original is looking at: " & objRS("au_fname").Value & _
               " " & objRS("au_lname").Value & "<BR>"

'I cancel the batch save here -- you don't have to
objRS.CancelBatch
%>
</BODY></HTML>
```

The output of this script looks like this:

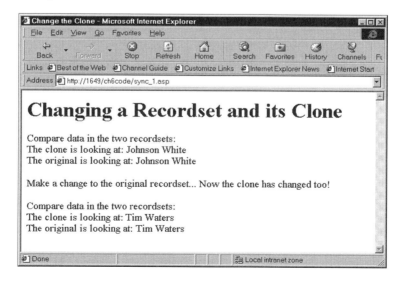

We can see that the change in the progenitor recordset is now reflected in the clone. Pretty cool, huh?

Recall that we called the BeginTrans *method – so all the code following the* BeginTrans *call is actually part of a transaction. We'd have to call the* CommitTrans *method in order to commit all the changes. However, you've probably noticed that we didn't call* CommitTrans *– therefore the transaction is rolled back at the end of the script, and none of the changes are persisted. I took this step to protect the* pubs *database from the changes that would otherwise have been enforced by the* Update *method in the script. Thus, you can run this sample as often as you like, without ultimately changing the underlying data in the* pubs *database.*

When the Clone gets Out of Sync with the Original Recordset

You need to be careful, because the clone doesn't remain synchronized with its original unconditionally. This next example shows how your original and clone can become out-of-sync, for example, if you requery the original recordset against the original database.

This sample builds onto the end of the previous example. Having shown the original and the clone in sync (the final Response.Write statement in the code above), we'll add some code to make the original recordset, objRS, requery the database:

```
Response.Write "<P>Now Requery the original and make a change to it...<BR>"
objRS.Requery
```

Note that we can't call the Requery *method for a recordset that is currently being edited. Therefore we must either cancel the edits that we'd made to* objRS, *or submit them to the database. In this case, you'll recall that we submitted them using the* Update *method.*

Once we've re-queried, we'll make some new edits to objRS, and update the changes to the database:

```
objRS("au_lname").Value = "Brown"
objRS("au_fname").Value = "Erin"
objRS.Update
```

Recall, as we mentioned at the end of the previous section, that the update is part of a transaction – we'll roll back the transaction at the end to protect the pubs *database from any actual changes.*

Now, we'll compare the data in objRS and objClone again:

```
Response.Write "...now the clone is out of synch and still has its old value!<P>"

Response.Write "<P>Compare data in the two recordsets:<BR>"
Response.Write "The clone is looking at: " & objClone("au_fname").Value & _
               " " & objClone("au_lname").Value & "<BR>"
Response.Write "The original is looking at: " & objRS("au_fname").Value & _
               " " & objRS("au_lname").Value & "<BR>"

'I cancel the batch save here -- you don't have to
objRS.CancelBatch
%>
</BODY></HTML>
```

You can see from the results that the `Requery` method throws the original and the clone out of sync – the changes made in the original recordset are not reflected in the clone:

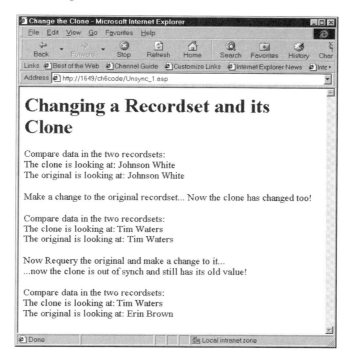

The lesson is this: Requerying breaks the link between the original and the clone. However, it's also worth noting that, if you have multiple clones and you requery the original recordset, the clones all remain synchronized with each other (though obviously not with the original).

Paging

Well, how do you like the book so far? No matter what your opinion of the book is, I bet you like the fact that it has many pages instead of just one big page. Because the book's information is broken into multiple pages, it makes the book easier to read and reference – the pages provide us with manageable units to work with. Now: wouldn't it be great if we had a method for looking at *data* one 'page' at a time?

Suppose we want to look through an employee database on the web. If we had to read down a long, seemingly interminable list of employees, it would be no fun. We'd prefer to see a nice orderly presentation of pages. It would take some custom programming to implement this – if the ADO recordset didn't give it to us for free.

There are five recordset properties that are used to implement recordset paging:

- ❑ **CursorLocation**: You must use a client-side cursor to enable paging (CursorLocation = adUseClient)
- ❑ **PageSize**: After you open your recordset, tell it a page size. How many records do you want on a page – 5, 10, 20, more? Choose how many you want. The last page will have the balance of the left-over records.
- ❑ **PageCount**: After you've set the page size, you can get the number of pages that your recordset makes up.
- ❑ **AbsolutePage**: This tells you what page you are on. You can set this number to turn to a specific page.
- ❑ **AbsolutePosition**: This tells you what record you are on in the recordset. You can set this number to go to a specific record or you can read it to see which record you are on.

An Example

You can use this code to view to list the people in the authors table of the pubs database – in a number of pages. We've coded three-per-page here. When the code executes the first time, we test the Session object – MyConnection – for an existing connection. If none exists, then the connection is established, the recordset is created, and the page size is set:

```
if not isObject(Session("MyConnection")) then
    set objConn = CreateObject("ADODB.Connection")

    'Initialize the string
    strSQL = "select * from authors"

    'Connect to database
    'You must use the Client side cursor
    objConn.CursorLocation = 3 'adUseClient
    objConn.Open "Provider=MSDASQL;" & _
                 "Persist Security Info=False;" & _
                 "User ID=sa;" & _
                 "Data Source=winbook;" & _
                 "Initial Catalog=pubs"

    'Create the recordset object
    Set objRS = CreateObject("ADODB.Recordset")
    objRS.CursorType = 3 'adOpenStatic
    Set objRS.ActiveConnection = objConn

    'Get the recordset and set the page size
    objRS.Open strSQL
    objRS.PageSize = 3
    set Session("MyConnection") = objConn
    set Session("MyResults") = objRS
    'The Initial Display
    Display
Else
    <deal with subsequent calls to this page, after the first>
    <we'll look at this in a moment>
End If
```

After setting the active connection and opening the recordset, we set the page size for three records per page. Then we cache the connection and the recordset. Most of the time you would refrain from caching a connection when possible, but for our example it's OK. Now we call the `Display` subroutine, and the user is shown the first page of data.

Let's have a quick look at the `Display` subroutine:

```
sub Display()
    dim intRecord
    Response.Write "<A HREF=""PageMe.asp?PrevOrNext=Prev"">Prev Page</A>"
    Response.Write "<A HREF=""PageMe.asp?PrevOrNext=Next"">Next Page</A>"

    Response.Write "<P>Page: " & objRS.AbsolutePage & "<P>"
    Session("Page")=objRS.AbsolutePage
    For intRecord = 1 To objRS.PageSize
        Response.Write objRS(2).value & " " & objRS(1).value & "<BR>"
        objRS.MoveNext
        If objRS.EOF Then Exit For
    Next
end sub
%>
```

This displays the user interface. The user is told what page is being displayed (on the first invocation the first page is displayed). The author's names are displayed; and the user is also provided with a couple of links that allow forward and backward direction through the pages. Of course, they can never page further than the beginning or end of the recordset.

When the page is executed subsequently (via the **Next Page** or **Prev Page** links), the request object (`PrevOrNext`) is read. If this equates to `Next` then we check to see whether we're on the last page (i.e. current page equals page count). If not, then the `AbsolutePage` property is set to the next page; otherwise we display an 'end' page:

```
if not isObject(Session("MyConnection")) then
    <deal with first execution of this page - see code above>
Else
    set objConn = Session("MyConnection")
    set objRS = Session("MyResults")
    intCurrentPage = Session("Page")

    if Request("PrevOrNext") = "Next" then
        'If we are not at the end of the pages then
        'go to the next page and display
        if not (intCurrentPage = objRS.PageCount) then
            objRS.AbsolutePage = intCurrentPage + 1
            Display
        else
            ' Display that we are at the end of the records and set the
            ' page count up so that the Prev will calculate the last page
            Response Write "<A HREF=""PageMe.asp?PrevOrNext=Prev"">Prev Page </A>"
            Response.Write "<P>No More Records"
            Session("Page") = objRS.PageCount + 1
        end if
    else
```

Walking backwards through the pages works very much the same way:

```
'If "Next" is not explicitly chosen, then assume "Prev"
'If we are not on the first page then turn back the page and display
if intCurrentPage <> 1 then
   objRS.AbsolutePage = intCurrentPage - 1
   Display
else
   'Display that we are at the start of the pages. Set the page number
   'to zero so that the next will increment to one
   Response.Write "<A HREF=""PageMe.asp?PrevOrNext=Next"">Next Page </A>"
   Response.Write "<P>At Start of Records"
   Session("Page") = 0
end if
  end if
end if
```

As you can see in the screenshots, paging output is simple and does not overwhelm the user with too much information.

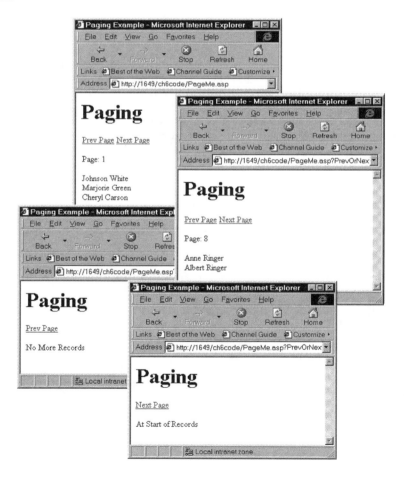

The Supports Method

Your recordset can tell you what properties are supported by its OLE DB provider. Keep in mind though, that while the provider may support some functionality, a particular recordset might not. For example, you might have a recordset that presents a calculated field that does not correspond to an actual field in the database. While the provider may support updating for a recordset of your configuration, it will not be able to update that particular recordset.

When you call the Supports method, you have a number of options:

```
booResult = objRS.Supports(Options)
```

The following table lists the options that you can query using the Supports method:

Attribute Name	Description	Option Constant
Add new	When Supports returns true, the provider allows for the AddNew method to be called for adding a new empty record to the recordset.	adAddNew
Approximate position	When true, the provider allows for the use of the AbsolutePage and AbsolutePosition properties.	adApproxPosition
Bookmarkable records	When true, the provider allows for the use of bookmarks in the recordset (a bokmark is a variant value returned from the Bookmark property, that uniquely identifies a record – bookmarks can be used to return to an exact location in a recordset).	adBookMark
Deletable records	When true, you may use the Delete method of a recordset to remove rows from the recordset.	adDelete
Find	When true, you can use the Find method to search a column in the recordset for a specific value.	adFind
Hold	When true, you can request more rows or move the row pointer without committing your edits.	adHoldRecords
Move back	When true, you can use MovePrevious, MoveFirst, GetRows and Move to move the record pointer backwards.	adMovePrevious

Table Continued on Following Page

Attribute Name	Description	Option Constant
Resynchronize recordset	When `true`, the provider allows you to call the `Resync` method. The `Resync` method refreshes the recordset with any changes in the underlying data in the database, no new records are included in the `Resync`.	`adResync`
Updateable	When `true`, the provider will allow for changes to be made with the `Update` method of the recordset.	`adUpdate`
Batch updateable	When `true`, the underlying provider supports `UpdateBatch` and `CancelBatch` methods for the cursor type.	`adUpdateBatch`

An Example

The code sample below is a neat way of creating recordsets with different permutations of cursor types, lock types, and cursor locations, and finding out what each recordset supports based on those choices.

It's quite straightforward really. We'll use a simple HTML form to choose the lock type, cursor type and cursor position of the recordset, like this:

```
<FORM NAME="Supports" ACTION="Supports.asp" METHOD="POST">
Cursor Type <BR>
<SELECT name="ct">
  <OPTION value=0 SELECTED>Forward Only
  <OPTION value=1>Keyset
  <OPTION value=2>Dynamic
  <OPTION value=3>Static
</SELECT><P>
Cursor Location<BR>
<SELECT name="cl">
  <OPTION value=2 SELECTED>Server Side
  <OPTION value=3>Client Side
</SELECT><P>
Lock Type<BR>
<SELECT name="lt">
  <OPTION value=1 SELECTED>Read Only
  <OPTION value=2>Pessimistic
  <OPTION value=3>Optimistic
  <OPTION value=4>Batch Optimistic
</SELECT><P>
<INPUT ALIGN=CENTER TYPE=SUBMIT VALUE="View Support">
</FORM>
```

So our page looks like this to start:

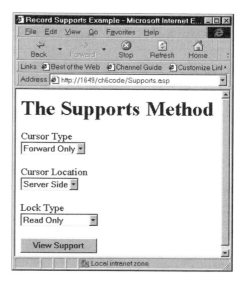

Hitting the View Support button will submit our form. After some unexciting variable declarations (which we'll skip here) we set the values for strLocation, strLock and strType – the variables that we'll use in a moment to open a recordset:

```
<%
if Request("ct") <> "" then
<variable declarations>
   SELECT CASE intCursorLocation
     CASE 2  strLocation = "Server Side"
     CASE 3  strLocation = "Client Side"
   END SELECT
   SELECT CASE intLockType
     CASE 1  strLock = "Read Only"
     CASE 2  strLock = "Pessimistic"
     CASE 3  strLock = "Optimistic"
     CASE 4  strLock = "Batch Optimistic"
   END SELECT
   SELECT CASE intCursorType
     CASE 0  strType = "Forward Only"
     CASE 1  strType = "Keyset"
     CASE 2  strType = "Dynamic"
     CASE 3  strType = "Static"
   END SELECT
```

We'll set the SQL string, and open the connection to the pubs database, as we've seen before in this chapter. Then we can query the recordset against the database – using the strLocation, strLock and strType variables for the recordset's settings:

```
strSQL = "SELECT * FROM authors"     'Initialize the string
objConn.CursorLocation = intCursorLocation    'Connect to database
objConn.Open "Provider=MSDASQL;" & _
             "Persist Security Info=False;" & _
             "User ID=sa;" & _
             "Data Source=winbook;" & _
             "Initial Catalog=pubs"
```

```
Set objRS = CreateObject("ADODB.Recordset")    'Create the recordset object
objRS.CursorType = intCursorType
objRS.LockType = intLockType
Set objRS.ActiveConnection = objConn
objRS.Open strSQL
```

In this example, we're not interested in the results of the query – we're interested in what funtionality the recordset supports. So the rest of the page is given over to presenting the attributes, and whether-or-not they are supported by `objRS`:

```
'Test Supports
Response.Write "<HR><H2>Previous test: </H2>" & _
               "Cursor Type = " & strType & "<BR>" & _
               "Lock Type = " & strLock & "<BR>" & _
               "Location = " & strLocation & "<BR>" & _
               "<H2>Supports:</H2>"
Response.Write "<TABLE BORDER=1>"
Response.Write "<TR><TD>AddNew</TD>"
Response.Write "<TD>" & objRS.Supports(&H1000400) & "</TD></TR>"
Response.Write "<TR><TD>Approx Position</TD>"
Response.Write "<TD>" & objRS.Supports(&H4000) & "</TD></TR>"
<etc>
Response.Write "<TR><TD>Update Batch</TD>"
Response.Write "<TD>" & objRS.Supports(&H10000) & "</TD></TR>"
Response.Write "</TABLE>"
end if
%>
</BODY></HTML>
```

Here are the results. The output contained in this table is dependent on the choices that the user makes for the recordset's cursor type, cursor location and lock type.

The figure shows the no-frills approach of using a forward-only, read-only cursor. This script will allow you to test any combinations that you wish – remember it is using the SQL Server OLEDB provider.

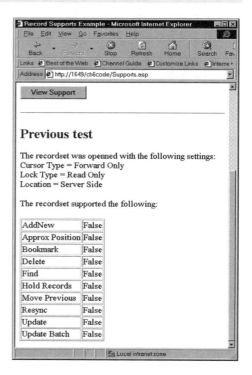

Filtering

One of the coolest features of the ADO recordset is the `Filter` property. We use the `Filter` property to narrow down the information the we can see in the recordset – according to the criteria we specify.

This is especially nice when there is a lot of data being returned. For instance, you could filter on all Last Names with the name of 'Smith', or all records with a State = 'NC'. You can filter your recordset to view just the information you want, without destroying the rest of the information. All the information is still there in the recordset – it's just hidden from view until you clear the filter.

By applying the filter, you get a subset of all the rows – only the filtered data (the subset) is displayed. So you can walk through the recordset from the first record to the last record and see *only* the records that match your criteria. If no rows match the filter then EOF and BOF will be true; otherwise you should be positioned at the first row in the record. You can use the `MoveNext`, `MovePrevious`, `MoveFirst` and `MoveLast` methods to navigate through the filter recordset. Once you're are done viewing your records, you need to set the filter to `adFilterNone`. This will clear the filter and display all the records. We'll have a look at an example in a moment.

How to use the Filter Property

The syntax of the Filter property is as follows:

```
objRS.Filter = Value
```

Value can take the form of a database query expression, or it can be one of the predefined constants. Let's take a closer look. *Value* can be any of the following:

❑ A SQL WHERE statement. You can supply what is essentially a SQL WHERE clause (contained within a pair of double-quotes), using field names from the recordset, logical operators (<, <=, >, >=, =, <>, LIKE), and values (dates, strings, wildcards (* and %), etc. when used with LIKE). We don't actually use the word WHERE – as you'll see in the code sample below.

❑ A bookmark array: You can supply an array of bookmarks – only the bookmarked records will be available in the recordset.

❑ A `FilterGroupEnum` value. These constants are described in the chart below:

Enumerator	Description
`adFilterNone`	Turns off filtering. With this setting, all records can be seen.
`adFilterPendingRecords`	When in batch update mode, this constant ensures that you see only those records that are pending updates – i.e. changes that have been made in the recordset but have not yet been sent to the server.
`adFilterAffectedRecords`	Allows you to see only those records affected by the `Delete`, `Resync`, `UpdateBatch` and `CancelBatch` calls.

Table Continued on Following Page

Enumerator	Description
adFilterFetchedRecords	Allows you to see only those records that are currently cached on the client machine – i.e the records retrieved in the most recent call to the database.
adFilterConflictingRecords	Allows you to see batch update collisions – those records updated in batch mode with concurrency conflicts on the server.

An Example

This example takes the contents of the authors table of the pubs database, and filters the contents by the first letter of the author's last name. We start by displaying links that will eventually filter our recordset by initial of last name:

```
'Write out the alphabet links
  for intLetter = 65 to 90
    Response.Write "<a href=""Filter.asp?letter=" & _
                   Chr(intLetter) & """>" & _
                   Chr(intLetter) & "</A>  "
  next
  Response.Write "<BR>"
```

Now we'll open the connection to the pubs database, and query the recordset objRS against the authors table:

```
if not isObject(Session("rs")) then
    set objRS = CreateObject("ADODB.Recordset")

    strSQL = "select * from authors"        'Initialize the string
    objRS.ActiveConnection = "Provider=MSDASQL;" & _
                      "User ID=sa;" & _
                      "Data Source=winbook;" & _
                      "Initial Catalog=pubs"      'Connect to database

    objRS.CursorType = 3 'adOpenStatic        'Create the record set object
    objRS.Open strSQL                         'Open and filter
```

Notice that the script only needs to go to the database once. The first time the user uses the page, he'll see the filtered contents of the recordset, showing only authors whose surnames begin with "A":

```
    Display("A")       'Display the A names first
    set Session("rs") = objRS
```

We'll have a look at the Display procedure in a moment. On subsequent queries (when the session object Session("rs") is non-null) we display the recordset filtered against a letter of the user's choosing – contained in the variable letter:

```
      else
        set objRS = Session("rs")
        strLetter = Request("letter")
        Display(strLetter)
      end if
```

OK. Let's have a look at the `Display` procedure. All we do is set the filter (using a `WHERE`-type SQL query), and display the contents of the filtered recordset:

```
  sub Display( strLetterToFilter )
    'Set the filter
    objRS.Filter = "au_lname Like '" & strLetterToFilter & "%'"

    Response.Write "<H2>" & strLetterToFilter & "<H2>"
    Response.Write "<TABLE Border=1><THEAD>" & _
                   "<TH>Name</TH><TH>Phone Number</TH><TH>Address</TH>" & _
                   "<TBODY>"
    do while not objRS.EOF
      Response.Write "<TR><TD>" & _
                     objRS("au_lname") & ", " & objRS("au_fname") & _
                     "</TD><TD>" & _
                     objRS("phone") & _
                     "</TD><TD>" & _
                     objRS("address") & _
                     "</TD><TD></TR>"
      objRS.MoveNext
    loop
    Response.Write "</TABLE>"
```

Then we tidy up, ready for the next query: we turn off the filter using the line `objRS.Filter = 0` (note that 0 = `adFilterNone`) and move the record pointer back to the first record of the un-filtered recordset:

```
    'Turn off the filter
    objRS.Filter = 0 'Turn Off Filter
    'Move to the first record
    objRS.MoveFirst
  end sub
%>
</BODY></HTML>
```

Here's a sample of what it all looks like. As you can see, filtering is perfect for an employee directory page, or a business directory:

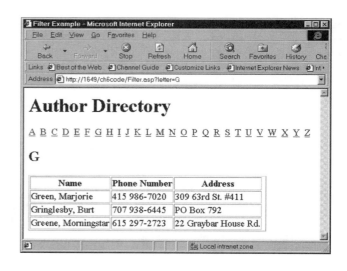

Indexing, Finding and Sorting

There are times when you might want to have your fields indexed. If your recordset becomes very large, having an index will decrease the amount of time it takes to search for a record, or sort a recordset. We will look into searching for a record and sorting a recordset (the Find method and Sort property respectively) later on this section. For now, it's worth noting that indexing will reduce processing time when performing either of these tasks.

Unfortunately, finding how to set the indexing property is not as straightforward as one might hope. Someday you might see an indexing property (scheduled for later releases of ADO), but for now you need to access it through the Field object's Properties collection.

Each Field object has a collection of its own, called Properties – it contains the settings of all the Field object's properties. The Field object's properties are dynamic in nature – by which I mean that they are created at runtime and they only exist under certain conditions. For example: if you have a server-side cursor, then you will not have a property for indexing a recordset. And this brings us to our point: the dynamic property that controls indexing is the Optimize property. To index a field, you need to set the property to True (and to remove an index on the Field object, you set the property to False). When the Optimize property is available, the default setting is False (no indexing).

> Note that the Optimize property is not available for all recordsets. If you attempt to access the Properties collection of a field with a recordset that is connected to a database, you will receive a nasty little error such as ADODB.Fields error '800a0cc1. So keep in mind that this only works with client-side cursors.

Your code for creating an index might look something like this:

```
objRS.Fields(0).Properties("Optimize") = True
```

Alternatively (because the Fields collection is the default collection of the Recordset object):

```
objRS(0).Properties("Optimize") = True
```

The index itself resides in the client-side cursor that ADO provides. That means you are not indexing the database itself – rather, you are indexing the Recordset object. These are not database indexes. This only works with client-side cursors because most data providers do not support your attempts at indexing their data through ADO. When you use Sort or Find within a Recordset object, the fields are not indexed – they get indexed temporarily (by ADO) to get the job done. But we'll get more into these methods later in this chapter.

Using the Find Method

The Find method will return one record at a time that matches your criteria. This method will search a specific column in the recordset for a specific value or criteria. The syntax for the Find method is as follows:

```
objRS.Find Criteria, [SkipRows], [SearchDirection], [Start]
```

The arguments are summarized in the table below:

Name	Type	Description
Criteria	String	Expression stating the value to search for and the field to search
SkipRows	Long	Boolean value stating whether to use the current row as part of the search. Optional. Default is 0
SearchDirection	SearchDirectionEnum	Indicates which direction to search the recordset. Optional. Default is adSearchForward (= 1)
Start	Variant	You can pass in a Bookmark as the starting position. Optional

Here's an example. Suppose you need a list of everyone in the authors table of the pubs database, whose last name begins with the letters Wil. You could do it using the following:

```
Const adSearchForward = 1      '-- Search Constant
Const adSearchBackward = -1    '-- Search Constant
objRS.MoveFirst
Do Until objRS.EOF
  ' Search Forward through the recordset
  objRS.Find "au_lname Like Like 'Gre%'",, adSearchForward
  If Not objRS.EOF And Not objRS.BOF Then
    Response.Write objRS("au_fname") & " " & objRS("au_lname")
    Response.Write "<BR>"
    ' Move to the Next record
    objRS.MoveNext
  End If
Loop
```

In this fragment, we start at the top of the recordset and search forward. (Incidentally, we could also use a filter to do this job.) Note that when the Find method hits EOF, it doesn't wrap back to the top. For a complete search, it's wise to start at the top – by calling MoveFirst, as we've done here. Searching backwards is just as simple, but requires that you start at the other end:

```
objRS.MoveLast
Do Until objRS.BOF
   ' Search Backward through the recordset
   objRS.Find "au_fname Like 'Gre%'",, adSearchBackward
   If Not objRS.EOF And Not objRS.BOF Then
      Response.Write objRS("au_fname") & " " & objRS("au_lname")
      Response.Write "<BR>"
      ' Move to the Previous record
      objRS.MovePrevious
   End If
Loop
```

Again, when the Find method hits BOF, it doesn't wrap back to the bottom – so we called MoveLast before running the search. If you do start at the bottom (objRS.MoveLast) then make sure you pass in the SearchDirection constant of adSearchBackward (= –1).

Sorting Data

To sort a recordset's data you must use its Sort property. The Sort property specifies one or more field names for the recordset to sorted on, and which direction the sort should be. The default sorting direction is ascending, which means you don't need to specify it if that is the direction you are planning on sorting.

The syntax for the Sort Property is as follows:

objRS.Sort = *Value*

Here, *Value* is a string of comma-separated field names, naming the fields to be sorted on. Additionally you may specify **after** each field name a blank space and the keyword ASCENDING or DESCENDING, which specifies the sort order. For example:

```
objRS.Sort = "LName ASCENDING, FName DESCENDING"
```

The default is ASCENDING, so the following two statements are functionally the same:

```
objRS.Sort = "LNAME"
objRS.Sort = "LNAME ASCENDING"
```

Note that the Sort property does not physically change the data – it simply allows you to access the data in a different order.

How does it work? A temporary index is placed on each Field object indicated in the Sort statement (provided one does not already exist on that particular field). If there is an existing index – created with the Optimize property – then that index is used.

To release the sort order, simply set the `Sort` property to an empty string. (Note that there's no enumerated constant for this, and that zero and `Nothing` don't do the job: you have to use an empty string.) For example:

```
objRS.Sort = ""
```

Any temporary indexes will also be released at this time.

Batch Updates

Batch updating allows you to request records, bring them to the client, make updates to the records on the client side, and then send the record updates back to the data source at some other time. We use batch updating when we cannot or do not wish to maintain a constant connection to the database. For example, if you write an employee expense system that can be accessed from anywhere around the world, you will fetch data from a data source and carry it back to the application. In an application like this, you neither want to nor can you keep a connection open to your database. Records must be sent back and forth in batches. Scalable applications require that connections be released as soon as possible; therefore updates should be done either through action queries or via disconnected recordsets. In this venue, and in multi-tier applications, batch updates become very important.

Cursor Location

For batch updating your cursor location *must* be client-side. By default, cursors are built on the server – so you must explicitly request that the cursor location be set to the client. You can set the cursor location on a `Connection` object, like this

```
Set objRS = CreateObject("ADODB.Recordset")
objRS.CursorLocation = adUseClient
```

Alternatively, you can set the cursor location on a `Recordset` object:

```
Set objConn = CreateObject("ADODB.Connection")
objConn.CursorLocation = adUseClient
```

When you use client-side cursors, note that only static cursor types are supported. If you choose another cursor type, then ADO will silently use a static type instead.

Lock Type

The next setting that is required to enable batch updating is the correct record locking type. Recall that record locking has to do with the concurrency of the data that you are changing. When we are requesting batch updates, we don't want a user to lock records back in the database while he's holding the records. That would be bad – a second user who need to access the same records would be unable to get at them. Even worse, if the first user failed to return and unlock the records, our other users might *never* be able to get at them.

Thus, we have a special setting for record-locking – adLockBatchOptimistic. Optimistic updating means that we will only lock records when a change comes through from a user (during the BatchUpdate call).

The lock type can be set one of two ways on the recordset. We can set the LockType property on the Recordset object:

```
Set objRS = CreateObject("ADODB.Recordset")
objRS.LockType = adLockBatchOptimistic
```

Alternatively, when we open the recordset we can send in the LockType as the fourth parameter of the Open method (notice that we also have a static cursor type):

```
objRS.Open strSQL, strConnect, adOpenStatic, adLockBatchOptimistic
```

When you are ready to send changes to the database you will call the UpdateBatch method of the recordset. If you need to cancel the changes that you made thus far to your recordset you use the CancelBatch method.

Here is an example that will tie together all of these steps for updating your data:

```
Set objRS = CreateObject("ADODB.Recordset")

'Use the correct location and cursor
objRS.CursorLocation = adUseClient
objRS.CursorType = adOpenStatic

'Open the recordset
objRS.Open "select Done from Tasks where date='12/12/98'", strConnect

Do While Not objRS.EOF
  objRS("Done") = "Y"
  'Use Update to update local recordset
  objRS.Update
  objRS.MoveNext
Loop
```

Now the user decides if the changes should go through:

```
If Request("CommitChanges") Then
  'Update the entire batch if the user has decided to
  objRS.UpdateBatch
  Response.Write "Changes sent"
Else
  'Cancel the update if the user changes his mind
  objRS.CancelBatch
  Response.Write "Changes canceled"
End If

'Close the recordset
objRS.Close
```

Remember that if some of the updates fail you can use the filter setting `adFilterConflictingRecords` to find out what records failed to update. There's more about conflicts in Chapters 5 and 8.

Multiple Recordsets

Many times, we need to get data in a static form (by this, I mean data that we can use for look-ups). Just as a database may have look-up tables, often we present our users with combo or list boxes that allow them to view options that we store in the database. These options are not subject to change and especially not subject to change by our users. What if we have a lot of data that we are using to populate lists and combos? What is the most efficient way of getting a lot of disparate data? The answer is to use multiple recordsets.

What are Multiple Recordsets?

Multiple recordsets are what I like to call 'stacked recordsets'. You issue multiple select statements at the same time, delimited by semicolons or spaces, and you are returned multiple recordsets in a stack. Like this:

```
strSQL = <SELECT ....> ; <SELECT ....>...
objRS.Open strSQL
```

After we call the recordset's `Open` method in the above lines of code, we now have a pop-only stack of recordsets. The stack is returned in order, so the first SQL `SELECT` is the first recordset immediately available.

Popping the Stack – the NextRecordset Method

To get at the next available recordset we use the `NextRecordset` method. The `NextRecordset` method returns a `Recordset` object. When you call `NextRecordset` your recordset object variable will drop its pointer to the current recordset and point to the next one. If no more recordsets are available, then `NextRecordset` returns `Nothing`.

Can I use Multiple Recordsets with Any Database?

Not every database, driver, and provider supports multiple recordsets. I've never been able to get them to work with Oracle. SQL Server works like a champ with them (in some cases – for example, when server-side cursors are used with ODBC, you get an unpleasant error message).

This screenshot shows a typical use for multiple recordsets. This is a display of some look-up tables from the pubs database in SQL Server. In this example we've populated some HTML SELECT boxes that the user might use to make static selections. Note that the data we retrieve in this way is data that the user needs for information purposes, not information that the user will necessarily be editing.

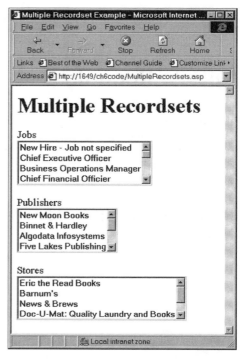

Let's look at the code. The first interesting thing is the instantiation of the Recordset object. We will give the recordset a connect string so that it can connect itself; however, notice the strSQL variable. This contains our three SQL statements for the retrieval of the multiple recordset. There is nothing special about the statements and they are concatenated into one space-delimited string:

```
<%@ LANGUAGE="VBSCRIPT" %>
<HTML><HEAD><TITLE>Multiple Recordset Example</TITLE></HEAD>
<BODY>
<H1>Multiple Recordsets</H1>
<%
  Dim objRS  ' as ADO Recordset
  Dim strSQL ' as string
  Set objRS = CreateObject("ADODB.Recordset")     'Create the recordset object

  'Initialize the string with 3 space delimited SQL statements
  strSQL = "SELECT Title='Jobs', job_desc FROM jobs " & _
           "SELECT Title='Publishers', pub_name FROM publishers " & _
           "SELECT Title='Stores', stor_name FROM stores "

  objRS.ActiveConnection = "Provider=MSDASQL;" & _
                           "Persist Security Info=False;" & _
                           "User ID=sa;" & _
                           "Data Source=winbook;" & _
                           "Initial Catalog=pubs"  'Connect to database

  objRS.CursorType = 0     'adOpenForwardOnly
  objRS.Open strSQL
```

Once we've opened the recordset, we have immediate access to the results returned by the *first* SQL string. Notice that entry to the While loop is dependent on the condition that our Recordset object, objRS, is not equal to Nothing – i.e. it hasn't gone past the last of our multiple recordsets. The loop depends on the call to NextRecordset. At the end of each run through the loop, we make the call to NextRecordset, to replace the exhausted recordset with the next one (always in the same order in which we issued the select statements). We populate three SELECT tags with varying amounts of disparate data. When we've looped through all the recordsets, the next call to NextRecordset returns Nothing, and the loop ends:

```
    Dim intCount
    'Loop through the multiple result sets
    Do While not (objRS is Nothing)
      intCount = 1
      Response.Write objRS(0).Value & "<BR>"
      Response.Write "<SELECT MULTIPLE>"
      Do While Not objRS.EOF
         Response.Write "<OPTION VALUE=""" & intCount & """>"
         Response.Write objRS(1).Value
         objRS.MoveNext
         intCount = intCount + 1
      Loop
      Response.Write "</SELECT><P>"
      'When we are out of recordsets we are set to nothing
      set objRS = objRS.NextRecordset
    Loop
  %>
  </BODY></HTML>
```

Summary

The sun is setting on this chapter. We have seen a lot of things going on with the Recordset object – the subjects that we've covered here help us to make better and faster use of ADO. Among other things, we've seen how:

❑ By cloning recordsets, we can take advantage of an efficient way of using ADO when we need to copy the Recordset object

❑ Paging makes good use of the data for our own code and for our users, by giving us a programmatically simple way of presenting data (which also aids user efficiency by giving them ways to look at logical data chunks)

❑ We can create an index on a recordset, provided it supports the Optimize property. The Find and Sort methods – which we can use to search and sort our recordset – use this property to create a temporary index if necessary

❑ The Filter property helps us to make more incisive, focused queries on an existing recordset (without having to requery the database)

❑ Multiple recordsets allow us to retrieve data with less network access

ADO recordsets offer us all these features and more (don't forget batch updating!). In the next chapter, we'll move onto look at the heady world of data shaping…

7

Data Shaping

Data shaping sounds like one of those mystical things that should be left to the 'more experienced' programmer. If this is what you're thinking then let me tell you now that there is nothing mystical or magical about it. Data shaping can appear daunting, especially when you start looking at the syntax. However, if you take the time to read this chapter from start to finish, any mystique will soon disappear, as you become proficient in the art of shaping your data.

In this chapter we will cover the following areas:

❑   Defining Data Shaping
❑   Hierarchical Recordsets
❑   Relational Shaping
❑   Parameter Shaping
❑   Group Shaping

Staying in Sync: The Definition of Data Shaping

DATA: da•ta(d•'ta) noun 1. Information

SHAPING: shap•ing(sh•p•ing) verb. To give form to

DATA SHAPING: Giving form to information.

Now that the formalities are out of the way we can begin our journey to shaping our data. Data shaping was a brand new feature with ADO 2.0. It uses ADO 2.0 and the Microsoft Client Cursor Engine to define hierarchical (parent-child) recordsets. Hold on! We just got you squared away with the term Data Shaping and now I'm throwing new terms at you! In fact, as we explain the topic of data shaping there are a few terms and expressions that will crop up. Don't worry, though, it will all become clear very soon.

Data shaping is, in essence, creating a hierarchical recordset, so when I talk about either, I'm talking about both. You can think of a hierarchical recordset in the same way as you view your files and folders in Windows Explorer. Each has a subset or child record. You start at the root (i.e. the C:\ Drive) or the parent records, and start working your way down (through folders or files). To get a picture of what I'm trying to convey, have a look at the screenshot below, which shows a hierarchical recordset from a Windows Explorer point of view.

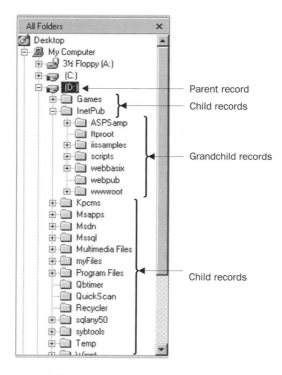

If you are an organized person then your file structure will actually make sense and you can easily find the information you are looking for. (However if you are like me you often have to use the Find utility to locate your files).

Understanding the Hierarchical Recordset

Now that you have a picture in your head of a hierarchical recordset (the Windows Explorer example from above), we can begin our discussion. Hierarchical records in themselves are not new; as programmers we use them all the time, although you may not be aware of it. The difference is that we usually implement ours through code rather than having the database take care of the grunt work for us.

Let's look at the following hierarchy: an Orders table that has many orders, and an Order_Items table with information about each ordered item, including an Order ID.

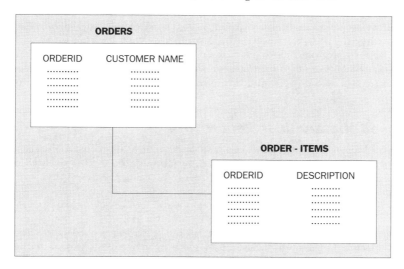

When using an application, web-based or otherwise, the first thing that is done is a query on the Orders table. All of the orders are then displayed on the screen. Next let's say you want to get the details of each item that was ordered from an Order_Items table. The next step would be to query the items based on an Order ID. Now, there are two possibilities open to you to accomplish these steps.

❑ You could use a SQL JOIN from the very beginning. With this method, the more layers you go down (say for details on the items) the more complex your JOIN statements become.
❑ You could use multiple SQL statements, or stored procedures. A hit will be made on the server multiple times to accomplish the lookup.

Both of these examples are very functional and are used everyday, but the key here is that they do not bring your data back in the useful tree-like structure that a hierarchical recordset does, and they cause much unnecessary network traffic. That's not to say that you can't produce a tree-like structure; however you're going to have to do all the work. Shaping changes that.

If we use data shaping to retrieve hierarchical recordsets, the parent recordset is only fetched once, as (depending on the type of hierarchical recordset) are the child recordsets. This allows for better performance, as well as the use of disconnected recordsets containing all the data you need. Let's take a look at the three different types of hierarchical recordsets to get a richer understanding of what I mean.

Types of Hierarchical Recordsets

When dealing with hierarchical recordsets we actually have three different sorts of recordset to choose from. These are relational-based hierarchical recordsets, parameter-based recordsets, and group-based recordsets. To make matters a little confusing, each has its own varying strengths and weaknesses. I want to point out that this is not a downside to hierarchical recordsets, it's really an upside. If we didn't have these three choices we would probably be saying, 'You know, I really like them, but I wish I could also do this, and this, and…'. That being said, let's begin our tour of the three types.

Relational-Based Hierarchical Recordsets

A relational-based hierarchical recordset can also be seen as a filter-based hierarchical recordset. With this type of recordset the data from both the parent (e.g. the Orders table) and the child (e.g. the Order_Items table) are fetched separately before creating the hierarchy.

When two records are related using the RELATE keyword (discussed shortly), an index is created on the related child (Order_ID in the Order_Items table) within the ADO cursor engine. A Field object then gets appended to the Fields collection of the parent recordset (Orders). This Field object holds a reference to the child table in its Value property. This way, when you access the child recordset, you only see the rows of data that are associated with the parent record. In the background, unbeknownst to you, a filter is being performed as each child recordset is created. (For more information on the Filter property, see the chapter on *Building on the Recordset Foundation*).

Here are the pros and cons of relational hierarchical recordsets:

Pros	Cons
Offers the highest performance for navigation.	The initial creation can be expensive (time and resource consuming for the server) since all the records are fetched before it can be created.
Since all the records are fetched up-front, the recordset could be disconnected once created.	
Allows for more flexible updating, by permitting updates to child recordsets (we'll discuss this in the next section on Updatability).	

Parameter Based Hierarchical Recordsets

A parameter-based hierarchical recordset provides the same functionality as a relational hierarchical recordset. The main difference between them is that the related rows are not fetched up front, meaning that the recordset can be created more quickly.

The difference between relational and parameter-based recordsets is shown in the commands that are used in the construction of the query (we'll see the query shortly). With a parameter-based hierarchical recordset the child query will have parameters that filter the result set, based on the current row in the parent. Unlike the filter in a relational hierarchical recordset, the filter here is executed back on the server. Each time the child recordset is accessed, the child recordset is re-executed based on the parameter values. The new rows are then accessed by the child recordset. The parameter recordset requires an active connection to the data source each time a child recordset is fetched or re-fetched. This type of re-fetching reduces the initial up-front investment, but can use a lot of bandwidth when the data is being reviewed, making it unsuitable for an Internet environment.

Here is a summary of the pros and cons of parameterized hierarchical recordsets:

Pros	Cons
Short time for the initial creation.	Could not be used as a disconnected recordset.
	Active connection must be maintained to get new child recordset.
	Performance penalty for each navigation.

Group Based Hierarchical Recordsets

A group-based hierarchical recordset differs from the previous two types in that only one recordset is involved. If more than one recordset needs to be involved then they will need to be created at the data source (i.e. with a View). Now for the big question – "If only one recordset is involved how can I have the tree-like structure that a hierarchical recordset is supposed to define?" I'll explain how this is possible. Firstly, think of a group-based hierarchical recordset as a GROUP BY clause in a standard SQL statement.

> *In case you are unfamiliar with the GROUP BY clause, the simplest explanation that I can give is that a GROUP BY is used in SQL to summarize data. Say, for example, you had a field in a table where the same value was repeated several times, such as an Order ID field in an Order_Items table. Grouping on fields with the same value, we could use GROUP BY to get the total amount for the items purchased.*

With a normal GROUP BY you would only get the total values of aggregate functions, or the values being grouped together. What you don't get is all the child data making up the summary or the parent. However, with a group-based hierarchical recordset, all of the aggregate or grouped values are stored in the parent record, and the records used to create the group or parent are placed in the child recordset. This is particularly useful when we want to do summary or detail reporting. We could use a group-based hierarchical recordset to produce a Master/Detail report. We'll have a look at using group-based hierarchical recordsets towards the end of this chapter.

Updatability

Among all the really great things you will read about in this chapter, updatability is possibly the most compelling reason to use hierarchical recordsets. The recordsets can be easily updated! Why is this so significant? Well, if we consider a normal SQL JOIN, you can update only one of the joined tables at a given time. With hierarchical recordsets you can update any or all of the recordsets, with the exception of groups where summaries are being used. In this latter case you need to update the child records in order to update the summary data.

Updating a hierarchical recordset is the same as updating any other recordset. By that I mean you simply issue the update method after giving a new value to a field. This chapter will focus only on retrieving the data, however keep in mind that you can treat a hierarchical recordset just like any other recordset.

Shaping

Now that you understand the concepts of a hierarchical recordset it's time to define, or shape it. Shaping has its own formal language. What do I mean, another language? In fact it only consists of some minor modifications to a normal SQL statement. Besides, I'll let you in on a secret: VB 6.0 comes with a utility called the Data Environment that you can use for creating shapes. So, if VB comes with a shape utility why am I wasting your time with the boring syntax? The answer to this is that the VB Data Shaper Tool also adds all the aliases, which can confuse (and bloat) your code, making the principles of data shaping harder to learn.

Once you get going with shaping, then using VB's Data Shaper will be a breeze. But I suggest that you stick with learning the syntax first before venturing into the realm of letting VB create your shaped recordsets. Most of you reading this do probably not use an editor that is exclusively drag and drop. In fact most of you probably use Visual InterDev or even Notepad as your editor, and to be proficient you need to understand what is actually going on in the code. With that said, let's take a look at this SQL-like shaping language.

The Shape Language

The shape language has its own formal grammar or command syntax used to build hierarchical recordsets. The new commands you will be using are SHAPE, APPEND, and RELATE. But before I scare you with a large example of this syntax, let's take a look at a couple of small real examples you can use against the Pubs database. In fact let's do one of each type so that you are not left out in the cold for a particular hierarchical recordset.

Relational Shape

A simple relational shape would have syntax like this:

```
SHAPE {parent_command} [ [AS] Parent_Table_Alias]
APPEND ({child_command} [ [AS] child_Table_Alias]
    RELATE Parent_Column TO child_Column) [ [AS] Column_Alias]
```

This will define how the parent and the child relate to one another. The `parent_command` and `child_command` are valid SQL statements. The `Aliases` are optional, as is the keyword `AS`. The `Parent_Column` and `child_Column` are the related fields that connect the two tables. Below is an example of how you might use this syntax:

```
SHAPE {SELECT * FROM publishers}
APPEND ({SELECT * FROM titles}
    RELATE pub_id TO pub_id as chTitle)
```

This is the most basic of the `SHAPE` commands you will see. Here we are using the `pubs` database that is installed with MS SQL Server. We'll see more complex commands later in this chapter, but let's go slowly to start with. The first line retrieves the parent records:

```
SHAPE {SELECT * FROM publishers}
```

Each publisher may have many titles that we want to list. To do this we `APPEND` a field to the `publishers` table:

```
APPEND ({SELECT * FROM titles}
```

So now we have both recordsets, but how do we put them together? Relating the recordsets is the key to making a hierarchical recordset. This will relate the appended `Field` object to the parent's `Fields` Collection. We also give it an alias (`chTitle`) so that we can reference it later:

```
RELATE pub_id TO pub_id as chTitle)
```

> So far we have been referring to the hierarchical relationship as parent and child. The Microsoft documentation also initially uses this terminology, but then suddenly starts talking about chapters without ever explaining this term. You come to realize that what they are talking about is a child (the `Type` property of a child recordset is `adChapter`), so if you see chapter think of it as a child.

Let's take a look at complete code sample that builds a relational hierarchical recordset.

Relational.asp – Building a Relational Hierarchical Recordset

```
<%@ Language=VBScript %>
<% Option Explicit %>
<%
   '----------------------------------------
   '-- Declare all variables used
   '----------------------------------------

   Dim objConn         '-- The ADO Connection to the Database
   Dim objRsParent     '-- The ADO Parent Recordset (Publishers)
   Dim objRsChild      '-- The ADO child Recordset (Titles)
   Dim strShape        '-- The SHAPE Syntax
   Dim strConn         '-- Connection String to the Database
```

```
'-- Create the ADO Objects
set objConn = Server.CreateObject("ADODB.Connection")
set objRsParent = Server.CreateObject("ADODB.Recordset")
set objRsChild = Server.CreateObject("ADODB.Recordset")

'-- Create Connection String - Data Provider is defined here
'-- Shape Provider is specified with the provider property
'-- Broken-up for better readability
strConn = ""
strConn = strConn & "Data Provider=SQLOLEDB;"
strConn = strConn & "Data Source=winbook;"
strConn = strConn & "Initial Catalog=pubs;"
strConn = strConn & "User Id=sa;Password="

'-- Define the Shape Provider
objConn.Provider = "MSDataShape"

'-- Open the Connection
objConn.Open strConn

'-- Create the Data Shape
strShape = ""
strShape = strShape & "SHAPE {SELECT * FROM publishers} "
strShape = strShape & "APPEND ({SELECT * FROM titles} "
strShape = strShape & "RELATE pub_id TO pub_id) as chTitle "

'-- Set the Parent Recordset Connection to the Active Connection
objRsParent.ActiveConnection = objConn

'-- Open the Data Shape
objRsParent.Open strShape

'-- Begin with the parent
Do until objRsParent.EOF
  '-- Display the Publishers Name
  Response.Write objRsParent("pub_name") & "<BR>"
  '-- Now set the child Recordset to the value of the appended Field
  '-- (aliased as chTitle)
  '-- IF value is not specified a runtime error will occur
  set objRsChild = objRsParent("chTitle").Value
  '-- Loop through the child Recordset
  Do Until objRsChild.EOF
    '-- Pad some spaces to show the relationship
    Response.Write "     "
    '-- Display the title
    Response.Write objRsChild("title") & "<BR>"
    '-- Move to the next Record in the child and then Loop
    objRsChild.MoveNext
  Loop
  '-- Move to the next Record in the Parent and then Loop
  objRsParent.MoveNext
Loop
'-- Clean up and Destroy used objects
objRsChild.Close
objRsParent.Close
objConn.Close
set objRsChild = nothing
set objRsParent = nothing
set objConn = nothing
%>
```

Now that you have the complete ASP file, to see how the code fits together, we'll walk through and look at it in detail. At this point I'm assuming that you know how to declare and to instantiate your objects, so let's begin with creating the connection string. The first line makes sure that the variable is cleared:

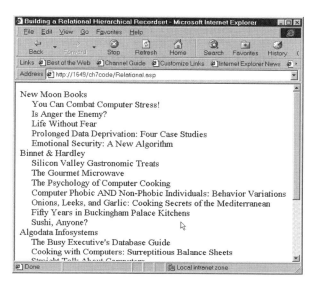

```
strConn = ""
strConn = strConn & "Data Provider=SQLOLEDB;"
strConn = strConn & "Data Source=winbook;"
strConn = strConn & "Initial Catalog=pubs;"
strConn = strConn & "User Id=sa;Password="
```

The first thing you may notice is:

```
objConn.Provider = "MSDataShape"
```

This sets the provider to `MSDataShape` provider, essential when doing shapes. We use the `MSDataShape` provider to shape the data it receives from the data provider. In other words OLE DB needs to pass the data off to another provider that will do the shaping. The data provider is specified in the connection string. When not shaping your data you could specify the data provider using the `Provider` property of the `Connection` object. (This can get confusing, and I don't know why Microsoft didn't just create a new `ShapeProvider` property).

The major work is done here in the loop:

```
'-- Begin with the parent
Do until objRsParent.EOF
```

We start this example by printing out each publisher's name. The publisher is the parent, and the children will be the title information we append to it:

```
'-- Display the Publishers Name
Response.Write objRsParent("pub_name") & "<BR>"
```

The code below may look strange and new to you. At this point, we set the child `Recordset` object (`objRsChild`) to the parent's appended `Field` object (which holds the child recordset).

> Since the new **Field** object is appended you know that it's the last **Field**
> object in the **Fields** Collection. As there are five **Field** objects in
> **publishers**, in this example a sixth **Field** object is appended, and since
> the collection is zero based it will be **objRsParent(5)**.

Keep in mind that you must specify the Value property! This is a default property and thus normally
there would be no need to specify it. However if you omit the Value property a runtime error no. 13
type Mismatch occurs when using hierarchical recordsets.

```
'-- Now set the child Recordset to the value of the appended Field object
'-- (aliased as chTitle)
'-- If Value is not specified a runtime error will occur
   set objRsChild = objRsParent("chTitle").Value
```

chTitle was defined as an alias during the RELATE command.

> The alias **chTitle** (you can name it whatever you want) is optional.
> However, if you do not create an alias then the **Field** object name defaults
> to the child alias, and if a child alias was not specified then the name
> defaults to Chapter1 (no spaces). You could also use the ordinal position of
> the newly appended Field.

You now have a new recordset containing the titles (or the children) to walk through, displaying each
in turn. When you reach EOF the inner loop ends. We do a MoveNext on the parent, which will go
to the next publisher and repeat this process until the end of the parent recordset.

If this is unclear look at the final outcome and then refer back to the code. Try to see this happening
visually. First you get a parent row of data. Then you set a Recordset object to the last field value
which we called chTitle (I could have named it chTitles, but thought that might be confusing).
Now the child recordset has a set of related data of it's own. It contains all the data from the Titles
table that relates to the pub_id (in other words it does this SELECT * FROM titles where pub_id =
the current pub_id in the parent recordset). Now you just walk through the child data like a normal
recordset. When you reach the EOF, you come out of the loop and move to the next parent recordset.
You then access that recordset's related child data, and so on, and so on... until you reach the EOF of
the parent recordset.

```
'-- Loop through the child Recordset
Do Until objRsChild.EOF
   '-- Pad some spaces to show the relationship
   Response.Write "     "
   '-- Display the title
   Response.Write objRsChild("title") & "<BR>"
   '-- Move to the next Record in the child and then Loop
   objRsChild.MoveNext
Loop
'-- Move to the next Record in the Parent and then Loop
objRsParent.MoveNext
Loop
```

The output should resemble this:

New Moon Books
  You Can Combat Computer Stress!
  Is Anger the Enemy?
  Life Without Fear
  Prolonged Data Deprivation: Four Case Studies
  Emotional Security: A New Algorithm
Binnet & Hardley
  Silicon Valley Gastronomic Treats
  The Gourmet Microwave
  The Psychology of Computer Cooking

…..and so on.

More Complex Shapes

You can create more complex shapes by adding multiple children, or adding children to children to create grandchildren.

Having Multiple Children

There is no golden rule to say you can have only one child. There may be many times that you wish to have multiple child recordsets. The figure below shows a graphical layout of how you can think of having multiple children with hierarchical recordsets:

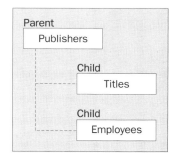

Creating multiple child recordsets requires only an additional argument to the APPEND command:

```
SHAPE {SELECT * FROM publishers}
APPEND ({SELECT * FROM titles}
  RELATE pub_id TO pub_id) as chTitles,
  ({SELECT * FROM employee}
  RELATE pub_id TO pub_id) as chEmp
```

As you can see, by simply adding a comma within the RELATE statement we can add another child recordset. Your recordset will now have two child Field objects, which can be accessed in the following manner:

```
'-- Create the Data Shape
strShape = ""
strShape = strShape & "SHAPE {SELECT * FROM publishers} "
strShape = strShape & "APPEND ({SELECT * FROM titles} "
'-- Make sure to notice the comma after chTitle ~ chTitle,
strShape = strShape & "RELATE pub_id TO pub_id) as chTitle, "
strShape = strShape & "({SELECT * FROM employee} "
strShape = strShape & "RELATE pub_id TO pub_id) as chEmp "

'-- Set the Parent Recordset Connection to the Active Connection
objRsParent.ActiveConnection = objConn

'-- Open the Data Shape
objRsParent.Open strShape
```

The loop will only add one more element. We've seen the code below in the example earlier, but it is included here (unshaded) to make sure you follow how to get the second child recordset.

```
'-- Begin with the parent
  Do until objRsParent.EOF
    '-- Display the Publishers Name
    Response.Write objRsParent("pub_name") & "<BR>"
    '-- Now set the child Recordset to the value of the appended Field
    '-- (aliased as chTitle)
    '-- IF value is not specified a runtime error will occur
    set objRsChildTitle = objRsParent("chTitle").Value
    '-- Loop through the child Recordset
    Do Until objRsChildTitle.EOF
      '-- Pad some spaces to show the relationship
      Response.Write "     "
      '-- Display the title
      Response.Write "<B>TITLE </B>"
      Response.Write objRsChildTitle("title") & "<BR>"
      '-- Move to the next Record in the child and then Loop
      objRsChildTitle.MoveNext
    Loop
```

At this point EOF is true for the first child recordset that contained all the titles for the current pub_id. Now we get the next child recordset. Setting the objRsChildEmp to the value of the chEmp field gives us another child recordset to loop through. We follow the same process as above and get all the employees associated with the pub_id:

```
'Do the Same thing with Employees
    set objRsChildEmp = objRsParent("chEmp").Value
    '-- Loop through the child Recordset
    Do Until objRsChildEmp.EOF
      '-- Pad some spaces to show the relationship
      Response.Write "     "
      '-- Display the title
      Response.Write "<B>Employee</B> "
      Response.Write objRsChildEmp("fname") & " "
      Response.Write objRsChildEmp("lname") & "<BR>"
      '-- Move to the next Record in the child and then Loop
      objRsChildEmp.MoveNext
    Loop
```

At this point we are out of the second child recordset. We move to the next parent row (or `pub_id`), getting the titles and employees associated with the next publisher. Remember this is only obtaining child records for the publisher. We are not making a correlation for titles to employees. To see a hierarchical structure of publisher to titles to authors you'll have to wait for a few minutes until we reach the next section on *Grand Children*.

```
'-- Move to the next Record in the Parent and then Loop
objRsParent.MoveNext
Loop
```

This example should produce results similar to:

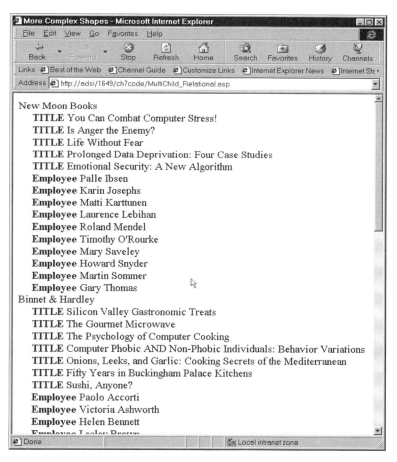

Having Grandchildren and Great Grandchildren

You say, this is nice, but what if you want to go to an even deeper level? No problem – have some grandchildren. This next shape connects to the `pubs` database and gets the publishers, the titles they carry, and the authors of those titles. This is where the shaping can get a little confusing and to be honest I didn't feel like figuring it out on my own, so I cheated a little on this one. I used VB to create the initial shape and then modified it for easier reading. (This is a good place to use the VB Shaper Tool to cheat, if you have access to Visual Basic 6.0.)

This tool can be found under the Project | Add Data Environment menu item in Visual Basic 6.0. We do not cover the Data Environment in this book. For a good example on how to use this tool, simply add the tool to your VB project, then click on the Data Environment (so that it has the current focus) and hit F1. This will launch the MSDN library (the new help for Visual Studio) and bring up the help for Data Designer. Make sure you see the section on the page about adding a child command.

The code to create this shape may look somewhat complex, but we'll go through it step by step so that it becomes clearer.

```
<%@ Language=VBScript %>
<% Option Explicit %>
<%



'----------------------------------------
'-- Declare all variables used
'----------------------------------------
```

So far there's nothing we haven't seen before. What you might notice here are a couple of new `Recordset` objects. The comments will list what each object contains, and as you can see we will be going down to great-grandchild level, which will display our authors. We won't be displaying anything at the grandchild level, but we do need to go through this level in order to reach the great grandchild level.

```
Dim objConn               '-- The ADO Connection to the Database
Dim objRsParent           '-- The ADO Parent Recordset (Publishers)
Dim objRsChildTitle       '-- The ADO child Recordset (Titles)
Dim objRsChildTA          '-- The ADO grandchild Recordset (titleauthors)
Dim objRsChildAuth        '-- The ADO Great grandchild (authors)
Dim strShape              '-- The SHAPE Syntax
Dim strConn               '-- Connection String to the Database

'-- Create the ADO Objects
set objConn = Server.CreateObject("ADODB.Connection")
set objRsParent = Server.CreateObject("ADODB.Recordset")
set objRsChildTitle = Server.CreateObject("ADODB.Recordset")
set objRsChildTA = Server.CreateObject("ADODB.Recordset")
set objRsChildAuth = Server.CreateObject("ADODB.Recordset")

'-- Create Connection String
'-- Data Provider is defined here
'-- Shape Provider is specified with the provider property broken-up
'-- for better readability
strConn = ""
strConn = strConn & "Data Provider=SQLOLEDB;"
strConn = strConn & "Data Source=winbook;"
strConn = strConn & "Initial Catalog=pubs;"
strConn = strConn & "User Id=sa;Password="

'-- Define the Shape Provider
objConn.Provider = "MSDataShape"
```

```
'-- Open the Connection
objConn.Open strConn

strShape = ""
strShape = strShape & "SHAPE {SELECT * from publishers} "
strShape = strShape & "APPEND (( SHAPE {select * from titles} "
strShape = strShape & "APPEND (( SHAPE {select * from titleauthor} "
strShape = strShape & "APPEND ({select * from authors} "
strShape = strShape & "RELATE 'au_id' TO 'au_id') AS chAuth) "
strShape = strShape & "RELATE 'title_id' TO 'title_id') AS chTitleAuth) "
strShape = strShape & "RELATE 'pub_id' TO 'pub_id') AS chTitles"
```

Hopefully the way I've chosen to display the shape makes it a little easier to follow. As you can see we start with the initial SHAPE command. Using the APPEND command we are appending Field objects to the parent recordset. If you follow the path of the parentheses you can see the shape (no pun intended) of the syntax. It works its way in and then it backs out again. The last APPEND goes to the first RELATE, the middle APPEND and RELATE go together and then the first APPEND matches the last RELATE.

At this point we take the current connection, and open the shape we defined above. Starting with the parent object we begin our loop:

```
'-- Set the Parent Recordset Connection to the Active Connection
objRsParent.ActiveConnection = objConn

'-- Open the Data Shape
objRsParent.Open strShape

'-- Begin with the parent
Do Until objRsParent.EOF
```

First let's write out the publisher, and establish where we are:

```
'-- Write out the Publishers
    Response.Write "<B>Publisher</B> "
    Response.Write objRsParent("pub_name") & "<BR>"
```

While on that row we reach the title data, and loop through its records. This will get the titles relating to the pub_id of the parent record.

```
    '-- Go to the Titles
    Set objRsChildTitle = objRsParent("chTitles").Value
    '-- Loop through the Titles
    Do Until objRsChildTitle.EOF
```

Here we pad some spaces for indentation, and display each title the publisher carries:

```
    '-- Pad some spaces
    Response.Write "    "
    Response.Write "    "
    Response.Write "<B>Titles</B> "
    Response.Write objRsChildTitle("title") & "<BR>"
```

Before we go to the next title we want to see who the authors are. Since there can be many authors for one book (co-authors), we need to access the `TitleAuthors` table to make any sense of the `Authors` table. We don't actually display any data from the `TitleAuthors` table, we just find a match (if any) for the title, then set a recordset to the appended field and loop through it for the author's first and last name.

```
'-- Go to the TitleAuthors
Set objRsChildTA = objRsChildTitle("chTitleAuth").Value
'-- Notice we don't write anything out
'-- We simply use it to relate to the author table
Do Until objRsChildTA.EOF
    '-- Go to the Authors table
    Set objRsChildAuth = objRsChildTA("chAuth").Value
    'Loop through the Authors
    Do Until objRsChildAuth.EOF
        Response.Write "    "
        Response.Write "    "
        Response.Write "    "
        Response.Write "    "
        Response.Write "<B>Authors</B> "
        Response.Write objRsChildAuth("au_fname")
        Response.Write " "
        Response.Write objRsChildAuth("au_lname") & "<BR>"
```

Make sure you do a `MoveNext` and then perform your loop, otherwise you'll get stuck in an infinite loop, which is not a good thing! This can rapidly get confusing, so stay alert. Here we move to the next item and continue the loop. Once all the authors for the current title are displayed we hit `EOF` and exit the loop. This puts us back inside the `TitleAuthors`, which does a `MoveNext` (and repeats the inner process). Once the `TitleAuthors` hits `EOF` it exits the loop and goes to the next title under the current publisher (and repeats the inner process). Once the titles run out for the current publisher a `MoveNext` is performed. The whole process is repeated until there are no more publishers.

```
        'Move to the next author for this title
        objRsChildAuth.MoveNext
    Loop
    '-- Move to the next titleauthor
    objRsChildTA.MoveNext
Loop
'-- Move to the next Title
objRsChildTitle.MoveNext
Loop
'-- Move to the next Publisher
objRsParent.MoveNext
Loop
```

Let's be nice and do a little clean up. Close the recordsets and destroy the object by setting them to nothing:

```
'-- Clean up and Destroy used objects

objRsChildAuth.Close
objRsChildTA.Close
objRsChildTitle.Close
objRsParent.Close
objConn.Close
```

```
set objRsChildAuth = nothing
set objRsChildTA = nothing
set objRsChildTitle = nothing
set objRsParent = nothing
set objConn = nothing
%>
```

The output with grandchildren will look something like this. As you can see we display a title and authors for each book under each publisher:

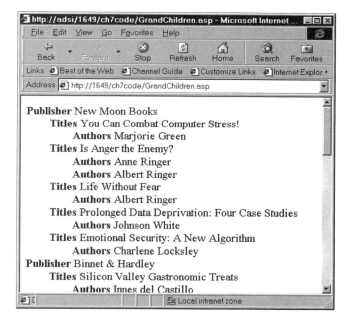

Parameter Shaping

For a refresher, parameter shaping is functionally the same as relational shaping, the main difference being the number of trips to the server. Using a parameter shape you are making a trip to the server for each child request. The following command, using parameter shaping, produces the same results as the relational shaping command shown in the example at the beginning of this chapter:

```
'-- Create the Data Shape
  strShape = ""
  strShape = strShape & "SHAPE {SELECT * FROM publishers} "
  strShape = strShape & "APPEND ({SELECT * FROM titles where pub_id = ?} "
  strShape = strShape & "RELATE pub_id TO PARAMETER 0) as chTitle "
```

> The question mark (?) after **pub_id** = is not something you fill in. Type your code exactly how it is here. The ? is used by the shape engine (**MSDataShape**). This basically tells the engine to grab the child recordset when we hit that row. In other words we will only fetch on demand, not all at once.

We can compare this to the relational shaping SQL statement:

```
SHAPE {SELECT * FROM publishers}
APPEND ({SELECT * FROM titles}
   RELATE pub_id TO pub_id as chTitle)
```

As you can see we have a few subtle but key differences. First you will notice the WHERE clause which wants a pub_id as a parameter, then next we send in a parameter to match the current pub_id.

All the examples in this chapter could be done with parameter-based hierarchical recordsets. That being the case, I won't show all the code again, but I will show all the shape commands as parameter based, just in case you want to try them out. The one above was from the first example. Here is the parameter-based shape command to create multiple children:

```
'-- Create the Data Shape
  strShape = ""
  strShape = strShape & "SHAPE {SELECT * FROM publishers } "
  strShape = strShape & "APPEND ({SELECT * FROM titles where pub_id = ?} "
  '-- Make sure to notice the comma after chTitle ~ chTitle,
  strShape = strShape & "RELATE pub_id TO PARAMETER 0) as chTitle, "
  strShape = strShape & "({SELECT * FROM employee where pub_id = ?} "
  strShape = strShape & "RELATE pub_id TO PARAMETER 0) as chEmp "
```

And here is the parameter-based shape command to create grandchildren and great-grandchildren:

```
'-- Create the Data Shape
strShape = ""
strShape = strShape & "SHAPE {SELECT * from publishers} "
strShape = strShape & "APPEND (( SHAPE {select * from titles where pub_id = ?} "
strShape = strShape & _
    "APPEND (( SHAPE {select * from titleauthor where title_id = ?}"
strShape = strShape & "APPEND ({select * from authors where au_id = ? } "
strShape = strShape & "RELATE au_id TO PARAMETER 0) AS chAuth) "
strShape = strShape & "RELATE title_id TO PARAMETER 0) AS chTitleAuth) "
strShape = strShape & "RELATE pub_id TO PARAMETER 0) AS chTitles"
```

Controlling the Freshness of your Data

As we mentioned earlier the main difference between relational and parameter based hierarchical recordsets is that the parameterized hierarchical recordsets fetch data on demand. The default setting of the cursor engine is to reuse cached data that has already been collected. This saves the performance hit you would experience if you were constantly checking the same sets of records. However, this may not be what you are looking for. Your whole intention in using parameterized hierarchical recordsets may be to ensure you are getting a fresh set of data every time even on the rows already visited. To accommodate you, the Properties collection of the Recordset object includes a property called Cache Child Rows (spaces included after each word) which can be set to False:

```
ObjRsChild.Properties("Cache Child Rows") = False
```

This will ensure that the child recordset does not cache its values, thus yielding a fresh set of data.

Group Shaping

When we introduced the term group shaping, we said its real strength lay in doing reporting, or any sort of grouping. One of the most useful applications is an online order form, which tallies all the values, creates subtotals and totals, and then gives a line by line item listing. I'm currently doing just that for a company. Group shaping will return all of the summary data as the parent, and the detailed data as the child making my life much, much easier. Here's the syntax:

```
SHAPE {parent_command] [ [AS] table_alias]
COMPUTE aggregate_field_list
BY group_field_list
```

This shouldn't look difficult to you (unless you've never done a GROUP BY SQL statement). Let's see some example values for the syntax statement above:

```
SHAPE {select * from titles} AS SalesFromTitles
COMPUTE SalesFromTitles, SUM(SalesFromTitles.ytd_sales) as TotalSales
BY type
```

The first line of this code snippet should be very familiar. You are simply creating a shape and aliasing it as SalesFromTitles. Next we want to use the aggregate function SUM, which will add together each ytd_sales field value that satisfies the BY command. The BY command will GROUP BY the field type, which is a category field containing values such as business, psychology, mod_cook and so on. To give you a better understanding, let's take a look at some code, and the results.

Creating a Report with Group-Based Hierarchical Recordsets

We'll separate this code example into blocks so that we can discuss the code as we go through it. The first section should be familiar to you by now. The only difference will be the names and the number of variables declared. We will still show it (unshaded), so that the new sections will still make sense to you and you won't get stuck when trying this on your own.

```
<%@ Language=VBScript %>
<% Option Explicit %>
<%


    '----------------------------------------
    '-- Declare all variables used
    '----------------------------------------

    Dim objConn              '-- The ADO Connection to the Database
    Dim objRsSummary         '-- The ADO Parent Recordset (Titles Summary)
    Dim objRsDetail          '-- The ADO child Recordset (Titles Detail)
    Dim strShape             '-- The SHAPE Syntax
    Dim strConn              '-- Connection String to the Database

    '-- Create the ADO Objects
    set objConn = Server.CreateObject("ADODB.Connection")
    set objRsSummary = Server.CreateObject("ADODB.Recordset")
    set objRsDetail = Server.CreateObject("ADODB.Recordset")
```

```
'-- Create Connection String
'-- Data Provider is defined here
'-- Shape Provider is specified with
'-- the provider property
'-- Broken-up for better readability
strConn = ""
strConn = strConn & "Data Provider=SQLOLEDB;"
strConn = strConn & "Data Source=winbook;"
strConn = strConn & "Initial Catalog=pubs;"
strConn = strConn & "User Id=sa;Password="

'-- Define the Shape Provider
objConn.Provider = "MSDataShape"

'-- Open the Connection
objConn.Open strConn
```

The first new section of code is where we define the group shape. As noted earlier, `SalesFromTitles` is the alias, using the SUM function to total the fields `ytd_sales`, grouped BY the field `type`:

```
'-- Create the Data Shape
strShape = ""
strShape = strShape & "SHAPE {select * from titles} AS SalesFromTitles "
strShape = strShape & "COMPUTE SalesFromTitles, "
strShape = strShape & "SUM(SalesFromTitles.ytd_sales) as TotalSales "
strShape = strShape & "BY type "

'-- Set the Parent Recordset Connection to the Active Connection
objRsSummary.ActiveConnection = objConn

'-- Open the Data Shape
objRsSummary.Open strShape
```

Next we start displaying the report, beginning with the details. We get the type of book and the totals for the given type:

```
'-- Begin with the detail ~ parent
Do until objRsSummary.EOF
  '-- Display the type (category)and the YTD for the type
  Response.Write "YTD Sales for Book Type  "
  Response.Write "<B>" & objRsSummary("type") & "</B>"
```

Since some fields will be null, and since a null will display nothing we want to check for this and act accordingly. I've decided to display is 0 for the YTD value if a null is found.

```
  '-- Do some error checking
  '-- If a field is null we want to display a Zero instead of no value
  if isNull (objRsSummary("TotalSales")) then
    Response.Write "is <B>0</B>"
  else
    Response.Write "are <B>"
    Response.Write objRsSummary("TotalSales")
    Response.Write "</B>"
  end if
```

Let's break the line, set the `onjRsDetail` recordset to the value of the new field `SalesFromTitles` and start looping through the details of the child recordset:

```
    Response.Write "<BR>"
    '-- Now set the child Recordset to the
    '-- value of the appended Field
    '-- (aliased as SalesFromTitles)
    '-- IF value is not specified a runtime
    '-- error will occur
    set objRsDetail = objRsSummary("SalesFromTitles").Value
    '-- Loop through the child Recordset
    Do Until objRsDetail.EOF
```

For a nice indentation we pad some spaces, and display the title and year-to-date sales for that title:

```
    '-- Pad some spaces to show the relationship
    Response.Write "     "
    '-- Display the Title
    Response.Write "YTD Sales for Title  "
    Response.Write "<B>" & objRsDetail("title") & "</B> "

    '-- If the field is Null display a zero
    '-- Otherwise display the value
```

We check for nulls in this section of code as well, and act accordingly. We loop through the recordset, and once at the end of the child (the detail recordset), we move to the next parent row and start again.

```
    if isNull(objRsDetail("ytd_sales")) then
      Response.Write "is <B>0</B><BR>"
    else
      Response.Write "are "
      Response.Write "<B>" & objRsDetail("ytd_sales")
      Response.Write "</B><BR>"
    end if
    '-- Move to the next Record in the child ~ Detail
    '-- And then Loop
    objRsDetail.MoveNext
  Loop
  '-- Move to the next Record in the Parent ~ Summary
  '-- And then Loop
  objRsSummary.MoveNext
Loop

'-- Clean up and Destroy used objects

objRsDetail.Close
objRsSummary.Close
objConn.Close

set objRsDetail = nothing
set objRsSummary = nothing
set objConn = nothing
%>
```

The results should look something like this:

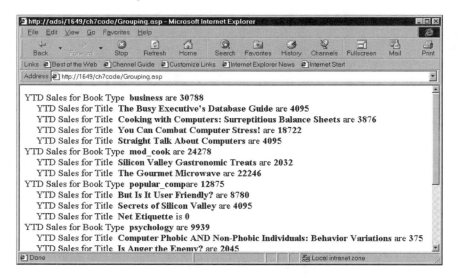

Staying in Sync

You are given a number of alternatives to refreshing your data. These are `Requery`, `Resync`, and a `StayInSync` property that applies only to group based hierarchical recordsets.

Using Requery()

You can refresh your data by executing `Requery()` on any recordset in the hierarchical chain, with the command:

```
ObjRsParent.Requery()
```

This will close and re-open the recordset connected to that recordset, and all the associated data. (This has exactly the same effect as closing and opening the `Recordset` object.) This is great for getting the latest results for your reports or any information from a system with a lot of transactions occurring; however you will utilize a good share of bandwidth when using this method. (So don't tell your network admin that I told you to use it).

Using Resync()

When you really do not want to reissue the entire recordset's command to refill the recordset with data, an alternative is to use the `Resync` method. When `Resync` is issued on a parent row the child recordsets will be cleared and re-fetched. (This is useful for parameter-based queries in making sure you get a fresh batch of data.)

An alternative to `Resync` *is the* `Properties` *collection's* `Cache Child Data` *property mentioned above.*

Using StayInSync

The StayInSync property applies only to group-based hierarchical recordsets. This is a boolean property – its default value is True. When this property is set to True the group parent (the summary dataset) updates itself when its children (the detail) are changed:

```
ObjRs.StayInSync = True
```

Setting the property value to False has the opposite effect, that is telling the parent not to update itself. You can think of these settings in much the same way as the difference between relational and parameterized hierarchical recordsets. Relational hierarchical recordsets get the data once, and will not receive a fresh set of data until instructed to, while the parameterized hierarchical recordset will get a fresh set of data every time it moves to a new child.

Summary

You should now have a good foundation for using and applying data shapes. Hierarchical recordsets give you the power and the functionality to make once complex tasks much easier. Even if the code seemed complex to you today, once you start experimenting with it you will soon find the only complexity involved is going back to using JOINs. Given time you will become proficient in the art of shaping your data. Any time you need parent to child based reporting, navigation or lookups, you should strongly consider using Data Shaping. Keeping that in mind, tomorrow you can go into work with a big smile and impress your boss and your co-workers, maybe even ask for a raise.

Disconnected Recordsets

The term 'disconnected recordset' may be a bit unsettling for some developers. A disconnected recordset may seem to go against everything we have learned about data access. After all, doesn't our data necessarily come from a database, or some other sort of data store? Don't we need a connection, in order to copy the data from the data store to our recordset? How can this be? It doesn't seem quite right. How can a "disconnected recordset" be of any use to me? Maybe if we ignore it they will just go away, right? No, of course not…and you would not want them to. Disconnected recordsets open up an entire new avenue of functionality. Because they can be disconnected, we can do things like

❑ Persist the recordset to disk, for data archiving or transport
❑ Send the recordset over networks using HTTP (such as the Internet) for use on the receiving system
❑ Use the `Recordset` object completely without a data store, using it like a "super-array", for storing temporary application data

At first glance, it may seem to be a complicated, bizarre and obscure technology, but disconnected recordsets are very useful and the idea behind them is quite simple. Disconnected recordsets are easy to create and easy to use. Even if you have never used a data access object model (such as DAO or RDO) before, you will find it easy to create and use disconnected recordset in your projects. In fact, if you haven't used disconnected recordsets before, I hope that by the end of this chapter you are asking, "It's so simple…why didn't anyone think of this before?"

In this chapter we will discuss the following topics:

❑ What are disconnected recordsets?
❑ Why use disconnected recordsets?
❑ The Active Connection
❑ Disconnecting a recordset
❑ Re-attaching to a database
❑ Re-synchronizing a disconnected recordset with a database

This chapter also explains how disconnected recordsets can help developers write scalable, distributed solutions. In addition, we will discuss the implementation details and objects involved in disconnected recordsets.

What is a Disconnected Recordset?

In simple terms, a disconnected recordset is an independent programming entity that is used to temporarily store data at run-time – i.e. when your code is executing. Admittedly, that's a fairly broad definition. In fact, the same definition could also be used to describe a standard programming variable – after all, variables are entities that are used to temporarily store data at run-time. However, a variable can only hold one unit of data at a time.

The above definition could also be used to describe a standard programming array. Arrays are also used to store data at run-time. Of course, arrays have an advantage over variables in that they can store *multiple* units of data simultaneously, but they usually do not do much more than that.

A disconnected recordset can store multiple units of data simultaneously, in much the same way as an array can. However, a disconnected recordset is much, much more functional. For example, a disconnected recordset provides built-in support for sorting data, filtering data, saving and retrieving data from disk, and much more. You can think of a disconnected recordset as the better-designed version of a programming array. In fact, you can use disconnected recordsets anywhere that you might otherwise use arrays, and benefit from their advanced features. In short, a disconnected recordset is a standard ADO recordset without an associated connection to a database. The data that is in the recordset could have originated from a data store, but not necessarily. The following diagram shows the range of temporary storage items:

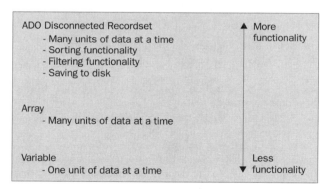

ADO disconnected recordsets can be created as stand-alone objects. There is no strict requirement dictating that recordsets must be created as a result of retrieving data from a data store, although they certainly can be. This means that recordsets can be created in a number of ways. For example:

❑ We can create a recordset without a persistent data store. In this case, we would add our own data to the recordset at run-time and take advantage of advanced recordset features, such as sorting.

❑ We can create a recordset as a result of retrieving data from a data store. In this case, the recordset will use a connection to the data store, through which data will be passed. Even in this case, we can later sever the connection between the recordset and the data store.

There are also other ways of creating disconnected recordsets – we'll look at some more later in this chapter. Regardless of how the recordset was created, a disconnected recordset is an ADO recordset that can be viewed and updated, but does *not* have a live and active connection to a data store. As a consequence, it does not carry the overhead required to maintain a live connection to the data store.

Definition of Terms

In ADO, we use the term 'disconnected recordset' to mean any one of a number of things:

- ❑ A recordset that was originally derived from a data store with a connection, and the connection was then dropped.
- ❑ A recordset that was opened from a disk file, without a connection to a database.
- ❑ A recordset used in Remote Data Services (RDS).

We will be covering the first two of these in this chapter. We'll see how recordsets are used in RDS in chapter 10. We can also create a recordset as a stand-alone object, used in place of an array, without a source data store. This is known as a custom recordset, and we'll be going into these in more detail in the next chapter.

An ADO disconnected recordset is either an `ADODB.Recordset` object or an `ADOR.Recordset` object, depending on how it was created. Applications using RDS usually work with the `ADOR.Recordset`, while non-RDS applications using disconnected recordsets usually use the `ADODB.Recordset`. The `ADOR.Recordset` is smaller than the `ADODB.Recordset` and was created specifically for passing over the low-bandwidth connections that are indicative of the Internet. The `ADOR` version of the `Recordset` object does not include the overhead of the `Connection` object or the `Command` object. Since the `ADOR` object is smaller than the `ADODB` object, it can more easily be passed over the Internet

When a disconnected recordset has been created as a result of retrieving data from a data store, it uses a connection to that data store, over which the data is passed. That connection can be manipulated through an `ADODB.Connection` object.

> *Disconnected recordsets are part of **Microsoft's Universal Data Access (UDA)** strategy. The UDA is based on data sources that expose their data through OLE DB providers, and applications that use ADO or OLE DB to access the data in a uniform way. The tools of MDAC (Microsoft Data Access Components) include ADO, RDS, ODBC and OLE DB. Together, it's the tools of MDAC that make UDA possible.*

A Disconnected Recordset's Place in the World

Disconnected recordsets will play an increasingly significant role in Internet, Intranet and LAN-based applications. Speaking for myself, I no longer use programmatic arrays in any but the simplest of applications. The superiority of ADO `Recordset` objects over programmatic arrays for holding data makes choosing easy. For example, I may never write another sort routine again – since that functionality comes as part of the `Recordset` object.

Where They Fit Into the Microsoft Universal Data Access Strategy

The UDA strategy defines technologies that enable developers to access data from virtually any type of data store located virtually anywhere in the world, in virtually the same way. I say 'virtually' because with UDA, as with anything, there are exceptions. Disconnected recordsets fit into the UDA strategy as the piece that enables data to be passed over TCP/IP networks like the Internet to web clients (satisfying the *'from virtually anywhere in the world'* criteria). In addition, disconnected recordsets make data portable. If you're so inclined, you can easily save a recordset and re-open it later on another system. When the recordset is re-opened, it is still a fully-functional disconnected recordset.

> *We'll discuss saving a recordset in the following chapter.*

Disconnected recordsets also assist enterprise applications in achieving scalability. Because they are manipulated on the client, disconnected recordsets do not require any running server code to support them. Since there is no code running on the server in support of the recordset, server resources are freed for other tasks. Distributing the processing load in this way helps application servers support more simultaneous user applications.

We can extend this idea of distributed processing and scalability even further. By creating COM (Component Object Model) objects and installing those objects into MTS (Microsoft Transaction Server), we can help applications distribute processing load and recycle server resources. If those components also access a data store and return disconnected recordset to their respective clients, server scalability increases even more.

What Disconnected Recordsets Can and Can't Do

So you're building your Web application, and you're thinking, "Should I implement disconnected recordsets, or shouldn't I?" As with many other application-building tools, this decision is tantamount to making a trade-off. The trick is to be savvy enough to know what those trade-offs are – then you can be sure to use disconnected recordsets only when what you are getting is more valuable to you than what you are giving up. (It's a sensible plan, but then it's hardly limited to disconnected recordsets.)

What Disconnected Recordsets Can Do

Disconnected recordsets enable you to use data in a structured manner and store related data in a single location: the `Recordset` object. As we've seen in the previous chapters: the ADO `Recordset` object stores data in a two-dimensional format. This format defines a recordset as the combination of horizontal rows and vertical columns of data – much like a spreadsheet stores data. Just as you'd expect, we use a **field** to represent a single type of data that can be included in the recordset – for example, we might have a field called `LastName` that is reserved for referring to the last name of any person (or, indeed, all people) defined in the recordset. A column represents every instance of a single field, and a row represents a single instance of each field in the recordset.

Client vs Server Load-Balancing

Disconnected recordsets enable our applications to do a kind of 'load-balancing' act – by offloading recordset management responsibility from the server to the client. Let's look at this more closely. When a computer performs an action, it is because it has received instructions to do so – usually in the form of code. An ADO recordset functions because code runs that supports the recordset. Because the recordset is running on the client (and not on the server), support code does not need to run on the server. The server is free to do other things. If an application's recordsets all run on the client-side, your server administrator will be happier because the server will run more smoothly. Moreover, it will make your users happy because the response to the recordset will be very fast. In fact, this is true for both LAN clients and Web clients. The following diagram illustrates this comparison between client-side and server-side recordsets and the associated cursors:

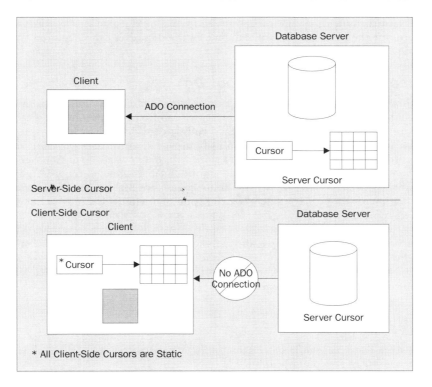

Persisting Recordset Data on Disk

Disconnected recordsets can be persisted as a recordset to a disk file. It is amazing but true: you can put a recordset on a disk, put the disk in your pocket and carry it with you. This can be a great boost for applications used by sales staff and other mobile users. For example, imagine a sales-tracking application, in which you can retrieve the structure of a recordset derived from a Sales table and other related tables. As the salesperson travels, he can enter sales information into the Sales application, which passes that information into a disconnected recordset. When the application is shut down, the disconnected recordset is saved to disk. The next time the application is started, the recordset will be re-opened from the disk file and the data loaded into the Sales application. When the salesperson returns to the office and connects to the LAN, the recordset data will be copied from the disk file directly to the master database. And it all occurs through built-in functionality of the Recordset object – no special coding is required on the part of the programmer.

Sorting, Filtering, Navigating and Editing Functionality

You can sort and filter the data in the recordset. As we saw in Chapter 6, the ADO `Recordset` object comes with features that enable us to do these things, and they apply equally to disconnected recordsets. For example, assume that you have a recordset populated with records of customers. If you want to see data for customers living in London, you can filter the recordset on that value. All other records will be present, but hidden. You can also sort on any column in the recordset. In addition, you can sort in ascending or descending order. (Like I said before, I may never write another sort routine again!)

You can also navigate through the data, one record at a time. You can use all of the standard `'Move'` methods of the recordset object to navigate through the recordset. Finally, disconnected recordsets allow for inserting new rows of data into the recordset, deleting rows from the recordset and updating existing data in the recordset. Data manipulation features are built right into the `Recordset` object. These features provide the mechanism by which data in the recordset can be altered. We will talk more about this later in this chapter.

What Disconnected Recordsets Cannot Do

By definition, a disconnected recordset derived from a data store is disconnected from its data store – so there are some things that it can't do. For example, we cannot use a disconnected recordset to modify data on the source data store without special coding considerations. We must take into account that other users might change the contents of the data store while we're using the disconnected recordset. When we update the data store with our revised recordset, our code must check for this. If we have changed an item of data within our disconnected recordset, and another user has also changed the same item of data (in the time since we first generated and disconnected our recordset), then there will be a conflict. We need code that will decide how to handle such a conflict.

When I am using a recordset that has a live and active connection to the source data store, I can change data on the data store with very little regard to possible conflicts. To truly use disconnected recordsets effectively, your code should check for and handle these occurrences. We will describe details of how this works later in this chapter.

Who is Really the Client?

ADO is very flexible. There is usually more than one way to accomplish a task. Such is the case with disconnecting recordsets in a web application.

> *A Web application is a collection of related web pages at a single web site that contain HTML, scripting code and objects that work together for a specific purpose.*

Persisting the Recordset on the Web Server

Our scripting code can be executed in server-side script – in which case the code runs on the IIS server. If our server-side code opens a recordset and disconnects it from the database server from within that server-side script, the web server is playing the role of 'client' to the database server. For each instance of the web application, each recordset will run on the web server. Of course, in this case, the disconnected recordset may off-load work from the database server, but this work is all dumped onto the web server – the client only receives web pages that are generated on the web server, not the actual recordset. This scenario is probably a simpler model – but does not *fully* exploit the idea of the disconnected recordset, since the recordset itself is never sent to the web browser.

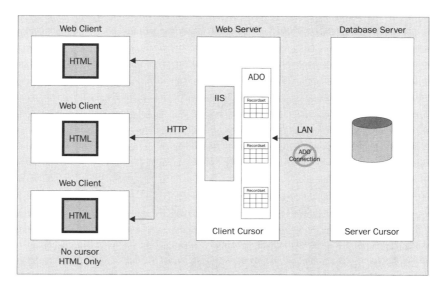

This diagram shows a disconnected recordset in which the IIS server is the client to the database server. In this model, the web browsers do not receive the actual recordset. They receive pages that were built using data from recordsets that are on the IIS server.

> **In an application that must support hundreds of users, this model might not be the most efficient. However, it may be the only way to go if the target browser is not Microsoft's IE 4.0 (or later). The ability to send an actual ADO recordset to a web client is *Internet Explorer-specific*.**

This model would also work well if the Web server needs to save recordsets out to network drives, for the traveling salesperson to pick up just before they leave on a trip. It's also the simplest model, and as such we will focus on this model in this chapter.

Persisting the Recordset on the Browser

If the browser is IE 4.0 or later (or IE 3.0, if the MDAC is installed on the client system), we can send the recordset to the Web client machine.

> *The MDAC is the set of data access tools including ADO and RDS. It is free and downloadable at http://www.microsoft.com/data.*

This transfer can occur across a LAN, or across an HTTP connection (such as the Internet). In this case, the recordset is passed from the database server to the IIS server via a LAN connection. Then, IIS breaks down the recordset into a MIME (text) format that can be sent to the browser. When received, IE reassembles the recordset so that it can be used within the client-side scripting. The following diagram shows this process:

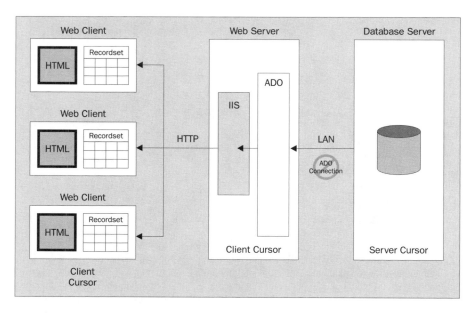

Note that both while the recordset is on the IIS server, and after the recordset is passed to the client machine, it uses a client-side cursor.

Using MTS and COM Components

Alternatively, we can use client-side script to access COM server components that are running on an application server and installed into MTS. In this case, code running within the COM component will create the recordset and disconnect from the database. The additional benefit is that the database access can participate in MTS transactions when there is a connection.

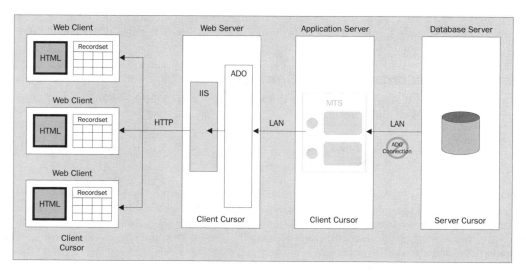

Here you see an MTS component passing an ADO recordset to client-side script through the IIS web server.

Using VB Client Applications

For completeness, I will mention Visual Basic client applications and how they work with disconnected recordsets. As you can see in the image below, the recordset travels a path that is very similar to the path traveled when using Web clients and MTS. An additional benefit to discussing ASP-only, as we are doing in this chapter, is that nearly all of the code can be copied and pasted directly into a Visual Basic project and it will run. The exception to this is when we use the following line in our ASP code:

```
Server.CreateObject(...)
```

In the Visual Basic code, this line should be changed to simply:

```
CreateObject(...)
```

In addition, although the objects will get created with the code as-is, Visual Basic provides the New keyword that would ideally be used to more efficiently create the object. The following diagram shows a disconnected recordset on a local area network, as in a VB client application:

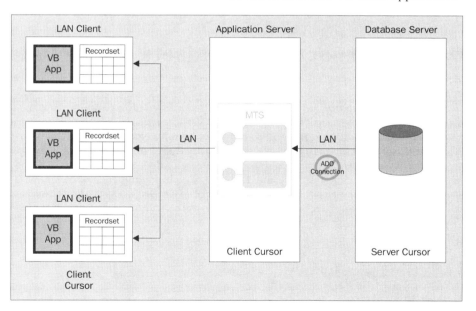

When Should I use Disconnected Recordsets?

'There is a time and place for everything under the sun'... Isn't that how it goes? There is a time and place for disconnected recordsets. This section talks about when we should disconnect.

In general, we can disconnect any time we want the client to have an ADO Recordset object for manipulating the data, and are willing to spend the resources to keep the recordset active. Also, with regard to performance, one of the primary benefits of disconnected recordsets is that while the client works on the data, the database server is not tied up with any open connections.

As a rule of thumb, you can almost always use disconnected recordsets anytime your application needs a snapshot of your data. For example, if your application needs to retrieve your company's product information (e.g. name, description and retail price), use a disconnected recordset. Because that information is relatively static, let the server generate the recordset and send it down to the client, then disconnect from the data store and forget about the recordset. Let the client deal with managing it.

You may also want to consider using disconnected recordsets even if the data *does* change frequently. If the data that you retrieve (or the changes you make to the data) don't need to be in real-time, or anything resembling real-time, consider using disconnected recordsets. Look at the traveling salesperson example again. In that example, the data originated from a master database and the salesperson used the disconnected recordset on his laptop while physically disconnected from the LAN. When ready, the recordset was sent back up to the master database, complete with changes that get integrated back into the master data. The sales data did not have to be up-to-the-minute accurate, so a disconnected recordset worked well assuming no conflicts.

If you need to store data on your running application code and want to take advantage of advanced features like sorting, filtering and navigation, you can use a disconnected recordset. That recordset will not have been created as a holding place for results when retrieving data from a data store. Instead, it will be created with the explicit purpose of holding data that is generated internal to the application and will be destroyed when the application is closed. This use of the disconnected recordset enables it to act as a replacement for the programmatic array.

How to Use Disconnected Recordsets from a Data Store

In this section, we'll get into the nitty-gritty details of how you will go about creating and using disconnected recordsets. This is the really interesting part! What might surprise you is that you, as a programmer, are required to do little in relation to all of the benefits that come with using them. You have just a couple of property settings to adjust, and presto…a disconnected recordset! The properties that determine whether a recordset is connected or disconnected affect the choice of recordset cursor type, cursor location and active connection to the database. The following code shows how to disconnect a recordset from a data store. Don't worry about the details just yet, but do look at the code. We'll talk about the details throughout the remainder of the chapter.

```
Dim strSQL
strSQL = "SELECT AU_FName, AU_LName FROM Authors"
Dim objRecordsetAuthors
Set objRecordsetAuthors = Server.CreateObject("ADODB.Recordset")

objRecordsetAuthors.CursorLocation = adUseClient
objRecordsetAuthors.CursorType = adOpenStatic
objRecordsetAuthors.LockType = adLockBatchOptimistic
objRecordsetAuthors.Open strSQL, objConnectionPubs

Set objRecordsetAuthors.ActiveConnection = Nothing
objConnectionPubs.Close
```

Cursors and Disconnected Recordsets

Let's recap the topic of cursors briefly, before we look at how they relate to disconnected recordsets. A cursor is a piece of code that performs management functions for a recordset. For example, you can choose a cursor that enables your application to navigate forwards and backwards through a recordset – or you can choose one that allows forward-only navigation. A cursor can enable records to be modified, or can make them read-only. A cursor can dictate many attributes of your recordset, so it is not surprising that cursors affect how your disconnected recordset behaves.

Of course, we are talking about ADO disconnected recordsets in this chapter, so it's a short mental leap to understand that we'll need ADO itself running on both the client and the server machines. ADO on the server can generate the recordset, populate it with data from a data store, and then pass that recordset off to ADO running on the client machine. Since ADO is running on both the client and the server, I can configure my recordset to use the cursor that is running on the client, or the cursor that is running on the server. The cursor I choose will handle applying the recordset attributes mentioned above and more.

Client-side or Server-side

In general, cursors can run on the client or the server machine. By default, ADO will use a server-side cursor unless you specify otherwise. If you intend to disconnect a recordset, you must use a client-side cursor (without a connection, there is no mechanism by which the server-side cursor and the recordset could communicate!).

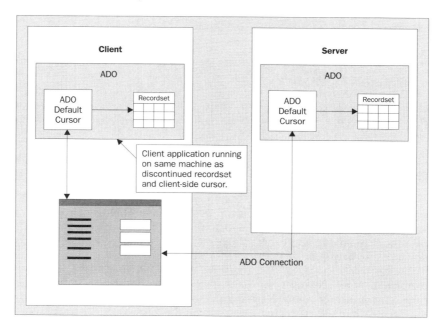

An ADO cursor can run on the client-side or the server-side. When the server cursor runs, the client communicates with it through the ADO connection. When the client cursor runs, the client application and the cursor run on the same machine and communicate via local procedure calls.

The `CursorType` and `CursorLocation` properties of the ADO `Recordset` object determine the functionality of that recordset. Available cursor types are `forward-only`, `static`, `keyset` and `dynamic`. We will not go through the details of the cursors here – although it's worth remembering that the `forward-only` cursor is the least resource-intensive – and also the least functional. The `dynamic` cursor type is the most resource-intensive and the most functional:

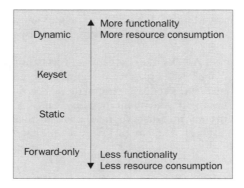

When working with disconnected recordsets, we must use a `static` cursor. The data contained in the data store cannot be changed while the recordset is disconnected, which is typical of static cursors, but once the recordset reconnects, the data can be updated. The following code segment shows a recordset object whose cursor properties have been set to work with disconnected recordsets:

```
Dim objRecordsetAuthors
Set objRecordsetAuthors = Server.CreateObject("ADODB.Recordset")
objRecordsetAuthors.CursorType = adOpenStatic
objRecordsetAuthors.CursorLocation = adUseClient
```

Assume that we have just instantiated the `Recordset` object but have not yet opened a recordset. We will build on this piece of code to get a complete picture of how to open a disconnected recordset. To specify that the recordset should be built on the client, we'll use the `adUseClient` parameter with the `Recordset` object's `Open` method.

Locking It Up (or is it Down?)

Whenever data is changed on a database, that data must be locked for exclusive use. Only the process that is changing the data should have the access to the data as it is being changed. All other processes must wait until the update is complete and the lock is released. Can you imagine what would happen if two different processes attempted to access the exact same memory location at the same time? Let's just say that it would not be pretty.

Whenever we open an ADO recordset, we can use the `LockType` property of the `Recordset` object to determine the type of locking that will be applied to the recordset. The behavior of the chosen lock will take effect when data in the recordset is updated on the database.

There are four different types of locks to choose from. They are as follows:

Lock Type	Description
Optimistic	Locks the data as late as possible in update process. Allows updates to only one row at a time.
Pessimistic	Locks the data as soon as possible in update process. Allows updates to only one row at a time.
LockBatchPessimistic	Used with multiple recordsets and disconnected recordsets. Allows updates to multiple rows at a time.
Read-Only	The only one of the four that is not updateable.

When creating a recordset that will be disconnected, you should use the `adLockBatchOptimistic` value for the `LockType` property of the recordset. This will enable the data in your recordset to be passed from server to client and back again. You might be wondering, "If we're only retrieving a single recordset, why do we need batch locking?" Later in this chapter, we'll see that there are in fact *three* copies of your recordset (not one) returned to the client.

Let's expand on the code we've seen so far. We'll add the `LockType` property and set it to `LockBatchOptimistic`:

```
Set objRecordsetAuthors = Server.CreateObject("ADODB.Recordset")
objRecordsetAuthors.CursorLocation = adUseClient
objRecordsetAuthors.CursorType = adOpenStatic
objRecordsetAuthors.LockType = adLockBatchOptimistic
```

Note that the sequence in which we set these property values does not affect the behavior of the recordset. Also, remember that when you are executing this code from within ASP, the 'client' machine is the web server, not the machine where the web browser is running.

Choosing the Right ADO Cursor and Lock Settings in Visual Basic Applications

There are quite a number of different combinations of cursor and lock settings, and this may make choosing the right ones confusing. Here are a few tips that will help you pick the correct combination. The overall theme to cursors is this: *take only what you need; and always choose the least resource intensive combination.*

If you need an updateable recordset but do not need real-time data, use a client-side, static, updateable cursor. This will off-load cursor processing from the server to the client and will help the overall application run more efficiently. Remember that since the recordset is stored locally, you will need enough RAM & hard-disk space (Windows will decide exactly where to put it) to store it.

If you need a snapshot of the data at a given point in time, choose the client-side, static cursor with a read-only lock. Since the data will not change, a read-only lock type is sufficient. The application will perform better since the read-only lock-type is less resource intensive than the other Lock Types.

When you need a snapshot of the data and just want to read it from beginning to end use a server-side, forward-only cursor, with a read-only lock. Because the forward-only cursor is the least expensive cursor and the read-only lock is the least expensive locking mechanism, the application should perform quite well.

The following diagram illustrates the points just made. Note that all client-side cursors also use the static type.

| | Cursor Location | | Cursor Type | | | | Lock Type | |
	Client (distributed load)	Server (server-side cursors for all users)	Forward-only	Static	Keyset	Dynamic	Updateable*	Readonly
Updateable Recordset	✓			✓			✓+	
Snapshot of the data that does not change	✓			✓				✓
Snapshot, retrieve data from beginning to end		✓	✓					✓

* (Pessimistic, Optimistic, BatchOptimistic)
\+ (use BatchOptimistic for disconnected recordsets)

The Active Connection

You can think of the connection as being information about a database and the underlying relationship that is created between components on the database client and components on the database server. In the case of an ASP application, the 'database client' is in fact the middle-tier web server – as we saw in the 3-tier illustrations earlier in the chapter. Information from the database server can then be sent from the web server to a web-client embedded in an HTML page.

In order to disconnect the ADODB.Recordset object (or, indeed, ADODB.Command object) from its source database, we use the recordset's ActiveConnection property. By changing the value of this property, the ADODB.Recordset can exist and function normally, but without the overhead (and connectivity) associated with live and active database connections. In this section, we'll describe the relationship between the ADODB.Recordset and ADODB.Connection objects, and how their relationship can be created, broken and re-created on a whim.

A Tumultuous Relationship

At any given time, the `ActiveConnection` property of the `ADODB.Recordset` object indicates to which `ADODB.Connection` object the specified `ADODB.Recordset` object currently "belongs". However, this sense of belonging is somewhat tentative – it's like an on-again/off-again relationship between a dating couple. It seems that they are constantly breaking up and getting back together. Something similar can occur between the connection and recordset. They can break up at any time, but they can also get back together at a moment's notice. Even when they get back together, conflicts can occur, which need to be resolved.

In this relationship, it is the `Recordset` object that tends to want to go it alone. The `ADODB.Recordset` does not need the `ADODB.Connection` to perform, so it likes to go out and have fun by navigating data single-handedly. However, if the `ADODB.Recordset` intends to make a serious commitment (such as committing changed data back to a database) then it does need the `ADODB.Connection`. Note that when re-connecting, the `ADODB.Connection` object used by the `ADODB.Recordset` may not actually be the same `ADODB.Connection` object previously used.

The `ADODB.Recordset` breaks it off with the `ADODB.Connection` object by changing the `ActiveConnection` property. The `ActiveConnection` property accepts two types of values:

❏ A string that contains the definition for a connection. This is the connection string that names a specific database server, DSN or OLE-DB provider (among other things).
❏ An `ADODB.Connection` object. You can create an object of this type, and pass the reference to the object to the `ActiveConnection` property.

The `Connection` object used by the recordset is flexible. We can pass a string or an object reference to the `ActiveConnection` property; alternatively, we can use either when we first create the recordset and the other when reconnecting. The default value of the `ActiveConnection` property is an object type that has a value of `Nothing`.

Disconnecting the Recordset

In this section, we will discuss how the disconnection occurs. You will find it very easy. We will look at how to disconnect a recordset from within ASP, and also how to disconnect a recordset from within a business object. While the mechanics of these two are quite similar, there are some subtle differences of which you should be aware. You are likely, and encouraged, to use both in your projects.

Disconnecting a Recordset in Active Server Pages

To support a disconnected recordset, you must specify that the recordset will be built on the client. When using ASP, remember that the 'database client' is the web server, not the browser. Let us continue with the example that we started earlier in this chapter. So far, we have created a `Recordset` object and set properties of the object that will enable us to disconnect. Now let's discuss the `Connection` object that's used to retrieve the recordset.

In the following code, we'll connect to the `Pubs` database through the native OLE DB provider for SQL Server:

```
Dim objConnectionPubs
Set objConnectionPubs = Server.CreateObject("ADODB.Connection")

' Establish a connection
objConnectionPubs.Provider = "SQLOLEDB"
objConnectionPubs.ConnectionString = "User ID=sa;" & _
                        "Data Source=MyServer;" & _
                        "Initial Catalog=Pubs"
objConnectionPubs.Open
```

This provider ships with OLE DB, so there is no need to procure it from elsewhere. If you have ADO 2.0 or later, you have this provider (as well as providers for Oracle and Jet databases). You can use these native OLE DB providers to access your data faster and with lower disk and memory footprint.

In this example, we have chosen to use the native OLE DB provider rather than the OLE DB provider for ODBC databases. If you have a choice between using the OLE DB provider for ODBC databases and the native OLE DB provider for your specific database (such as Microsoft SQL Server), use the native provider. It does not have to go through the extra layer of processing. It communicates with the database in a more direct manner and will provide enhanced performance to your application. In the sample code above, pay particular attention to the value we are assigning to the `Provider` property of the `Connection` object. This syntax may look strange if you are familiar with the process of creating connection strings. The `Data Source` parameter defines the database server. The `Initial Catalog` parameter defines the specific database on that server.

Now let's add the code that will open the recordset – then we will disconnect. Assume that `objConnectionPubs` is a `Connection` object variable that contains a valid `Connection` object to the SQL Server 6.5 `Pubs` sample database and was created in a manner similar to that described above. We'll add some new lines of code, shown with the shaded background:

```
Dim strSQL
strSQL = "SELECT AU_FName, AU_LName FROM Authors"
Dim objRecordsetAuthors
Set objRecordsetAuthors = Server.CreateObject("ADODB.Recordset")

objRecordsetAuthors.CursorLocation = adUseClient
objRecordsetAuthors.CursorType = adOpenStatic
objRecordsetAuthors.LockType = adLockBatchOptimistic
objRecordsetAuthors.Open strSQL, objConnectionPubs

Set objRsAuthors.ActiveConnection = Nothing
objConnectionPubs.Close
```

The last two lines of this code fragment disconnect from the data source and close the connection. By setting the recordset's `ActiveConnection` property to `Nothing`, we disconnect the recordset from the active connection. Your application can then close the active `Connection` object using the `Close` method. If the `CursorLocation` property of the recordset is set to `adUseClient`, the client will have a copy of the recordset data and can begin navigating or updating the records. If `CursorLocation` was not set to `adUseClient`, the recordset will be destroyed when the connection is closed.

Disconnecting a Recordset in a COM Object

In this section, we'll discuss the subtle differences between disconnecting a recordset in ASP (as demonstrated above) and doing it from within a Visual Basic-built COM object. The image under *Visual Basic Client Applications* (earlier in this chapter) shows a COM object, running in MTS, that will pass a `Recordset` object to a Visual Basic client. When a recordset is marshaled to a client computer, the data connection is *not* marshaled with it.

The term **marshalling** is used frequently when discussing COM. It refers to the passing of data from an application in one execution process to a second application in a second execution process. When this happens, the data must be copied and recopied multiple times before it reaches its destination. Passing data in this way is generally slower than passing data between applications running in the same execution process. Because a COM object, running on the server, and the client application, running on the client, are in separate execution processes, the recordset is marshaled between them. Because of this, the recordset must be disconnected from the database server. We'll discuss marshalling in detail in chapter 10.

The example shows how to create a disconnected recordset inside a COM object for use in Visual Basic client:

```
Dim objConnectionPubs as ADODB.Connection
Set objConnectionPubs = New ADODB.Connection

' Establish a connection
With objConnectionPubs
  .Provider = "SQLOLEDB"
  .ConnectionString = "User ID=sa;" & _
                      "Data Source=MyServer;" & _
                      "Initial Catalog=Pubs"
  .Open
End With

Dim strSQL
strSQL = "SELECT AU_FName, AU_LName FROM Authors"

Dim objRecordsetAuthors as ADODB.Recordset
Set objRecordsetAuthors = New ADODB.Recordset
With objRecordsetAuthors
  .CursorLocation = adUseClient
  .CursorType = adOpenStatic
  .LockType = adLockBatchOptimistic
  .Open strSQL, objConnectionPubs
End With

Set objRsAuthors.ActiveConnection = Nothing
objConnectionPubs.Close
```

Note the differences in the way that the objects are created. In addition, this code assumes that the developer has set a reference to the Microsoft ADO Library 2.0, from within the Visual Basic environment.

You can see that the code for a COM object is very similar to code for ASP. Pay particular attention to the use of the `New` keyword. There are a number of ways to instantiate objects in Visual Basic, but we have declared the variable on a line of code and are creating the object on another. If you are familiar with Visual Basic, you know that we also could have combined the two steps to declare and create the object reference on a single line of code.

```
Dim objConnectionPubs As New ADODB.Connection
```

This is a form of early binding (i.e. telling Visual Basic about the object before the code runs) and is faster than using the `CreateObject` function. While this code does work, because of the way Visual Basic creates the objects internally, it is not as fast as splitting the operation into two separate lines of code, as we have done above.

Making Offline Changes

Once a recordset has been disconnected from the data source, your application can use any of the data update and navigation features provided by ADO recordsets. You can add new records using the `AddNew` method, you can delete records using the `Delete` method, and you can edit existing records using the `Update` method. However, all changes are cached on the client until the connection is re-established.

The following sample code builds upon the previous examples by using the now disconnected recordset object:

```
<%
Sub MoveToNextRecord
   objRecordsetAuthors.MoveNext
End Sub

Sub MoveToPrevRecord
   objRecordsetAuthors.MovePrevious
End Sub

Sub DeleteCurrentRecord
   objRecordsetAuthors.Delete
End Sub
%>
```

These demonstrate our ability to navigate through a disconnected recordset and our ability to make changes to the data. The use of the `Delete` method of the recordset object will delete the currently visible row of data. This change only affects the locally cached version of the recordset. It does not yet affect the master data store. It is important to understand that offline changes made to the same record by more than one user will cause a conflict when the data is saved back to the data source. We will talk about how to handle those conflicts later in this chapter.

Reconnecting to the Data Store

After a connection has been closed, it can be reopened and any changes the user made offline can be saved to the data source. The original connection information, such as the data source provider, is retained as long as the `Connection` object was disconnected using the `Close` method. If the `Connection` object is set to `Nothing`, all connection information must be re-established. In our sample code above, the connection object is closed but *not* destroyed:

```
objConnectionPubs.Close
```

Because the `Connection` object is not destroyed, it retains connection information and can be re-used when we want to reconnect to the data store.

However, if we had set the object variable to `Nothing`, the `Connection` object would have been destroyed and we would have to recreate a connection object with identical information in order to re-connect. The following example shows this:

```
objConnectionPubs.Close
Set objConnectionPubs = Nothing
```

This code destroys the `Connection` object and frees resources associated with its maintenance.

Reconnecting from within ASP

If your application will re-open the `Connection` within the same user session, you can consider keeping the connection around by not destroying it with the `Nothing` keyword. The following example code reconnects to a data source and associates the `Recordset` object with the connection:

```
objConnectionPubs.Open
Set objRecordsetAuthors.ActiveConnection = objConnectionPubs
```

In the preceding code, the existing recordset is re-attached to a database connection. This recordset may have been disconnected or it may have been saved out to disk and restored. We'll discuss saving a recordset to disk, in Chapter 9, next. In either case, the recordset can easily be reattached by setting the `ActiveConnection` property to a `Connection` object reference.

The Three Copies of Data

Since these recordsets are not connected to the underlying database from which they were created, it is possible that other users may make changes to the master copy of the data while we have a disconnected copy. The questions that beg to be answered are:

1. How do we know if changes have been made to the underlying data?

2. How do we resolve the differences?

3. What features are built-in to assist me with resolving the differences?

To help resolve potential conflicts, the recordset maintains three different views of the field values in the records. They are the **original value** view, the **value** view, and the **underlying value** view:

❑ The Original Value view accesses the original values contained in the recordset, *before* any changes were made. These are the values that originally came from the database.

❑ The Value view accesses the *current* values in the recordset. Any changes you made to data in the disconnected recordset will be reflected in this field.

❑ The Underlying Value view contains the values as they are currently stored in the database. Note that, because we are dealing with disconnected recordsets, the Underlying Value fields may not always accurately reflect the actual contents of the corresponding fields in the database. To update the contents of the Underlying Values view with the most recent data, use the `Resync` method of the recordset object. For more information about the `Resync` method, see the section below entitled, "That Sync'ing Feeling".

When the recordset first arrives at the client, all three views are the same, like this:

Original_Value	Values	Underlying_Values
White	White	White
Green	Green	Green
Carson	Carson	Carson
O'Leary	O'Leary	O'Leary
Straight	Straight	Straight
Smith	Smith	Smith
Bennet	Bennet	Bennet
Dull	Dull	Dull
Gringlesby	Gringlesby	Gringlesby

Disconnected recordsets are delivered to the client with not one but three different copies of the data. When the recordset first arrives at the client, all three are the same. The three views of the data are accessible programmatically, through the `Original`, `Value` and `Underlying` properties of the `Recordset` object.

Sending Changes Back to the Data Store

When your application is ready to send data changes from the disconnected recordset to the back-end data store, your code must take into account the possibility that the changes may not initially make it to the data store. There are a few things that could hinder the process, and necessitate that your application should be prepared to acknowledge those hindrances and re-try (or take action then re-try).

Among the events that could get in the way of sending changes to the data store are user intervention and concurrency issues. If your application makes the functionality available to cancel changes to the disconnected recordset data, your code should be prepared for the possibility that the user might actually use it. If they do, changes should not be saved back to the database. Your code should implement that functionality. In addition, if other users have made changes to the data store data, your code should be able to handle that also.

How to use UpdateBatch

When your application is ready to send changes back to the data store from which the original data came, you can implement the `UpdateBatch` method of the `Recordset` object to handle sending the data to the data store. Note that you would only call `UpdateBatch` *after* you have set the `ActiveConnection` property of the `Recordset` object back to an open connection, as shown in the section titled, *Reconnecting from within ASP* above. The following sample code can be used to initiate the process of sending data back to the data store:

```
objRecordsetAuthors.UpdateBatch
```

The `UpdateBatch` method of the `Recordset` object works similarly to its cousin method, `Update`. `Update` and `UpdateBatch` are both designed to save changes made in a recordset to a back-end data store. The difference between the two methods is that the `UpdateBatch` method is specifically designed for use with multiple recordsets and disconnected recordsets.

172

If your application has not yet called UpdateBatch, it can cancel all the changes that are in the client's cache. This means that if a user makes a change to the data in the disconnected recordset, they can 'roll-back' those changes so that the data returns to its original state. This functionality is made possible by the Original Value view of the data in the recordset. We use the Recordset object's CancelBatch method to reset the Value view of the recordset to its original state. Immediately after CancelBatch is called, the Original Value view and the Value view will be identical.

The following example code will submit and save all batched changes, or abort the save and lose all recent (from the time the recordset was last opened) changes based on the value of blnSubmitChanges:

```
If blnSubmitChanges = False Then
   objRecordsetAuthors.UpdateBatch
Else
   objRecordsetAuthors.CancelBatch
End If
```

Conflicts

When UpdateBatch is called, it creates a separate SQL query for each changed record – these SQL queries will modify the original values in the database. Part of the SQL query checks to see if the record has changed since the recordset was first created. It does this by comparing the Underlying Value view in the recordset against the values of the corresponding fields in the database. If they are the same, then the database has not changed, and the update can proceed. If they are different, then someone has recently changed the database, and the update fails.

When a record fails to update because of a conflict with the database, UpdateBatch flags it by changing its Status property of the Recordset. After UpdateBatch returns, you can include code that checks to see if there were any conflicts – by setting the recordset's Filter property to adFilterConflictingRecords. Then, in order to find out whether there were any conflicting records, you check the number of records in the filtered recordset. There will be one record in the filtered recordset for each conflict. If there are no records present, no records conflicted. If there are conflicting records, you can check the Status property to determine why the update failed.

> *For more information about the* Status *property, check out* ADO 2.0 Programmer's Reference *(Wrox, ISBN 1-861001-83-5).*

That Sync'ing Feeling

As a developer, you must include code in your application that will decide how to handle conflicts. The handling of conflicts is not automatic, but there is enough available information to make writing this piece easy. If there are conflicts, your code must decide how best to resolve them. Some options include:

- ❑ Overwrite the conflicting records in the database
- ❑ Decide not to change the conflicting records
- ❑ Take other action depending on custom business rules

All of these options are available to your code. Factors that dictate which path you take may include personal preference, and the policy of the organization that owns the data. To help make this decision, you can update the underlying values in the disconnected recordset to examine the conflicting values in the database. To update the underlying values, call the Resync method with the adAffectGroup and adResyncUnderlyingValues parameters (as shown in the code below). The Resync method copies the current data in the data store fields into the corresponding fields of the Underlying Values view. After calling the Resync method, the data in the Underlying Values view will be identical to the data in the database. Afterwards, Updatebatch can be called again. At this point, there will be no conflicts (assuming no other users have made changes as Resync was called), and the updates will be made.

The following figure illustrates the procedure. When the recordset is first created, the three records contain the values 1, 2, 3 respectively. The recordset is then disconnected from the data store; then the value of Record1 is changed from 1 to 2, and the value of Record3 is changed from 3 to 8. When we call UpdateBatch, we find that the value of Record3 in the data store has been changed from 3 to 6 – effectively, two amendments to Record3 have taken place simultaneously. The Conflict flag is set – and when UpdateBatch is finished, we can run the code that decides how to resolve the conflicts.

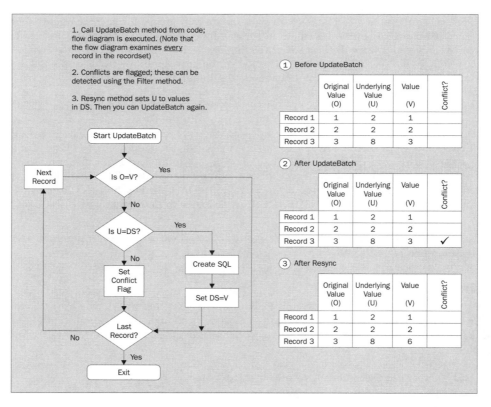

The process of sending changes back to a database and synchronizing changes to a database can seem confusing at first, but it is really easy if you know what is going on.

And Sync'ing Further...!

So before we enforce our local changes onto the database, we check to see whether there are conflicts – if there are no conflicts then we go ahead, and if there are conflicts then we resolve them before updating. But what happens if someone updates the database while we're resolving our conflicts, and that update causes further conflicts that we didn't account for?

For example, suppose your code calls UpdateBatch, and finds some conflicting records. You can Resync the recordset, to set the underlying values equal to the values in the database, then call UpdateBatch again to save those originally conflicting records. Ideally, that would work, but if *another* user makes changes to the database – between your Resync call and your second UpdateBatch call – that causes a second conflict. If your code does not check for conflicting records again, you might not actually make the changes to the database that you think you have.

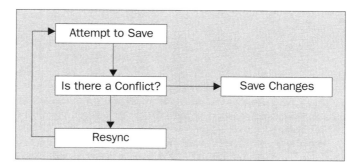

Here we're attempting to save changes, then resync'ing if conflicts occurred.

The thing to take away from this is that you should not call the UpdateBatch method without also checking for conflicting records. Conflicts can occur when you least expect them.

The following example code shows one way to resynchronize the underlying values in a recordset and ensure that the changes actually get made. In the sample code below, the Filter property of the Recordset object is set to check for conflicting records. In addition, the Resync method of the Recordset object is called. This sample code will check for conflicts after calling UpdateBatch and will loop until there are no more conflicts. When there are no more conflicts, the application can call UpdateBatch, which will overwrite any changes that may have been made by other users. As the programmer, I have the option to write code that overwrites other users changes, or not, depending upon the design of the application.

```
objRecordsetAuthors.UpdateBatch
Do
    objRecordsetAuthors.Filter = adFilterConflictingRecords

    If objRecordsetAuthors.EOF And objRecordsetAuthors.BOF Then
        ' NO CONFLICTING RECORDS
        Exit Do
    Else
```

```
      ' RECORDS CONFLICTED
      objRecordsetAuthors.Resync adAffectGroup, adResyncUnderlyingValues

      ' OTHER USERS COULD MAKE CHANGES HERE.
     ·' CHECK FOR CONFLICTS, AGAIN, AFTER
      ' CALLING UPDATEBATCH.
      objRecordsetAuthors.UpdateBatch
   End If
Loop
```

Once the underlying values are synchronized with the database, you can see the changes other users have made through the Underlying Value property and decide if you want to overwrite them or not. If you decide to overwrite the conflicting records, simply call UpdateBatch again. Now that the underlying values match the database, there are no conflicts, and the updates occur.

Summary

Disconnecting recordsets is a functional alternative to maintaining open connections to databases in conditions where it's either expensive or impossible to maintain the connection – such as a Web environment, or a scenario where a recordset is held open for a long period of time. As we'll see in the next chapter, ADO recordsets can be created without the presence of a database at all. By creating a stand-alone recordset, you can traverse and manipulate data from a text file, or other non-database source, using the recordset functionality that has, in the past, been reserved for data derived from a database. We'll also see how to save the recordset to disk.

This chapter introduced you to disconnected recordsets and showed the basics of how to disconnect a recordset from a data store. We have seen the process of disconnecting a recordset, re-attaching to a database and resync'ing a disconnected recordset to a database. I am sure that you can find a use for disconnected recordsets in your next Web application.

Custom Recordsets

Welcome to the chapter that is going to change your life as you know it – at least as far as dealing with custom data is concerned. If you are just glancing through this book at home, in the office or even at the bookstore, make sure you read this section!

This chapter is all about custom recordsets and what they can do for you. If you've ever tried persisting data in a structured way (but without a database – for example, using an array or a collection) – and if you've been frustrated by the lack of functionality available to manage that data – then custom recordsets could well be what you're looking for.

We will be covering:

- ❑ What is a custom recordset?
- ❑ The `Fields` collection
- ❑ Adding, updating and deleting records
- ❑ Making persistent records – saving them to disk
- ❑ Creating custom objects (a shopping cart example)
- ❑ Ad hoc reporting

What is a Custom Recordset?

Maybe the question on your lips is "What does he mean by a 'custom recordset'?" – after all, don't we create custom recordsets every single day of our working lives? Every time we access a database with a different SQL statement isn't *that* a custom recordset? Yes, every time you request data from the database you are creating a custom recordset from the database! So what's so new about what I'm saying?

I'll try to answer that question with another question. Have you ever wanted to create a recordset *without* the use of a database? With a custom disconnected recordset, you can define the fields and their types on the fly, and then populate the fields as if they were actually recordsets. Naturally, because it *is* a recordset it can do all the things that any other recordset can do – such as adding, updating, deleting and sorting data.

If that hasn't got you excited, maybe this will. Until I started using custom recordsets, all my temporary data was held either in an array or in a collection. Now I have nothing against holding data in either. The headaches begin however, when the time comes to sort this data. There's a plethora of array-sorting algorithms out there, and each one becomes significant when the size of your array changes. And you can basically forget about trying to sort a collection; besides, I think I've found collections are better at holding objects rather than individual data elements (although I'm sure there are people out there that will disagree with me).

As we go through this chapter, keep in mind that working with a custom recordset (once it has been created) will be no different than working with any other kind of recordset. Use this chapter as a guide to understanding how a custom recordset can be used in your own application.

Creating a Custom Recordset

Creating a custom recordset is actually quite simple. In this section we'll walk through the elementary steps involved in creating a recordset and customizing it to our needs. You'll have seen some of the methods we use here, in other parts of the book – they're included here for completeness here but in less detail, and I'll direct you to other chapters for the detail instead of going over it again.

The first and most basic thing we need to do is create a `Recordset` object. We've seen the code for creating a recordset before:

```
Dim objRS                           ' The ADO Recordset that will store our data
set objRS = Server.CreateObject("ADODB.Recordset")   ' Create the ADO Objects
```

The first thing you may notice is that we haven't talked about the `Connection` object (or even a connection string). The reason we haven't discussed connections is that we won't be using one. We are going to create recordsets based on what we (the programmer) or someone else (the user) defines. We only want to create the `Recordset` object.

> *Later in this chapter, we'll look at how to make our recordsets persistent by using the `Save` method.*

Appending Fields and Adding Data

When you create your `Recordset` object, its `Fields` collection will be empty. So the next step is to append one or more fields to the recordset – by adding `Field` objects to the `Fields` collection. By appending a field we are simply defining a new column, in which values will be held – i.e. we're not adding any records (rows) or any data yet. If you are accustomed to creating tables within a database, you'll know that it works the same way when you create a table. You define one or more field names (column names), the data type that each field will store, and maybe the size and/or whether the value should be unique. When using the `Append` method of the `Fields` collection, the same set of rules apply.

Here's an example. If we need an integer field called `ID` in our application, here's how we can add the field to our custom recordset:

```
objRS.Fields.Append "ID", adInteger
```

We can use lines like this one to build a recordset object that contains all the fields we need. Here's the syntax for the `Append` method:

```
objRS.Fields.Append Name, Type, [DefinedSize], [Attrib]
```

Name	Type	Description
Name	String	The name of the new `Field` object
Type	DataTypeEnum	The data type of the new field. The default value is `adEmpty`
DefinedSize	Long	**Optional**. The size, in bytes or characters. The default uses the `adEmpty` type, which evaluates to 0
Attrib	FieldAttribEnum	**Optional**. Specifies the attributes for the new field. The default is `adFldDefault`.

You can find the complete listings of the DataTypeEnum and FieldAttributeEnum types in Appendix G.

Note that `DefinedSize` is not optional when the `Type` argument is set to `adVarChar` (a variable character data type) or other character data types. Remember that the default evaluates to zero, and you cannot have a character field that is of zero length (you receive an error number 3001). If you try doing the same thing manually in MS Access, it sets your field size to 255 without even telling you.

Also, note that `adFldDefault` (the default type for the `Attrib` argument) doesn't seem to exist externally (if you use it from within Visual Basic); however, since you need to declare you constants with ASP you can declare `adFldDefault` as 0. If you try to use this constant (from within Visual Basic without declaring it yourself) you will receive a compile error – "variable not defined".

Adding Data

We use the `AddNew` method to add data to a recordset. For full disclosure on the AddNew method refer back to Chapter 5. However, just to make sure you are not left out in the cold let's walk through an example of using the AddNew method with a custom recordset.

Using the Append and AddNew Methods

Now for the fun stuff! Let's create a custom recordset, add some fields and populate it with data. We'll define the ADO constants we need (we could have included the `adovbs.inc` file instead), and open the `Recordset` object:

```
<%@ Language=VBScript %>
```

```
<% Option Explicit %>
<%
 ' Declare all ADO 2.0 constants to be used
 Const adUseClient = 3  ' Cursor Location Constant
 Const adVarChar = 200  ' Data Type Constant
 Const adInteger = 3    ' Data Type Constant

 ' Declare all variables to be used
 Dim objRS                        ' The ADO Recordset that will store our data
 set objRS = Server.CreateObject("ADODB.Recordset") ' Create the ADO Object
 objRS.CursorLocation = adUseClient       ' Set the Cursor Location to Client
```

We've also set the cursor location to the client (we'll look at how the cursor location works with a custom recordsets shortly). Now we can start to build the custom recordset by appending the fields we need:

```
 ' Append some Fields to the Fields Collection
 objRS.Fields.Append "ID", adInteger
 objRS.Fields.Append "FName", adVarChar, 25
 objRS.Fields.Append "LName", adVarChar, 35
 objRS.Fields.Append "MInit", adVarChar, 1
```

Here we've created an integer field and three character fields, with sizes 25, 35 and 1 respectively. Before we add any data, we need to open the recordset:

```
 ' We must have an open recordset in order to add records
 objRS.Open
```

> Note that *defining* the recordset and *populating* the recordset are two separate tasks. You can only append fields to the recordset when it's closed (not open). Also, you can only add data to the recordset when it's open.

Once the recordset is open we can then add values to each field:

```
 objRS.AddNew               ' Adding by name reference
 objRS.Fields("ID").value = 1       ' Have specified the default properties here
 objRS.Fields("FName").value = "Eric"
 objRS.Fields("LName").value = "Wilson"
 objRS.Fields("MInit").value = "C"
 objRS.Update               ' Update the Recordset

 objRS.AddNew               ' Adding by ordinal position
 objRS(0) = 2               ' (Have used shorthand by omitting the default
 objRS(1) = "Jim"           '                   properties in these lines)
 objRS(2) = "Zimmer"
 objRS(3) = ""
 objRS.Update               ' Update the Recordset
%>
```

First, we call the `Recordset` object's `AddNew` method. Notice that we called `AddNew` without specifying any parameters – this sets the recordset's `EditMode` property to `adAddEdit`. It will remain this way until the `Update` method is executed – which changes the `EditMode` property to `adEditNone`.

In between the `AddNew` and `Update` method calls, we specify the new data to be added. You'll have noticed that there are a couple of differences between the first and second blocks here:

❑ The first block uses the field names to specify in which field the data should be stored, while the second block uses the ordinal positions of the fields (field 0 is `ID`, field 1 is `FName`, etc – it's zero-based)

❑ The first block specifies the `Fields` collection and the `Value` property – but we can omit them (as we have in the second block) because they are the defaults

When referencing the ordinal position of a custom recordset, the ordinal position is dependent on the order in which the field names were appended to the `Fields` collection. It's worth contrasting this with referencing the data fields of a database: in this case the ordinal position is defined either by the order in which the fields are represented in the table, or by the order in which they appear in the SQL statement (depending on the method used to opened the recordset).

Passing Data as an Array

The `AddNew` method has two optional parameters – `FieldList` and `Values`. This gets only slightly complicated since we need to pass the arguments as arrays. Even when passing the arguments we have a couple of choices:

❑ We can create the array first, assign values to the arrays, and then pass them into the `AddNew` method

```
Dim aryFields(3)                    ' Declare the Arrays to be used
Dim aryValues(3)
aryFields(0) = "ID"                 ' Populate the arrays
aryFields(1) = "FName"
aryFields(2) = "LName"
aryFields(3) = "MInit"
aryValues(0) = 3
aryValues(1) = "Erik"
aryValues(2) = "Johnson"
aryValues(3) = "H"
objRS.AddNew aryFields, aryValues   ' Add passing arguments
```

As you can see this adds more code and more complexity to your application. If you pass the values directly into the `AddNew` method like this, oyu don't need to call the `Update` method – `AddNew` method knows that it should complete the operation on its own. In this case, the `EditMode` property is changed internally to `adEditNone`.

❑ Alternatively, we can passing in the arguments be creating the array as we pass the values in:

```
' Add passing arguments in one line
objRS.AddNew Array("ID", "FName", "LName", "MInit"), _
  Array(4, "Christine", "Spiess", "A")
```

This takes the complexity and lengthy code out of the previous example; however, neither of these are as flexible as assigning to the fields directly (using the `AddNew` and `Update` methods in tandem).

Updating A Record

Chances are the data you entered will change throughout the course of the application. Updating a record is fairly straightforward. Issuing an update on a custom recordset works the same is it does for any other type.

Here's an example of updating the 'current' record (i.e. the record pointed to by the cursor) of a custom recordset:

```
objRS("FName") = "Johnny"
objRS("LName") = "Papa"
objRS("MInit") = ""
objRS.Update
```

For a complete listing refer to Chapter 5.

Deleting A Record

Sooner or later we'll probably need to delete one or more of the records we have added. Just like the `AddNew` and `Update` methods, the `Delete` method on a custom recordset is no different than deleting a record from any other type of recordset. Once your cursor is on the record you wish to be deleted simply issue the delete method:

```
objRS.Delete
```

Cursor Location

The Microsoft documentation says that you need to specify a recordset cursor location value of `adUseClient`, changed from a default value of `adUseServer`. I have noticed with my own testing (which equates to forgetting to set the location to `adUseClient`) that this doesn't seem to pose a problem, even if I use the default server-side cursors. This is because the ADO will actually set the `CursorLocation` to `adUseClient` once we open a recordset that we defined using the `Append` method.

However, I have not found this to be a documented feature – so I won't guarantee that your code won't blow up on you with the next release of ADO. Therefore, at this point I would suggest proceeding with caution and take the recommend route – by setting the `CursorLocation` to `adUseClient` (which evaluates to 3).

As an aside, it's worth noting that you can check cursor location when you are developing, by writing it to the screen:

```
Response.Write objRS.CursorLocation & "<BR>"
```

That Data is Persistent! – Saving Data to Disk

There are times that we as programmers might want to make our data persistent *without* the need of a database. The `Recordset` object's `Save` method will allow you to save your recordset to a local binary file – which you can then retrieve later with the `Open` command. There's no need for file parsing – or any extra work for that matter – when dealing with a saved recordset.

This is great when you want to leave your work and return to it at a later date. It's also a useful tool if you have a disconnected recordset which you have updated – and you want to update your changes on the database. Instead of opening up the database connection immediately, you can save your amended recordset to a file and update the database at a time that is convenient to you.

In future versions of ADO, we will be able to save recordsets to different formats such as XML, using the Save *method. For the time being, the only format is the proprietary format of ADO, denoted by* adPersistADTG *(the default).*

An Example

To see how the save method works, let's look at an example. Imagine a sales force application that needs to operate both while connected and disconnected from the network. Members of the sales force save a disconnected recordset to their local hard drive; then they go off on a sales trip (during which they update the disconnected recordset). When they're back online they update the central database with the data from the recordset.

Let's now take a look at how we might make use of the Save method. This next application will open a recordset that is saved to a file (creating it first if it does not exist); then it writes data to the recordset, displays the data, and then closes it. You can even close out your session, turn off your machine, leave for the weekend and when you come back all your data is still there the next time you open the page. It's a great alternative to a database for small amounts of information.

In this example we're going to use On Error Resume Next:

```
<%@ Language=VBScript %>
<% Option Explicit %>
<% On Error Resume Next %>
```

This is the best you can do when handling errors in VBScript. We *will* be getting some errors on this page, but we'll handle them when the time is right. If the On Error Resume Next was omitted, then we'd experience a lot of problems – because errors will occur that can't be handled.

Here are the constants and variables we'll use. We'll also initialize the recordset object, and set a client-side static cursor:

```
<%
' Declare all ADO Constants
   Const adUseClient = 3      ' Client Side Cursors
   Const adOpenStatic = 3     ' Static Cursor
   Const adVarChar = 200      ' Variable Character

   ' Declare all ADO Objects to be Used
   Dim objRS                  ' ADO Recordset Obejct

   Set objRS = Server.CreateObject("ADODB.Recordset")    ' Create the Recordset
   objRS.CursorType = adOpenStatic       ' Specify the cursor location and type
   objRS.CursorLocation = adUseClient
```

Now we reach the first area where we might get an error. We try to assign a saved recordset, by assigning the contents of the file data.dat to objRS. If the file has not been created yet we'll get an error. We check the error number to see if it matches the one we are looking for: 3709. If the error matches it proves that the file doesn't exist – so we clear the error (in this way we don't pick it up later when it didn't actually happen). Then we build a new recordset with the Append method:

```
' Attempt to opend the file
' If the File does not exist an error will be raised
objRS.Open "C:\data.dat"
' If the file does not exist we will get error no 3709
If err.number = 3709 Then
  err.number = 0                                    ' Clear the error number
  objRS.Fields.Append "FName", adVarChar, 25        ' Create the Recordset
  objRS.Fields.Append "LName", adVarChar, 35
  objRS.Fields.Append "EMail", adVarChar, 65
  objRS.Open
End If
```

If error handling is turned off (no `On Error Resume Next`*), you will not receive error
number 3709. Instead you get a generic ADO error. You can find out more about your error
using* `Response.Write Err.Number & " " & Err.Description`*.*

Next we call a method, `AddFormData`, that will add data to the recordset. The function grabs values
from <FORM> fields, and places then in the recordset. We'll look at the function itself in a moment.
Then we sort the recordset by the 'last name' field:

```
Call AddFormData()       ' Call a function to add some data
objRS.Sort = "LName"     ' Sort the Recorset
```

Now we'll try to save the recordset to the file `data.dat`. If the file doesn't exist, then the `Save`
method creates the file. However, if the specified file already exists (from previously entering the
page) then we get an error number 58. In that case we must have opened the file using `objRS.Open`
`"c:\data.dat"`, then all we need to do is issue the save command without the parameter to save
the recordset back to its original file location:

```
' Save the File with the name
' This will create the file if does not exist, or cause an error if it does
objRS.Save "C:\data.dat"
' If the file exist we will get an error no 58
If err.number = 58 Then
  ' If it exist we can just issue the save method
  ' to save it the currently opened path
  objRS.Save
End If
```

Let's sidestep for a moment and find out what happens in the `AddFormData` function. This function
adds the data from the <FORM>:

```
Public Function AddFormData()
  Dim strFName  ' String Variable for First Name
  Dim strLName  ' String Variable for Last Name
  Dim strEMail  ' String Variable for Email

  strFName = Request.Form("txtFName")
  strLName = Request.Form("txtLName")
  strEMail = Request.Form("txtEMail")
```

```
    ' You might want to check for all variable lengths to be greater than zero
    If Len(Trim(strFName)) <> 0 Then
      ' Prepare to add new record
      objRS.AddNew
      objRS("FName") = strFName
      objRS("LName") = strLName
      objRS("EMail") = strEMail
      objRS.Update        ' Commit new record
    End If
  End Function
  %>
```

We're only doing a little checking here, to see if the First Name was entered – you may wish to implement strong requirements. Checking at least one value for an empty string ensures that an empty record does not get entered when the page first loads.

OK, let's get back to the page. The layout of the data is fairly simple HTML, so we won't cover it here. You can see a sample of it in the following screenshot, and the code is available for download from http://webdev.wrox.co.uk/books/1649.

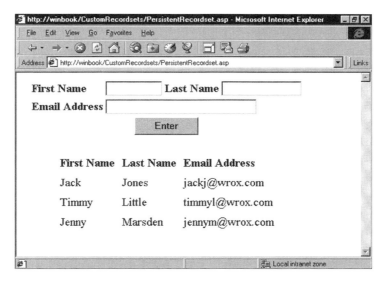

You'll recall that we saved the recordset earlier on, but we did not close it. So the last thing we'll do here is a little clean up – closing the recordset and setting it to `Nothing` (of course, we couldn't close it before we'd displayed the records on the page):

```
<%
  ' Close the Recodset
  objRS.Close
  '-- Set the Recordset object to nothing
  Set objRS = Nothing
%>
```

Implementing Flexible Business Objects

All of this would just be a lot of fluff if we couldn't actually come up with some serious business uses for custom recordsets. In this section were going to talk a little bit about the uses for custom recordsets – even in a compiled business object. For example:

Idea	Short Description
Small sets of data	Replace arrays and collections
Shopping Cart/Order Entry	Hold orders in custom recordset until they've been committed to an order.
Patient Entry/Data Entry	Hold all patient information in custom recordset until administrator commits the entry.

There's a few scenarios in which we might take advantage of custom recordsets – and I'm sure you can come with a whole load more. This gets even more intriguing when we discover how much overhead it will save us. In the remainder of this chapter, we'll focus on a complete example.

A Shopping Cart Application

Let's consider for a moment what goes on in an order entry application such as a web-based shopping cart application:

- ❑ A user comes to a place an order.
- ❑ The user starts placing items in the shopping cart.
- ❑ The user adds items, deletes items or updates quantities.
- ❑ The user commits or aborts the transaction.

With this type of application you have a couple of choices with conventional methods. We could:

- ❑ Use a connection to the database, which remains open for the course of the session – and lock in a transaction that can be committed or aborted when finished.
- ❑ Track various session objects or collections across the session.

The first of these options is easier to track. However, it adds a lot of overhead as far as the database is concerned – what if the user leaves the office, closes the browser, or loses their connection with their ISP, in the middle of the session? My point is this: we often don't know how long the user will be around during a web application. If the user leaves and the database is left supporting a connection that's not being used, it's a waste of resources – we have to wait for the session to time out before we can destroy that connection (if we pass the connection in the session variable).

And if you have a lot of users, then session variables are just as hungry when it comes to eating server resources.

Wouldn't it be great to get the best of both worlds? Keeping the data in a recordset for easy updates to the database – but also having an object that's not connected to the database... It's similar to using a disconnected recordset – except for the fact that no connection is needed until the final update occurs. Why bother the database until it is time to create a permanent record? Sure – for a fully-functioning shopping cart, we will need to get some data from the database first (like the items for sale, prices etc), but the orders themselves won't hit the database until the sale is committed.

The CustomRecordObject

Let's take a look at how we might set up something like this. What we want is an object that we can add, edit, and delete data from a list of values (and of course get the data back out, once it has been added). The object isn't concerned about getting data from the database or storing it to the database (we would use other more specific objects, or use VBScript in our ASP page for that). This object needs the following functions:

Name	Description
CreateFields	This creates a field to store data. This will be a private function, and will be called by the object when it is created (in the initialize event).
AddRecord	This will add a record to the custom recordset. It will also serve as the update. If the value is passed in again, we will update the quantity.
DeleteRecord	This deletes a record using the ID field of the custom recordset.
GetRecords	This retrieves all records.

Creating the CustomRecordObject

Fire up Visual Basic, and create a new ActiveX DLL. Use Project | Properties... to change the name of the project to CustomRecordObject. Now add the class cBasket, which contains these methods (select Project | Add Class Module, and select cBasket.cls from the Existing tab; remove the default class, Class1 too). Also make sure to add a reference to the ADO 2.0 Library (select Project | References.... and then ensure that Microsoft ActiveX Data Objects 2.0 Library is checked). Then compile the DLL by selecting File | Make CustomRecordObject.dll...

Let's have a quick look through the code in cBasket.cls, which defines the CustomRecordObject.

> *We don't cover all the code in the book – but we will walk through the most important parts. The complete code listings (including cBasket.cls) are available as part of the source code download for this book – at http://webdev.wrox.co.uk/books/1649.*

We have only one declaration – the recordset object – which is defined and declared within a single statement:

```
Private objRS As New ADODB.Recordset
```

When the object is created, a special event – Initialize – is automatically fired. We'll look at that shortly. For now, just remember that the Initialize event is executed for you every time a new object is created.

The CreateFields Function

This function is declared as private – because it's only used internally. Its purpose is to create the fields in which we plan to store data. There are four fields defined here: ID, Description, Quantity and Price. The first two are strings of characters, and the third is integer type. The fourth – Price – is type double. This allows for the use of decimals – always handy when storing units of currency.

```
Private Function CreateFields ()
   ' Use the append method to create a Field in the Fields Collection
   objRS.Fields.Append "ID", adVarChar, 20
   objRS.Fields.Append "Description", adVarChar, 100
   objRS.Fields.Append "Quantity", adInteger
   '-- Use type adDouble to allow for decimal values -- e.g. 29.95
   objRS.Fields.Append "Price", adDouble
End Function
```

The AddRecord Function

The AddRecord function accepts all the values we defined in our CreateFields method, and is used to add and edit records. If it finds an existing match for the ID, it will update the Quantity field; otherwise it will add a new record.

First we use the AddNew method to get the Recordset object ready for incoming data. A little error handling is added to this one, (in fact, a production version of this application would contain error handling in all of our methods – but this one specifically needs it). We'll take a closer look at why when we get to the specific lines of code.

We declare a Boolean value that indicates if we have found a matching record – if so then we update the quantity of the existing record, otherwise we add a new record:

```
Public Function AddRecord(strID, strDescription, intQuantity, dblPrice)
   On Error GoTo Err_AddRecord
   Dim booMatchFound As Boolean   '-- Boolean value indicating a found record
   booMatchFound = False          '-- Default booMatchFound to false
   objRS.MoveFirst
```

This is where the error handling comes in. The first time you use the AddRecord method, no records exist in the recordset – so when we try to move to the first record (using MoveFirst) we'll get an error. When the error occurs (i.e. only with the first entry) you can just Resume Next (which is what the error handler does – see the code below).

> Note that we could implement the above by checking for BOF and EOF – but then we'd be checking for that every time we added a new record.

Now we perform a Find. If a match is found, we set the booMatchFound flag to true:

```
objRS.Find ("ID = '" & strID & "'")
If Not objRS.EOF Then
   booMatchFound = True       '-- We found a match
End If
```

Now, we check the booMatchFound flag: if it's true we update the Quantity field, and if it's false we add a new record:

```
      If booMatchFound Then
         '-- If a match was found then the cursor is on the found record
         objRS("Quantity") = intQuantity
         objRS.Update                            '-- Lock in the change
      Else
         '-- No match was found add a new record
         objRS.AddNew
         objRS("ID") = strID
         objRS("Description") = strDescription
         objRS("Quantity") = intQuantity
         objRS("Price") = dblPrice
         objRS.Update                            '-- Lock in the change
      End If
   Exit Function

   Err_AddRecord:
      Debug.Print Err.Number & " " & Err.Description
      If Err.Number = 3021 Then      '-- No records are in the recordset
         Resume Next
      End If
   End Function
```

The DeleteRecord Function

Deleting a record is fairly straightforward. Since we are using the `Find` method to locate the record we want to delete, we need to move to the first record before performing the find. The `Find` will work from the top of the recordset all the way down to the bottom. We place an index on the `ID` field (the field we are searching on), by setting its `Optimize` property to `True` – this is done in the `Class_Initialize` event, which we will cover shortly. The `Find` should be lightening fast!

```
   Public Function DeleteRecord(strID)
      objRS.MoveFirst
      objRS.Find ("ID = '" & strID & "'")
      If Not objRS.EOF Then      '-- We found a record now let's delete it
         objRS.Delete
      End If
   End Function
```

A little error checking is being done. If we hit the `EOF` doing a forward search (the default direction when doing a `Find`), this means that no match was found. In this case, we don't want to attempt to delete a record (we'll get an error message). However if we find a match, `Not objRS.EOF` is true, we can safely perform the deletion.

The GetRecords Function

We definitely want to retrieve our records, and the method to do this is simple. We also want to be polite and return the recordset with the cursor sitting on the first row. However, if no records exist when we issue the `MoveFirst` method, we get an error – that's why we've added the `On Error Resume Next`. We need to pass the object back, even if there are no records, and since we are returning an object we use the `Set` command.

```
   Public Function GetRecords() As Recordset
   On Error Resume Next
      objRS.MoveFirst
      Set GetRecords = objRS
   End Function
```

Initializing the Page – the Class_Initialize Event

Finally, we have the `Class_Initialize` event, which gets fired every time a new object is created (strictly speaking, it's executed when the new object is *referenced* for the first time).

We use this event to set up our object. We call the `CreateFields` method (which defines our fields), then we open the `Recordset` object so it can receive data. We also add an index on the `ID` field (by setting its `Optimize` property to `True`) – as we noted above, we use the `Find` method within the `Delete` method, and `Find` performs faster on an indexed field.

```
Private Sub Class_Initialize()
  Call CreateFields          '-- Create the Fields to hold our data
  objRS.Open                 '-- Open the recordset
  objRS("ID").Properties("Optimize") = True   '-- Create an index on the ID field
End Sub
```

The User Interface

Now we have an object, let's create a web page that will use it to store values like an online shopping cart. With this object, it doesn't matter where we get our products (or items) from. So, for the purposes of this demonstration, we'll get our items from the `Titles` table of the `pubs` database.

We'll implement this page in three frames. It's probably not what the finished product would look like, but it will make it much easier to follow and debug. When you've got the inards ready for a production environment, you can work on having pages instead of frames, with nice graphics and so forth.

To start with we'll have a `default.htm` (or `default.asp`, if you need any processing done). This page will simply define the frame layout:

❑   Frame 1 will contain the products (in this case, the titles from the authors page).
❑   Frame 2 will contain the details once a title is selected.
❑   Frame 3 will contain the orders page, consisting of all the orders made by the user thus far. A user can delete an item or place an order from within Frame 3.

Ultimately, this is what it will look like:

Default.asp

The Default page is about as basic as your going to get. We simply create a frameset with three frames:

```
<FRAMESET rows="100, 100, *" FRAMEBORDER=NO SCROLLING=NO>
  <FRAME src="Titles.asp" name="titles" >
  <FRAME src="TitleDetails.asp" name="details">
  <FRAME src="Orders.asp" name="orders">
</FRAMESET>
```

Titles.asp

We start with the normal process of declaring all of the variables and ADO constants we need; then we instantiate an `ADODB.Connection` object and an `ADODB.Recordset` object (`objConn` and `objRS` respectively). We then define a connection string, `strConn`, that defines a connection to the `pubs` database, and use it to open a connection:

```
strConn = ""
strConn = strConn & "Provider=SQLOLEDB;"
strConn = strConn & "Data Source=winbook;"
strConn = strConn & "Initial Catalog=pubs;"
strConn = strConn & "User Id=sa;"
strConn = strConn & "Password="
objConn.Open strConn              '-- Open the ADO Connection
```

The SQL statement will be retrieving the `Title_ID`, `Title` and `Price` from the `titles` table of the database (there's no sense in doing a `SELECT *` when we know we only need three columns). Now, if you skipped Chapter 8, 'Disconnected Recordsets', the next set of code could look a little strange. In short, we're telling the `Recordset` object to get ready to be disconnected from the connection once we get the recordset back. We do this before opening the connection by setting the cursor location to use client-side cursors and the cursor type to open a static recordset:

```
strSQL = ""
strSQL = strSQL & "SELECT title_id, title, price FROM titles"

objRS.ActiveConnection = strConn   '-- Set the Recordsets Connection
objRS.CursorLocation = adUseClient '-- Set cursor location to client-side
objRS.CursorType = adOpenStatic    '-- Set the cursor type to open static
objRS.Source = strSQL              '-- Set the Source to the SQL statement
objRS.Open                         '-- Open the Recordset
```

After we issue the `Open` command we have all the data we need – so now we want to cut the cord from the database. To do this, set the active connection to the recordset equal to nothing. To save resources we also close the connection:

```
set objRS.ActiveConnection = nothing   '-- Disconnect the Recordset
objConn.Close                          '-- Close the Connection
%>
```

Now we have the recordset, we can begin to build the page. I used some `<STYLE>` tags simply to help with the sizing of the rendering in the browser (I won't go into that issue here; if you're unfamiliar with `<STYLE>` tags, you don't need to use them – the application is functionally the same without them).

We display a form, `frmProducts`, which will be used in some client-side scripting at the bottom of the Titles page. The target screen will be the center frame named `details` (defined in `default.asp`), and the Action (i.e. the page we will be posting to) is `TitleDetails.asp`:

```
<FORM name="frmProducts" action="TitleDetails.asp" method=post target="details">
   <TABLE><TR>
     <TD>Title Name</TD>        <!-- Place a title above the combo box -->
   </TR>
```

We loop through the recordset and display all the titles in a combo box. The `<SELECT>` tag will monitor the onchange event which will occur whenever a new selection is made from the combo box. When that happens, a JavaScript function called `submitForm` will be executed:

```
<% If Not objRS.EOF And Not objRS.BOF Then %>
   <TR><SELECT name="lstTitles" onchange="submitForm();">
   <% Do Until objRS.EOF %>
     <OPTION value="<%=objRS("title_id")%>">
     <%=objRS("title")%>
     </OPTION>
     <%
     objRS.MoveNext        '-- Do not forget to movenext and continue the loop
   Loop%>
   </SELECT>
   </TR>
<% End If %>
</TABLE></FORM>
```

The `submitForm` function simply submits the form, and no other intervention (like hitting a button) is required.

Below is the JavaScript function. We simply navigate through the document object model to the `<FORM>` which we named `frmProducts`. We use the form's `submit` method to submit the form using the Action and Method specified in the `<FORM>` tag:

```
<SCRIPT>
function submitForm(){
  document.frmProducts.submit();
}
</SCRIPT>
```

The purpose of creating a disconnected recordset was to use it in other pages – so that we won't have to bother the database with simple look-ups. With this in mind, we need to save or store the disconnected recordset – by placing a clone of the recordset object in a session variable.

```
<%
  set session("objRSTitles") = objRS.Clone
  objRS.Close
  set objRS = nothing
%>
```

As we saw in Chapter 6, a clone recordset is just a copy of another recordset. I have found that it's worth using a clone to ensure that you capture the complete recordset to disk. For example, by performing a MoveNext on objRS, and then saving the recordset into the session variable, I've found that the recordset contains only *the records between the 'current' record and the EOF.*

TitlesDetail.asp

Next we'll look at the creation of the `TitleDetails.asp` page (the middle frame of our screen). While the top frame, `Titles.asp`, simply allows us to select a book title, the middle frame will display more information about our selection – in this case just the price. (We could extend it to show the author's name, ISDN etc – of course, we'd need to add `Append` fields to our custom recordset but in principal it's not a difficult exercise.)

We begin by declaring and instantiating a recordset object. Then we find out whether our session-level `Recordset` object exists (it should have been created in the `Titles.asp` page). If so, we simply pull it out of the session and use it; if not, we tell the user to refresh the `Titles.asp` page which will re-create the object:

```
Dim objRS                        '-- The ADO Recordset that stores the data
Set objRS = Server.CreateObject("ADODB.Recordset") '-- Create the ADO object
If isObject(Session("objRSTitles")) Then
  Set objRS = Session("objRSTitles")
Else
  Response.Write "You need to Refresh the Titles Frame"
  Response.End
End if
```

Now we want to know which book title was selected from the combo/list box. First a little checking to see if we have any records in the recordset brought in from the session. If so, we then check to make sure a value was passed from the `frmProducts` form, by checking the length of the value from the `lstTitles`. If a value is found, we execute a `Find`:

```
If not objRS.EOF and not objRS.BOF Then
   if len(trim(Request.Form("lstTitles")))<>0 then
     objRS.MoveFirst
     objRS.Find "title_id = '" & Request.Form("lstTitles") & "'"
   end if
End if
%>
```

Now we'll start building the page layout. The `frmDetails` form will be posted to `orders.asp` (the lower frame) and it will target the `orders.asp` frame named `orders` (defined in `default.asp`):

Title ID	Title	Price	Quantity	
PC9999	Net Etiquette		3	Add to Basket

```
<FORM name="frmDetails" method=post action="orders.asp" target="orders">
  <TABLE cellspacing=3>
    <TR>
      <TD>Title ID</TD><TD>Title</TD><TD>Price</TD><TD>Quantity</TD>
    </TR>
    <TR>
```

We check that we have a record, before trying to display it. Display the values, we also want to place them in `<input>` tags of type `hidden`. Placing them in these tags will allow their values to be posted when the form is submitted. We use hidden tags to make sure that the values being sent weren't edited.

```
<% If Not objRS.EOF and Not objRS.BOF then %>
  <TD><%=objRS("title_ID")%>
  <INPUT type=hidden name="txtTitle_id" value="<%=objRS("title_ID")%>">
  </TD>
  <TD><%=objRS("title")%>
  <input type=hidden name="txtTitle" value="<%=objRS("title")%>"></TD>
  <TD><%=objRS("Price")%>
  <INPUT type=hidden name="txtPrice" value="<%=objRS("price")%>"></TD>
  <TD><input type=textbox name="txtQuantity" size=3></TD>
  <TD><input type=submit value="Add to Basket"></TD>
<% End If %>
</TR>
```

In a production environment, you might want to implement security measures to ensure that an imposter can't fake a POST request.

Since the `orders` page will process information posted from this page (`TitleDetails.asp`) and from itself (`Order.asp`), we add a hidden tag named `frmName` (for Form Name) that tells `Orders.asp` which form we are coming from. This will help us decide what course of action to take on the `Orders.asp` page:

```
<TR>
  <TD><input type=hidden name="frmName" value="details"></TD>
</TR>
</TABLE>
</FORM>
```

Orders.asp

The final page in this example is `orders.asp`. This page processes the information entered and uses the custom recordset object that we built earlier. This page can add items to the custom object, delete items, and display all items in the order. We'll use a stub (i.e. a function with no actual processing) called `PlaceOrder`, which will allow us to add our own routine to save the order to a database. We'll also use a shopping basket object called `objBasket` – an instance of the `cBasket` class.

We start off with the usual declarations. Then we instantiate a recordset object:

```
set objRS = Server.CreateObject("ADODB.Recordset")
```

First we'll deal with the **Add to Basket** button from the `details` page, which sends data to `Orders.asp`. When we first come into `Orders.asp`, the shopping basket object will not exist, so we'll create one. Each subsequent visit to `Orders.asp` (after the first) will use the one created. The shopping basket object will contain all the items for our order:

```
If isObject(Session("objBasket")) Then  '-- Check to see if one already exists
  Set objBasket = session("objBasket")  '-- Use the Object from the Session
Else
  '-- Create one if we can't find it
  Set objBasket = Server.CreateObject("CustomRecordObject.cBasket")
End If
```

We need to check which page we just came from. The `TitleDetails.asp` page has a hidden tag named `frmName` with a value of `details`, and the `Orders.asp` page has the same hidden tag with a value of `orders`.

```
strPage = Request.Form("frmName")
```

If we are coming to `Orders.asp` from `TitleDetails.asp` then we will add a record using a function named `AddRecord`. If we are coming from `Orders.asp` then we have a couple of choices on which action to take. Depending on which button is selected, we either delete (one or many) record(s), or we place the order. A hidden tag name `hdnTag` will contain the value `delete` or `order`, depending on which button was pressed. If the **Delete** button was pressed, we call the `Delete` function; if the **Order** button was pressed then we will call the `PlaceOrder` function:

```
SELECT Case strPage
  Case "details"
    Call AddRecord()
  Case "orders"
    If Request.Form("hdnTag") = "delete" Then
      Call DeleteOrder()
    ElseIf Request.Form("hdnTag") = "order" Then
      Call PlaceOrder()
    End If
End SELECT
```

Finally (and before we look at the `AddRecord`, `DeleteOrder` and `PlaceOrder` functions), we retrieve all the items in our shopping basket that we will then display on the page.

```
set objRS = objBasket.GetRecords        '-- Get the Records from the Object
```

The functions

The `AddRecord` function adds a record to our shopping basket. This function pulls each value from the form collection. We also add a little error checking on the value of the `Price` field (some of the titles in the `pubs` database don't have a price – if we come across a title with no price then we assume a default price of $29.95). Then we add the item to the object changing the data type (using `CInt()`, or `CDbl()` if necessary) to match the type defined by the custom recordset:

```
Public Function AddRecord()
  <declarations...>
  strID = Request.Form("txttitle_id")
  strDescr = Request.Form("txttitle")
  intQuantity = Request.Form("txtQuantity")
  dblPrice = Request.Form("txtPrice")
  If trim(dblPrice) = "" then        '-- Books title has no price
    dblPrice = "29.95"               '-- use a default price
  End if
  objBasket.AddRecord strID, strDescr, CInt(intQuantity), CDbl(dblPrice)
End Function
```

The `DeleteOrder` function deletes one or many items, depending on how many checkboxes were selected. The function itself is actually pretty slick. We loop through the `Forms` collection and find any items with a value of `on` (this is the value of a checkbox when it is checked). If we find one, then we simply call the `DeleteRecord` method of our `objBasket` object, passing in the variable item (the value of the checkbox, which contains the `title_id`):

```
Public Function DeleteOrder()
  Dim item
  for each item in Request.Form
    if Request.Form(item) = "on" then
      objBasket.DeleteRecord item
    end if
  next
End Function
```

This is quite hard to visualize; to see what's happening I would suggest adding the following line inside of the `for` loop to see the values being passed:

```
Response.Write item & " = " & Request.Form(item).
```

`PlaceOrder` is the stub that I was talking about earlier. It has code in it that really doesn't do anything in particular right now. Here you would need a table in your database that accepted orders. You should also set all the session objects you are using to equal nothing if the order was confirmed.

```
Public Function PlaceOrder()
  '-- Place your code here to place an order. At this point you would
  '-- hit the database and clear all objects from the session
  Response.Write "<CENTER>"
  Response.Write "<B>Thank you for Placing your order."
  Response.End
End Function
%>
```

The form

Now for creating the layout for `Orders.asp`. We'll just look at the key points of this.

```
<FORM name="frmOrders" action="Orders.asp" method=post>
  <TABLE cellspacing=0 >
```

First we check to see if we have any records to add (if we don't have any records then we shouldn't show any column names – we'll come to that in a moment):

```
<% if not objRS.EOF and not objRS.BOF then %>
  <TR>
    <TD><B>Delete Item</TD><TD></TD><TD></TD><TD><B>Description</TD>
    <TD></TD><TD><B>Quantity</TD><TD></TD><TD><B>Unit Price</TD>
    <TD></TD><TD><B>Price</TD>
  </TR>
```

Here we create a Boolean variable, `booColor`, which will alternate values allowing us to alternate the background color of the table rows. Then we start to loop through the recordset:

```
<%Dim booColor          '-- Boolean value to help track color
  booColor = true
  Do Until objRS.EOF    '-- Let's loop through the recordset
    If booColor then %> '-- Decide on the background color
      <TR bgcolor="#336699">
    <% else %>
```

```
      <TR bgcolor="#eeeecc">
  <% end if %>
    <TD><input type=checkbox name="<%=objRS("ID")%>"></TD>
    <TD>   </TD>
    <TD><input type=hidden name="ID" value="<%=objRS("ID")%>"></TD>
    <TD><%=objRS("Description")%></TD>
    <TD>    </TD>
    <TD><%=objRS("Quantity")%></TD>
    <TD>    </TD>
    <TD><%=FormatCurrency(objRS("Price"))%></TD>
    <TD>   </TD>
    <TD><%=FormatCurrency((objRS("Quantity") * objRS("Price")))%></TD>
  </TR>
```

Note that the name field for the checkbox (the first column of the table, above) will hold the
title_id. When the **Delete** button is pressed, we will query the Request.Form collection for a
value of on. If one is found, we get the associated name – which holds the title_id. Then, we
simply need to issue the delete method, passing in the title_id.

Shopping Basket				
Delete Item	Description	Quantity	Unit Price	Price
☐	The Gourmet Microwave	5	$2.99	$14.95
☐	Net Etiquette	7	$29.95	$209.65
☐	Sushi, Anyone?	10	$14.99	$149.90
☐	But Is It User Friendly?	15	$22.95	$344.25
Delete				Order

Now we need to change the value of booColor:

```
    <% booColor = not booColor
    objRS.MoveNext   'Move to the next record
Loop%>
```

Now we create the two buttons – **Delete** and **Order**. When clicked, each button executes a JavaScript
function called submitME, passing in different values which will change the value of the hdnTag.
(You'll recall that hdnTag is used inside of the SELECT CASE statement to determine the course of
action to take when coming from the Orders.asp page.)

```
    <TR>
      <TD colspan=4 align=left><input type=button value=" Delete "
        onclick="submitME(0)" id=button1 name=button1></TD>
      <TD colspan=4 align=right><input type=button value="  Order  "
        onclick="submitME(1)" id=button2 name=button2></TD>
    </TR>
    <INPUT type=hidden name="hdnTag" value="">
    <INPUT type=hidden name="frmName" value="Orders">
```

So that's what we do if there are records found. If there are no records found, we display a message announcing that the shopping cart is empty:

```
<% else %>
  <TR><TD> You have no items in your shopping cart</TD></TR>
<% end if %>
</TABLE>
</FORM>
```

This message will be displayed the first time you enter the application; it will also be displayed if and when the user deletes all the items in the shopping basket.

The submitME function

The JavaScript function submitME changes the value of the hdnTag based on the value of the incoming parameter:

```
<SCRIPT>
<!--
function submitME(value){
  switch(value){
    case(0):        //The delete button was pressed
      document.frmOrders.hdnTag.value = "delete";  //set the hdnTag to delete
    break;
    case(1):        //The order button was pressed
      document.frmOrders.hdnTag.value = "order";  //set the hdnTag to order
    break;
  }
  document.frmOrders.submit();      //submit the form
}
//-->
</SCRIPT>
```

The final order of business is to put the objBasket object into the session. The first entrance into this page will create the session variable; after that we will replace the existing basket with the one used in the page. We also want to destroy any other objects created, like the local copy of the titles. We don't need to store the local copy of the titles recordset. We never changed any of the values, and it will stay in the session until we destroy it, or the session times out:

```
<%
  Set  session("objBasket") = objBasket
  Set objRS = nothing
%>
```

Phew! We've been through quite a bit of code to complete the shopping cart application. But as you can see, ADO can be used quite extensively and effectively in e-commerce solutions on the Web. We'll look at another solution in the following section when we delve into AdHoc reporting with ADO.

Creating a Flexible Ad hoc Report

Creating flexible reporting simply translates into finding a way to get some data back to the user, to allow them to view the information the way *they* want to see it. As all developers know, no two users want to see the same data in exactly the same way.

In this section, we will continue with the shopping basket example from the previous section. We're going to allow the user to sort by the title (description), price or quantity. We'll do all this by adding code to the `Orders.asp` page only. The finished product will look like:.

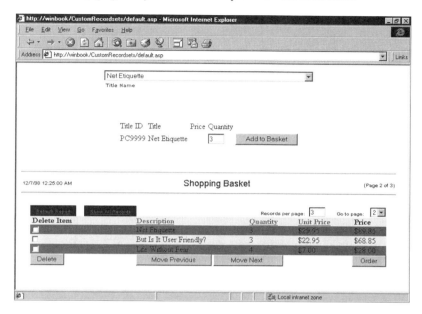

For the most part we will only show the code you need to add. However, in some instances that might make it confusing. So, in places where the new and old code are well intermixed, we will display it all. There's a hefty list of new variables – I'll list their declarations here so you know what they are:

```
dim intCurrentPage    '--- The current page.
dim intPageSize       '--- The amount of pages.
dim intRow            '--- A loop counter variable.
dim intCol            '--- A loop counter variable.
dim intPos            '--- Position of a square bracket within a string.
dim intDisplayRows    '--- Display this many rows on a page.
dim strSort           '--- The column to sort by.
dim strSortDir        '--- The direction of the sort.
dim strLastSort       '--- The column we sorted by last time.
dim strLastSortDir    '--- The direction of the sort we used last time.
```

Sorting

We'll add sorting capabilities, which will allow the user to view the report in ascending or descending order on the fields we specify. We will track which direction was last used and then reverse the direction. We even allow for the user to specify table names with spaces in the name.

```
If Trim(Request("SortBy")) <> "" and Trim(Request("Resort")) <> "" Then
    '--- Retrieve the field the user chose to sort by.
    strSort = Request("SortBy")
    '--- Get the field (and direction) we used to sort the recordset the last time.
    '--- The column name is enclosed within brackets, in case it has multiple words.
    intPos = Instr(2, objRS.Sort, "]")
    If intPos > 0 Then
```

```
      strLastSort = Left(objRS.Sort, intPos)
      strLastSortDir = Trim(Mid(objRS.Sort, intPos + 2))
   End If
   '--- Check if the sorting field has changed.
   If Trim(strSort) <> Trim(strLastSort) then
      '--- The sorting field has changed, so we will sort in ascending order.
      strSortDir = "asc"
   Else
      '--- The sorting field is the same.
      '--- Determine which sort direction we used last time (so we can switch it)
      If strLastSortDir = "asc" Then
         strSortDir = "desc"
      Else
         strSortDir = "asc"
      End If
   End If
   objRS.Sort = strSort & " " & strSortDir
End If
```

Paging

This section will control how many records we view per page. We set the default to 10. If the user
specifies a new size then the new value will be used instead.

```
intPageSize = 10                            '--- Set the default page size
'--- Determine if the user entered a page size.
If Trim(request("txtPageSize")) <> "" then
   intPageSize = request("txtPageSize")   '--- Set pagesize to user's choice
End If
```

We check to see if we need to show all the records or by page.

```
If Trim(Request("lstPages")) <> "" and Trim(Request("AllRecs")) = "" then
   '--- Set the current page to what the user chose.
   intCurrentPage = Request("lstPages")
Else
   '--- Since we are showing all records, set the current page to the first page
   intCurrentPage = 1
End If
```

Now we make sure we have records and set the page size, it is also important that we do some error
checking to make sure the current page does not exceed the page count:

```
If Not (objRS.BOF and objRS.EOF) Then   '--- As long as there are records...
   objRS.PageSize = intPageSize           '--- Set the page size
   '--- If the page we were on is no longer valid,
   '--- set the current page to the last page available.
   If CInt(intCurrentPage) > CInt(objRS.PageCount) Then
      intCurrentPage = objRS.PageCount
   End If
   objRS.AbsolutePage = intCurrentPage
End If
```

Displaying

Next we start laying out the page. This section would be hard to explain without showing the page in its entirety. This is where you will find plenty of new code intermixed with code form the original page. This should hopefully make the transition smoother.

The Title

The first section adds a little to the report by indicating the time using the VBScript `Now()` function, and by giving the page a title. We also tell the user how many pages are contained in the report, and which page we're looking at – to do this we refer to the `intCurrentPage` variable and the `objRS.PageCount` property:

```
<body bgcolor="#ffffff" link="#336699" alink="#336699" vlink="#336699">
<HR>
<TABLE border="0" width="100%">
  <TR>
    <TD align="left">
      <font face="helvetica,verdana,arial" size="1" color="#000080">
      <B><%=Now()%></B></FONT>
    </TD>
    <TD align="center">
      <FONT face="helvetica,verdana,arial" size="4" color="#000080">
      Shopping Basket</FONT>
    </TD>
    <TD align="right">
      <%If Not (objRS.BOF and objRS.EOF) Then%>
             
        <font face="helvetica,verdana,arial" size="1" color="#000060">
        <B>(Page <%=intCurrentPage%> of <%=objRS.PageCount%>)</B>
        </FONT>
      <%End If%>
    </TD>
  </TR>
</TABLE>
<HR>
```

Refresh and ShowAllRecords

The next section sets up two links – one that refreshes the report and one that shows all the records. When clicked, the links **Refresh Report** and **Show All Records** will execute JavaScript functions called `Refresh` and `ShowAllRecs` respectively. We will see both of these functions in a few moments:

```
<% if not (objRS.EOF and objRS.BOF) then %>
<form name="frmOrders" action="Orders.asp" method=post>
<table cellspacing="0" cellpadding="0" border="0" width="95%">
  <TR>
    <!-- Display the menu options. -->
    <TD align="center" bgcolor="#000060" nowrap>
        <font face="helvetica,verdana,arial" size="1" color="#99cccc">
      <a href="javascript:Refresh()">Refresh Report</a></font>  
    </TD>
```

```
<TD nowrap>   </TD>
<TD align="center" bgcolor="#000060" nowrap>
    <FONT face="helvetica,verdana,arial" size="1" color="#99cccc">
  <A href="javascript:ShowAllRecs()">Show All Records</A></FONT>  
</TD>
```

Implementing the Paging Options

We allow the users to indicate how many records they want to see per page. Since we know we are going to have multiple pages, it would be nice to be able to get to any one, page at any given time. This is done with a combo box. When the user selects a new page number, the onchange event is fired (executed) calling the Refresh() function written in JavaScript:

```
<TD align="right" valign="top" width="100%" nowrap colspan=10>
  <%If Not (objRS.BOF and objRS.EOF) Then%>
    <FONT face="helvetica,verdana,arial" size="1" color="#000060">
    <B>Records per page:</B></FONT>
     <INPUT type="text" size="3" name="txtPageSize"
    value="<%=intPageSize%>">
    <FONT face="helvetica,verdana,arial" size="1" color="#000060">
         
    <%If objRS.PageCount > 1 Then%>
      <B>Go to page:</B></FONT> 
      <SELECT size="1" name="lstPages" onChange="Refresh();">
        <%For intRow=1 To objRS.PageCount%>
          <%If CInt(intCurrentPage) = CInt(intRow) Then%>
            <option selected value="<%=intRow%>"><%=intRow%>
          <%Else%>
            <option value="<%=intRow%>"><%=intRow%>
          <%End If%>
        <%Next%>
      </SELECT>
    <%End If%>
  <%Else%>
    <INPUT type="hidden" name="txtPageSize" value="<%=intPageSize%>">
  <%End If%>
</TD>
</TR>
```

Implementing the Sort Facility

We need a ReSort function that receives the name of a field, and sorts the table by that field. Using the brackets [ ] will allow us to send in a field name that contained spaces (although we don't actually do that here).

```
    <TR>
      <TD  bgcolor="#eeeecc"> <B>Delete Item</TD>
      <TD  bgcolor="#eeeecc"> </TD><TD  bgcolor="#eeeecc"> </TD>
      <TD bgcolor="#eeeecc">
        <A HREF="javascript:ReSort('[Description]')" ><B>Description
      </TD>
      <TD  bgcolor="#eeeecc"> </TD>
      <TD bgcolor="#eeeecc">
        <A HREF="javascript:ReSort('[Quantity]')" ><B>Quantity</TD>
      <TD  bgcolor="#eeeecc"> </TD>
      <TD bgcolor="#eeeecc">
        <A HREF="javascript:ReSort('[Price]')" ><b>Unit Price</TD>
      <TD  bgcolor="#eeeecc"> </TD><TD  bgcolor="#eeeecc"><B>Price</TD>
    </TR>
    <%Dim booColor            '-- Boolean value to help track color
      booColor = true
```

It's generally not a good idea to specify field names that contain spaces – however, in this case it offers a distinct advantage. The adhoc reporting page we are discussing allows for us to dynamically render fields in a report. To accomplish this task, the ASP and ADO code uses the name of each field for the column heading. So if we wanted to have 'prettier' column headings, we could alias our fields using SQL like this:

```
SELECT au_fname AS 'First Name', au_lname AS 'Last Name' FROM pubs
```

Again, I suggest that you carefully weigh your options before using this aliasing technique.

We create the value for `intDisplayRows` (the number of rows to be displayed on a single page) using the `AbsolutePosition` and `PageSize` properties of the recordset object. We then loop through the recordset until we've displayed that many records – no more – or we hit the EOF:

```
      intDisplayRows = objRS.AbsolutePosition + objRS.PageSize - 1
      For intRow = objRS.AbsolutePosition to intDisplayRows
        If booColor then %>  '-- Decide on the background color
          <TR bgcolor="#336699">
        <% else %>
          <TR bgcolor="#eeeecc">
        <% end if %>
          <TD><INPUT type=checkbox name="<%=objRS("ID")%>"></TD>
          <TD>    </TD>
          <TD><INPUT type=hidden name="ID" value="<%=objRS("ID")%>"></TD>
          <TD><%=objRS("Description")%></TD>
          <TD>    </TD>
          <TD><%=objRS("Quantity")%></TD>
          <TD>    </TD>
          <TD><%=FormatCurrency(objRS("Price"))%></TD>
          <TD>    </TD>
          <TD><%=FormatCurrency((objRS("Quantity") * objRS("Price")))%></TD>
        </TR>
        <% booColor = not booColor
        objRS.MoveNext  'Move to the next record
        if objRS.EOF then exit for  '-- If we are at the end exit the for loop
        'Continue with the loop
      Next%>
```

For navigation we display a **Move Previous** button – provided `intCurrentPage` is greater than 1 (if it is equal to 1 then there is no previous page). When this button is selected we pass the selected index of the combo box (holding the current page number) minus one to the `MovePage` function.

More Paging Options – Implementing MoveNext and MovePrevious

We also display a Move Next button (unless we're on the last page – i.e. `intCurrentPage` is not equal to `PageCount`. Clicking the Move Next button passes the selected index of the combo box (holding the current page number) plus 1:

```
<TR>
    <TD colspan=3 align=left><input type=button value=" Delete "
        onclick="submitME(0)" id=button1 name=button1></TD>
    <TD colspan=4>
      If (intCurrentPage > 1)  Then%>
        <input type=button value="  Move Previous   "
        onclick="MoveToPage(document.frmOrders.lstPages.selectedIndex - 1)">
      <%End If%>
      If CInt(intCurrentPage) < CInt(objRS.PageCount) Then%>
        <INPUT type=button value="      Move Next         "
        onclick="MoveToPage(document.frmOrders.lstPages.selectedIndex + 1)">
      <%End If%>
    </TD>
    <TD colspan=4 align=right><input type=button value="  Order   "
        onclick="submitME(1)" id=button2 name=button2></TD>
</TR>
<INPUT type=hidden name="hdnTag" value="">
<INPUT type=hidden name="frmName" value="Orders">
```

We use hidden values to keep track of the `SortBy`. `ReSort` and `AllRecs` do not need value holders since they are only used to execute a function. We are only passing a value of `yes`, in essence saying "execute this function on the server" (in fact, any value other than a zero length string will do the job):

```
    <!-- column to sort by -->
    <INPUT type="hidden" name="SortBy" value="<%Response.Write(strSort)%>">
    <!-- should the columns be resorted -->
    <INPUT type="hidden" name="ReSort">
    <!-- should all of the records be displayed on one page -->
    <input type="hidden" name="AllRecs">
  <% else %>
    <TR><TD> You have no items in your shopping cart</TD></TR>
  <% end if %>
</TABLE>
</FORM>
```

The Functions

The `Refresh` function simply resubmits the page's form, causing it to be redisplay itself. All the values are still the same – the page simply re-executes itself:

```
function Refresh()    // Refresh the recordset by submitting the form.
{
  document.frmOrders.submit();
}
```

The `MoveToPage` function receives a page number that we want to navigate to. Then through JavaScript code we set the combo box's selected index to the value being passed in. Then by invoking the Refresh button, we refresh (or resubmit the page). The new value from the combo box (along with any other values) is sent to the server causing the next page to be shown.

```
function MoveToPage(PageNumber)   // Select the page number, then submit the page
{
   if (PageNumber != -1)
      {document.frmOrders.lstPages[PageNumber].selected = true;}
   else
      {document.frmOrders.lstPages[0].selected = true;}
   Refresh();
}
```

`ShowAllRecs` simply passes the value of `RecordCount` to the `txtPageSize` text box and places a value of `yes` in the `AllRecs` hidden field. On the server-side script, if `AllRecs` has any value then the current page is set to the first page. This will ensure that we in fact see all the records.

```
function ShowAllRecs() //Show all records on 1 page, then submit the page
{
   document.frmOrders.txtPageSize.value = <%=objRS.RecordCount%>;
   document.frmOrders.AllRecs.value = "yes"
   Refresh();
}
```

The `ReSort` function receives the `SortString` and places it in the hidden `SortBy` hidden field. Then it changes the value of `ReSort` to `yes` and calls the `Refresh` function.

```
function ReSort(SortString)       //Sort the recordset, then submit the page
{
   document.frmOrders.SortBy.value = SortString;
   document.frmOrders.ReSort.value = "yes";
   Refresh();
}
```

Food for Thought...

Think about a real-world application that processes a request from the user and performs a comparison with the database. For instance, back on that American Express Gift check tracking system. A manager will receive large batches of checks to assign (or to hand out to their minions, for *them* to assign!) for recognition purposes.

One of our requirements is that the system will allow a manager to assign checks to another manager. This information needs to be tracked. For audit purposes, at any given time we need to know exactly how many gift checks each manager has.

The checks have sequential serial numbers that are entered into the database. A manager can select a check he wants to reassign via an option box – for large trades, he can fill in a range. Now: what happens if, somewhere in that range, there's a check that the manager does not own? Instead of kicking out the entire batch, we should track which checks that the system says he doesn't own, and we should then notify the manager that those checks weren't reassigned – because they weren't his to assign.

To do this, we could create an array and ReDim it each time we wanted to add a new value to it; alternatively, we can create a custom recordset and add a new record for any match not found. When the code for the reassignment is complete, we simply examine the recordset to see if any records were added – and if so we act accordingly.

We can write a customizable report that allows the manager to review the data in different ways. He could sort by denomination or by serial number. He could sort by matches, if you indicate a field that contains 'yes' for a match and 'no' for a no-match.

Once you start thinking about it, you'll find yourself being able to accomplish many tasks much quicker than before. Perhaps you'll even implement ideas that were once thought as too complex, simply because now it's within your reach!

Summary

We covered a lot in this chapter. We've seen that, in essence, you can just think of a custom recordset simply as a database without a connection. Disconnected recordsets function in just much the same way as a regular recordset – in that they allow for inserts, updates, deletes, sorts, finds, filters, indexing and so on.

Custom recordsets can be a great asset to your coding needs. You'll no longer need to use arrays to store your temporary data. No more ReDim-ing, and no more headaches when you need to sort or search your data, or when you need to retrieve the data from complex multidimensional arrays. Speaking of this, if you've read Chapter 7, 'Data Shaping', I'll let you in on a little secret: you can create data shapes of hierarchical recordsets using custom recordsets! Think about the possibilities of that one for a moment; especially when it comes to flexible reporting!

10

Meet RDS

Remote Data Services (RDS) is a powerful technology from Microsoft that adds a new type of arrow to our application development quiver. We can use RDS to retrieve recordsets from remote databases and manipulate these databases in client-side script – in a way that also succeeds in reducing network traffic (compared to other methods) and gives us a great set of functionality.

In this chapter we will discuss ways that RDS can benefit your applications and we will begin the discussion of how to bring RDS into your applications. RDS consists of a set of objects: we'll be looking at the `DataControl`, `DataFactory` and `DataSpace` objects of the RDS object model. We will cover the following topics:

- ❑ An introduction to RDS – what can RDS do for me?
- ❑ The structure of RDS
- ❑ Business Object Proxies
- ❑ RDS objects and their properties and methods

In subsequent chapters we will continue the discussion and show more advanced techniques. We'll introduce several techniques that you can use to build distributed applications that run across Internet-type networks – such as Intranets, Extranets and traditional local area networks (LANs). These distributed applications will have the ability to retrieve information from virtually any type of data store, from virtually anywhere in the world. In addition, they will run in Microsoft's Internet Explorer web browser and can do so in an inviting, interactive manner and with exceptional speed.

Using RDS – an Introduction

So, this chapter is essentially an overview of RDS and how it can help you build high-performance data-aware application. By 'data-aware application', I mean an application that can retrieve and/or modify data in a data store. The data store could take many forms, but for this chapter we will assume that it is a traditional RDBMS.

We'll also look at the RDS objects – so that by the end of the chapter you'll know enough to be able to work effectively with them in your applications. In subsequent chapters I'll show you specific techniques that you can use to build an ADO and RDS application that, when finished, can be used as a springboard into your own projects. But before you find out how to implement RDS, you should know why you might want to, and what RDS can do for you.

Why Use RDS? An Example

Let's consider an example that will give us a feel for the power of RDS. Suppose that you must write a web application that will allow users to retrieve and display information about cars. A typical user might be a potential car-buyer, using browsing information in their purchase decisions. This web application should allow the user to select from a list of automobile makers – BMW, Nissan, Ford etc. They might then choose a specific model about which they want information.

Alternatively, the application should be able to group vehicles by price range, by type of vehicle, by horsepower, or by a number of other attributes. In addition, it should have a feature that allows customers to compare an attribute – e.g. estimated fuel economy – from several cars, perhaps by multiple manufacturers, in an appropriate visual form like a bar chart. Obviously, an application like this would need to manage a tremendous amount of information. There are plenty of car manufacturers out there, even more models of cars, and lots of attributes to consider before we buy one of them.

On the web, this type of application might involve a series of listboxes – each one narrowing the user's selection and each one initiating a round trip to the server. Using a very fast Internet connection, each round trip might take about three seconds to complete. Functionally, this design works fine, and in fact, the vast majority of web applications that are currently in use today provide this type of functionality and employ this method for bringing data back to the user.

However, there may be a better choice. We could use RDS to build this application – because it would dramatically increase the performance of the application. For example, if our customer selects Audi cars, he should be able to immediately see every single Audi model – without waiting for a page to reload with new information. We can achieve this with RDS – while using ASP or CGI script alone would require that the browser request new data, wait for a response from the server, receive the new data and then reload the page. RDS can help eliminate the pause that occurs each time the web browser displays different information. Using RDS, the speed of web applications approaches that of more traditional desktop applications

The following two screenshots demonstrate this difference. Without RDS, viewing data in multiple ways usually means many trips to and from the server:

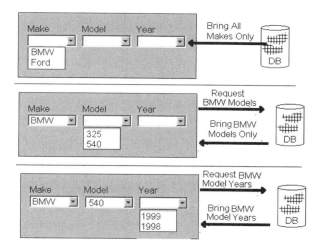

However, using RDS, an entire set of data can be returned to the client. This enables client code to filter and manage the recordset without the server:

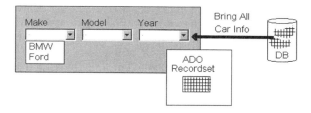

RDS Eases the Network Burden

Using RDS, we can create applications that can receive an entire recordset from a remote database and manipulate this database in client-side script. This can happen over the HTTP protocol. Note that this is not just an HTML page that has data embedded in it – rather, it's an actual ADO recordset that exists in the client's PC memory and provides sorting, filtering and other features. In addition, once the data has been retrieved it exists physically on the client – so there's no need for additional trips over a network to the web server. Fewer trips to the server means less network traffic.

We can also combine the client-side functionality with another client-side feature – Dynamic HTML – to display the data. The end result can be a web application that provides an abundance of information in a visually appealing manner, and that can provide this information with virtually zero wait time between views of the data (except of course for the initial data fetch).

Using HTTP

Delivering web pages via HTTP means that those pages – text, images and all – are physically copied from the server to the client machine. If a Web application requires round trips to the server in order to display new information, it's a potential headache to network administrators who want to minimize network traffic (especially with increasing numbers of users). RDS can help to minimize the impact the application has on the company LAN. So how can we build an application that will run across HTTP, if we want to limit the amount of network traffic the application generates? Simple – that feature is built right in! Because RDS applications store the application data on the client-side, there is no need to request the server for more data. Fewer requests translate into less traffic on the network. This fact becomes more significant as the number of users of the application increases.

We still use a browser to receive and display information – whether we use RDS to retrieve a recordset, or we download ASP to pages with this information embedded. The difference is that we manage to keep the number of network transmissions down, in two ways:

❑   RDS enables us to retrieve *all* of the information at once, rather than piece-by-piece

❑   RDS gives us the functionality to query and manipulate the data on the client, not the server

Each network transmission requires a certain amount of overhead – using RDS to keep the number of transmissions down translates to lower overhead, which translates into an overall lighter network load. For the client, it also translates to faster response time! Of course if the user only wants to examine a few records, downloading all of them to the client would be wasteful of bandwidth. In this case, you can use a query on the server to select a subset of all the records and then send just this subset via RDS. Moreover, if the data in your database doesn't change frequently, your application can save the recordset to the local hard drive of the client machine. Each time the client starts the application, it can check with the server to find out whether there's any new information to download. If not, the previously saved local recordset can be used – further reducing the load on the network.

Data on the Client

The Expires property of the ASP Response object also allows your application to save information on the client-side. The Expires property determines how long a particular page should be cached on the client-side. As long as the page has not expired, the locally saved copy of the page (rather than the actual page from the web site) will be viewed in the browser when the user browses to it. The difference between the two approaches is that the Expires property allows saving only HTML pages, whereas RDS allows an actual recordset to be saved on the client. Saving the actual recordset on the client allows for much more functionality and flexibility than just pure HTML.

Of course, this assumes that security settings allow this. For more information about saving a recordset to disk, see the previous chapter.

Web Clients don't Need a Constant Data Connection

RDS allows you to build web applications that can display and update information derived from a data store. This data will be held in an ADOR Recordset object. The ADOR Recordset object is a smaller, lightweight version of the full ADO Recordset object (it doesn't have the explicit Command or Connection objects). The ADOR Recordset object is designed for transmission over the relatively low-bandwidth connections of the Internet and, thus, has a smaller memory footprint. Your application won't require a constant data connection, because the connection that brought the data to the client can be severed without affecting the data. This is because RDS is very closely associated with ADO, which provides disconnected recordsets.

For more information about using disconnected recordset in ADO, see chapter 8, Disconnected Recordsets.

The fact that the web client does not consume a data connection benefits your application because no resources are required to maintain a data connection. The client can then use the stand-alone `Recordset` object and all of the methods and properties that come with it. This means that you can sort, filter, update, insert and delete records without a live connection to the source database. Your application can later reconnect and send data changes back to the source server.

Data Can Be Accessed From Virtually Anywhere

RDS enables your applications to retrieve ADO recordsets across HTTP. HTTP is the protocol of the Internet, so your applications can retrieve recordsets across the Internet. This is possible because the recordset can be broken down into a text-like format on the server, sent over HTTP, and reassembled into an ADO `Recordset` object on the client. We will talk more about this later in this chapter.

Since HTTP is running on the Internet, and it is probably also running on your organization's LAN, you have the pathways by which you can retrieve data. This functionality enables applications running in Web browsers to retrieve and update data from nearly anywhere in the world! Of course, there are other factors (such as security permissions) that will determine whether or not your application can actually retrieve the recordset, but assuming those are configured properly, RDS makes it work.

RDS Improves the User's Experience

Because RDS can bring a recordset to the client, web pages do not make round trips to the server when new information needs to be displayed. Instead, the new data is simply loaded from the recordset locally. This makes for a very smooth transition. In fact, the page on which the data is displayed does not change at all. It is not reloaded. The only changes are to the data being displayed by intrinsic HTML controls or objects such as applets and ActiveX controls. This enables the user-perceived speed of web applications to rival that of standard Windows applications.

What's more, because the recordset is accessible to client-side script, Dynamic HTML can present information. The data does not have to be confined to controls like text boxes or listboxes. Data can be presented in a very rich and interactive manner. For instance, if you like data to smoothly fade in, in response to a "mouseover" event or after a specified amount of time: no problem. Would you like to enable drag-and-drop on information that has been loaded from a database? That can be done as well. In fact there are innumerable presentation options provided by Dynamic HTML. By combining that functionality with data from a data store, you can build applications that are information-rich, interactive and highly satisfying for users of your application.

The Structure of RDS

Although primarily used to retrieve data over HTTP, the more generic purpose of RDS is to allow the creation and use of COM objects over HTTP. When retrieving data, the ADOR `Recordset` is the vehicle by which the data travels from server to client. Other objects could also be involved, depending on how the application is built.

RDS can be used from within a web client, such as IE 4.0, or from within a more traditional LAN-based client, such as one built with Visual Basic. There are many ways to write code to provide the benefits of RDS to an application.

❑   *We can write to the RDS data control.* The `RDS.DataControl` uses other RDS objects without requiring you, the programmer, to interact with those other components. It is a quick and easy way to bring a disconnected recordset to the client, but is less flexible than other techniques.

❑   *We can write directly to the RDS.DataSpace and RDS.DataFactory objects.* These objects also enable us to retrieve data but provide us with more flexibility in terms of what we can do in our applications.

❑   *We can write to ADO only.* RDS functionality has been rolled into ADO so that I can retrieve a disconnected recordset from a remote server by writing to ADO objects only. I do not have to write directly to any RDS object.

Any of these approaches could bring a recordset from a server to a client and each has its own set of benefits and drawbacks. We'll move on to looking at the RDS objects a little further on in this chapter.

ADO and RDS are very flexible in terms of exactly how their services can be included in our applications. There are many different ways to write code to implement their functionality. The purpose of this section is to provide you with enough information to get you started using RDS – but not so much detail that you feel overwhelmed. So we won't cover *every* way of writing RDS code, but we will enable you to use RDS to bring data from a data store to a web client (and we'll show you easy ways to do so). In later chapters, we will cover more particulars and how to get even more use from RDS.

As stated earlier, the purpose of RDS is to provide access to remote data sources from client applications and COM components. RDS is used to transport ADO recordsets from a server to a client computer. However, to appreciate the principle behind RDS we need to have an understanding of multi-tier applications – so let's revisit that first.

RDS and Multi-Tier Applications

Applications built with RDS fit very nicely with the multi-tier (or n-tier) application model, as do all Internet applications. The great thing about multi-tier application design is that it can greatly enhance scalability– the application's ability to support more and more users. It can do this by relieving the server from maintaining recordsets and from executing supporting code, such as cursors. In addition, the multi-tier approach encourages simplified application management (if implemented correctly) – so when the time comes to update the application, the job should be easier.

Multi-tier Applications in General

RDS applications are built as n-tier applications. Let's have a quick revision of n-tier applications. An n-tier application separates the various components of a client/server system into three layers: client, middle (or business-level) and data source.

These tiers are logical tiers that do not necessarily map to physical machines. For example, the Web Server and the components it uses (middle tier) can often be on the same machine as the data store (data tier). The tiers do not necessarily map to specific types of software, either. Code that defines the reason the application was created usually runs in the middle tier(s), such as code that processes orders in a shopping cart application. These are the business rules and are often associated with COM objects running on an application server, although you can find these business rules in other places. This diagram shows a traditional three-tier model:

Simple 3-tier Application

The three tiers can be described as follows:

- ❑ User services typically run on the client computer. This tier handles displaying data and implements code that supports displaying data. Also, code in the client tier will, usually, manage the client application itself, in such ways as opening and closing windows and showing visual cues to the end-user. In the case of a web application, it is where the browser is running, with RDS stored data and DHTML. In the case of a standard client-server Window application, it is where that client is running.

- ❑ The middle tier typically relates to a server that is running COM components. This server might be a dedicated application server, or it might be a web server, or many others types of servers. These COM server components will handle managing, processing, and passing data from a data store to the client and vice-versa. These components sit between the user and the data, transforming the raw data from the data store into usable information for display on the client. These are the business rules that are implemented as code running in the middle (business) layer. A business object is an ActiveX component that can retrieve and process data or can perform just about any other work that the code can support. Business objects are usually on the middle tier. The middle tier, also known as the application server tier, is the logical layer between a user interface or Web client and the database. This is typically where the Web server resides, and where business objects are instantiated.

- ❑ The data tier (or data layer) usually maps to where the data store is located, together with all of the associated processes that support management of the raw data. Insert, update and delete operations are in the data tier. Do not be mislead: those operations can be initiated from within the business layer, but the actual functionality is controlled in the data layer.

Although these three tiers are generally implemented as a user computer, an application server, and a database server (with the appropriate software at each level), there is no rule that requires it. Business rules can appear on any computer involved in the application and can take forms other than COM components. For example, if you have added code to your client application that ensures only numbers will be keyed into a "Product ID" text box, you have added a business rule that will be executed by the client computer. If you create a SQL Server stored procedure that aggregates financial data before sending the results to the caller of the stored procedure, you have created a business rule that will be executed by the database server. Remember that the N-tier application model defines logical layers for your application, not physical ones.

The Place of RDS in Multi-tier Applications

RDS is the set of components that allows your applications to access data across HTTP. When you create an RDS application (an application that uses RDS functionality), you can partition your application into two or three logical tiers. In fact, RDS itself is partitioned into client-side and server-side components.

In order to accomplish its work, RDS uses some components that run on the client and some that run on the web server (we'll see a diagram of this a little further on). In addition, the data that RDS delivers is derived from a back-end data store. This short description roughly follows the multi-tier application development model described above. Thus, you could say that all RDS applications are multi-tier applications. However, the server-side component is somewhat limited in what it can do and there are some drawbacks to using it, as we will see. In addition, there is no custom business logic running in the default server-side business component. This default server-side business component is known as the RDSServer.DataFactory object.

It is possible to build your own server-side component. You can build a COM server and install it on the server-side to access a data store and return the results to the client. You can implement your own functionality, but even when writing such a custom server-side business object, you can create an instance of an RDSServer.DataFactory object (we'll meet this formally in a moment) and use some of its methods to accomplish your own tasks.

> For more details about the limitations of the default business object, (the
> RDSServer.DataFactory) and how to build your own server-component for use with RDS, see the
> next chapter, "Building COM Servers for Use with RDS"

RDS Architecture

So, RDS consists of client-side components and server-side components. Typically, the client-side components are hosted in an IE browser, using HTTP to communicate with the server components. Alternatively, they could be used in an application built using Visual Basic. The client-side RDS components are installed with IE 4.01, thus simplifying your custom application deployment. In other words, if you build an application using IE 4.01 and RDS, you can expect that the application will work on other systems with IE 4.01. There is usually no need to distribute additional software.

The diagram below shows how RDS works from a very high-level perspective. The idea is that client-side scripting code can use ADO to access a database through an IIS server. The client could be the actual web browser client or it could be a middle tier component acting as the client to the database. The code provides the name of the IIS server and information about the database. If the information is correct, a recordset can then be retrieved from the database and sent over the HTTP connection back to the client. Note that it's the recordset object that is sent to the client, not the database connection.

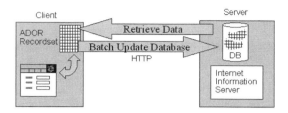

This is a high-level overview of an RDS application. It can be broken down into more detailed pieces, some of which we will discuss below.

Note that the client will receive an ADOR `Recordset` object, not just a web page with information derived from a database. This will enable the web page to display data from the recordset and to use client-side script to execute the `Move` methods, such as `MoveNext` and `MovePrevious`, as well as other features of the `Recordset` object. As previously mentioned, one of the best and most visible effects of this design is that the web page is not re-loaded when new data is displayed. Only the contents of the control that is displaying the data changes. The actual page does not. There are other ways to implement RDS in enterprise applications, but this is one of the simplest.

The RDS Information Flow

Let's look at the flow of information with an RDS application. The following diagram shows the flow of data from a web client, across HTTP to the web server, into the database, and back to the client. Glance briefly at this diagram. We will discuss each step in more detail later in this chapter.

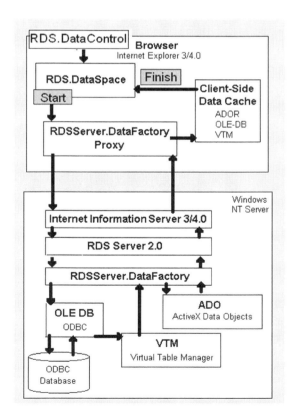

An RDS application accepts input from a user. The `RDS.DataControl` will make requests on behalf of the user for various sets of data. When the user enters the request, the client-side RDS components send the query to the Web server. The server-side RDS components process the request and send it to the DBMS.

The DBMS responds to the request, sending back the data. The RDS components on the Web server transform that data into an ADOR `Recordset` object. The data is converted into MIME format for transport to the client and sent back across the network to the client computer. Among other things, it may be bound and displayed in a data-aware or data-bound control, such as a text box or grid control. The control can then be bound to the data using the `RDS.DataControl` object. The `RDS.DataControl` object can provide fields of data to controls on the page. In fact, one `RDS.DataControl` can channel data to many data-aware controls.

The resulting data is cached on the client computer – this reduces the number of connections to the Web and makes it easier for a user to manipulate the data. The only calls requiring a trip to the server are those to the default RDS business object (the DataFactory) or a custom object of your own creation. Those calls might include those that perform updates to the data server, or requests for new data.

The RDS Object Model

When using RDS, objects running on multiple computers will interact with one another to bring data to your client. In this section, we will discuss the RDS object model and we will talk about which objects run where and when. The object model itself looks like this:

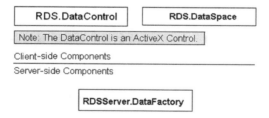

RDS Object Model

For a complete listing of the RDS object model, see Appendix B.

The RDS objects that you will work with include the `RDS.DataSpace`, and the `RDS.DataControl`. In addition, the `RDSServer.DataFactory` object always provides services, but your code will not interact with it directly. The `RDS.DataSpace` and the `RDS.DataControl` are installed on the client and are the objects that your code will manipulate to bring data down from a server. The difference between the two is that `RDS.DataSpace` is an object, in the sense that it must be instantiated, and provides methods and properties. The `RDS.DataControl` is also an object but it acts more like an ActiveX control than a COM server object. Although the most obvious difference between an ActiveX control and a COM server is that the ActiveX control provides a graphical user interface while the COM server does not, the `RDS.DataControl` is an ActiveX control and yet it does not provide a graphical user interface (similar to the VB Timer control). It can get confusing, so continue reading.

First we'll discuss the RDS.DataSpace object, and the related subject of business object proxies. Next we'll cover the RDS.DataFactory object and four of its most commonly used methods. Finally we look at the methods and properties of the RDS.DataControl. In all our syntax examples we'll use objDF, objDC and objDS to represent instances of RDS.DataFactory, RDS.DataControl and RDS.DataSpace objects respectively.

The RDS.DataSpace Object

The RDS.DataSpace object runs on the web client. The job of the RDS.DataSpace object is to create COM objects on an IIS server, and return an object reference from the server to the web client application. These references are called proxies and are a bit like your television remote control. In a similar manner that you can press a button on your remote control to make something happen on your television, your client application can call a method provided by the proxy to make something happen on the server object. This client-side proxy object is the remote control that can be used to control a server-side object across the Internet. When the client uses the business object proxy, it can manipulate that object as if it were there on the client.

RDS.DataSpace is the object that is used to instantiate COM servers that are located on remote IIS servers. In addition, the RDS.DataSpace object can instantiate objects on the same computer, the same local area network, or from across the Internet, assuming security allows this. For information about security considerations when creating server-side objects, see Chapter 11, *Building COM Servers For Use With RDS*. Under the hood, the location of the object does matter in that the reference that is returned is different. Let's look at business object proxies in detail before we move on to the RDS.DataSpace object's CreateObject method.

Business Object Proxies

What are business object proxies, and why do we need them? To answer this let us start this section with some information related to COM objects.

- ❑ In general, a process is a space in memory that has been allocated to a COM object for its use
- ❑ More than one COM object can run in a single process space simultaneously
- ❑ COM objects can communicate directly only if they are running in the same process space
- ❑ COM objects cannot communicate directly if they are not running in the same process space

The third and fourth bullet points are different ways to say the same thing. I repeated it because this is important and is the reason that business object proxies exist.

Because objects cannot communicate with one another unless they are running in the same process, there needs to be a mechanism by which they can communicate when they are running in different processes. The proxy serves this purpose. A proxy is itself an object that provides a pointer to another object in another process. The other object that is in the other process is known as a stub. The proxy and the stub point to each other across processes. This is an exception to the rule about objects not being able to communicate across processes.

This idea of a business object proxy is similar to the idea of a vote-by-proxy in an election. When an individual can not be present at an election, a proxy vote can be cast for that individual. A business object proxy works in a similar manner. When an object cannot be present in the same process space as the caller, a proxy object can be created to represent the business object in its absence. When a caller needs to communicate with a business object running in another process space, the following sequence of steps occur:

1. The caller communicates with the business object proxy that is running in the same process as the caller.

2. This proxy will, in turn, communicate with another object that is running in the other process. That object is called a stub.

3. The stub receives the message from the proxy and passes the message on to the destination business object.

As you can tell, the caller cannot talk to the business object from separate processes, but the caller can talk to a business object proxy. The business object proxy will assume the functionality of the business object and it will appear to the caller that it actually IS the business object. The caller never knows that it is not communicating with actual object, but is actually communicating with a proxy object that is emulating that actual business object.

Similarly the stub object runs in the same process space as the business object and assumes the place of the caller. The business object never knows that it is not talking to the actual caller. The proxy sends the message to the stub, the stub sends the message to the business object. This means that when a client instantiates an object that is running in another process, the client receives a reference to the proxy rather than to the actual object. Talking to the business object proxy will enable the client to communicate with the business object.

Let's look at a diagram that will make all this a little clearer:

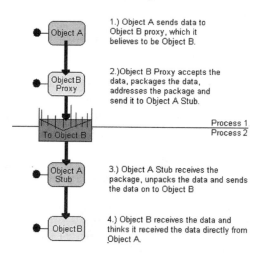

As you may notice, this diagram shows not only how proxies and stubs bridge the process gap, but also provides an illustration of marshalling. Marshalling is the process that must occur when a proxy communicates with a stub. When they communicate with one another, the message must be packaged for transport across process boundaries. After the message is packaged, it is sent (copied) from the proxy to the stub. When the stub receives the message, it must be unpackaged and sent on to the business object. This practice of packaging and unpackaging messages and copying them across processes is known as marshalling. Marshalling does not include the instantiation or destruction of objects, but is the activity of passing data across process boundaries.

Proxies and Stubs – an Analogy

The idea is a bit like a telephone. If you want to communicate with a friend, but that friend is in his own house, you might use the phone to call that friend and have a conversation. Assume that you and your friend are both objects. You cannot communicate directly because you are in different houses. Let us call each house a process. You need a mechanism by which to communicate. Your telephone at your house will be the proxy. Your friend's telephone at his house will be the stub. Your proxy is in your process and his stub is in his process. When you pick up and dial, you enter in the number that will connect you to the other object, your friend.

The phone number is like the class ID that uniquely identifies an object. Each person has a unique phone number and each object has a unique class ID. You, as a caller, are not concerned with exactly where the other object (your friend) is but the unique number will ensure that you get connected properly. When you begin to have a conversation with your friend over the phone, you have connected. However, you are not actually talking to your friend, you are actually talking to the telephone (the proxy). When your friend talks, he too, is talking to a telephone (the stub), not you. The telephones and underlying switched network take care of sending your speech, your message, to the other telephone, where your friend the COM object can hear it and respond to it.

The DataSpace.CreateObject Method

The `RDS.DataSpace`'s `CreateObject` method creates a proxy for the business object and returns a reference to it, as we discussed above. The proxy marshals data to the server-side stub when it needs to communicate with the business object. This happens when the client needs to send requests and data over the Internet.

RDS supports the following protocols:

- ❑ HTTP – the standard Web protocol
- ❑ HTTPS – a secure Web protocol (HTTP over Secure Socket Layer)
- ❑ DCOM (Distributed COM) – Microsoft's technology that enables COM components to communicate with each other across a network. DCOM is language neutral. This means that any language that can produce COM components can have those components run over DCOM. Use DCOM when running COM components on a local-area network without HTTP.
- ❑ In-process – a local dynamic-link library (DLL); it runs as a local process and it does not use a network.

The syntax to use the `CreateObject` method across HTTP is:

```
Set MyObj = DataSpace.CreateObject("ProgramID", "http://MyWebServer")
```

You can find the syntax for HTTPS and DCOM in Appendix B. Both are similar to HTTP; for HTTPS the second parameter is an `https://` URL, and for DCOM it is a machine name. The syntax for in-process is slightly different:

```
Set MyObj = DataSpace.CreateObject("ProgramID ", "")
```

- For in-process, MyObj is an object variable holding a reference to the ProgramID object. For the other three protocols, MyObj holds a reference to a client-side proxy object that has been created on the named server.

- DataSpace is an object variable that represents an RDS.DataSpace object, used to create an instance of the new object. The RDS.DataSpace object runs on the client.

- ProgramID represents a string that is the programmatic ID identifying a server-side business object, which implements your application's business rules, eg "MyComponent.Class".

- MyWebServer is a string that names a URL (if the machine is across the Internet), or UNC machine name (if on the same LAN), identifying the IIS web server where an instance of the server business object is created.

The DataSpace.InternetTimeout Property

The InternetTimeout property indicates the number of milliseconds to wait before a request times out. Requests in a three-tier environment can take several minutes to execute. Use this property to specify additional time for long-running requests. This property sets or returns a Long value and applies only to requests sent with the HTTP or HTTPS protocols.

The RDSServer.DataFactory Object

RDSServer.DataFactory is the RDS server-based object that talks to the data source. When you use RDS, this is the object that does the bulk of the work. It can do either of the following:

- Perform a SQL query against the data source and return a Recordset object
- Take a Recordset object and update the data source

In addition, this object has a method for creating an empty Recordset object that you can fill programmatically, and another method for converting a Recordset object into a text string to build a web page.

The server program is sometimes called a business object. You can write your own custom business object that can perform complicated data access, validity checks, and so on. Let's look at some of the methods of the RDSServer.DataFactory object: ConvertToString, Query, SubmitChanges and CreateRecordset.

The ConvertToString Method

The ConvertToString method converts a recordset to a MIME string.

> *MIME is a standard that allows binary data to be published and read on the Internet. The header of a file with binary data contains the MIME type of the data; this informs client programs (Web browsers and mail packages, for instance) that they will need to handle the data in a different way than they handle straight text. For example, the header of a JPEG graphic file is image/jpeg. This allows a browser to display the file in the web page or in its JPEG viewer, if one is present.*

The syntax of the method is:

```
objDF.ConvertToString(MyRecordset)
```

In this syntax MyRecordset represents the recordset we want to convert.

`ConvertToString` can be used to send a recordset generated on the server to a client. It converts the recordset by generating a stream that represents the recordset in MIME format. When the MIME data reaches the client, RDS can convert the MIME string back into an ADO recordset.

When a recordset is passed from a server to a client, that recordset is passed in MIME format. The browser receives the MIME-format data and rebuilds the recordset from the MIME data. The recordset that will be created on the client side, from the MIME data is the ADOR `Recordset` object. In this scenario, there are functional size restrictions, due to the way the MIME handler works. If data exceeds these limits, poor performance will result. They are:

- ❑ Less than 400 rows of data
- ❑ 1024 max bytes per row.

The Query Method

The `Query` method, as you might guess, executes a query against a data source, and returns a recordset. The query should be a valid SQL string, appropriate for the specific data source, as this method does not check the SQL syntax. The syntax of the method is:

```
Set objRS = objDF.Query(txtConn, txtMyQuery)
```

Here,

- ❑ `objRS` is an object variable which will contain our recordset.
- ❑ `txtConn` is a string containing the server connection information. This is similar to the `Connect` property.
- ❑ `txtMyQuery` is a string containing the SQL query that defines the recordset to be returned.

Let's look at an example using `ConvertToString` and `Query` methods:

```
Sub MyRDSConvert()
    Dim objRS
    strMyServer = "http://<%=Request.ServerVariables("SERVER_NAME")%>"
    set DS = CreateObject("RDS.DataSpace")
    Set objDF = DS.CreateObject("RDSServer.DataFactory", strMyServer)
    ' objRS WILL BE AN ADOR RECORDSET
    Set objRS = objDF.Query (txtConn.Value, txtQueryRS.Value)
    strRsAsMIME = objDF.ConvertToString(objRS)
End Sub
```

The sample code above is running in ASP. The `SERVER_NAME` value is passed into the `ServerVariables` method of the ASP `Request` object, to retrieve the name of the web server on which this code is running. Next, the VBScript version of `CreateObject` is used to instantiate an `RDS.DataSpace` object. There are actually multiple versions of `CreateObject`. Usually, the `CreateObject` method of the `Server` object should be used when creating objects in ASP. However, I have seen occurances where that version did not correctly create an object and the VBScript version did. If one of these versions does not work, use the other. Next, the `CreateObject` method of the `DataSpace` object is used to create an instance of the `RDSServer.DataFactory` object. After that, the `Query` method of the `RDSServer.DataFactory` is called to return an ADO recordset. Finally, the `ConvertToString` method of the `RDSServer.DataFactory` object will convert the recordset to text in MIME format. In other words, the recordset is converted to text just before it is sent over HTTP. The text is used to create a recordset on the client as the text is received.

The CreateRecordset Method

The `CreateRecordset` method creates an empty, disconnected recordset. The syntax for using the method is:

```
MyObject.CreateRecordset(ColumnInformation)
```

Here,

❑ `MyObject` can represent either a `RDSServer.DataFactory` or an `RDS.DataControl` object – we call this method with either.

❑ `ColumnInformation` is a variant array of arrays, defining each column in the recordset being created. Each column definition contains an array of four required attributes: the column header name, the data type of the column, the width of the field and a boolean value indicating whether the field can be NULL.

The set of column arrays is then grouped into an array, which defines the recordset. This recordset can then be populated with data by the business or `RDS.DataFactory` object on the server.

Remember, there are two types of ADO recordsets, the ADODB recordset and the ADOR recordset. We can explicitly create either type. (the R signifies reduced and is more lightweight). The full ADODB recordset cannot be used to transfer data over HTTP, but the ADOR recordset can. Even if your code creates an ADODB recordset on the server-side, the client will not receive it. The client will receive an ADOR recordset.

The `RDSServer.DataFactory` object's `CreateRecordset` method supports a number of data types, which can be fixed length or variable length. Fixed-length types are defined with a size of –1. Variable-length data types sizes can range from 1 to 32767.

> For a complete list of the data type constants (and their values) supported by the `CreateRecordset` method, see the **DataTypeEnum** class in Appendix G, *ADO 2.0 and RDS 2.0 Enumerators*.

Here's a code example that creates an `ADODB.Recordset` on the server side. The recordset is then assigned to an RDS control. The recordset has two columns. The `CreateRecordset` method will automatically create the ADODB type.

```
Sub CreateRecSet
   Dim ColInfo(1),
   Dim ColDef0(3)
   Dim ColDef1(3)

   ' Define Column 1.
   ColDef0(0) = "CustomerID"       ' Column name.
   ColDef0(1) = CInt(3)            ' Column type (3 = adInteger)
   ColDef0(2) = CInt(-1)           ' Column size.
   ColDef0(3) = True               ' Is the column nullable?
```

```
    ' Define Column 2.
    ColDef1 (0) = "Customer"            ' Column name.
    ColDef1 (1) = CInt(129)            ' Column type (129 = adChar).
    ColDef1 (2) = CInt(40)             ' Column size.
    ColDef1 (3) = False                ' Is the column nullable?

    ' Add the columns to the recordset definition.
    ColInfo (0) = ColDef0
    ColInfo (1) = ColDef1

    ' Set the recordset definition to a DataControl Object Variable.
    MyDC.SourceRecordset = MyDF.CreateRecordset(ColInfo)
End Sub
```

The RDS.DataControl Object

The RDS.DataControl is used to bind query results with HTML controls, such as textboxes. It uses the functionality of the RDS.DataSpace and RDSServer.DataFactory objects. It also enables visual controls to easily use the Recordset object returned by a query from a data source. RDS attempts, for the most common case, to do as much as possible to automatically gain access to information on a server and display it in a visual control. The RDS.DataControl has two aspects.

One aspect pertains to the data source. If you set the Command and Connection properties of the RDS.DataControl, it will automatically use the RDS.DataSpace object to create a reference to the default RDSServer.DataFactory object. Then the RDSServer.DataFactory will use the Connection property value to connect to the data source, use the Command property value to obtain a recordset from the data source, and then return the Recordset object to the RDS.DataControl.

The second aspect pertains to the display of returned recordset information in a visual control. You can associate a visual control with the RDS.DataControl (in a process called binding) and gain access to the information in the associated ADOR Recordset object, displaying query results on a web page in Internet Explorer. Each RDS.DataControl object binds one Recordset object, representing the results of a single query, to one or more visual controls (for example, a text box, combo box, grid control, and so forth). There may be more than one RDS.DataControl object on each page. Each RDS.DataControl object can be connected to a different data source and contain the results of a separate query.

The RDS.DataControl object also has its own methods for navigating, sorting, and filtering the rows of the associated Recordset object. These methods are similar, but not the same as the methods on the ADO Recordset object. The required syntax for instantiating the RDS.DataControl is:

```
<OBJECT CLASSID="clsid:BD96C556-65A3-11D0-983A-00C04FC29E33" ID="MyDC">
<PARAM NAME="Connect" VALUE="DSN=MyDSN;UID=Admin;PWD=password;">
<PARAM NAME="Server" VALUE="http://MyWebServer">
<PARAM NAME="SQL" VALUE="Select * from Customers">
</OBJECT>
```

For a basic scenario, you need to set only the SQL, Connect, and Server properties of the RDS.DataControl object, which will automatically call the default business object, RDSServer.DataFactory. All the properties in the RDS.DataControl are optional because custom business objects can replace their functionality.

Using the RDS.DataControl object

The RDS.DataControl is used only in Web-based applications – a Visual Basic client application has no need for it. You can use one RDS.DataControl object to link the results of a single query to one or more visual controls. For example, suppose you code a query that requests customer data such as Name, Residence, Place of Birth, Age, and Priority Customer Status. You can use a single RDS.DataControl object to display a customer's Name, Age, and Region in three separate text boxes, Priority Customer Status in a check box, and all the data in a grid control.

Use different RDS.DataControl objects to link the results of multiple queries to different visual controls. For example, suppose you use one query to obtain information about a customer, and a second query to obtain information about employees. You want to display the results of the first query in three text boxes and one check box, and the results of the second query in a grid control. If you use the default business object (RDSServer.DataFactory), you need to do the following:

4. Add two RDS.DataControl objects to your web page.

5. Write two queries, one for the SQL property of each of the two RDS.DataControl objects. One RDS.DataControl object will contain a SQL query requesting customer information; the second will contain a query requesting a list of employees.

6. In each of the bound controls' <OBJECT> tags, specify the DATAFLD, DATASRC and optionally the DATAFORMATAS parameter values in each visual control (we'll be looking in detail at data-binding in Chapter 13). There is no count restriction on the number of RDS.DataControl objects that you can embed via <OBJECT> tags on a single web page.

When you define the RDS.DataControl object on a web page, use non-zero height and width values such as 1 (to avoid the inclusion of extra space). RDS client components are already included as part of the Internet Explorer 4.0 installation; therefore, you don't need to include a CODEBASE parameter in your RDS.DataControl object tag.

It is possible to use data-aware controls with the RDS.DataControl, to provide an interface for working with the data. A data-aware control is a control that is able to use data from a database. Once you bind the control to a database via the RDS.DataControl object, the control is referred to as a bound control. The term data-aware is used interchangeably with data-bound.

> *The Sheridan data-aware grid control has been tested to work with the RDS.DataControl object and associated client-side components. Other controls may also work with RDS, but they have not been tested. The file name of the grid control is SSDATB32.ocx and the class id is AC05DC80-7DF1-11d0-839E-00A024A94B3A.*

With Internet Explorer 4.0, you can bind to data by using HTML controls and ActiveX controls only if they are apartment-threaded controls. The apartment-threading model enables each thread of a process to be created and run in its own "apartment" that is isolated from other threads. This makes the control thread-safe and more fault-tolerant. The Sheridan data-aware grid control is not distributed with RDS, but ships as part of Microsoft Visual Basic, Enterprise Edition.

DataControl Methods and Properties

For the rest of this section we'll cover some of the methods, properties and events belonging to the `RDS.DataControl` object. Among other things, we'll see how to use the `Refresh` method to run a query (contained in the `SQL` property) against a data source (specified in the `Connect` property). We can also update the data source (using the `SubmitChanges` method), or cancel changes made to the recordset (using the `CancelUpdate` method). In addition, the `RDS.DataControl` object provides mechanisms to specify synchronous or asynchronous execution and fetching (the `ExecuteOptions` and `FetchOptions` properties), or to cancel asynchronous operations (the `Cancel` method). We'll also look at using the `Reset` method to execute a filter specified by the various `Filter` properties.

Methods of the RDS.DataControl object

The methods of the `RDS.DataControl` object include `Cancel`, `CancelUpdate`, `CreateRecordset`, `MoveFirst`, `MoveLast`, `MoveNext`, `MovePrevious`, `Refresh`, `Reset`, `SubmitChanges`. Some of these methods apply to the `RDSServer.DataFactory` as well as to the `RDS.DataControl`. I won't repeat the explanation of those methods that we've already seen in the section above.

The SubmitChanges and CancelUpdate Methods

When you have made changes to a recordset, you can choose to either save these changes, or to discard them. With the `SubmitChanges` method, any data changes that are pending will be sent back to the datasource. With the `CancelUpdate` method all pending changes will be discarded, and the data in the recordset will revert to the last values that were retrieved from the data source.

You can use the syntax:

`objDC.SubmitChanges` or `objDC.CancelUpdate`

With the `SubmitChanges` method you can also specify:

`objDF.SubmitChanges strConn, objRS`

`strConn` is a string value that represents the connection created with the `RDS.DataControl` object's `Connect` property. `objRS` represents the `Recordset` object containing the changed data. As you can see above, you can call `SubmitChanges` with an instance of either an `RDS.DataControl` object (`objDC`) or an `RDSServer.DataFactory` object (`objDF`), although this may only be the default `RDSServer.DataFactory` object. Custom business objects can't use the `SubmitChanges` method. We will talk more about building your own custom business object for use with RDS in Chapter 11, *Building COM Servers For Use With RDS*.

To call the `SubmitChanges` method with the `RDS.DataControl` object there are three properties that must first be set: `Connect`, `Server`, and `SQL`. We'll see these in the *Properties* section a little further on. When you call `SubmitChanges`, only the changed records are sent for modification, and either all of the changes succeed, or all of them fail together. If you call the `CancelUpdate` method after you have called `SubmitChanges` for the same `Recordset` object, the `CancelUpdate` call fails because the changes have already been committed. The Client Cursor Engine keeps both a copy of the original recordset values, and a cache of the changes. When you call `CancelUpdate`, the cache of changes is reset to empty, and the bound controls are refreshed with the original data.

The Move Methods

The `MoveFirst`, `MoveLast`, `MoveNext`, `MovePrevious` methods move the cursor to the first, last, next, or previous record in a recordset. The syntax for using the methods is:

```
objDC.Recordset.MoveFirst
objDC.Recordset.MoveLast
objDC.Recordset.MoveNext
objDC.Recordset.MovePrevious
```

You can use the `Move` methods with the `RDS.DataControl` object to navigate through the data records in the data-bound controls on a Web page. For example, suppose you display a recordset in a grid by binding to an `RDS.DataControl` object. You can then include First, Last, Next, and Previous buttons that users can click to move to the first, last, next, or previous record in the displayed recordset. You do this by calling the `MoveFirst`, `MoveLast`, `MoveNext`, and `MovePrevious` methods of the `RDS.DataControl` object in the `onClick` procedure of each button. Once these are called, the data-bound controls automatically refresh themselves to show the current record.

The Refresh Method

You can execute the SQL query defined in the `SQL` property, by issuing the `Refresh` method. This will run the query against the data source specified by the `Connect` property. The syntax for using the `Refresh` method is:

```
objDC.Refresh
```

As with the `SubmitChanges` method, you must set the `Connect`, `Server`, and `SQL` properties of the `RDS.DataControl` before you use `Refresh`. All data-bound controls on the form associated with an `RDS.DataControl` object will reflect the new set of records. Any pre-existing `Recordset` object is released, and any unsaved changes are discarded. The `Refresh` method automatically makes the first record the current record.

It's a good idea to call the `Refresh` method periodically when you work with data. If you retrieve data, and then leave it on your client machine for a while, it is likely to become out of date with respect to the server. For more information about negotiating differences when updating recordsets, see Chapter 8, *Disconnected Recordsets*.

The Reset Method

You use the `Reset` method to execute a sort or a filter on a recordset held on the client. The actual sort or filter performed will depend on the value of the `Sort` or `Filter` properties. The syntax for using the `Reset` method is

```
objDC.Reset([blnValue])
```

`blnValue` is an optional Boolean value that is `True` if you want to filter on the current "filtered" rowset. `False` indicates that you filter on the original rowset, removing any previous filter options. If you do not set the value of `blnValue`, it will be set to `True` by default.

We'll see how to use the `Reset` method in the section *Filtering and Sorting* further on in the chapter.

Properties of the RDS.DataControl object

The properties of the RDS.DataControl object include Connect, ExecuteOptions, FetchOptions, FilterColumn, FilterCriterion, FilterValue, InternetTimeout, Recordset and SourceRecordset, ReadyState, Server, SortColumn, SortDirection, and SQL.

The Connect Property

The Connect property specifies the source of the data for the RDS.DataControl object. When you are authoring web pages, you can set properties at design time in HTML tags. To set the data source at design time you would use:

```
<PARAM NAME="Connect" VALUE="DSN=MyDSN;UID=UserName;PWD=password;">
```

The data source name should be a system DSN, for the data source to which you want to connect. Alternatively you can set the connection information at run time in scripting code, using:

```
objDC.Connect = "DSN=MyDSN;UID=UserName;PWD=password;"
```

The ExecuteOptions Property

With the ExecuteOptions property you can choose to execute recordset refreshes either synchronously or asynchronously. By default, it is set to a value of AdcExecAsync, which means that asynchronous execution is enabled. To execute Refresh synchronously you need to specify:

```
objDC.ExecuteOptions = adcExecSync
```

This is the run time syntax. As with the previous property, you could also specify this at design time. Each client-side executable file that uses these constants must provide declarations for them. You can cut and paste the constant declarations you want from the file Adcvbs.inc, located in the \Program Files\Common Files\System\MSADC folder.

The FetchOptions Property

The FetchOptions property determines the type of fetching that the RDS.DataControl object will perform. As with the previous property, by default asynchronous fetching is enabled (a value of adcFetchAsync). This means that control returns immediately to the application while records are fetched in the background.

The alternative values are adcFetchUpFront, which means that the application will wait until all the records have been fetched before continuing, or adcFetchBackground, where the application only has to wait for the first batch of records to be fetched.

In a web application, you will usually want to use adcFetchAsync (the default value), because it provides better performance. In a compiled client application, you will usually want to use adcFetchBackground.

The InternetTimeout Property

With the InternetTimeout property you can specify, in milliseconds, how long the DataControl object should wait for the server to respond to a request when the Refresh or SubmitChanges method is called. This enables your application to wait sufficiently for operations you know will take a long time. It also enables your applications to abort quickly for operations you know should execute quickly; that way, your users don't have to wait for an unacceptable length of time, or see a timeout error message displayed.

This property applies only to requests sent via HTTP or HTTPS, and its value is of datatype Long.

The ReadyState Property

As an RDS.DataControl object pulls data into its recordset, the value of its ReadyState property will change. At each change it will fire the onReadyStateChange event – we'll see this event in the *Events* section below. When the recordset is complete and ready for use, the value of this property will be adcReadyStateComplete. Confusingly enough, this will also be the value if the recordset is not initialized, or if there was an error preventing the data from being fetched.

If data is still being fetched, but some rows are ready for use, the ReadyState property will have a value of adcReadyStateInteractive. The third and final possible value, adcReadyStateLoaded, indicates that the query has not yet finished executing and that no data has been fetched into the recordset.

The Recordset and SourceRecordset Properties

These properties indicate the ADOR.Recordset object that is returned from a custom business object. You can set the SourceRecordset property or read the Recordset property at run time in scripting code (for instance, VBScript). The syntax is

```
Set objDC.SourceRecordset = objRS
```

or

```
Set objRS = objDC.Recordset
```

These properties allow an application to handle the binding process by means of a custom process. They receive a rowset wrapped in a recordset, so that you can interact directly with the recordset, performing actions such as setting properties or iterating through the recordset. (A rowset is the set of rows returned in a single fetch by a block cursor).

The Server Property

The Server property specifies the location of the server where server-side objects are created, as opposed to where the data is located, if they differ. You use this property to set or return the IIS URL and communication protocol, or the machine name, of the server. The syntax for using the property, whether at design time or run time, varies depending on the protocol. For each protocol, the server value should be of the following format:

HTTP	`"http://MyWebServer"`
HTTPS	`"https://MyWebServer"`
DCOM	`"machinename"`
In-process	`" "`

`MyWebServer` or `machinename` should be a string containing a valid Internet or intranet path and server name.

The SQL Property

The `SQL` property holds the query string with which we query the data source and retrieve the recordset data. You can choose to set the SQL query string at either design or run time. We must set this property (as we said above) before we can execute either the `Refresh` or the `SubmitChanges` methods.

Filtering and Sorting

The `SortColumn`, `SortDirection`, `FilterValue`, `FilterCriterion`, and `FilterColumn` properties of the `RDS.DataControl` object provide sorting and filtering functionality on the client-side cache. The sorting functionality orders records by values from one column. The filtering functionality displays a subset of records based on a criteria, while the full recordset is maintained in the cache. The `Reset` method will execute the criteria and replace the current recordset with a read-only recordset.

If there are changes to the original data that have not yet been submitted, the `Reset` method will fail. First, use the `SubmitChanges` method to save any changes in a read/write recordset, and then use the `Reset` method to sort or filter the records.

If you want to perform more than one filter on your recordset, you can use the optional Boolean argument with the `Reset` method. The following example uses the default SQL Server `Pubs` database to show how to do this:

```
MyDC.SQL = "Select au_fname from authors"
MyDC.Refresh          ' Get the rowset.

MyDC.FilterColumn = "au_fname"
MyDC.FilterCriterion = "<"
MyDC.FilterValue = "'C'"
MyDC.Reset            ' Rowset now has First Names < "C".

MyDC.FilterCriterion = ">"
MyDC.FilterValue = "'L'"

' TRUE is the default property so this call is not required.
MyDC.Reset(TRUE)      ' Rowset has First Names < "C" and > "L".

MyDC.FilterCriterion = ">"
MyDC.FilterValue = "'H'"

' Filter on the original rowset. Reset the previous filter options.
MyDC.Reset(FALSE)    ' Rowset now has all Last Names > "H".
```

Events of the RDS.DataControl Object

Two events are supported by RDS.DataControl, which are independent of the ADO Event Model. The onReadyStateChange event is called whenever the RDS.DataControl ReadyState property changes, thus notifying you when an asynchronous operation has completed, terminated, or experienced an error. The onError event is called whenever an error occurs, even if the error occurs during an asynchronous operation.

The onReadyStateChange Event Procedure

When the value of the ReadyState property changes this event will be fired. As we saw above, this property has three possible values, depending on whether data has been fetched into the recordset and whether the recordset is available. You should use the onReadyStateChange method to monitor changes in the ReadyState property whenever they occur. This is more efficient than periodically checking the property's value.

The onError Event Procedure

The onerror event was one of the features that was new with ADO 2.0, and is called whenever an error occurs during an operation. The syntax for the onError event procedure is

```
Sub_onError(intStatus, strDesc, strSrc, blnCancelDisplay)

End Sub
```

intStatus is an integer, which contains the status code of the error. strDesc is a string, which contains a description of the error. strSrc is a string containing the query or command that caused the error. blnCancelDisplay is a Boolean value, which when set to False prevents the error from being a VB-trappable error. (Defaults to True).

You can declare your instance of the RDS.DataControl as a WithEvents variable in the (Declarations) section of a VB module:

```
Private WithEvents objDC As DataControl
```

When you declare this, notice the variable objDC appears in the object list in your module's code window. If you select your object, you'll see the two events: onreadystatechange, and onerror. The onerror event enables you to perform error trapping on your DataControl object without having to use VB OnError... code. This sample onerror event procedure displays the error description, status code, and source in a message box and prevents VB from seeing the error

```
Private Sub objDC_onerror(ByVal Scode As Integer, ByVal Description As String,
ByVal Source As String, CancelDisplay As Boolean)
    MsgBox "Description. " &
        Description & vbCrLf &
        "Scode: "  & CStr(SCode) &
        vbCrLf &   "Source: " & -
        Source,    vbexclamation, "DataControl Error", CancelDisplay = False
End Sub
```

Putting the Pieces Together

We have talked about so many objects, methods, and properties that you may be unclear as to exactly where each piece fits in the overall picture. I think it is time for a fly-by, looking at each piece from above. We saw this diagram earlier in the chapter – let's now describe the flow of data in detail, and see what's happening behind the scenes, as control passes from object to object.

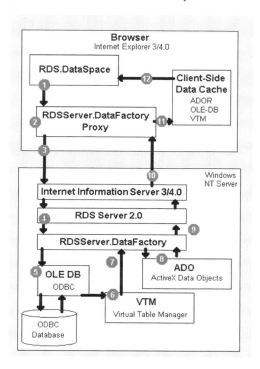

This is a representation of the process flow when the RDS.DataFactory object is used. We'll walk through and look at each step in the following list, corresponding to the numbers on the diagram.

1. The client application creates an instance of the RDS.DataSpace object to handle a database request.

2. The RDS.DataSpace object creates an instance of the RDSServer.DataFactory Proxy.

3. The RDSServer.DataFactory Proxy translates the call into an HTTP request. The parameters to the method are passed across the Internet via HTTP to the Web Server specified in the RDS.DataControl object's Server property. IIS then passes the HTTP request to a server extension called the RDS Server component ADISAPI (Advanced Data Internet Server API).

4. The web server receives the request. The RDS server component examines the contents of the call. It creates an instance of the RDSServer.DataFactory object and makes the requested method call. When using the RDSServer.DataFactory object the requested method call is the Query method.

5. The RDSServer.DataFactory object executes the query via OLE DB or ODBC by passing in the SQL statement and DSN information. It sets the properties for the requested rowset so that OLE DB uses the Virtual Table Manger as the buffering component. The VTM manages the data before it is passed to ADO and converted to a recordset.

6. OLE DB passes the rowset containing the results of the query to the virtual table manager(VTM). The VTM populates its buffers with the rowset data and stores all of the metadata information for all base tables that are part of the resultset. It also implements the marshaling interfaces for the rowset.

7. The VTM passes the marshalable rowset back to the RDSServer.DataFactory object.

8. The RDSServer.DataFactory object creates an instance of an ADO recordset and passes it the VTM marshalable rowset. ADO wraps the rowset into a recordset, which is then returned as the return value of the original query call from step 4.

9. The RDSServer.DataFactory passes the recordset back to the RDS server component, which packages the return value of the recordset into MIME 64 Advanced Data Tablegram format by calling the VTM to create a tablegram stream.

10. The RDS server component (ADISAPI) sends the tablegram (it's not really a recordset when it is passed over the Internet...it's a tablegram) over HTTP, as multi-part MIME packets to the business object proxy on the client side.

11. The client-side RDSServer.DataFactory Proxy unpacks the results of the method call from HTTP format, and recreates the recordset in the client side VTM. The VTM on the client side temporarily holds the data just before it is inserted into a recordset.

12. The application now has access to the recordset.

Conclusion

The purpose of this chapter was to introduce you RDS and to help you begin to get familiar with the various objects that are available in RDS and the methods, properties and events that belong to those objects. In later chapters we will look more closely at these objects and I will show you specific techniques for using these objects in your own code.

11

Building COM Servers For Use With RDS

This chapter is about creating instances of business objects remotely. We will talk about creating server-side COM components and instantiating them from remote clients. We'll then see how to use that component to deliver data to the user from a Web server, without the help of the default (middle tier) RDS business object, `RDSServer.DataFactory`. There are lots of good things about the `RDSServer.DataFactory` object. For example, it is the workhorse of the system, and is the object that allows you to execute database queries remotely. However, `RDSServer.DataFactory` has limitations – there may be cases in which `RDSServer.DataFactory` does not fully meet the needs of your application. In those cases, RDS allows us to build our own custom COM component that can provide both the functionality of the `RDSServer.DataFactory` object, and the functionality of additional custom features that you add to it.

We will use the terms "COM servers" and "business objects" interchangeably in this discussion. They will both refer to compiled applications or components running on a server that provides services to a client. As you work through this chapter, you'll see how to use Visual Basic to create an ActiveX COM-compliant DLL. We will install that COM DLL on a server, and instantiate it remotely from a client via HTTP, to provide services from the COM server to the client. So, in this chapter we will discuss the following topics:

- ❑   Why build your own business object?
- ❑   How to build your own business object
- ❑   How to replace the `RDSServer.DataFactory` object with your own custom data factory component
- ❑   A sample application
- ❑   Managing interactions with the server and client-side data control
- ❑   Interacting with the client-side data control
- ❑   The `DATASRC` and `DATAFLD` attributes

Our focus will be not so much on the RDSServer.DataFactory object as it will be on COM objects in general.

Why a Custom Business Object?

The Windows applications that you've used before probably had buttons, listboxes, option buttons and other controls. As a developer, you may have created Windows applications that used the same controls. Maybe you incorporated other controls into your applications. Maybe you bought an ActiveX control and used that control. Maybe you built your own.

An ActiveX control is a compiled, re-usable user-interface element that enables users to communicate with your application graphically (i.e clicking a button), and vice-versa (i.e displaying informative text in a label). If you develop your application with an ActiveX control that someone else built, it saves you time, because you do not have to take the time to implement the functionality of the control. You just use the methods and properties of the control. The control takes care of the rest. However, you do have to accept the methods and properties of the control "as is". You do not have the option of creating new methods or properties on that control.

If those methods and properties satisfy the needs of the application, life is good, but what if they do not? What if you need functionality that no control implements? What do you do?

If you use Visual Basic, Visual C++ or an other tool with similar functionality, you can build your own ActiveX control. If you build your own ActiveX control, you can build in any functionality that the language supports. You would create your own control when you need custom functionality from a control, and that functionality does not already exist in a control.

The same goes for the RDSServer.DataFactory object. If you need functionality that is not already supported, you can build your own. The exact reasons for building your own RDS-accessible COM server will depend upon the exact requirements of your application. It is possible that you could use RDS and receive adequate functionality from the RDSServer.DataFactory, however, if you need additional services, it is nice to know that you can build in any ability your application needs.

Hide The Connection String

Using RDS from within the browser involves executing code in the browser. This code will do such things as connect to a data store, retrieve data from the data store and manipulate the data at the client. Code that is running on the client will do things such as pass in a connection string. The connection string contains the name of the server where the data store is located, and database authentication information such as username and password.

Because my database authentication code is located in the client-side script, database security is an issue. Any user can select View | Source from within the web browser. I do not want users to be able to see connection information, such as the password. Creating my own custom business object will enable me to hide my database connection information inside the object. If the user selects View | Source, they can see the call to the business object but not database connection information. That information is stored in the business object. By wrapping my authentication information inside of my custom business object, I can make my business object, and my system as a whole, more secure.

Increased Functionality and Flexibility

Business objects and RDS make a powerful combination. RDS allows you to use HTTP to control and communicate with business objects. This enables your applications to create instances of these business objects on a server that is located down the hall or halfway around the world. You can also implement RDS applications on a local area network, without using HTTP. If the client-tier and middle-tier components are on different computers (a typical LAN implementation), you can use DCOM, through RDS, to marshal (copy and send) the interfaces and method arguments across the network. This enables the component to be used from a client while running on a server.

Business objects can provide services to RDS clients, and return virtually any type of data to the client. Among the most useful of these is an ADO `Recordset` object populated with data. When the client receives the recordset, it can read and manipulate the data almost as if the recordset was connected to the source data store, although it is not. This type of recordset is known as a disconnected recordset.

> *For more information about disconnected recordsets, see Chapter 8*

This functionality is quite useful. In fact, the `RDSServer.DataFactory` object can also return a recordset to an RDS client. However, the `RDSServer.DataFactory` object has certain limitations. It is a COM object that runs on an IIS web server. It is a small, light-weight object that has the job of accepting a SQL query, generating a recordset, converting the recordset object into a MIME (text) format and returning it to the client that initiated the query. (The client will always receive the `ADOR.Recordset` object, regardless of the type of recordset the server sends).

The architects of RDS built the `RDSServer.DataFactory` object with limited functionality, and had the foresight to see that it might not be the ideal object for every situation. As a result, we will often need to take advantage of the features of RDS to create our own middle-tier business object to replace the default `RDSServer.DataFactory` object.

Later, in the chapter, we'll look at how we design and implement our custom data factory object. First, let's talk about two limitations of the existing `RDSServer.DataFactory` object: the OLE DB simple provider, and security considerations.

RDSServer.DataFactory and the OLE DB Simple Provider

OLE DB is the cornerstone of Microsoft's current data access strategy. This technology allows data from many different types of data stores to be accessed through OLE DB providers. OLE DB providers are specific to the type of data store from which data will be retrieved. OLE DB providers exist for SQL Server databases, ODBC desktop databases and many other types of data stores (Microsoft Index Server, mail servers, spreadsheet applications and so on).

The **OLE DB Simple Provider (OSP) Toolkit** allows for creation of OLE DB providers, using Visual Basic, Visual J++ or Visual C++. However, if you are using an early version of `RDSServer.DataFactory` (version 1.0 or 1.5) in conjunction with an OSP built with the OSP Toolkit 1.5, you'll have problems with the 80004005 error.

This error occurs when you use the RDSServer.DataFactory's Query method, or when you return the disconnected recordset from a business object. It occurs because an OLE DB provider built with the OSP Toolkit can only return rowsets containing data of *variant* type. The process will fail whenever the OLE Simple Provider sends the variant data to be sent to the client. RDS is unable to remotely marshal variant-type data.

> *Marshalling refers to the process of passing objects across process boundaries – for a discussion of marshalling, see Chapter10.*

One option to workaround this is to use a full OLE DB provider, written with Visual C++ (instead of an OLE simple provider). If you're using Visual C++, you'll be happy to discover that the OLE DB 1.5 SDK includes SAMPPROV, a sample provider that may be used as a springboard for writing a full OLE DB provider in Visual C++.

A second possible workaround makes use of the fact that recordsets can be returned from RDS objects. This enables us to pass the recordset from a business object inside another Recordset object. To do this we use the RDSServer.DataFactory's CreateRecordset method (instead of the Query method). The steps for this workaround would be as follows:

- ❑ Create an ADO recordset from provider generated by OLE Simple Provider (including the SQL Server or Oracle Provider)
- ❑ Use the RDS CreateRecordset method to dynamically create a new recordset then copy data from the OLE Simple Provider records into the new recordset
- ❑ Pass the newly created recordset to your RDS client. If the recordset is returned from the client, use its Recordset.Status field to find out which of the records are new, and which are modified, and which are to be deleted. After that, you can generate a SQL statement against the OSP-provider-exposed datasource.

Security Configuration Issues

As you know, RDS is installed by default when you install IIS 4.0 using the Windows NT 4.0 Option Pack. However, there is a security issue, of which you should be aware. Microsoft's IIS team discovered that a potential intruder (with knowledge of a password, and the name of a target database) can use RDSServer.DataFactory to submit queries to that database and hence to access its contents. Of course, the obvious solution is to ensure that your passwords and database names are closely guarded; an additional security measure, if you are not using RDSServer.DataFactory functionality, is to disable that object.

What are the Advantages of Building your own Business Object?

There are many ways to build Windows applications. I can use C++, Pascal, C, Java, Visual Basic and more. Each approach has its own unique advantages and disadvantages. In general, the tools that are more flexible are usually more difficult to use. The tools that are easier to use, are usually more restrictive. A skilled C or C++ programmer has virtually no limits to what his application can do, but the language can be difficult. On the other hand, Visual Basic applications are generally easier to create, but there are some things that Visual Basic just cannot do.

The ease-of-use versus flexibility rule seems to hold true in many areas. For example, the `RDSServer.DataFactory` is very easy to use with either the `RDS.DataControl` or the `RDS.DataSpace` objects, but it does have limits as to what it can do for you. However, if you take some extra time to build your own server component, a replacement for the `RDSServer.DataFactory`, you can build in some extra functionality. The point to all of this is that I can take any COM object and use the services of that object from just about anywhere.

Control Over How Data Is Returned

The `RDSServer.DataFactory` can return data from a database, but you have no control over the internals of the RDSServer.DataFactory or how the data is returned. By creating your own business object to return data to the client, you can manipulate data before it reaches the client. This allows the control to decide where the data might get modified and how it gets modified.

Code Re-Use

Business objects are ideal for creating re-usable code blocks. You can create a business object and then re-use that object with RDS, in Visual Basic, from within stored procedures, and more.

Application Scalability

If you install the component into MTS, your application can achieve scalability such that the object can support many concurrent users. You can also distribute your objects so that many objects running on many servers work together to provide services to your application.

Development Tool Independence

An ActiveX DLL can be created with many different tools and from within many different development environments including Java, C++, Visual Basic (and even VB Script via scriptlets) and some versions of COBOL. Developers can choose the language that best suits them.

Platform Independence

ActiveX DLLs must be built to a specific platform, such as Windows NT or MacIntosh. Once built, a business object running on one platform can communicate with business objects running on another platform. This is platform independence from the standpoint that the application as a whole can include ActiveX DLLs running on any of those operating systems, and they can all communicate with one another as part of the same application.

Access To Data From Virtually Anywhere In The World

Through ADO and RDS, my COM objects can access data from any IIS server in the world. Although this can also be achieved using the `RDSServer.DataFactory`, my own component can implement other custom services that the `DataFactory` cannot. In fact, I do not have to return a recordset at all. I can use these same techniques discussed in this chapter to access a COM server that provides just about any service. The Internet is the network and HTTP is the protocol that can connect my applications to any IIS server (taking security into account), through which a recordset can be sent. The reach is nearly limitless.

How to Create a Custom Business Object for use with RDS

It is surprisingly easy to build a custom business object. In fact, if you use Visual Basic, you can create a COM object in less than 5 lines of code. When we've built a custom business object we can then instantiate that object over HTTP. In this section we'll discuss how to build a business object with Visual Basic for use with RDS. The first things we'll look at are Visual Basic project settings.

Visual Basic Project Settings

Creating business objects with Visual Basic is a relatively simple process because Visual Basic takes care of many details for you. You should, however, be aware of the property settings that make it possible. Most of these properties can be accessed by selecting Project | <Project Name> | Properties, then choosing the General tab. The following sections detail what these property settings are and what their values should be set to.

Project Type

The Project Type list box allows you to determine what Visual Basic will create when the project is compiled. If you select ActiveX DLL, Visual Basic will generate a COM DLL file. The ActiveX DLL is the project type that should normally be used, and is the only project that can be used if the business object is going to run under the control of MTS (MTS does not support any other types of component).

Startup Object

The Startup Object in an ActiveX DLL will most likely be set to (None). You will not want a form to be used in the DLL, as would be used in a Standard EXE project. If you want initialization code to run when the DLL is loaded, include that code in a subroutine named `Main`, then set the startup object to `Sub Main`. You can also include initialization code in the `Class_Initialize` procedure, which will run when an instance of the class is created. `Sub Main` would execute as the project that contains the class modules starts. `Sub Main` executes first. After that, as each class is instantiated and a corresponding object is created, the `class_initialize` event will run.

Project Name

When business objects are created programmatically, a programmatic identifier is most often used. When Visual Basic is used to create a business object, the programmatic id is created by concatenating the project name with a class name, separated by a period. A Visual Basic class is a single file (with a `.cls` extension) that is used to hold procedures. These procedures will become methods of the class if defined as Public procedures. For example, if the name of the project is `MyProject` and the name of the class is `MyClass`, the programmatic identifier of the resulting DLL will be `MyProject.MyClass`.

Project Description

The Project Description field allows you to enter a brief description about the project. The description will appear in the Visual Basic Object browser and in the References dialog box. The Object Browser window allows you to view information about COM objects including the methods and properties supported by the objects. The References dialog box allows you to inform the Visual Basic IDE (integrated development environment) about objects and allows variables to be declared as specific object types.

Upgrade ActiveX Controls

The Upgrade ActiveX controls checkbox will ensure that the newest version of ActiveX controls will be used in your project. If you add an ActiveX control to your project then a newer version is installed on the computer, the newer version will automatically be used. This is of less importance to ActiveX DLLs, since they normally do not include a user interface or ActiveX controls.

Unattended Execution

The Unattended Execution setting is normally ideal for an ActiveX DLL. This checkbox informs Visual Basic whether or not it should display any user interface elements, such as a message box. If the application does attempt to display a user interface element, that element will not be displayed, but instead information about it will be written to a log file.

Retained In Memory

Whenever a Visual Basic ActiveX DLL is created, internal data structures are also created in memory to support the object. Normally, those data structures are created when the object is created and destroyed when the object is destroyed. Creating and destroying these structures takes time. The Retained in Memory option tells Visual Basic not to destroy those data structures when the object is no longer referenced. In this case, the contents of those structures will be destroyed. This is beneficial when objects are often created and destroyed. Since the data structures for an object may already exist, they do not have to be re-created, which improves overall performance. This is especially important for ActiveX DLLs that are running under the control of MTS, where objects are constantly created, destroyed and re-created. When you install MTS Service Pack 1, this feature is automatically enabled, even if you do not select this check box.

Threading Model

Visual Basic ActiveX DLLs can be created as single-threaded or apartment-threaded. The analogy that works best to describe apartment threading describes each thread as isolated from other threads in their own "apartments". This threading model makes applications "thread-safe" and works best in ActiveX DLLs that will run in MTS.

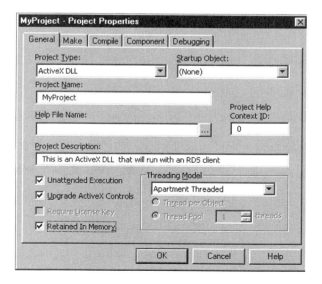

Class Module Settings

A Visual Basic class module is simply a text file that contains Visual Basic code. This Visual Basic code can consist of procedures, variable declarations, and other standard code elements. The thing that makes class modules special is the way that Visual Basic treats them when the ActiveX DLL is created. The class modules become the blueprints for objects that can be created from the ActiveX DLL. A single ActiveX DLL project can include one or more class modules. Each class module represents a separate object that the DLL can create. Properties of each Visual Basic class module can be set on each class module in the project independently of the other class modules in the project. The class module properties determine how the resulting object will get created and how it will behave.

Name

The Name property of the class is used as the second half of the programmatic identifier (ProgID) that we saw earlier.

Instancing Property

Instancing refers to creating an instance of the object. Using the Instancing property, you can determine how an object gets used. Objects can get used in the following ways. 1.) Clients can create your object, 2.) the object can be required to be created by other objects, 3.) an object can service multiple clients, or 4.) each client can get its own instance of the ActiveX DLL for its own use. The following bullets will explain this further.

The Instancing property can have the following values:

- ❑ Private – Private to a single project. Other modules in the same project can create instances of objects defined by the class, but clients cannot see or use them.
- ❑ PublicNotCreatable – Clients can use these objects, but only after they are created by another object in this same class. This is useful for building object hierarchies.
- ❑ MultiUse – This is the setting you should use with ActiveX DLLs. It allows a single instance of a COM server to provide objects to multiple clients
- ❑ GlobalMultiUse – Similar to MultiUse except that an instance of the object does not have to explicitly created. The methods of the object are automatically available and appear to be part of the Visual Basic language.

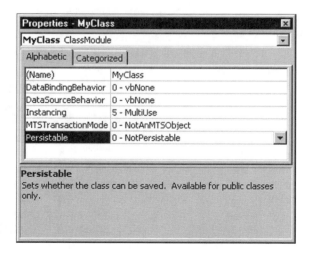

An ActiveX DLL's `Instancing` property should be set to `MultiUse`.

In the screenshot above we can see the `Instancing` property is set to `Multiuse`. The other properties visible on this screenshot are described below.

DataBindingBehavior

Determines if the class can be a data consumer or not. If it will be a data consumer, this property will determine if the class is simple bound (like binding a textbox) or complex bound (like binding with a grid).

DataSourceBehavior

Determines if the class can be a data source or not. If it will be a data source, it can provide data to bound controls in much the same way that a data control can provide data to bound controls.

MTSTransactionMode

If this component will be installed into Microsoft Transaction Server, this property allows the developer to set, at run-time, how this object will participate in MTS transactions. When the component is installed into MTS, the setting applied here will be picked up and assigned to the object. The four possible values include:

❑ **Requires a Transaction** – If Microsoft Transaction Server is already running a transaction when this object is created, this object may participate in that transaction. If no transaction is already running, one will be created.

❑ **Requires a New Transaction** - Whenever the object's code runs, it will have a new transaction created for it by Microsoft Transaction Server.

❑ **Supports transactions** – If a transaction has already been created before this object is created, it may participate in that transaction. Otherwise, the component will run without a transaction.

❑ **Does not support transactions** – This component may not participate in transactions.

Code that will Run Inside the Business Object

The great thing about using business objects in a multi-tiered application to implement business logic is that you can build any functionality into the object that the language will support. That benefit is further enhanced by RDS and its ability to instantiate (create) business objects from across HTTP. In fact, if you want to instantiate a business object from across HTTP, RDS is your only choice. This means that I can build a system that can do just about anything, from just about anywhere. When you add ADO to the mix, you realize that you can access just about any type of data store from just about anywhere as well.

RDS was designed to return an actual ADO recordset to a client application built using HTML and script, and running in a browser. You can build a business object to emulate this functionality and add custom functionality that RDS alone does not provide.

Is it an ADODB.Recordset or an ADOR.Recordset?

As you build your code, you can declare variables of type `ADODB.Recordset` or you can declare the variables of type `ADOR.Recordset`. When you send the recordset across the Internet to the client, that recordset is converted into text before it is sent, and then converted from text back into a recordset when it arrives on the client.

When a recordset is received on the client-side from across the Internet, the type of recordset that is received must be the `ADOR.Recordset`. This is true regardless of the type of recordset that is sent from the server. The following diagram demonstrates this:

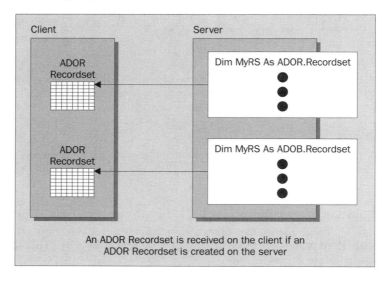

This means that the recordset that is created on the client will always be the ADOR type. Your server code can create the `ADODB.Recordset` or the `ADOR.Recordset`, it does not matter to the client.

> *When in your code would you choose to create an ADOR recordset? Maybe never. Since there is little difference between the two types of recordsets and the client will always receive an ADOR recordset, regardless, you may never need to explicitly create the ADOR recordset.*

The ADO Libraries

We have written our code in the Visual Basic IDE(Integrated Development Environment). We are able to define variables as specific ADO types because within the VB IDE we can refer to the ADO 2.0 library. To refer to such object libraries, select Project | References from within Visual Basic. This will display the References dialog box:

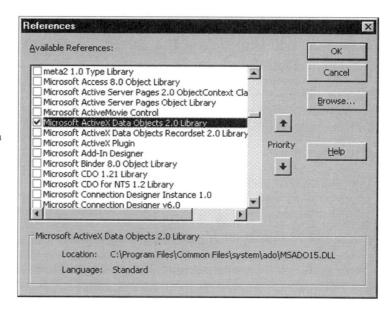

Note that there are two entries for ADO. The Microsoft ActiveX Data Objects 2.0 Library entry is the one you will use most often. If you should want to explicitly create an ADOR.Recordset, you will need to add the Microsoft ActiveX Data Objects Recordset 2.0 Library reference.

The Code

The code that runs inside a business object, and will return a recordset to a client, is quite similar to code that creates a disconnected recordset. In fact, it creates a disconnected recordset to be sent across HTTP to a web client or other type of client. Here is our business object code:

```
' THIS CODE WILL RUN WITHIN THE BUSINESS OBJECT
Function GetMyData() As ADODB.Recordset
    ' THE CLIENT WILL RECEIVE AN ADOR.RECORDSET EVEN THOUGH WE CREATED IT AS ADODB
    Dim MyRS As ADODB.Recordset
    Dim strConn As String

    strConn = "Provider=SQLOLEDB;Data Source=(local);User ID=sa;
        Password=;Initial Catalog=pubs"

    Set MyRS = New ADODB.Recordset
    MyRS.CursorLocation = adUseClient
    MyRS.CursorType = adOpenStatic
    MyRS.LockType = adLockBatchOptimistic
    MyRS.Open "Select * From Authors", strConn

    'Now disconnect the recordset
    Set MyRS.ActiveConnection = Nothing

    Set GetMyData = MyRS

End Function
```

What's Going On?

In the code above, we are executing code inside a COM object, to return a recordset from the server to the client. The COM object will be installed on and running on the server and may be separated from the client by the Internet. The client may be a client-server application or it may be a web application running in a browser.

We have created this procedure and given it a return type of ADODB.Recordset. When we return recordsets from a function from across the Internet the data type returned is not necessarily the data type that is specified in your code. In the code above, we have defined the return data type as the ADODB.Recordset, however, the recordset that the client will actually receive will be the ADOR.Recordset.

We define variables in the code that will hold the recordset and the connection string. We can define an object of type ADODB.Recordset as we are making use of the ADO 2.0 Library (shown in the References dialog box a little further back). After declaring the variables, we can use them. The strConn variable is used to hold information about the database to which we will connect. The syntax may look a bit odd if you are used to working with ODBC datasources. The information that is in strConn will be passed into ADO and used with OLE DB, rather than ODBC. The parameters are as follows:

- ❑ Provider – The name of the OLE DB provider that will be used to retrieve data from a data store; we're using SQLOLEDB.
- ❑ Data Source – The name of the machine on which the database is running. Our code and our database are both on the same machine, so we're using (local). Note that you need the parentheses.
- ❑ User ID – The name that will be used to authenticate the user to the database, here the system administrator.
- ❑ Password – The password for the user ID. We have no password set.
- ❑ Initial Catalog – The actual data store that provides the data.

After the database connection information is assigned to the strConn variable, I create an ADODB.Recordset object. The New keyword does the work of actually creating the object. Although we used Dim to declare the MyRS variable, the variable is created at that point, not the object. We would use New to create an instance of the Recordset object and return a reference to that object. There are other ways to create object in Visual Basic, but "Dimming" it on one line and "Newing" it on another, as we have done here, is the most efficient way.

The next two lines determine properties of the recordset cursor. We will be using the client-side, static-type cursor. Client-side cursors can only be of the static type.

Next we set attributes of the locking mechanism of the recordset. When records are updated, records in a database must be locked. We can choose when and how those records are locked. Batch-Optimistic is the required setting for recordset that will be sent over the Internet to clients.

The last three lines of code do a lot. To start, we will open the recordset using the Open method of the recordset. After we have the Recordset object, we can set the ActiveConnection property to Nothing. This disassociates the recordset from the database and enables the recordset to be a stand-alone object. Finally, we will return the recordset from this procedure to the client. Setting the name of the procedure to the Recordset object will accomplish that. The process of converting the recordset to MIME (text) format begins here.

Class Module Code and MTS

Class modules support methods, properties, and events. If your business object will be installed into MTS and run under its control, it is highly recommended that you **do not** create properties or events for those objects.

MTS objects are constantly created, destroyed and re-created. In fact, we can not rely on the existence of an object at a particular point-in-time. MTS will create objects when they are needed and will destroy them when they are not. Because of this, it would be unwise to store property values in MTS components. When MTS deactivates the object, the property values would be lost. For this discussion, the word "deactivate" is what MTS does to objects when they are no longer needed. For all intents and purposes, it has a similar effect as destroying an object by freeing associated resources, although the object is not actually completely destroyed.

Inputs to the Business Object from the Caller

It is one thing to be able to simply call a procedure or a method of an object and have that routine perform work or return results back to the caller. It is, however, more flexible to have a routine that can accept inputs from the caller and behave differently based upon the values of those inputs.

Creating object methods that accept input parameters is done in basically the same way as creating a function that accepts input parameters in a standard EXE project. You provide a name and a data type for each input parameter. The difference lies in the fact that when creating input parameters to an object function, it is highly desirable to create these parameters with the ByVal option.

ByVal will cause input parameters to be passed "by value". This means that the input parameter will receive a separate and distinct copy of the value that was passed to the method for that parameter. Changes to the value of the parameter made from within the method do not affect the original value of the variable that was passed to the method from the caller. ByVal is preferred because under the RDS model, the code that implements the method and the code that calls the method are likely to be executing on separate machines separated by an HTTP connection. Passing parameters ByVal is less likely to cause problems as opposed to the option ByRef.

ByRef is the default behavior for all input parameters in Visual Basic, and will pass input parameters "by reference" unless you specify otherwise. Passing parameters ByRef means that a pointer to a variable holding the input gets passed to the method, not a copy of the actual value. Because a pointer gets passed to the server object method, and the value that is being pointed to is on the client, and both are separated by HTTP, problems can arise.

> **Pass parameter values by value using the ByVal option.**

The following code shows this syntax:

```
Function SetValues(ByVal Param1 as Variant, ByVal Param2 as Variant)
     ' DO WORK HERE
End Function
```

Returning Data To The Caller

Returning data to the caller is done in a manner similar to returning data from a function in a standard EXE. The value that is to be returned is assigned to the name of the function. Let's look at two ways of returning values from a method. The first function assigns a numeric value to the name of the function. This will cause that value to be returned to the caller.

```
Function SetValues(ByVal Param1 as Variant, ByVal Param2 as Variant)

     ' RETURN intReturnValue TO THE CALLER
     SetValues = intReturnValue

End Function
```

The second function shows returning an object variable reference from a method. Notice the use of the Set keyword. The Set keyword is used anytime an object variable reference will be copied from one location to another. This is particularly useful when returning a recordset from a method.

```
Function SetValues(ByVal Param1 as Variant, ByVal Param2 as Variant)

     ' RETURN objRecordset TO THE CALLER
     ' objRecordset IS AN OBJECT, SO USE THE Set KEYWORD
     ' THE RECORDSET IS PASSED BACK HERE
     Set SetValues = objRecordset

End Function
```

Installing the Business Object on the Server

It's really not difficult to take a Visual Basic ActiveX component and make it run with RDS. There are just a few things to keep in mind, and to do, to make it work. Make sure that the component is registered in the Windows Registry of the system on which the component will run. If the component is not registered on that machine, use RegSvr32 to register the server DLL on the web machine. For more information, see *Registering the DLL*, below.

In addition to the registration, there may be some extra steps that are required, depending upon where the component is going to run. This section will discuss setting up your business object.

Physically Moving the DLL to Production

After the DLL has been created, you should have a physical DLL file. DLLs are typically built on a development machine and later copied to a production machine. You must make sure that a copy of your DLL exists on the system on which it will run. The location of the DLL on the production server really does not matter, although if you move it after you have registered it, you will have to make sure that the registry entry settings reflect the DLL's new location.

> *One strategy that many take is to create a folder named Applications, COMSERVERS, BusinessObjects or something similar. Inside that folder would be sub-folders for each specific DLL.*

Registering the DLL

After the DLL has been successfully copied to the production machine, it must be registered on that machine. Registering a DLL on a machine will write information about the DLL into the registry. This process typically involves using the following command

```
Regsvr32.exe C:\<Path to DLL>\MyProject.dll
```

This command can be executed from within the Start | Run dialog box or from within the Command Prompt window. The path to the DLL is required if you executed the command from within a folder other than the folder where the DLL is located. To unregister a DLL and remove the corresponding entries from the registry, add the /u switch to the command:

```
Regsvr32.exe /u C:\<Path to DLL>\MyProject.dll
```

The DLL can be registered in other ways. For example, if you install a DLL into an MTS package before it is registered on a system, MTS will take care of registering it for you.

As a shortcut, you can set up an association between files with the DLL extension and the Regsvr32.exe application. This will enable you to register DLLs by simply double-clicking on them rather than typing the entire command. To set up an association between DLLs and Regsvr32.exe:

1. Right-click over any file with a `.dll` extension.

2. Select Open With from the context menu, and click Other...

3. Navigate to `C:\Winnt\System32` and select `REGSVR32.EXE`.

4. Click Open. REGSVR32 will appear in the Open With dialog box.

Double-click the REGSVR32 entry. Make sure that the Always use this program to open this file box is selected.

You can now register a DLL in the registry by simply double-clicking on it. There are other third-party tools that can also assist in the registration of DLLs, but this method is simple, quick and easy.

Enabling the Business Object for use by RDS

When you create your business object, and install it on the Web server, you need to take further action before it is enabled for RDS. The additional modifications that you need to make depend upon where the business object will run in relation to the client application.

The business object can run in one of three locations from the perspective of the client application. The way you configure the business object will depend upon the location of the business object. The business object can be:

- ❑ **On The Same Computer As The Client** – The client application and the business object both run on the same machine.
- ❑ **On A Different Computer From The Client But On The Same LAN** – The client application and the business object run on the same local network, but on different computers. This might be two computers on the same Windows NT Domain. This business object will communicate with the client via DCOM through RDS.

❑ **On A Different Computer From The Client And On A Different LAN But On The Internet** – The computer running the client application and the computer running the business object are both connected to the Internet. There is no other connection between the two computers. The business object will communicate with the client via HTTP.

Each deployment scenario requires different configuration and there may be modifications required on both the machine running the business object and the machine running the client. The following section will detail the changes required on the client and the changes required on the server for each of the three deployment scenarios. First however, a brief note on registry editing.

About Manual Registry Modifications

To successfully launch a custom business object (DLL or EXE) through the Web server (known as remoting), the business object's ProgID must be entered into the registry.

> This feature protects the security of your Web server by running only COM servers that have been entered into the registry in this way. The default business object, RDSServer.DataFactory, is already fully registered.

There are two ways you can modify the registry. The text below can be copied into a text file and given a `.reg` extension, such as `AddBusObj.reg`. By double-clicking the `.reg` file on the server, these changes will be made to the server registry for you. Instead, as we've done below you can also use the `regedit` utility to navigate to the registry entry named below and add the name of the business object as a new key. You should always back up your registry files before manually editing them.

For more information on creating registry files, refer to Appendix H, Hints and Troubleshooting.

Running on the Same Computer

When running the client application and the business object on the same computer, there are no additional setup steps required. Registering the business object on the computer is sufficient for enabling the client and object to communicate.

There is, however, a particular syntax that should be used when instantiating the business objects from within the client. The `CreateObject` method of the `RDS.DataSpace` object should be used to create an instance of the business object. This `CreateObject` method accepts two input parameters. The first parameter names the business object, the second parameter names the machine on which the object is registered and will run.

When the client and the business object are on the same machine, however, the second parameter does not work. It cannot be used to identify a machine, and if you try, it will not correctly instantiate the object. The second parameter should be a zero-length string. The following sample code shows how the business object should be instantiated when the client and business object are running on the same machine. Assume `MyDS` represents a valid `RDS.DataSpace` object reference.

```
Set x = ds.CreateObject("MyObject.MyClass", "")
```

Running on the Same LAN via DCOM Through RDS

When running your business object on the same LAN as the client application, DCOM enables the communication between the two. In this scenario, the server running the business object needs some registry modifications before this will work. Also on the server, you'll need to grant DCOM Launch permissions to users. Finally you need to modify certain registry settings on the client.

Registering the DLL on the Server

First of all, the DLL that represents the business object needs to be registered on the server machine. After the DLL has been registered, a surrogate .EXE file needs to be named. Since DCOM works with .EXE files and not DLL files, an EXE needs to be used so that DCOM will work. If you install the business object into an MTS package, you do not need to take any additional steps to set up an surrogate EXE. Microsoft Transaction Server itself will be the surrogate EXE for the business object.

If you do not install the business object into MTS, you will need to tell DCOM which EXE file will be your surrogate EXE for the business object. Use the following file as the surrogate EXE: `c:\winnt\system32\dllhost.exe`.

You will need to add a `LocalServer` entry to one of your DLL's registry entries, to tell DCOM that that file will be your surrogate EXE for that business object. This is similar to the entry that Microsoft Transaction Server automatically makes when you install the business object into an MTS package. If you do not install the business object into a package, you must make this entry manually. To make the entry, do the following:

1. Start the registry editor by clicking Start | Run... and typing `regedit` into the textbox. Click OK to start the registry editor.

2. Select the `HKEY_LOCAL_MACHINE` registry hive by left clicking on it once.

3. Select Edit | Find to locate a business object entry

4. Enter the ProgID of the business object (eg. `MyObject.MyClass`)

When the registry editor locates the entry for your business object, click the plus sign next to your object's Class ID in the explorer pane of the registry editor. This will expand the information and will display where the new entry needs to go.

> **Important: Write down, or save to a file the ClassID. You will need to enter it later.**

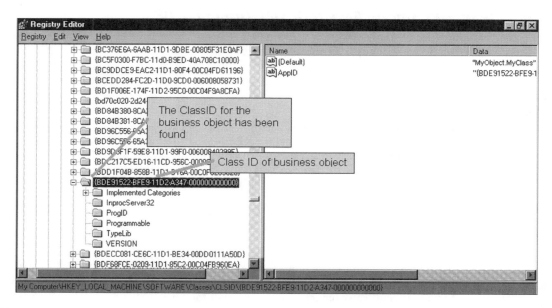

5. Right-click over the ClassID for the business object and select New | Key from the context menu that appears.

6. Enter `LocalServer` as the name of the new key.

7. Double-click over the "default" entry for `LocalServer` and enter the path and name of the surrogate DLL: `c:\winnt\system32\dllhost.exe`.
The following image shows how the registry entry should look when you finish.

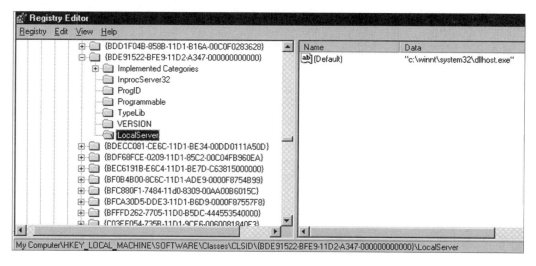

8. Close the Registry editor.

Granting DCOM Launch permissions

You now need to give DCOM launch permissions to the appropriate user. You will use the DCOM configuration editor to do this. The following steps show the details.

1. Select Start | Run... and enter `dcomcnfg` in the text box and click OK. The DCOM config window will open.

2. Scroll down the list until you find your business server object.

3. Double-click the business object entry or select it and click Properties.

4. Select the General tab on the Properties dialog box. Note that the local path to your DLL is the surrogate EXE that you listed in the registry.

5. Select the Security tab. Click the Edit button that is in the section labeled Use Custom Launch Permissions

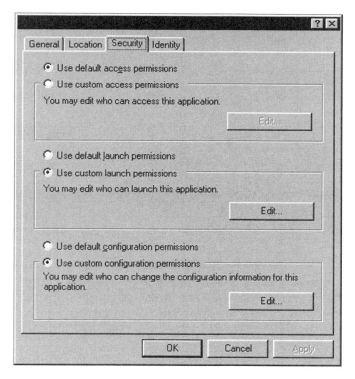

6. Use the Windows NT user dialog box that appears to choose users and groups who have launch rights to your business object

7. After you have selected the user(s), click OK. Click OK again to close the `dcomcnfg` application.

That is all there is to setting up the server. Now you need to set up the client.

Configuring the Client Registry

You will need to make two changes to the registry of the client in order for instantiation via DCOM to work. First you need to enter the ClassID of the business object. To do this follow these steps:

1. Right-click over the HKEY_CLASSES_ROOT hive

2. Select New | Key and enter the ProgID of the business object (eg MyObject.MyClass).

3. Right-click over the new ProgID entry and select New | Key

4. Enter Clsid as the name of the new key

5. Set the default value of the Clsid key to the ProgId that you wrote down or saved to a file (see step 5 of *Registering the DLL on the Server*, above)

6. Make sure the changes were saved

An example of how the registry editor should look afterwards is shown in the next secreenshot:

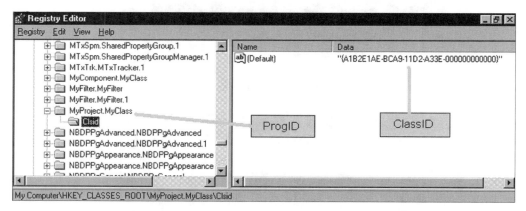

The next step is to mark the object as safe for initialization and scripting. Here's what you need to do for this:

1. Add the following two registry entries to the registry. Note that <Clsid> below will have the same value as the class ID referenced in step 5 above:
    ```
    HKEY_CLASSES_ROOT\CLSID\<Clsid>\Implemented Categories\{7DD95801-
    9882-11CF-9FA9-00AA006C42C4}
    ```

    ```
    HKEY_CLASSES_ROOT\CLSID\<Clsid>\Implemented Categories\{7DD95802-
    9882-11CF-9FA9-00AA006C42C4}
    ```

2. Close the registry editor.

Clients will now be able to use your business object via DCOM through RDS.

Running Over the Internet

To enable your business object to be accessed over the Internet, there is only one required step past the standard registration process. Middle-tier components must have ADCLaunch permission if they are to be invoked using RDS over HTTP connections. On the server you will need to enter an additional entry into the registry. The following key in the Web server's registry will enable that component to be created over RDS. Here's the key:

```
HKEY_LOCAL_MACHINE\SYSTEM\CurrentControlSet\Services\W3SVC\Parameters\ADCL
aunch\ProjectName.ClassName
```

There are no changes to make to the client.

Using the Business Object in Client Script

When creating an instance of a business object, there are several situations in which using the RDS.DataSpace object on the client is preferable to using the RDS.DataSpace object in an ASP page on the server. The RDS.DataSpace object provides the following advantages:

- ❑ We can make numerous requests to multiple business objects from a single web page without having to retrieve new pages. This gives us more flexibility in the design of a web page. (ASP can also call multiple business objects; however, they can only get information from a submitted HTML form, which is more limiting in that when new information needs to be displayed, a round trip to the server must be made)

- ❑ We can use the RDS.DataSpace object to retrieve the data and cache it on the client. This improves performance by reducing the load on the server, and is especially useful if business objects return large amounts of data.

However, you should use an ASP page (instead of an RDS.DataSpace object) to create your business object in the following situations:

- ❑ When the business object must perform secure transactions. Using the RDS.DataSpace object exposes the code of the business object by creating it on a web page, where it could be misused. When the code is placed in server-side script in an ASP page, it is not returned to a client

- ❑ When the security settings of the client are set so that it is unable to run ActiveX controls

As you know, RDS can be used to create distributed, three-tier applications. You can do this with the default RDSServer.DataFactory object or you can replace the RDSServer.DataFactory object with an object of your own creation. You can use ASP to retrieve data as well, but with RDS I can pass the actual recordset to the client, whereas the ASP page would usually send an HTML page with data embedded into the page. The main difference here is that when building a three-tier (n-tier) application, the client components of the distributed application typically contain all the presentation-related logic and local validation checks for user input and actions.

As described in Chapter 10, components hosted at the middle tier typically contain the business logic, integrated validation checks, and all the code to work with underlying data sources. The third tier is composed of stored procedures and triggers residing inside the data source. This approach offers more scalability for your server. The lifetime of middle-tier components invoked by using RDS is limited to the time it takes to complete the function call. The components are released as soon as the function call finishes; thus server resources are freed at the same time. Middle-tier components invoked by RDS can easily run inside the MTS (MTS) environment to increase scalability and fault-tolerance. In addition, MTS components can participate in ODBC connection pooling, although this functionality is currently implemented by ODBC, not MTS.

Creating Remote Instances of Business Objects with RDS

Using RDS, we can do explicit remoting. By **explicit remoting**, we mean the process of creating an instance of a remote business object. If our code is executing on the client, how do we create an object located on the server? Within our HTML document, we must first create the RDS.DataSpace object. Then we can use its CreateObject method to create an instance of the business object on the Web server. If the business object in question is an out-of-process component, this creates a proxy on the client-side to marshal method calls to the object. CreateObject returns an object reference, which we use to invoke methods of the business object.

The syntax for calling the CreateObject method is as follows:

```
RDS.DataSpace.CreateObject ProgID, ServerName
```

In the following example, we use the CreateObject method to create an instance of a business object. It then invokes the MyMethod method of the object to perform work on behalf of the client. This code will execute within the client. More specifically, it might run inside of Internet Explorer and client-side script, although it could run in other types of clients. In this code snippet, the explicit remoting is contained in the fact that I can name a remote server (such as MyServer) and name a component that is on that server (such as MyObject.MyClass), then instantiate that object remotely.

```
set objMyObject = objMyDataSpace.CreateObject("MyObject.MyClass","MyServer")
objMyObject.MyMethod(Parameter1, Parameter2)
```

Checklist for Business Objects with RDS

When building your COM servers, keep in mind that these middle-tier components must meet the following criteria:

- ❑ **IDispatch is required**. Middle-tier components can be written using any language, but they must be implemented as Automation servers. That is, they must implement the IDispatch interface. Visual Basic COM servers implement this interface by default and do not require additional steps.
- ❑ **If using ODBC DSNs, they should be defined as System DSNs**. System DSNs (Data Source Names) are available to every user and service on that machine. If accessing ODBC data from the middle-tier component, define all such DSNs as system DSNs. This is also true for ODBC data sources accessed through the RDSServer.DataFactory object. The reason is that when you log on to the server over an HTTP connection, the Anonymous user logging on through IIS cannot view user DSNs. This means that if I access this component though other means, such as DCOM, the IIS anonymous user is not used for authentication and this is not an issue. Also, you are not required to use a DSN at all. To enhance portability, and reduce complexity, a lot of users use DSN-less connections. This just means that there is no DSN defined on the machine; instead the connection information is built in code and passed to ADO as text. The following sample code shows an example of a DSN-less connection.

```
    strConn = "Provider=SQLOLEDB;Data Source=(local);User ID=sa;
        Password=;Initial Catalog=pubs"

    Set MyRS = New ADODB.Recordset
    MyRS.CursorLocation = adUseClient
    MyRS.CursorType = adOpenStatic
    MyRS.LockType = adLockBatchOptimistic
MyRS.Open "Select * From Authors", strConn
```

❑ **Use Client Cursors**. Recordsets created on the server that are to be passed to the client must be opened using a client-side cursor (a CursorLocation property value of adUseClient), and the cursor type must be static (currently, client-side cursors support only the static type). This allows the recordset to be disconnected from the ADO connection. In addition, if data in the recordset will be updated, the lock type must be batch-optimistic. The following code shows an example of this:

```
Public Function ReturnRS(strConnect As String, _
                       strQuery As String) As ADODB.Recordset
  ' An ADOR recordset will be received on the client
  Dim objAdoCon1 As New ADODB.Connection
  Dim objAdoRs1 As New ADODB.Recordset

  ' Open a connection to the Database
  objAdoCon1.Open strConnect

  ' Set the CursorLocation to adUseClient
  objAdoCon1.CursorLocation = adUseClient

' Set the CursorType to static
' All client-side cursors are static
' but it is good to set it anyway.
  objAdoCon1.CursorType= adStatic

  ' Open an ADO Recordset
  objAdoRs1.Open strQuery, objAdoCon1, adOpenStatic, adLockBatchOptimistic

  ' Return ADO Recordset object to Client
  '       (returns the actual recordset, not just a pointer to it)
  Set ReturnRS = objAdoRs1

  ' Cannot close the ADO Recordset object here,
  '       but it can be disconnected
  Set objAdoRs1.ActiveConnection = Nothing

  ' Close ADO Connection object
  objAdoCon1.Close
End Function
```

❑ **Recordsets Must Re-Connected When Updating the Underlying Data Store**. If a method on the business object accepts a disconnected recordset as an input parameter, to apply the changes to an underlying data source a new connection to the data source must be opened. This connection must be set as the ActiveConnection property of the recordset. This is known as re-connecting. After this the UpdateBatch method can be called to update the recordset.

The following code fragment is an example of what might run on the client to call the custom business object on the server. The fragment shows how the RDS.DataSpace object can use the GetRecordset method to invoke middle-tier components. This method would be defined inside the custom object. The object is identified by the PROGID MyObject.MyClass, running on MyServer, to which the client connects over an HTTP network. The GetRecordset method takes a parameter, TheParam, and returns a disconnected recordset:

```
Dim objRdsds as new RDS.Dataspace
Dim objMycustobj as new object
Dim objMyrs as new ADOR.Recordset

Set objMycustobj = objRdsds.CreateObject('MyObject.MyClass','http://MyServer')
Set objMyrs = objMycustobj.GetRecordset(TheParam)
```

Programming Example for RDS

The following code sample demonstrates the concepts and processes we have been describing in this chapter. We'll look at two sections of code, one running on the client and the other running on the server. First here's the client code.

What's Happening on the Client?

```
------------------------------------------------
Client Call. This code runs on the client:
------------------------------------------------
Private Sub cmdGetData_Click()

' Create an instance of the DataSpace
  Set objDs = CreateObject("RDS.DataSpace")

  ' Use the DataSpace version of CreateObject here
  ' Pass in the name of your custom object
  ' Pass in the name of the IIS server on which
  ' the custom object is registered and will be created.
  Set objBo = objDs.CreateObject("MyBusObject.MyClass", "http://MyWebServer")

  Dim objADORs
' Call custom method of the object
Set objADORs = objBo.GetRecordset(strConnectionString, strSQL)
End Sub
```

There are only three lines of code executing in the sample code above. The first executing line of code uses the VBScript CreateObject function to instantiate the RDS.DataSpace object. That object will be used to create the RDS default server object, RDSServer.DataFactory. After the first line of code executes, the code will hold a reference to the RDS.DataSpace object in the objDs variable. The objDs variable can then be used to gain access to the RDS.DataSpace object. In the next line of code, the CreateObject method of the RDS.DataSpace object is called to instantiate the MyBusObject.MyClass business object. That business object is located on the http://MyWebServer server. Note that the CreateObject method of the RDS.DataSpace object accepts two parameters. The first parameter names the business object. The second parameter names the server.

When the object is created, the objBo variable will hold a reference to that object. Note that the object is created on another machine. My code can control that object. In this case, my code is executing the custom GetRecordset method of my object. This method will return a recordset. The recordset was created on the server, and returned, from across the Internet, to the client.

Now we'll see the code running on the server.

What's Happening on the Server?

```
-------------------------------------------
Server Object. This code runs on the server:
-------------------------------------------
' Notice that the input parameters are passed
' in ByVal.
' Also, notice that the return type is ADOR
' type recordset instead of ADODB.Recordset
Public Function GetRecordset(ByVal strConnect As String,
ByVal SQL As String) As ADOR.Recordset

  On Error GoTo errGetRecordset
  Dim objADORs As New ADOR.Recordset

  ' Very Important!!! This allows the recordset
  ' to be disconnected and sent to the client
  objADORs.CursorLocation = adUseClient
  objADORs.Open SQL, Connect, adOpenUnspecified, adLockBatchOptimistic, _
        adCmdUnspecified

  Set GetRecordset = objADORs
Exit Function
ErrGetRecordset:
'Handle Error
End Function
-------------------------------------------
```

The server code above will run as part of the custom business object. The custom business object runs on an IIS server, named in the client call above. The GetRecordset procedure is created with a return-type of ADOR.Recordset.

We could also have used an alternative (more efficient) method of instantiation, by using two separate calls, as we saw earlier on in the chapter (first using Dim and then Set).

In the rest of our example code above, we declare a variable that will store the object reference, and create an instance of that object on the declaration line. Afterwards, the cursor is set to use the client-side cursor and the recordset is opened. Finally, the recordset is returned from the server to the client by setting the name of the procedure to the recordset object reference variable.

Summary

In this chapter we have discussed the limitations of the RDSServer.DataFactory object, and the advantages of building your own business object with RDS capabilities. We showed how to build a business object with Visual Basic, and looked at the code that would run in it. Finally we learnt how to enable a business object for use with RDS, whether on the same machine, over a LAN, or over the Internet.

This was a complex and detailed chapter, but you now have the tools required for building your own business object, if the need arises. In the following chapter we'll look at further possibilities with RDS, with data binding and Dynamic HTML.

DHTML's Role in RDS

DHTML is one of the most exciting application development technologies in a long time. Most end users thoroughly enjoy using well-designed, interactive web applications built with DHTML. For the first time, Web developers have a chance to create highly functional and user-friendly applications, that standard Windows developers have enjoyed for years in languages such as Visual Basic. Even if you have not had an opportunity to develop web applications with DHTML, chances are that you have browsed to a page that uses it. Using DHTML we can provide drop-down menus, font roll-over effects (font changes when the mouse rolls over them) and other techniques designed to make our Web pages more functional, enjoyable and easy to use.

As if DHTML by itself was not impressive enough, we have the ability to factor data access into the equation. The data-access capabilities of RDS combined with the presentation features of DHTML provides a powerful one-two punch that enables you to create knockout web applications.

This chapter is designed to provide you with the understanding of how these two technologies work together to produce highly interactive and dynamically data driven Web pages. We'll discuss the basic features of DHTML that allow us to create simple data bound web pages using the Tabular Data Control and the RDS `DataControl` object. The main concept we'll concentrate on in this chapter is how we can employ DHTML's features to enhance our data driven Web pages. We'll tackle this topic by first looking at the `RDS.DataControl` object and tabular data control objects, and then see how we integrate DHTML into the equation.

In this chapter we will discuss the following topics:

- ❑ Using DHTML with Data
- ❑ New Features of the RDS DataControl
- ❑ Using the RDS DataControl
- ❑ Using the Tabular Data Control
- ❑ A Simple Data Bound Selection Page

Using DHTML with Data

DHTML is a powerful new development platform. It will be to your advantage to learn to use DHTML to build powerful Intranet applications. DHTML is extremely important because of the many changes it brings to HTML. For instance, you can do these things with DHTML quite easily while they would be difficult or impossible with HTML:

❑ Accurately position elements on a page

❑ Bind intrinsic HTML controls to a data source

❑ Access remote data from client-side script

❑ Programmatically change the style characteristics of a page without refreshing the page in the browser

❑ Programmatically reload images, data, and other page elements without refreshing the page in the browser

❑ Apply custom multimedia effects to elements on a page

I think of DHTML as a version of HTML that provides developers with some features that plain HTML does not provide. You no longer need to make a round-trip to the server and redisplay the page for each action. Instead, your application can contain client-side script that runs in the browser and uses DHTML to completely handle the updates to the page. The user will see an interface that appears to execute smoothly just like a traditional VB application.

Basic DHTML

Let's take a look at an extremely simple page. You can create a page with the idea of letting the user toggle between two images. The functionality for the page is implemented by using an HTML <IMG> tag and a VBScript function. When the user clicks on the image, the image itself changes to show a different graphic.

This simple functionality is achieved by implementing a few lines of code. The image tag inserts the image and links the `toggle` function to the `onclick` event for the image. This is how we trigger the action when the user clicks the image:

```
<IMG SRC="images/Image1.gif" id="logo" style="LEFT: 268px; POSITION: absolute;
TOP: 54px; Z-INDEX: 101" onclick="toggle()" WIDTH="81" HEIGHT="81">
```

The `IMG` tag also includes another feature that we can easily overlook. The `style` attribute includes parameters for `TOP`, `LEFT`, and `POSITION`. This example includes `POSITION: absolute`, which allows us to specify the exact location of the `IMG` on the page. Using this one DHTML feature, you can create Web pages with discretely positioned elements such as aligned data entry boxes. The positioning features make it easier to position elements and streamline your HTML code. We can accomplish this because we can simply specify exactly how our elements should appear. For example, without the `POSITION` attribute, this image would have appeared wherever we placed it within the HTML page relative to all of the other HTML within the page.

Next, we use a script block to contain the VBScript procedure `toggle`. In this function, we check the value of the `src` attribute of the image which we named `logo`. If the `src` attribute is set to `Image1.gif`, then we reset it to `beach.gif`. If it is not `Image1.gif`, then we reset it to `Image1.gif`.

```
<SCRIPT language=vbscript>
sub toggle()

  if (logo.src = "http://MyServer/images/Image1.gif") then
      logo.src = "http://MyServer/images/beach.jpg"
  else
      logo.src = "http://MyServer/images/Image1.gif"
  end if
End Sub
</SCRIPT>

</BODY>
</HTML>
```

This code is quite simple, but illustrates one of the most useful aspects of DHTML. You can use client script (VBScript in our case) to accomplish many tasks and do it all within the browser without ever making a trip back to the server. This makes developing applications easier and gives you more tools to create robust Web pages.

How DHTML Compliments RDS

It may not be clear as to why we might use DHTML with RDS. To answer these questions, it is useful to know exactly what DHTML is. Once we understand what DHTML is, we can more effectively answer the question, "How do RDS and DHTML relate to one another".

We know that DHTML has the ability to access certain client-side objects. You might be asking yourself, "What are these objects? And what do they mean to me?" Without going into an extended discussion of DHTML, let us focus on those components that provide data access functionality.

> *For comprehensive DHTML coverage with IE4, see Instant IE4 Dynamic HTML by Alex Homer and Chris Ullman (Wrox, ISBN 1861000685).*

The most valuable features of DHTML that allow you to use RDS easily include the fact that intrinsic HTML controls can be easily bound to the RDS.DataControl. By simply identifying the RDS.DataControl to be used and the field from the RDS.DataControl, our page can display data from any data source from anywhere in the world. In addition, because we can access data from the RDS.DataControl in code, we can use DHTML to display the data in any way that we choose.

Using the RDS.DataControl object

So how do we tie an HTML element to an RDS.DataControl? We bridge the gap by setting the DATASRC property of specific HTML elements to bind the recordset's fields directly to these elements. But before we can bind the RDS.DataControl to any elements, we must first define it by embedding it using the <OBJECT> tag, as shown in the following code:

```
<OBJECT CLASSID="clsid:BD96C556-65A3-11D0-983A-00C04FC29E33" ID="objDataControl"
      <PARAM NAME="Connect" VALUE="Provider=SQLOLEDB;Database=pubs;">
      <PARAM NAME="Server" VALUE="http://Myserver">
      <PARAM NAME="SQL" VALUE="Select * from authors">
</OBJECT>
```

Now that we have defined the RDS.DataControl, we can move on to binding the data fields themselves to individual HTML elements.

Adding Data to the Mix

The most important feature of any Intranet application is probably the ability to access and analyze data. DHTML provides several features that we can use to easily access data. RDS is a COM object built directly into IE4 that provides a recordset within a Web page that is accessible via DHTML.

DHTML provides data binding attributes on several elements. For instance, the TABLE tag has a DATASRC attribute that is used to specify the data source (such as an RDS.DataControl). Other tags such as INPUT fields have a DATAFLD attribute which is used to bind to the recordset fields you are using. Other data attributes are DATAFORMATAS (a format specifier) and DATAPAGESIZE (controls the number of rows to display at one time in a table).

The easiest way to use the data binding features is with RDS, although we can also use the tabular data control. We'll cover both routes in this chapter, however we definitely prefer the RDS.DataControl. You simply place an RDS control on the page, set its properties, then bind the DHTML tags to it or programmatically drive it. The first example we will look at uses RDS and a DHTML table.

Check Out the Code

Let's take a look at how this code works. First, we create a new page. This example uses an ASP page. Then we add the object tag for the RDS tag:

```
<!-- RDS Control -->
<OBJECT classid="clsid:BD96C556-65A3-11D0-983A-00C04FC29E33"
ID="objSControl" WIDTH="1" HEIGHT="1">
    <param NAME="SERVER"    VALUE="http://
            <%=Request.ServerVariables("SERVER_NAME")%>">
</OBJECT>
```

The classid will be the same for each instance of RDS. Notice that it is not an intuitive classid whatsoever. In fact, I suggest that if you use Visual InterDev 6.0 that you create an item in your toolbox for the RDS.DataControl so you can simply drag and drop the RDS.DataControl into your Web pages. The ID property is set to the name we want to use for the control (objSControl). The code uses the ServerVariables collection to set the SERVER parameter with the correct name of the server. The reason we used the ServerVariables collection instead of hard coding the server name was to allow us to move the page from one system to another.

Next, we created the BODY tag for the page and set it to execute the "Load" subroutine when it loads:

```
<BODY language="VBScript" onload="Load">
```

We included a bit of code to set several RDS constants from the file adovbs.inc that we've seen before. We pulled the following constants from that file:

```
'---- enum Values ----
Const adcExecSync = 1
Const adcExecAsync = 2

'---- enum Values ----
Const adcFetchUpFront = 1
Const adcFetchBackground = 2
Const adcFetchAsync = 3
```

All of the enumerators for ADO and RDS can be found in Appendix G

The `Load` subroutine creates the recordset for the page when it loads. This is quite similar to using the `Form_Load` event in a VB form. The first step is to set up the options for RDS. We set the `ExecuteOptions` to `adcExecSync` to set RDS to synchronous execution.

```
objSControl.ExecuteOptions = adcExecSync
```

Then we set the `FetchOptions` to `adcFetchBackground` so fetching can occur in the background.

```
objSControl.FetchOptions = adcFetchBackground
```

Now we can define the SQL to retrieve the records for our page. The SQL is set just like any other VB or VBScript SQL statement:

```
objSControl.SQL = "Select au_FName, au_LName, Phone, city from authors"
```

Next, we set the DSN setting. I used a System DSN that points to the `Pubs` sample database that ships with SQL Server. You can also use a File DSN or a DSN string. We like the File DSN as it totally hides the connection information and credentials from the user. We used the System DSN in this case for the sake of simplicity only.

```
objSControl.Connect = "dsn=pubs;UID=sa;PWD=;"
```

Next, we execute the `Refresh` method to open the recordset.

```
objSControl.Refresh
```

That's it! Now we have an active recordset that we can use right in our HTML page. Now, let's take a look at how we put data on the page.

Displaying the Data

First, we create a new HTML table. This sample uses data binding to link the HTML elements to the RDS control. The next line creates the table and sets the `datasrc` property to point to our RDS control. Note the # prefix to the control's name:

```
<TABLE border="1" datasrc="#objSControl" style="LEFT: 69px; POSITION: absolute;
TOP: 187px; Z-INDEX: 100">
```

The next two lines are `Table` tags that create the table detail body and the first table row:

```
<TDBODY>
<TR>
```

Now, we simply bind the HTML elements to the recordset field. We accomplish this by setting the `datafld` property to the field name:

```
<TD width="50"><INPUT
    datafld="au_fName" size="15"
```

We simply repeat this line for each field in the table, then close the table detail body and the table. That's it!

RDS and the DHTML data binding are quite powerful. You can access the fields in the RDS recordset using this syntax:

```
SFirst.Value = objSControl.Recordset("au_FName")
```

This would place this value of `au_Fname` in the `Sfirst` field (an Input Textbox). You set values using the opposite syntax:

```
objSControl.Recordset("au_FName")
  = SFirst.Value
```

This sets the value in the recordset to the value in the textbox.

Updating the Data

Since RDS is working over HTTP, you do not need a LAN connection to use these features. RDS pulls the data down to the client where it remains until you are through using it or you execute code to update the database.

Users can continue to work with the recordset locally as long as they need to. They can even change data in the recordset locally. When you are ready to update the server, you execute the `SubmitChanges` method:

```
objSControl.SubmitChanges
```

This method performs a batch update to the server, sending all the changes at one time. You can also update the server as each change is made – it's your choice as a developer.

You can cancel an update action with this method:

```
objSControl.CancelUpdate
```

To navigate through an RDS recordset, you use the standard navigation features (`MoveNext`, `MoveLast`, `BOF`, and `EOF`). The syntax for navigation is:

```
objSControl.Recordset.MoveLast
```

Complete Code

The complete code listing follows below, so that you can see how everything we've looked at so far fits together (you can also obtain the code from the Wrox website). Notice the use of the `<OBJECT>` tag to include the object on the page. Also, notice the use of the `id` parameter on the `<OBJECT>` tag. Notice how the value of this tag is used on the HTML table tags to identify the source of the data.

```
<HTML>
<HEAD>
<!-- RDS Control -->
<OBJECT classid="clsid:BD96C556-65A3-11D0-983A-00C04FC29E33"
ID="objSControl" WIDTH="1" HEIGHT="1">
     <param NAME="SERVER"     VALUE="http://
             <%=Request.ServerVariables("SERVER_NAME")%>">
</OBJECT>

<TITLE>Consultant Listing</TITLE>
</HEAD>

<BODY language="VBScript" onload="Load">

<H1 align="center"> </H1>
<CENTER>
<TABLE border="0" cellPadding="1" cellSpacing="1" height="80" style="HEIGHT: 80px;
LEFT: 106px; POSITION: absolute; TOP: 20px; WIDTH: 308px; Z-INDEX: 102"
width="48.58%">
<TR>
     <TD><STRONG><FONT size="6">Master Consultants</FONT></STRONG>
     </TD>
</TR>
</TABLE>

 

<H1 align="center"><FONT color="#160b5a">

<TABLE border="0" cellPadding="1" cellSpacing="1" height="56" style="HEIGHT: 56px;
LEFT: 23px; POSITION: absolute; TOP: 125px; WIDTH: 223px; Z-INDEX: 103"
width="35.17%">
<TR>
     <TD><STRONG><FONT size="4">Consultant Listing</FONT></STRONG>
     </TD>
</TR>
</TABLE>

<BR>

</H1>
 

<H2>
```

```
<TABLE border="1" datasrc="# objSControl" style="LEFT: 69px; POSITION: absolute;
TOP: 187px; Z-INDEX: 100">
<TDBODY>
<TR>
     <TD width="50">
          <input datafld="au_fName" size="15" id="text0" name="first">
     </TD>
     <TD width="50">
          <INPUT datafld="au_lName" size="15" id="text1" name="last">
     </TD>
     <TD width="50">
          <input datafld="Phone" size="15" id="text2" name="Phone">
     </TD>
     <TD width="50">
          <input datafld="City" size="15" id="text3" name="City">
     </TD>
</TR>
</TDBODY>
</TABLE >

<SCRIPT language="VBScript">

'---- enum Values ----
Const adcExecSync = 1
Const adcExecAsync = 2

'---- enum Values ----
Const adcFetchUpFront = 1
Const adcFetchBackground = 2
Const adcFetchAsync = 3

SUB Load
     'Change the asynchronous options such that execution is synchronous
     'and Fetching can occur in the background
     ObjSControl.ExecuteOptions = adcExecSync
     ObjSControl.FetchOptions = adcFetchBackground

     'Define SQL
     ObjSControl.SQL = "Select au_FName, au_LName, Phone, city from authors"

     ObjSControl.Connect = "dsn=pubs;UID=sa;PWD=;"
     ' System  DSN must be installed on this system

     ObjSControl.Refresh

END SUB

</SCRIPT>

<IMG src="images/Image1.gif" style="LEFT: 21px; POSITION: absolute; TOP: 7px; Z-
INDEX: 101" WIDTH="81" HEIGHT="81"></h2></font>
</BODY>
</HTML>
```

Using the Tabular Data Control

The Tabular Data Control is another object that allows you to provide data to your DHTML application. It works very similarly to the way that the RDS.DataControl works. However, the Tabular Data Control is not part of RDS. The Tabular Data Control is not as robust or functional as the RDS.DataControl, however we have included it for the sake of completeness.

Although the Tabular Data Control cannot do most of what the RDS.DataControl can do, it is a simple, lightweight alternative to the RDS.DataControl. The Tabular Data Control is designed to take, as its only form of input, a flat comma-delimited text file. (You can get a sample file on the Wrox website.) This file must exist on the same local area network as the client-side application that is using it. In other words, if you are using a web-browser, the text file must exist on that side of the Internet (on the client PC or some drive the client PC can access). If your application is running on an Intranet, the file can exist anywhere on the same local area network.

The Tabular Data Control on your Web Page

The process of using the Tabular Data Control to bring data to your web page follows 6 simple steps:

1. Add the <OBJECT> tag for the Tabular Data Control to that page.

2. Set the properties of the Tabular Data Control that will inform it which text file to use as the source of data.

3. Add elements to the page that will display the data from the Tabular Data Control.

4. Set the datasrc property of those elements to the name of the Tabular Data Control.

5. Set the datafld property of those elements to the column to which that element will bind.

6. Set the dataformatas property of any text-based elements, such as text boxes.

The use of the Tabular Data Control is very similar to using the RDS.DataControl. The remainder of this section will describe the specific settings of the Tabular Data Control, most of which will also apply to the RDS.DataControl. Both controls have a non-visible ActiveX control that is used to implement functionality. They both use an <OBJECT> tag to add the control to the page. Although some properties and property values are different between the two controls, their use is nearly identical.

Setting the Properties

The minimal properties of the <OBJECT> tag that will display the Tabular Data Control are as follows:

```
<OBJECT id="objMyTDC" CLASSID="CLSID:333C7BC1-460F-11D0-BC04-0080C7055A83">
</OBJECT>
```

There are also other properties that will need to be set before we can actually get to our data. (We will cover these as we go.)

First of all, the Tabular Data Control must know where it can find the data that will be added to the page. The `DataURL` property tells the Tabular Data Control from where to retrieve the data. The following example adds this new property to the `<OBJECT>` tag above. The file named `MyData.txt` is the comma-delimited file that contains the data that will be displayed on the page.

```
<OBJECT id="objMyTDC" CLASSID="CLSID:333C7BC1-460F-11D0-BC04-0080C7055A83">
    <PARAM NAME = "DataURL" VALUE="MyData.txt">
</OBJECT>
```

The `<OBJECT>` tag has only a few arguments that can be passed to it. The `id` argument is one and `CLASSID` is another. Since the `<OBJECT>` tag can be used to instantiate a virtually infinite number of objects with any number of properties, the `<PARAM>` tag can be used to assign property values to those objects. The `<PARAM>` tag takes two arguments, `NAME` and `VALUE`. `NAME` represents the name of a specific property that belongs to the object being created by the `<OBJECT>` tag. `VALUE` represents the value of that property.

Be aware of the fact that the actual value of the `CLASSID` parameter is pre-defined. You must find a copy of this class id and enter it into the `<OBJECT>` tag. To find the `CLASSID` of the Tabular Data Control, you can locate some sample code (like that above), or search your Windows registry for "Tabular Data Control".

Data Aware Elements

The next step is to add intrinsic HTML controls and tags to the page for displaying the data. These controls will bind to the Tabular Data Control and will have the ability to display to the user whatever data the Tabular Data Control exposes. Examples of controls and tags that can be used to display data from a Tabular Data Control follows. Please remember that, as impressive as this list is, it is not an all-inclusive list. There are more HTML tags that can be bound.

For a comprehensive discussion of the tags that can be bound, see the next chapter, DHTML's Role in RDS.

The following list applies to both the Tabular Data Control and the `RDS.DataControl`:

❑   <A>
❑   <APPLET>
❑   <DIV>
❑   <FRAME>
❑   <IFRAME>
❑   <IMG>
❑   <INPUT TYPE=Checkbox>
❑   <INPUT TYPE=Hidden>
❑   <INPUT TYPE=Password>
❑   <INPUT TYPE=Radio>
❑   <INPUT TYPE=Text>
❑   <MARQUEE>

- ❑ `<OBJECT>`
- ❑ `<SPAN>`
- ❑ `<TABLE>`
- ❑ `<TEXTAREA>`

Using the Input Tag

The following example shows how you might use the `<INPUT>` tag to display data exposed from the Tabular Data Control in an intrinsic textbox. Note the use of the `datasrc` argument to specify the name of the Tabular Data Control to which to connect. The syntax of this argument requires that the name of the control (whether this is the Tabular Data Control or the `RDS.DataControl`) be preceded by a pound sign (#).

```
<INPUT TYPE =text datasrc="#objMyTDC">
```

The tag that will display the data must also know which column (or field) from which to pull the data. The `datafld` argument allows us to identify it. The following extension to the above code allows us to specify the specific field to display.

```
<INPUT TYPE="text" datasrc="#objMyTDC" datafld="FirstName">
```

That is all that is required to display data from a text file in Internet Explorer 4.0 (or above) using the Tabular Data Control. Again, these steps also apply to the `RDS.DataControl`.

One final step is optional and applies only if you are using an HTML tag that can display text and pure HTML, such as a `<SPAN>` tag or a `<DIV>` tag. The `dataformatas` argument allows us to tell the page how to format the data coming in from the Tabular Data Control. By default, the data is formatted as text. You can, however, tell the page to format the data as HTML. As mentioned above, this is really only useful for those tags that understand pure HTML. The following example shows how we might use a `<DIV>` tag to display the same data as shown above. This tag and arguments are used in exactly the same way as the `<INPUT>` tag:

```
<DIV datasrc="#objMyTDC" datafld="FirstName" dataformatas="html">
```

The complete example would look like the following code. Notice that there are no formatting HTML tags included below. The textbox and the `<DIV>` tag would appear side-by-side on the web page.

```
<HTML>
<OBJECT id="objMyTDC" CLASSID="CLSID:333C7BC1-460F-11D0-BC04-0080C7055A83">
  <PARAM NAME = "DataURL" VALUE="MyData.txt">
</OBJECT>

<INPUT TYPE="text" datasrc="#objMyTDC" datafld="FirstName">
<DIV datasrc="#objMyTDC" datafld="FirstName" dataformatas="HTML"></DIV>
</HTML>
```

275

Navigating through the Data

Once you have a Tabular Data Control on your page and you are displaying data, it would be nice to be able to move through the data and display each record (row of data) one at a time. The example (as written) above would not allow this, but we can easily make this happen.

The code syntax that will allow you to move from one record to the next is shown below. Note that the first word will be the name of the Tabular Data Control, the second word is `Recordset` and the third word is one of the move methods.

```
MyTabularDataControl.Recordset.MoveMethod
```

The move methods include those methods that allow your application to display a specific record in the data from the Tabular Data Control. Whenever you use one of the `Move` methods (`MoveNext`, `MovePrevious`, `MoveFirst` and `MoveLast`), the contents of all of the HTML elements on the page that are linked to the Tabular Data Control will automatically be updated. This happens regardless of where on the page those elements are located.

An example of when we might use a `Move` method with the above example is shown below. Note that the first word is the name we used to identify the Tabular Data Control, and the last word indicates the specific `Move` method we have chosen.

```
objMyTDC.Recordset.MoveNext
```

We can also use two read-only properties using nearly identical syntax to determine if we have traveled beyond the scope of the data exposed by the control. These properties are shown below:

Property Name	Description
EOF	The user has traveled one position past the last record in the data exposed by the control. This property is set to TRUE if the dataset has moved to this position, and FALSE if the dataset has not moved to this position.
BOF	The user has traveled one position before the first record in the data exposed by the control. This property is set to TRUE if the dataset has moved to this position, and false if the dataset has not moved to this position.

These properties are usually used to determine if any data has been returned from the control, to manage the process of looping through all records or to determine if the user has moved past the last record or above the first record. The following code demonstrates the use of the `Move` methods and the read-only properties. We have implemented a page that displays data and uses buttons to provide the user direct control over which record is displayed from the underlying recordset.

```
<HTML>
<OBJECT id="objMyTDC" CLASSID="CLSID:333C7BC1-460F-11D0-BC04-0080C7055A83">
    <PARAM NAME = "DataURL" VALUE="MyData.txt">
</OBJECT>
```

```
<INPUT TYPE="text" datasrc="#objMyTDC" datafld="FirstName">
<DIV datasrc="#objMyTDC" datafld="FirstName" dataformatas="HTML"></DIV>

<SCRIPT language="VBScript">
    Sub comMoveNext_OnClick()
        ObjMyTDC.Recordset.MoveNext

        ' Prevent the user from moving past the last record.
        If ObjMyTDC.Recordset.EOF Then
            ObjMyTDC.Recordset.MoveLast
        End If
    End Sub
'-------------------------------------------
    Sub comMoveFirst_OnClick()
        ObjMyTDC.Recordset.MoveFirst
    End Sub
'-------------------------------------------
    Sub comMoveLast_OnClick()
        ObjMyTDC.Recordset.MoveLast
    End Sub
'-------------------------------------------
    Sub comMovePrevious_OnClick()
        ObjMyTDC.Recordset.MovePrevious

        ' Prevent the user from moving above the first record.
        If ObjMyTDC.Recordset.BOF Then
            ObjMyTDC.Recordset.MoveFirst
        End If
    End Sub
</SCRIPT>

<INPUT TYPE="BUTTON" ID="comMoveNext" Name="comMoveNext" VALUE=">"><BR>
<INPUT TYPE="BUTTON" ID="comMovePrevious" Name="comMovePrevious" VALUE="<"><BR>
<INPUT TYPE="BUTTON" ID="comMoveFirst" Name="comMoveFirst" VALUE="<<"><BR>
<INPUT TYPE="BUTTON" ID="comMoveLast" Name="comMoveLast" VALUE=">>">

</HTML>
```

This is a very easy way to bring data from an external source and display it on the page. The icing on the cake is the fact that the methods used to interact with the Tabular Data Control and the `RDS.DataControl` are nearly identical. The difference lies in the source of data. The Tabular Data Control uses the `DataURL` property, while the `RDS.DataControl` uses the `SQL`, `SERVER` and `CONNECT` properties.

What is the Source of The Data?

Up to this point, we have discussed how to use data that is exposed from a flat text file through the Tabular Data Control. We now need to talk about the structure of that text file. The file itself is a simple comma-delimited text file that can be opened in any text editor. Some applications, like Microsoft Excel, make it easy to create a comma-delimited text file. The following example shows the typical structure of a comma-delimited text (`csv`) file that might be used as the source of data for a Tabular Data Control.

```
FirstName, LastName, FavoriteCity, FavoriteCookie
Sharon, Love, Greensboro, ChocolateChip
London, Hairston, Tampa, ChocolateChip
Cynthia, Williams, Tampa, ChocolateChip
Gwen, Love, Winston-Salem, ChocolateChip
```

The previous example displays text that might be part of `MyData.txt`, or any text file that might be the source of data for the Tabular Data Control. Note that the first row contains only words that will be used as column (or field) names. This row is optional, but helpful if it is included because it makes identifying individual fields easier.

Other properties are as follows:

Tabular Data Control Property Name	Description
FieldDelim	Set the character that will be used as the field delimiter. By default, the value of this property is the comma ",".
RowDelim	Set the character that will be used as the row delimiter. By default, the value of this property is the non-printing carriage return (cr) character. Using this property you can use a text file that contains text in a single line, then read it into a page as multiple records.
UserHeader	We can tell the Tabular Data Control that the first row of the text file will contain column headings by setting the UseHeader property to TRUE.

An example of using these properties follows. Notice that we can set the value of all of these properties in a single <OBJECT> tag. Note the value of the UseHeader property is set to 1, which indicates a value of TRUE.

```
<OBJECT id="objMyTDC" CLASSID="CLSID:333C7BC1-460F-11D0-BC04-0080C7055A83">
     <PARAM NAME = "DataURL" VALUE="MyData.txt">
     <PARAM NAME = "FieldDelim " VALUE=";">
     <PARAM NAME = "RowDelim " VALUE="|">
     <PARAM NAME = "UserHeader" VALUE="1">
</OBJECT>
```

> The properties **DataURL**, **FieldDelim**, **RowDelim**, and **UseHeader** do not apply to the **RDS.DataControl**. They apply only to the Tabular Data Control.

This <OBJECT> tag identifies `MyData.txt` as the source file whose contents will be displayed on the web page. The row delimiter of that file is a semi-colon (;) and the column delimiter of that file is the pipe (|). In addition, the file will use the first row as the heading of all of the columns of data in the file.

The RDS.DataControl and the Tabular Data Control Contrasted

The Tabular Data Control is not nearly as powerful as the RDS.DataControl for accessing data. While the RDS.DataControl can access nearly any type of data from nearly anywhere in the world, the Tabular Data Control can access data from only delimited text file. The advantage to learning to use the Tabular Data Control is that it provides a good introduction to using data-bound controls (and can also be useful in those situations in which your application actually needs access to a delimited text file!). In addition, you can easily leverage your knowledge to the RDS.DataControl; the process of adding the control to the page is identical and many of the methods for interacting with the control are the same.

To illustrate this let's look at a simple data-bound selection page that demonstrates the use of the RDS.DataControl object. We'll use the RDS.DataControl object to connect to a database, then display the contents of a data set on the web page.

The RDS.DataControl on your web page

```
<HTML>
  <HEAD>
    <STYLE>
      TD {font-size:18pt}
      INPUT {font-size:18pt}
    </SYTLE>

    <TITLE>RDS and DHMTL Example</TITLE>
  </HEAD>

  <BODY>

    <P>
      <OBJECT classid="clsid:bd96c556-65a3-11d0-983a-00c04fc29e33"
              id=objRds1 height=10 width = 10>
        <PARAM name="SQL" value="select * from authors">
        <PARAM name="SERVER" value="http://Myserver">
        <PARAM name="CONNECT" value="dsn=pubs;UID=sa;PWD=;">
      </OBJECT>

    <H1 style="color:#0000CD">AUTHOR NAMES</H1>

    <TABLE style="table-layout:fixed" border datasrc="#objRds1">
      <COL width=150>
      <COL width=150>
      <COL width=100>

      <THEAD>
        <TH>First Name</TH>
        <TH>Last Name</TH>
        <TH>Phone</TH>
      </THEAD>
      <TR>
        <TD>
          <INPUT type=text datasrc=#objRds1 datafld="First Name" size=15>
        </TD>
```

```
            <TD>
                <INPUT type=text datasrc=#objRds1 datafld="Last Name" size=15>
            </TD>
            <TD>
                <INPUT type=text datasrc=#objRds1 datafld="Phone" size=10>
            </TD>
        </TR>
    </TABLE>

    <BR>
    <BR>
    <INPUT type=button id=updateDB name=updateDB value="Update">
</BODY>

<SCRIPT language=VBScript>
    Const adFilterConflictingRecords = 5

    Sub updateDB_onclick()
        On Error Resume Next

        objRds1.recordset.update
        objRds1.recordset.updateBatch

        IF (Err.Number <> 0) Then
            HandleError()
        End IF

    End Sub

    Sub HandleError()
        Msgbox "Conflict detected during update"
        Set myRecordset = objRds1.recordset
        myRecordset.Filter = adFilterConflictingRecords

        MsgBox "Recordset could not be updated.  " & _
               "Update conflicts occured on " & _
               CStr(myRecordset.RecordCount) & " records."

        myRecordset.Resync 4,1

        myRecordset.moveFirst()

        While Not myRecordset.EOF
            MsgBox "The original salary (" & _
                   myRecordset.fields("Salary").OriginalValue & _
                   ") has already been changed to " & _
                   myRecordset.fields("Salary").UnderlyingValue
            myRecordset.moveNext()
        Wend

        objRds1.sql = "select au_fname, au_lname, phone from authors"
        objRds1.refresh
    End Sub
</SCRIPT>

</HTML>
```

In the above code, the <OBJECT> tag is used to add the RDS.DataControl to the page. The tag takes the usual Identifier string (the GUID) for the control. It also takes an id parameter, which is the value that client-side scripting will use to reference and command the RDS.DataControl. The SQL, SERVER and CONNECT properties are required. The RDS.DataControl cannot retrieve the data without proper values in these properties.

This control can be bound to many different types of intrinsic HTML controls and tags. In the case of this code, the RDS.DataControl is bound to an HTML <TABLE> tag. The <TABLE> tag has a property named datasrc that is used as the property that names the RDS.DataControl that will be used as the source of the data. This parameter uses a pound (#) sign on the RDS.DataControl object name, even though that actual name does not include that character.

The specific fields of data, that come from the RDS.DataControl, can be specified using the datafld property of the <INPUT> tag. In this case, the <INPUT> tag is defining a text box that will display a field of data from the database. The value of the datafld property must be the same as a field defined in the SQL statement of the RDS.DataControl.

Building Object Tags at Run-Time

Using ASP, you can dynamically generate any HTML and script that will run in the browser. You have complete control over what code does and does not get downloaded to the client. It is awesome!

For example, the following code allows me to generate an <OBJECT> tag that will instantiate and run a RDS.DataControl object. Because this <OBJECT> tag is not hard-coded into the HTML page, it can get treated in different ways depending upon conditions, or not included all. The decision is completely up to us and the ASP script code that we write. This allows you to target the specific browser version and type. For example, if it does not support RDS you can do something else.

```
<HTML>
<HEAD>
</HEAD>
<BODY>
    <%
    Dim strServer
    Dim strConnectString
    Dim strSQL

    strServer = "http://www.MyServer.com"
    strConnectString = "dsn=pubs"
    strSQL = "SELECT au_Lname From Authors"
    ' booCreateObjectTag IS SET IN ANOTHER PLACE
    If booCreateObjectTag = True Then
      Response.Write _
         "<OBJECT classid='clsid:BD96C556-65A3-11D0-983A-00C04FC29E33'"
      Response.Write " ID=objMyDataControl Width=1 Height=1>"
      Response.Write "<PARAM NAME='CONNECT' VALUE='" & StrConnectString & "'>"
      Response.Write "<PARAM NAME='SERVER' VALUE='" & strServer & "'>"
      Response.Write "<PARAM NAME='SQL' VALUE='" & strSQL & "'>"
      Response.Write "</OBJECT>"
    Else
    End If
    %>
</BODY>
</HTML>
```

Notice that in the code on the previous page, we are generating HTML from the server-side at run-time. This HTML will be returned from the server to the client so that the browser can run the code. We can generate any HTML code from the server side because it is just text. In the example, we are generating an <OBJECT> tag that will have the duty of running our RDS.DataControl . We have separated the SQL, CONNECT and SERVER properties from the rest of the hard-coded pieces to the <OBJECT> tag. The reason is that I may want to change servers or databases at run-time. In this case I can easily do that by changing the values of the strServer, strConnectString and strSQL variables before concatenating those variables to the rest of the <OBJECT> tag. This is a very convenient and flexible way to exercise complete control over the content of your web pages.

Summary

In this chapter we have seen how a little DHTML mixed in with RDS in a Web application can create a powerful and user friendly application. We've also seen how some of DHTML's features compliment RDS and how those key features of DHTML can be used to jump start RDS development.

You can take advantage of DHTML with, RDS, and its data features only if your users are using IE4 or greater. Many organizations are standardizing on IE4 in order to take advantage of these features. RDS is powerful, fast, and can take a load off your overworked database and web servers. In the next chapter, we will continue with our exploration into the RDS.DataControl by showing how we can create some powerful and robust web pages based on RDS.

13

Data-Consuming Elements

We have looked at a few of the different ways we can procure data. In this chapter, we'll move on to talk about the page elements that can use (or consume) the data, when it arrives at the page. As we saw in the previous chapter, data-consuming HTML elements (such as the <INPUT> tag) can be bound to an RDS.DataControl object or the Tabular Data Control. What does this mean exactly? It means that we can take the data from an RDS.DataControl object and relate its fields directly to HTML elements on a Web page. These HTML elements will then contain data values from the RDS.DataControl's underlying recordset.

We have seen how to bind to an <INPUT> tag, but that leaves the data value wide open for editing. What if we want to simply display the values from an RDS.DataControl? In this chapter we'll see how we can bind data to just about any element on a web page. There are many types of HTML tags that can be bound to a RDS.DataControl object – we will discuss some of them in this chapter. First we'll take a look at the tags and how to bind the data to them. Then we'll look at how to display multiple records at a time.

In this chapter we will look at:

- ❑ Various <INPUT> tags
- ❑ The <TEXTAREA> tag
- ❑ The <DIV> and <SPAN> tags
- ❑ The <A> and <IMG> tags
- ❑ <SELECT> and <INPUT TYPE=RADIO> binding
- ❑ <TABLE> tags
- ❑ A case study

The most common way for an RDS.DataControl to expose data to a data consumer, is a row at a time. We use the methods of the data control object to navigate from one record to the next – however we never work with more than a single record at a time. (Even if we are going to display multiple records at once, we still never actually work with more than one record at a time). We'll look at some sample code that should allow you to work with your row data in nearly any form that you desire.

Data-Bound <INPUT> Tags

The <INPUT> tag can create many different types of page elements. In this section we'll look at the use of text, password, checkbox and hidden elements.

<INPUT TYPE=TEXT>

Binding is supported by the VALUE attribute of the input text. In the example below, the web page shows a text box, which is bound to the current record of the data set. The user can choose a different record by clicking on the arrow buttons – this also changes the value displayed in the text box to reflect the value of the current record. (The current record is managed by the underlying recordset within the MS Cursor Engine via RDS.)

Here's an example web page, which displays data binding with HTML elements. We'll reuse this web page in most of the examples in this chapter, making small changes to the code each time. The source of our data is the sample pubs database in SQL Server. We have also included basic navigational features to move from record to record within the recordset.

For this first example, we are populating the web page's data bound text boxes with all of the authors from the authors table of the pubs database:

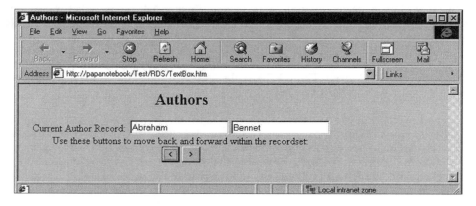

Here's the code which produces this sample web page. We begin by including the <OBJECT> tag for the objDC (RDS.DataControl) object.

```
<!-- RDS DataControl -->
<OBJECT classid="clsid:bd96c556-65a3-11d0-983a-00c04fc29e33"
id="objDC" width="0" height="0">
</OBJECT>
```

We have to set the RDS.DataControl's properties to valid values from within the window_onload event. This event fires automatically when the web page is first loaded. We set the Server property to the name of the server preceded by HTTP://, the SQL property to the database query, and the Connect property to the database connection string. Then we issue the Refresh method to populate the Web page with the data from the RDS.DataControl's recordset.

Next, we need to outline a couple of simple routines that control the forward and backward movement of the arrow buttons, as shown below. We are simply moving forward or backward one record at a time. If we move past the end or before the beginning of the recordset, we display a message and readjust the current record.

```
<SCRIPT LANGUAGE=VBScript>
Sub Window_OnLoad()
   objDC.Server = "http://papanotebook"
   objDC.SQL = "select au_fname, au_lname, city, contract, state from authors order
by au_lname, au_fname"
   objDC.Connect = "Provider=SQLOLEDB.1;User ID=sa;Password=;Initial
Catalog=pubs;Data Source=papanotebook"
   objDC.Refresh
End Sub

Sub GoForward()
   objDC.Recordset.MoveNext
   If objDC.Recordset.EOF Then
      Msgbox("You cannot move past the last item")
      objDC.Recordset.MoveLast
   End If
End Sub

Sub GoReverse()
   objDC.Recordset.MovePrevious
   If objDC.Recordset.BOF Then
      MsgBox("You cannot move above the first item")
      objDC.Recordset.MoveFirst
   End If
End Sub
</SCRIPT>
```

Now we're ready to write the data onto the web page. We bind the data to the two text boxes using the DATASRC and DATAFLD tag attributes. The DATASRC attribute represents the name of the RDS.DataControl, and the DATAFLD attribute represents the name of the field within the RDS.DataControl's recordset.

Finally, we create two buttons for forward and previous record navigation. Each button has an onclick event that calls the appropriate function to either go forward one record or go backward one record.

```
<TITLE>Authors</TITLE>
</HEAD>

<BODY bgcolor=#add8e6>
<CENTER>
<H2>Authors</H2>

Current Author Record: 
<INPUT type="text" datasrc="#objDC" datafld="au_fname">
<INPUT type="text" datasrc="#objDC" datafld="au_lname">
<BR>
Use these buttons to move back and forward within the recordset: 
<BR>
```

```
<INPUT type="button" value="  <  " onclick="GoReverse">
<INPUT type="button" value="  >  " onclick="GoForward">
<HR>

</CENTER>
</BODY>
</HTML>
```

This example uses RDS to marshal the data (the recordset) from the web server to the client PC (within the browser). Just because we do not see all of the records at once doesn't mean that they are not all there on the client! The records are on the client, embedded within the browser's page. That is why we can go forward and backward throughout the recordset without refreshing the page.

<INPUT TYPE="CHECKBOX">

Check boxes are traditionally used in HTML to determine whether a value is returned to the server when the page is submitted. Data binding uses the check box slightly differently. When we use checkboxes in tandem with data binding, the checkbox binds a Boolean value from the data set. Our code example will demonstrate how we add a data-bound checkbox to our previous example, as shown in the figure below:

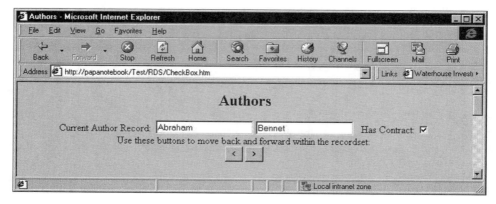

Much of the code for this example is similar to the code in textbox.htm, so we'll focus on the differences. Below is the <BODY> section of the HTML:

```
<BODY bgcolor=#add8e6>
<CENTER>
<H2>Authors</H2>

Current Author Record: 
<INPUT type="text" datasrc="#objDC" datafld="au_fname">
<INPUT type="text" datasrc="#objDC" datafld="au_lname">  
Has Contract: <INPUT type="checkbox" datasrc="#objDC" datafld="contract">
<BR>
Use these buttons to move back and forward within the recordset: 
<BR>
<INPUT type="button" value="  <  " onclick="GoReverse" >
<INPUT type="button" value="  >  " onclick="GoForward" >

</CENTER>
</BODY>
```

Notice how we added the checkbox and simply set its DATAFLD attribute to the contract field. This takes the boolean value of either 1 or 0 from the recordset and sets the checkbox either on or off.

<INPUT TYPE="HIDDEN">

Although they are invisible in the browser display, hidden input elements can also be data bound. Binding is to the VALUE attribute of the hidden element. In the sample code below, we move the current record by clicking on the arrow buttons, as we have in the previous examples. You can reveal the hidden value by clicking on the Show Hidden Value button (which produces a message box). Notice that the message box displays the current record's First Name value from the current record:

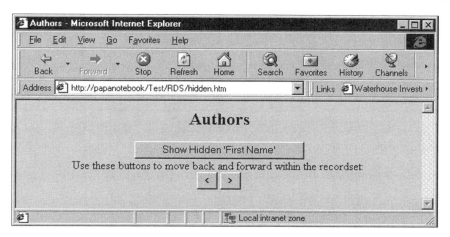

Here is the line of code that creates the hidden text box. This is simply a text box that is invisible on the web page.

```
<INPUT type="hidden" datasrc="#objDC" datafld="au_fname" name="txtFirstName">
```

We then can click the new button to show the hidden value by using a little DHTML in the button's onclick event, as shown below:

```
<INPUT type="button" value="Show Hidden 'First Name'" onclick="MsgBox
txtFirstName.value">
```

<INPUT TYPE="PASSWORD">

The VALUE attribute of a password input element can also be bound. Security is not compromised as the data is inaccessible external to the web page. However, I would not suggest using data binding with <PASSWORD> tags.

The code below shows how to bind a field to a password input element:

```
<INPUT type="password" datasrc="#objDC" datafld="au_fname" name="txtFirstName">
```

The <TEXTAREA> Tag

We can bind the contents of a text area to the current record of a data set. The bound data is displayed in the multi-line textbox. Here is an example of a text area bound to the current record:

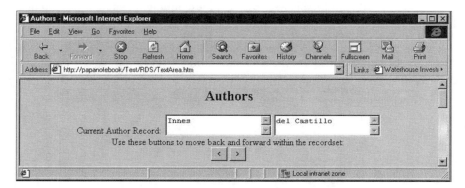

Clicking on the arrow buttons will move the current record. This results in the text area changing to display the values from the current record.

Notice the code below simply binds the data fields to the individual <TEXTAREA> tags.

```
Current Author Record: 
<TEXTAREA datasrc="#objDC" datafld="au_fname"></TEXTAREA>
<TEXTAREA datasrc="#objDC" datafld="au_lname"></TEXTAREA>
```

If you wanted to put a concatenation of both the first and last names in a <TEXTAREA> tag, you could create a derived field in your SQL Statement, like this:

```
objDC.SQL = "select au_fname + au_lname AS FullName from authors"
```

Then you would bind the <TEXTAREA> element to the FullName data field:

```
<TEXTAREA datasrc="#objDC" datafld="FullName"></TEXTAREA>
```

The <DIV> and <SPAN> Tags

At this point you are probably wondering how you can display a data bound value on a web page without having it appear in an editable element such as an <INPUT> tag. This is where <DIV> and <SPAN> tags step in. The big difference between the two is that a <DIV> tag puts a line break after itself while a <SPAN> tag does not. Therefore, if you wanted to put a display-only data bound field on the web page on the same line as some fixed text, you would want to use the <SPAN> tag.

The <DIV> tag

The <DIV> tag is an HTML container tag that contains other HTML. Data binding binds the content of a <DIV> to the data from a column in the data set. The column can contain either plain text or HTML. To render HTML, the <DIV> tag must include the DATAFORMATAS attribute set to a value of HTML.

A <DIV> tag can be bound to a column of the current record of a data set. Here's what this would look like – as before, you can click on the arrow buttons to change the current record:

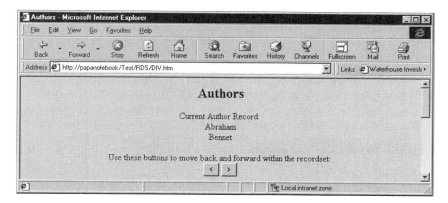

The value displayed in the <DIV> tag changes to match the value in the current record. Notice that the first and last name are on separate lines. This is because a <DIV> tag inserts a line break immediately following itself.

The only code that has changed from our previous examples is where we have been placing the HTML element. The two lines of code to place the <DIV> element in our page are these:

```
<DIV datasrc="#objDC" datafld="au_fname"></DIV>
<DIV datasrc="#objDC" datafld="au_lname"></DIV>
```

The <SPAN> tag

You can use the <SPAN> tag to bind data directly into the text of the page. Keep in mind that the <SPAN> tag is functionally the same as a <DIV> tag for our purposes, except that the <SPAN> tag does not place a line break after itself.

The example below shows two <SPAN> tags used to insert the first and last name into a sentence. Although not shown in the current record example below, <SPAN> can also display HTML when present in the data by adding the DATAFORMATAS attribute (just like <DIV> tags can).

Again, clicking on the arrow buttons will move the current record. This results in the content of the <SPAN> tags changing to display the values from the current record.

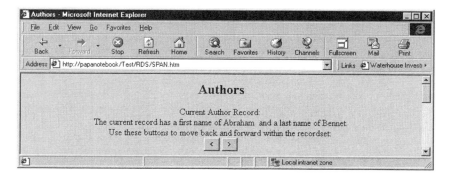

The lines we need to change in our original example to display a <SPAN> HTML element are these:

```
The current record has a first name of
<FONT color="blue">
<SPAN datasrc="#objDC" datafld="au_fname"></SPAN> </FONT>and a last name of
<FONT color="blue"><SPAN datasrc="#objDC" datafld="au_lname"></SPAN >.
</FONT>
```

Notice how we placed plain text beside the <SPAN> tags. Doing this makes the <SPAN> data blend right in with the plain text (we have made the <SPAN> data blue merely for effect.)

The <A> and <IMG> Tags

The <A> or anchor and <IMG> tags can both be used to create hyperlinks to new pages, using RDS and data binding. In this section we'll show how we can use them to create dynamic, data driven hyperlinks.

The Anchor <A> Tag

Data binding is supported by the HREF attribute of an anchor tag. Binding to the anchor tag is supported in both current record mode and repeated table mode. In our example below we can click on the arrow buttons to move from record to record, and the anchor tab will display the changing values. In the screenshot below Abraham is a link to the current record:

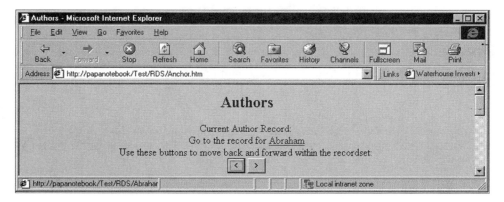

Here we changed the key lines of code by putting an <A> tag in the midst of other text. The <A> tag is a hyperlink to whatever data is bound to the <A> tag. Typically, we would bind a field from a database that was a valid URL (such as www.bluesand.com).

```
Go to the record for <A datasrc="#objDC" datafld="au_fname">
<SPAN datasrc="#objDC" datafld="au_fname"></SPAN >
</A>
```

Did you notice that we put a <SPAN> within the <A> and </A> tags? We did this so we could have some text to use for the hyperlink, just like you would for standard HTML.

The <IMG> Tag

The DATASRC element of the <IMG> tag can be bound to the current record of a data set. The bound data should consist of a URL to an image file.

To display an <IMG> tag that is bound to the current record in our standard example, we need the following line of code:

```
<IMG DATASRC="#objDC" DATAFLD="au_fname"></IMG>
```

Keep in mind that normally you would place a database field that is a path to a valid image in the DATAFLD attribute.

Combo Box and Radio Button Data Binding

We can also bind data directly to radio buttons (<INPUT TYPE=RADIO> tags) and/or combo boxes (<SELECT> tags). These types are similar in that they both accept multiple values.

<SELECT>

The <SELECT> tag allows the user to select a single item from a list of pre-defined choices. Within the <SELECT> element, we use one <OPTION> tag for each of the choices on offer. We can bind to the <SELECT> tag but can not bind to the <OPTION> tag. It would be great if we could bind to the <OPTION> tag with a different RDS.DataControl to fill it with a valid list of cities. However, this is not possible at this time, so we have to manually type in the values (or use ASP to fill the list).

Also, keep in mind that only single select mode is supported. This is because it only makes sense that a single value is bound to the database field. Both the combo/drop-down and list box formats are supported for display purposes by changing the SIZE attribute.

The code snippet below is used to display the city combo box. Here, we bind the DATASRC and DATAFLD attributes to the <SELECT> tag:

```
City: 
<SELECT NAME="cboChoices" SIZE=1 DATASRC="#objDC" DATAFLD="city">
    <OPTION SELECTED VALUE="Albany">Albany</OPTION>
    <OPTION VALUE="Raleigh">Raleigh</OPTION>
    <OPTION VALUE="Tampa">Tampa</OPTION>
    <OPTION VALUE="Davos">Davos</OPTION>
</SELECT>
```

If we use the above code in our same example page we should see the following output:

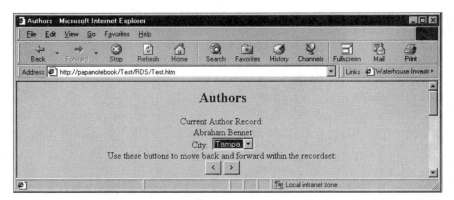

If you use the arrow buttons to move through the recordset, the value displayed in the HTML <SELECT> element will change accordingly. Keep in mind that the value will only appear if the same valid value exists in the list and in the current record.

<INPUT TYPE=RADIO>

A radio button or group of radio buttons can be bound to a column in the data set. The binding stores the VALUE attribute from the selected radio button. If the value in the data set matches no VALUE attributes on the radio button group, then no radio buttons are selected.

Lets look at an example of a radio button group with a current record binding. The code below binds the radio buttons to the City field, and then uses the value from the VALUE attribute to save to the recordset.

```
<FORM name="frmTest">
City: 
<INPUT type="radio" name="optChoices" value="Albany" DATASRC="#objDC"
DATAFLD="City">
<INPUT type="radio" name="optChoices" value="Raleigh" DATASRC="#objDC"
DATAFLD="City">
<FORM name="frmTest">
```

If you use this code in our web page example you'll see the following result:

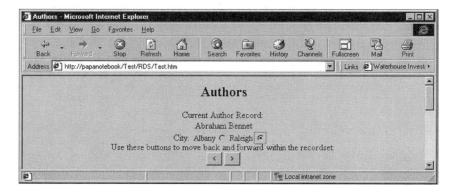

Clicking on the arrow buttons will move the current record, which results in the radio button with the matching value being selected. Radio buttons can also be used within a repeated table. However, you must ensure that a named form surrounds buttons to ensure correct operation.

The <TABLE> Tag

Repeated tables are a key feature of the data binding functionality included in DHTML. Repeated tables allow a page author to merge data with an HTML table on the client. The HTML table is used as a template for repeated rows, and the content of the table is repeated once for each record in the data set. The data set is supplied by a data source object on the web page. The table (template) is bound to the data source using the DATASRC attribute of the <TABLE> tag.

The key advantage of repeated tables is that the repetition is done on the client without requiring round-trips to the server or storing state on the server. The data can subsequently be sorted, filtered, or manipulated in any fashion, and the page will dynamically be redrawn to reflect the changes – without writing complicated scripts, server-side CGI processes, or Java code.

In the example below, you can click on the table headers to sort by that column. The sorting is done by a small snippet of client-side VBScript. Note that the sort is done on the client, without a round-trip to the server. Let's take a look at the output, then we'll examine the code.

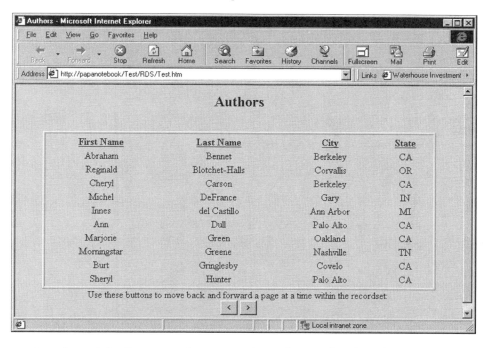

Here we have bound the first name, last name, city and state of each author to each row of an HTML table. Because we bound the RDS.DataControl to the <TABLE> tag in addition to binding the fields to the individual table cells, every row in the authors table has a row in the HTML table.

If you click on a column heading, the table will sort itself by that column in ascending order. If you click the same column heading again, the table will then re-sort itself by that column in descending order. Keep in mind that the data is all on the client (within the browser) so each time we sort we are not going back to the Web server. This yields fast sorting results!

We also have added a new feature that allows us to see *n* amount of records per page. In our case, we are displaying 10 records per page. When we click on the next and previous buttons, the next or previous pages of data are displayed, respectively.

Let's take a look at the source code:

```
<HTML>
<HEAD>

<!-- RDS DataControl -->
<OBJECT classid="clsid:bd96c556-65a3-11d0-983a-00c04fc29e33"
id="objDC" width="0" height="0">
</OBJECT>

<SCRIPT LANGUAGE=VBScript>
Sub Window_OnLoad()
    objDC.Server = "http://papanotebook"
    objDC.SQL = "select au_fname, au_lname, city, state from authors order by
au_lname, au_fname"
    objDC.Connect = "Provider=SQLOLEDB.1;User ID=sa;Password=;Initial
Catalog=pubs;Data Source=papanotebook"
    objDC.Refresh
End Sub


Sub SortTable(strColumn)
    if objDC.SortColumn <> strColumn then
        objDC.SortColumn = strColumn
        objDC.SortDirection = true
    else
        objDC.SortColumn = strColumn
        objDC.SortDirection = Not objDC.SortDirection
    end if
    objDC.Reset
End Sub

Sub spnFirstName_onclick()
    SortTable "au_fname"
End Sub
Sub spnFirstName_onmouseover()
    spnFirstName.style.cursor = "hand"
End Sub
Sub spnFirstName_onmouseout()
    spnFirstName.style.cursor = ""
End Sub

Sub spnLastName_onclick()
    SortTable "au_lname"
End Sub
Sub spnLastName_onmouseover()
    spnLastName.style.cursor = "hand"
End Sub
```

```
Sub spnLastName_onmouseout()
     spnLastName.style.cursor = ""
End Sub

Sub spnState_onclick()
     SortTable "state"
End Sub
Sub spnState_onmouseover()
     spnState.style.cursor = "hand"
End Sub
Sub spnState_onmouseout()
     spnState.style.cursor = ""
End Sub

Sub spnCity_onclick()
     SortTable "city"
End Sub
Sub spnCity_onmouseover()
     spnCity.style.cursor = "hand"
End Sub
Sub spnCity_onmouseout()
     spnCity.style.cursor = ""
End Sub
</SCRIPT>

<TITLE>Authors</TITLE >
</HEAD>

<BODY bgcolor=#add8e6>
<CENTER>
<H2>Authors</H2>

<BR>

<TABLE border="1">
<TR>
<TD>
<TABLE id="tblAuthors" border="0" datasrc="#objDC" width="640" datapagesize="10">
<THEAD >
  <TR align="CENTER">
    <TD><FONT color="#0000FF">
      <B><U><SPAN id="spnFirstName">First Name</SPAN></U></B>
    </FONTt></td>
    <TD><FONT color="#0000FF">
      <B><U><span id="spnLastName">Last Name</SPAN></U></B>
    </FONT></td>
    <TD><FONT color="#0000FF">
      <B><U><FONT id="spnCity">City</SPAN></U></B>
    </FONT></TD>
    <TD><FONT color="#0000FF">
      <B><U><SPAN id="spnState">State</span></U></B>
    </FONT></TD>
  </TR>
</THEAD>
<TBODY>
  <TR align="CENTER">
    <TD><SPAN datafld="au_fname"></SPAN></TD>
    <TD><SPAN datafld="au_lname"></SPAN></TD>
    <TD><SPAN datafld="city"></SPAN></TD>
    <TD><SPAN datafld="state"></SPAN></TD>
  </TR>
```

```
  </TBODY>
  </TABLE>
  </TD>
  </TR>
  </TABLE>

  Use these buttons to move back and forward a page at a time within the
  recordset: 
  <BR>
  <INPUT type="button" value="  <  " onclick=" tblAuthors.previousPage">
  <INPUT type="button" value="  >  " onclick="tblAuthors.nextPage">

  </CENTER>
  </BODY>
  </HTML>
```

There are a lot of new concepts you may notice in this code. First, let's concentrate on the table itself. The <TABLE> tag has a DATASRC attribute that we set to the name of the RDS.DataControl object preceded by the # character. This tells the browser that you are binding repeated rows to the HTML table. Within the table's rows, we bind each individual field to a <SPAN> tag. This way, we have repeated rows, and each field value knows to go in each cell of the table.

We have also included sorting features by using some DHTML. Notice that there is a client-side VBScript method called spnFirstName_onclick. This is the common naming convention that is used to refer to the event name of an object. For example, spnFirstName_onclick is the event that fires when the element known as spnFirstName is clicked. We create a similar event procedure for each of the columns, and each of these procedures calls the SortColumn method.

The SortColumn method sorts the recordset using the name of the column passed in to it and then it determines how to sort (i.e. ascending or descending). Setting the SortDirection to True is ascending, and False is descending. After we are done setting the sorting properties, we issue the Reset method of the RDS.DataControl so the web page will display the data in its new sort order.

The paging features of this web page are implemented by doing a few small things. First, we give our data bound table an ID attribute value (I chose tblAuthors). Second, we set the DATAPAGESIZE attribute of the data bound table to 10 to signify that we want the table to show 10 data rows at a time. Third, we create the buttons for the previous and next pages. (Make sure you give them Ids, too!) Finally, we issue the tblAuthors.nextPage and tblAuthors.PreviousPage methods in the onclick events of the next page and previous page buttons, respectively.

Finally, we include some code to turn the mouse cursor into a hand when the mouse is hovering over column heading. We do this by using the event procedures such as spnFirstName_onmouseover and spnFirstName_onmouseout. These event procedures set the cursor property of the <SPAN> tag's style property.

Case Study: Creating a Flexible Pick List

So far we've discussed how to create dynamic and data driven web pages using the RDS.DataControl object, a sprinkle of DHTML and by data binding some common HTML elements. These are all great tools that we can use in real world applications. In this section I'll show you when and where you might want to use these features in your applications. We'll take a look at some code that you can easily integrate into a real-world business solution, that will make your application soar!

Why do I Care about the RDS Pick List?

The **RDS Pick List** is ideal in situations where you need to allow a user to select a record based upon several criteria. For example, suppose you are creating an order entry system, and on the order header page you want the user to be able to select a customer number. Now, suppose the user is dealing with a customer (by telephone, say) and the customer doesn't remember their customer number. In this case, the user needs to search for the customer number using the customer's name and address.

Based on this example, a combo box just doesn't handle the problem. We wouldn't want to list all of the customers, their addresses and their customer numbers in the combo box, would we? That list could be huge! So we need to find another way to allow a user to search for the customer, without leaving the current page.

This section will show you how to integrate a search page into your application that will:

- ❑ Allow you to search for a record by bringing up a separate search screen
- ❑ Enter criteria to search upon
- ❑ Load a screen displaying the search results
- ❑ Allow you to sort and select the record from the search results
- ❑ Return the selected data to the original screen and populate HTML elements with it

Confused? That's OK – if you're anything like me then you'd prefer to see what I am talking about before you see how it works. Let's begin by taking a look at the RDS Pick List technique with a short sample web page that I'll call Caller.htm.

From a User's Standpoint

I've called it Caller.htm because the page calls the search criteria entry and the search results web pages. The Caller.htm web page is merely a snippet of code that helps us demonstrate the RDS Pick List technique. How will this help you? When you create your own pages that display data from a search screen, you can use this code as a template.

Beginning the Search

Because Caller.htm is simply intended as a template for you to follow, I have forgone the fancy web page theatrics and made the page contain the basic features that we will need. Here's what the user will see:

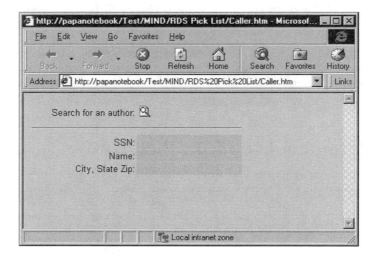

Entering the Search Criteria

As you can see, `Caller.htm` is quite simple. It allows you to initiate a search for an author by clicking on the 'find' icon, 🔍. (Once you've found and selected an author record, the application fills the gray read-only boxes with the author's information.)

When you click on the icon to initiate the search, you are presented with the `SearchCriteria.htm` page:

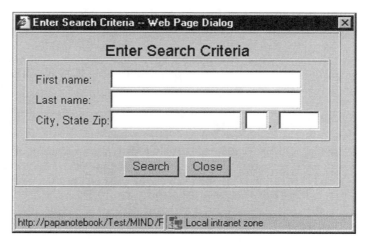

In `SearchCriteria.htm` you enter any combination of search fields – including partial fields. For example, let's say we wanted to find all authors in California in the zip code beginning with '94'. To do this, enter the criteria as shown below, and click the Search button:

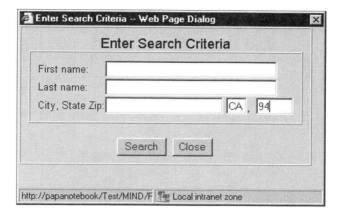

Displaying the Search Results

Once we click the Search button, the generic `RDSPickList.asp` is displayed. This page shows all of the search results, as shown below. Notice that there are a total of 12 records found, so the results span two pages. We can navigate to the second page of results by clicking the next page button in the lower left corner of the page:

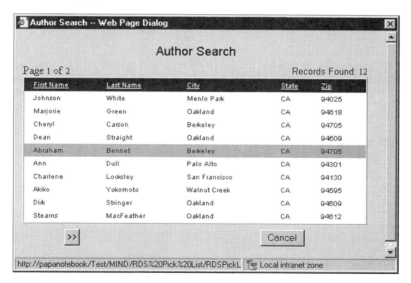

In addition to paging, this page also allows us to sort by any one column at a time. To do this, we simply click on the column header and the page re-sorts itself by that column. (Notice that when you put your mouse over a row in the table the row is highlighted and the cursor turns into a hand. We accomplish this by using a little DHTML to fancy up the page.)

To select the author record you want, simply click on the appropriate row. The data for that record is sent back to the calling web page, `Caller.htm`, and displayed on the form in a read-only fashion:

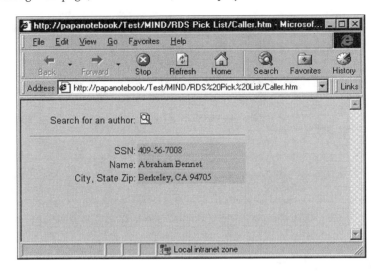

None of this is rocket science, as I am sure you have guessed. All I have done here is combined several simple concepts to create a reusable template for complex searches where a simple combo box just doesn't fit the bill. So now that we've seen what we can accomplish, let's take a behind-the-scenes look.

Backstage

By now you must be thinking about how we tied all of this chapter's topics together into the RDS Pick List. So far in this chapter, we've seen how to bind data to a web page's table using the DATASRC and DATAFLD attributes and how to sort and use paging on the data in the HTML table. These are all wonderful tools that can be used together to create a reusable and generic pick list with RDS. First, let's take a look at the HTML behind `Caller.htm`.

Inside Caller.htm – the HTML

`Caller.htm` is simply the jump-off point where we allow the user to select an author. Now we could have loaded a combo box with all of the authors and their address, but that would look ugly – and it could take a long time if there were a lot of authors. Besides, then we wouldn't have the ability to narrow the search or sort by a particular column.

Here's the body of the HTML for `Caller.htm`. A lot of the code deals with styling – we use some cascading style sheets here – so I've picked out the main logical points of the pick list by highlighting those lines:

```
<BODY bgcolor="#ffffc0">
<LINK rel="stylesheet" type="text/css" href="PickListStyles.css">
<TABLE name="tblAuthor" border="0" cellpadding="1" cellspacing="1">
  <TR>
    <TD nowrap align="right" width="150px">
      <FONT class="DataLabelFont">Search for an author:</FONT>
    </TD>
```

```
      <TD width="150px">
        <IMG name="imgFind" src="Find.gif" alt="Find an author"
          border="0" onclick="CallPickList"
          onmouseover="me.className='Point'"
          onmouseover="me.className='DontPoint'"
          WIDTH="20" HEIGHT="20">
      </TD>
    </TD>
    <TD>
      <TD align="right" nowrap colspan="2"><HR>
      </TD>
    </TR>
    <TR>
      <TD align="right" nowrap><FONT class="DataLabelFont">SSN:</FONT>
      </TD>
      <TD nowrap bgcolor="silver"><FONT class="DataFont">
        <DIV id="divSSN"></DIV></FONT>
      </TD>
    </TR>
    <TR>
      <TD align="right" nowrap><FONT class="DataLabelFont">Name:</FONT>
      </TD>
      <TD nowrap bgcolor="silver"><FONT class="DataFont">
        <DIV id="divName"></DIV></FONT>
      </TD>
    </TR>
    <TR>
      <TD align="right" nowrap><FONT class="DataLabelFont">
        City, State Zip:</FONT>
      </TD>
      <TD nowrap bgcolor="silver"><FONT class="DataFont">
        <DIV id="divCityStateZip"></DIV></FONT>
      </TD>
    </TR>
  </TABLE></BODY>
```

The HTML in the Caller.htm simply displays an HTML table that contains several <DIV> tags. Each <DIV> tag represents a piece of information about the selected author. This is where we place the selected row's data from the RDS pick list later on. Until then, these <DIV> tags remain empty. There's also an image, Find.gif – the user clicks this image to initiate a search. The search is executed via the CallPickList function. We'll have a look at this function in a moment.

Styling – an Aside

The <LINK> tag (right below the <BODY> tag) links or embeds the HTML that defines the cascading style sheet for this page. Just in case you don't already know, a style sheet is simply a predefined definition of a formatting style that we can apply to HTML elements. We use these styles in our sample pages to keep the fonts and colors consistent throughout the pages. We have included the styles from PickListStyles.css. Here's a sample (you can download the whole file from http://webdev.wrox.co.uk/books/1649):

```
.Point
{
    CURSOR: hand
}
.DontPoint
{
```

```
        CURSOR: default
    }
    .UnHighlight
    {
        BACKGROUND-COLOR: #ffffff;
        CURSOR: default
    }
    .Highlight
    {
        BACKGROUND-COLOR: #cc99cc;
        CURSOR: hand
    }
```

We've created two styles – called `Point` and `DontPoint` – that simply change the appearance of the cursor depending on whether or not the cursor is floating over a button. More significantly, we use the `Highlight` and `UnHighlight` styles to create the 'row highlight' effect in the `RDSPickList.asp` page (the selected row has a purple background, while the others have a white background).

The other styles in `PickListStyles.css` are used to format the fonts with the same colors and sizes throughout our web pages. Our font styles – `DataLabelFont`, `DataFont`, `HeadingFont`, `ReportFont`, `HeadingTitleFont` and `ReportHeadingFont` – have definitions that look similar to this one:

```
FONT.DataLabelFont
{
    COLOR: black;
    FONT-FAMILY: Arial, Verdana;
    FONT-SIZE: x-small
}
```

And we define a background color:

```
BODY
{
    BACKGROUND-COLOR: #ccccff
}
```

You don't have to use these styles at all – alternatively, you can expand on the styles to create a more dynamic effect. But let's not get off of the point here; let's get back to the HTML.

Calling out the Search Party – the CallPickList Method

We've seen the HTML part of `Caller.htm`; now let's have a look the client-side VBScript part. The `CallPickList` method is the driving routine of this page. The `CallPickList` method function calls the `SearchCriteria.htm` page – it's on this page that the user will enter his search criteria. Then, the script turns around and passes the criteria to the `RDSPickList.asp` page, to display the results based upon that criteria. Get it? Well, you will after we look at the VBScript for the `Caller.htm` page.

Here's the VBScript code for the `CallPickList` function. First we define all the necessary variables:

```
<SCRIPT language="vbscript">
<!--
option explicit

sub CallPickList()
   '--- Use RDS to get the SQL for the search.
   dim strConnString
   dim strData
   dim strFeatures
   dim strSearchString
   dim strServer
   dim strSQL
   dim strTitle
   dim strURL
   dim strFirstName
   dim strLastName
   dim strCity
   dim strState
   dim strZip
```

Getting the Search Criteria

Then we define the features for the modal browser window we will open. What modal window am I talking about? I am referring to the SearchCriteria.htm page. We have to open the SearchCriteria.htm page modally so that the user can not ignore the page. Otherwise, it would be quite difficult to ensure that the user followed the flow of the pages:

```
strURL = "SearchCriteria.htm"
strFeatures = "dialogWidth:400px;dialogHeight:260px;help:no;center:yes;"
strFeatures = strFeatures & _
              "border:thin;status:no;scrollbars=yes;toolbar=no;menubar=no;"
strData = window.showModalDialog(CStr(strURL), , CStr(strFeatures))
```

Also, because we open the page modally, execution of CallPickList freezes after the line of code that opens the modal window using the window.showModalDialog method. It freezes because it is waiting for the modal page to be closed. So, at this point we're actually showing SearchCriteria.htm to the user, and waiting for him to enter the criteria before we continue. We'll take a look at the SearchCriteria.htm shortly.

When SearchCriteria.htm is closed, control returns to the CallPickList subroutine. You might notice that we store the return value of the window.showModalDialog method in the variable strData. This is how we grab the search criteria from the SearchCriteria.htm page to pass to the RDSPickList.asp page.

Building the Query – the Connection

Execution of CallPickList continues by preparing the connection to the database. We place the name of the web server in the strServer variable, and the connection string (to the pubs database) in the strConnString variable. We'll need to pass these to the RDSPickList.asp a little later:

```
if len(trim(strData)) > 0 then
   strServer = "http://papanotebook"
   strConnString = "Provider=SQLOLEDB.1;Initial Catalog=pubs;"
   strConnString = strConnString & "Data Source=papanotebook;"
   strConnString = strConnString & "User ID=sa;Password="
```

We parse the data from the `strData` string variable (that came from the `SearchCrtiteria.htm` page) and store them in local variables. To do this, we use the `RetrieveValue` function, which accepts the `strData` variable and the ordinal position of the field we want to grab. We need to do this because we have passed the data back delimited by the pipe character:

```
strFirstName = RetrieveValue(strData, 1)
strLastName = RetrieveValue(strData, 2)
strCity = RetrieveValue(strData, 3)
strState = RetrieveValue(strData, 4)
strZip = RetrieveValue(strData, 5)
```

Building the Query – Generating the SQL

Now we formulate the SQL statement that we will use to retrieve the authors that match the specified criteria. We store the SQL in the `strSQL` variable and pass it to and from the `EncodeURL` function. This function simply parses the SQL and replaces any special characters with their corresponding HTML encoding characters. We need to do this because we are going to pass the SQL as a URL to the `RDSPickList.asp` page and the special characters would not transfer without the encoding:

```
strSQL = "SELECT au_id, au_fname, au_lname, city, state, zip FROM authors"
strSQL = strSQL & " WHERE au_fname LIKE '" & strFirstName & "%'"
strSQL = strSQL & " AND au_lname LIKE '" & strLastName & "%'"
strSQL = strSQL & " AND city LIKE '" & strCity & "%'"
strSQL = strSQL & " AND state LIKE '" & strState & "%'"
strSQL = strSQL & " AND zip LIKE '" & strZip & "%'"
strSQL = EncodeURL(strSQL)
```

Building the Query – Calling the Pick List

Now that we have gathered all of this information, we need to put it together and pass it to the `RDSPickList.asp` page. Notice that we pass the server variable and the connection string so that the `RDSPickList.asp` can process the SQL, as it needs to know where the Web server is and how to contact the database from there. Then we pass the names of the database fields, separated by the pipe character, and then their corresponding captions. We use the captions as the HTML table's columns headings for the pick list, because the real field names are often undesirable:

```
strURL = "RDSPickList.asp?Server=" & strServer & "&Connect=" & strConnString
strURL = strURL & "&FieldNames=au_id|au_fname|au_lname|city|state|zip"
strURL = strURL & "&FieldCaptions=ID|First Name|Last Name|City|State|Zip"
```

Now we pass the names of the hidden columns and the number of hidden columns. Why hide them? Because we might not want to see them in the search results, but we do want to retrieve them back at the `Caller.htm` page. In our case we do not want to see the authors' SSNs in the search results, but we *will* need the SSN when we get back to the `Caller.htm` page:

```
strURL = strURL & "&HiddenFields=au_id&HiddenFieldCount=1"
```

A better scenario is when we use an `IDENTITY` column as the primary key. In that case we would not want to see it as it means nothing to the user, but we definitely need it at the calling page to identify the record we chose if we ever want to go back to the database.

Finally, we pass in the total number of fields, a title for the search results page and the SQL that we formulated earlier. Then we pass all of this information to the `RDSPickList.asp` using the `window.showModalDialog` method:

```
        strURL = strURL & "&FieldCount=6&Title=Author Search" & "&SQL=" & strSQL
        strFeatures = "dialogWidth:550px;dialogHeight:375px;help:no;center:yes;"
        strFeatures = strFeatures & _
                    "border:thin;status:no;scrollbars=no;toolbar=no;menubar=no;"
        strData = window.showModalDialog(strURL, , CStr(strFeatures))
```

Once again, the `CallPickList` function freezes and waits for the user to choose from the list of customers. When this choice is submitted, the pick list closes and control returns to the `CallPickList` routine. We'll look at what happens in `RDSPickList.asp` shortly.

Returning the Data to Caller.htm

When control returns to `CallPickList`, it completes its tasks by calling the `FillData` method to fill the `<DIV>` tags on `Caller.htm` with the data from `RDSPickList.asp`, and hence fill in the gray read-only boxes:

```
        if Len(Trim(strData)) > 0 then
            FillData strData
        end if
      end if
    end sub
```

The Supporting Functions

That's how the query works! Let's have a look at the supporting functions that we mentioned above. First, the `RetrieveValue` method. When the value is returned from `RDSPickList.asp`, it contains a string value separated by the pipe character (|). The `RetrieveValue` method returns the nth value contained in `strData`, where n is the value of the `intFieldNumber` parameter. The values of `strData` are separated by pipe (|) characters.

```
    Function RetrieveValue(strData, intFieldNumber)
      Dim intCurrentField, intFoundPos, strValue, strNames
      strNames = strData
      intCurrentField = 0
      Do While intCurrentField <> intFieldNumber
        intFoundPos = InStr(strNames, "|")
        intCurrentField = intCurrentField + 1
        if intFoundPos <> 0 then
          strValue = Left(strNames, intFoundPos - 1)
          strNames = Mid(strNames, intFoundPos + 1, Len(strNames))
        else
          if intCurrentField = intFieldNumber then
            strValue = strNames
          else
            strValue = ""
          end if
          exit do
        end if
      loop
      RetrieveValue = strValue
    End Function
```

Now, the `Encode` method – which encodes the URL for transport:

```
function EncodeURL(strText)
  dim intPos
  dim strChar
  const cCodeChars = "%#_&="

  intPos = 1
  do while intPos <= Len(strText)
    strChar = Mid(strText, intPos, 1)
    if InStr(1, cCodeChars, strChar) > 0 then
      strChar = "%" & Hex(Asc(strChar))
    end if
    strText = Left(strText, intPos - 1) & strChar & Mid(strText, intPos + 1)
    intPos = intPos + Len(strChar)
  loop
  EncodeURL = strText
end function
```

Last, the `FillData` method, which takes the returned string from the center pick list, and parses it to fill the author's information into the gray boxes:

```
sub FillData(strData)
  dim strCityStateZip
  divSSN.innerHTML = RetrieveValue(strData, 1)
  divName.innerHTML = RetrieveValue(strData, 2) & " " & RetrieveValue(strData, 3)
  strCityStateZip = RetrieveValue(strData, 4) & ", "
  strCityStateZip = strCityStateZip & RetrieveValue(strData, 5) & " "
  strCityStateZip = strCityStateZip & RetrieveValue(strData, 6)
  divCityStateZip.innerHTML = strCityStateZip
end sub
```

Stepping Through SearchCriteria.htm

The `SearchCriteria.htm` page has the sole purpose of returning the search criteria to the `Caller.htm` page. We set up a simple HTML table and form to grab the criteria and we then use some client-side script to return that data to the calling page.

The HTML in this page consists of an HTML <FORM> with first name, last name, city, state and zip fields. Then, when the user clicks the Search button, the client-side script's `Search` method is called. This method simply gathers the HTML form's input and puts in the string variable `strData`, with each form variable separated by the pipe character (|). We then pass this string back to the `Caller.htm` form by setting the `returnValue` property of the window object before we close the browser window. Once this window is closed, control goes back to the `Caller.htm`'s `CallPickList` subroutine, right where it left off.

Let's take a look at the whole page's code. We have a `window_onload` routine that sets the focus to the First Name box:

```
<SCRIPT language="vbscript">
<!--
option explicit

sub window_onload()
  frmSearch.txtFirstName.focus
end sub
```

We also have the search routine, that gathers the criteria and returns it to the calling page, delimited by the "|" character:

```
sub Search()
   dim strData
   strData = strData & trim(frmSearch.txtFirstName.value) & "|"
   strData = strData & trim(frmSearch.txtLastName.value) & "|"
   strData = strData & trim(frmSearch.txtCity.value) & "|"
   strData = strData & trim(frmSearch.txtState.value) & "|"
   strData = strData & trim(frmSearch.txtZip.value) & "|"
   if strData = "|||||" then
     alert "Search criteria too broad. You must enter some search criteria."
   else
     window.returnValue = strData
     window.close
   end if
end sub
//-->
</SCRIPT>
```

The HTML form looks like this.

```
<FORM name="frmSearch" method="post" action="SearchCriteria.htm">
<TABLE border="1" cellpadding="10" cellspacing="0" width="100%">
<TR>
<TD>
<TABLEname="tblCenter" border="0" cellpadding="0" cellspacing="0" width="100%">
  <TR>
    <TD align="center">
      <FONT class="HeadingFont">Enter Search Criteria</FONT><BR>
    </TD>
  </TR>
  <TR>
    <TDalign="center">
      <TABLE border="1" cellpadding="10" cellspacing="0">
        <TR>
          <TD nowrap>
            <TABLE border="0" cellpadding="0" cellspacing="0">
              <TR>
                <TDnowrap><font class="DataLabelFont">First name:</FONT></TD>
                <TD></TD>
                <TD nowrap>
                  <INPUT name="txtFirstName" type="text" maxlength="30" size="30">
                </TD>
              </TR>
              <TR>
                <TD nowrap><font class="DataLabelFont">Last name:</FONT></TD>
                <TD></TD>
                <TD nowrap>
                  <INPUT name="txtLastName" type="text" maxlength="30" size="30">
                </TD>
              </TR>
              <TR>
                <TD nowrap><FONT class="DataLabelFont">City, State Zip:</FONT>
                </TD>
                <TD></TD>
                <TD nowrap>
```

309

```
                    <INPUT name="txtCity" type="text" maxlength="50" size="20">
                    <INPUT name="txtState" type="text" maxlength="2" size="2">, 
                    <INPUT name="txtZip" type="text" maxlength="5" size="5">
                      </TD>
                    </TR>
                  </TABLE>
                </TD>
              </TR>
            </TABLE>
          </TD>
       </TR>
       <TR>
         <TD align="center" nowrap><BR>
           <BUTTON id="btnSearch" onclick="Search()"
                   alt="Search" onmouseover="btnSearch.className='Point'"
                   onmouseout="btnSearch.className='DontPoint'">Search</BUTTON>
           
           <BUTTON id="btnClose" onclick="window.close"
                   alt="Close" onmouseover="btnClose.className='Point'"
                   onmouseout="btnClose.className='DontPoint'">Close</BUTTON>
         </TD>
       </TR>
     </TABLE>
</TD></TR></TABLE></FORM>
```

Stepping Through RDSPickList.asp

The RDSPickList.asp page is completely generic code that can be used from any calling page. If you choose to use this pick list, you will not have to change any code within this page; however, you will want to create your own Caller.htm and SearchCriteria.htm to customize your search.

The HTML

Enough said, let's take a look at the HTML within RDSPickList.asp. First we define the RDS.DataControl object, and link to the stylesheet file:

```
<object CLASSID="clsid:BD96C556-65A3-11D0-983A-00C04FC29E33" ID="mobjADC">
</object>
<link rel="stylesheet" type="text/css" href="PickListStyles.css">
```

Next we build the first table. It's mostly formatting here but you can see in the shaded lines that we prepare to use the paging facilities:

```
</HEAD>
<BODY link="#ffff00" vlink="#ffff00" alink="#ffff00">
<DIV id="divTitle" style="position:absolute;top:20;left:200">
  <FONT class="HeadingFont"><%=Request("Title")%></FONT>
</DIV>
<DIV id="divList" style="position:absolute;top:50;left:10">
<TABLE border="0" cellpadding="0" cellspacing="0" width="95%">
  <TR>
    <TD align="left"><div id="divPaging"></DIV></TD>
    <TD align="right">
      <DIV id="divRecordCount"><FONT class="DataLabelFont">Records Found: 0</FONT>
      <FONT class="DataFont"></FONT></DIV>
    </TD>
  </TR>
</TABLE>
```

We'll use it to show the current page, number of pages and total number of records. We'll update the <DIV> tabs `divPaging` and `divRecordCount` later – see the section *Bells and Whistles* later in the chapter – the code above deals with the case before any records have been found.

```
Page 1 of 2          Records Found: 12
```

Now we build the main table:

```
<TABLE name="tblBorder" border="1" cellpadding="0" cellspacing="0" width="95%">
<TR>
  <TD>
    <TABLE id="tblList" name="tblList" datasrc="#mobjADC"
           datapagesize="10" border="0" cellpadding="3"
           cellspacing="0" width="100%">
      <THEAD bgcolor="#000080"><%
        for intField = 1 to CLng(Request("FieldCount"))
          strFieldName = RetrieveValue(CStr(Request("FieldNames")), intField)
          strIDName = "divCol" & strFieldName
          strFieldCaption = _
                  RetrieveValue(CStr(Request("FieldCaptions")), intField)
          Response.Write "<td align=left nowrap>" & vbCr
          Response.Write "<font class=ReportHeadingFont><u><div id=" & strIDName
          Response.Write " onclick=SortData('" & strFieldName & "')"
          Response.Write " title='Sort by " & strFieldCaption & "'"
          Response.Write " onmouseover=" & strIDName & ".className='Point' "
          Response.Write " onmouseout=" & strIDName & ".className='DontPoint'>"
          Response.Write strFieldCaption & "</div></u></font>" & vbCr
          Response.Write "</td>"
        next%>
      </THEAD>
      <TBODY bgcolor="#ffffff"><%
        for intField = 1 to Request("FieldCount")
          Response.Write "<td align=left nowrap>" & vbCr
          Response.Write "<font class=ReportFont><div "
          strFieldName = RetrieveValue(CStr(Request("FieldNames")), intField)
          Response.Write "id=divDataCol" & strFieldName
          Response.Write " datafld=" & strFieldName
          Response.Write "></div></font>" & vbCr
          Response.Write "</td>"
        next%>
      </TBODY>
    </TABLE>
  </TD>
</TR >
</TABLE>
```

We define a basic HTML table that is bound to the `RDS.DataControl` that we defined up top. We set the table `tblList`'s `DATASRC` attribute to the `id` of the `RDS.DataControl`, and the `DATAPAGESIZE` attribute to the number of records we want to see at a time (we used 10).

We don't know in advance how many fields the calling page might ask to see in the table, so we need to generate the HTML dynamically – to accommodate whatever the calling page requests to see. Since we dynamically generate the HTML for the RDS pick list, we've written this as an ASP page (not an HTML page).

That is why this page is so generic. You'll notice this code has two `For...Next` loops – one for the table header and one for the body – to create the headings and data rows respectively. These bits of server-side VBScript within the ASP call the server-side function `RetrieveValue`.

Finally we create a form, containing three buttons – for previous page, next page and Cancel:

```
<FORM name="frmList" method="post">
<BUTTON name="btnPreviousPage" id="btnPreviousPage"
  style="position:absolute;top:240;left:25"
  title="Go to previous page">&lt;&lt;</BUTTON>
 
<BUTTON name="btnNextPage" id="btnNextPage"
  style="position:absolute;top:240;left:60"
  title="Go to next page">&gt;&gt;</BUTTON>
<BR>
<BUTTON ="btnCancel" id="btnCancel"
  style="position:absolute;top:240;left:340"
  title="Cancel">Cancel</BUTTON>
</FORM>
</DIV>
```

The RetrieveValue Function

The server-side RetrieveValue function is the same as it was in the client-side VBScript in the Caller.htm page, except here it is intended to retrieve each value from the parameter list we passed into this page. I am referring to the long list of parameters we passed in through the URL to the RDSPickList.asp back from the Caller.htm. All of this combined generates the HTML to support the data bound pick list.

```
<%@LANGUAGE="VBScript"%>
<%Option Explicit%>
<%
Response.Expires = 0
dim intField
dim strIDName
dim strFieldName
dim strFieldCaption

Function RetrieveValue(strNames, intFieldNumber)
  dim intCurrentField   '--- The field number as we loop
  dim intFoundPos       '--- The position of the field delimiter
  dim strValue          '--- The value of the field we found
  intCurrentField = 0
  Do While intCurrentField <> intFieldNumber
    intFoundPos = InStr(strNames, "|")
    intCurrentField = intCurrentField + 1
    if intFoundPos <> 0 then
      strValue = Left(strNames, intFoundPos - 1)
      strNames = Mid(strNames, intFoundPos + 1, Len(strNames))
    else
      if intCurrentField = intFieldNumber then
        strValue = strNames
      else
        strValue = ""
      end if
      exit do
    end if
  loop
  RetrieveValue = strValue
End Function
%>
```

Bells and Whistles

The final piece of the RDSPickList.asp puzzle is the client-side script that creates all of the user friendly features that the pick list provides. Let's take a look at this code. There is a lot of code, but you'll see that most of it is quite simple.

```
<SCRIPT LANGUAGE="vbscript">
<!--
Option Explicit
'--- DECLARE ALL CLIENT-SIDE VARIABLES TO USE.
dim mobjRS           '--- Recordset used to fill the pick list
dim mintPageNumber   '--- The current page number
dim mlngLastRecord   '--- The last record the mouse was over
'--- DECLARE ALL CLIENT-SIDE CONSTANTS TO USE.
const adcExecSync = 1      '--- Execute Synchronously
const adcFetchUpFront = 1  '--- Fetch records, then return control
```

The first is the window_onload method. This code connects the RDS.DataControl to the database using the server and connection string parameters we passed in. Then it executes the SQL and retrieves the data set by issuing the Refresh method of the RDS.DataControl. We then show the appropriate page number, record count and navigation buttons based on the number of records and the page size. Finally, we hide the columns that we defined in the URL.

First we define local variables and set the server, connect and SQL strings from the QueryString we passed in:

```
sub window_onload()
   dim strServer
   dim strSQL
   dim strConnString

   strServer = "<%=Request("Server")%>"
   strConnString = "<%=Request("Connect")%>"
   strSQL = "<%=Request("SQL")%>"
   mobjADC.Server = strServer
   mobjADC.SQL = strSQL
   mobjADC.Connect = strConnString
```

Now we refresh the HTML data bound table. Note that we execute synchronously so the DHTML events will fire after the recordset is returned. We also fetch synchronously so the record count will reflect the total number of records fetched:

```
mobjADC.ExecuteOptions = adcExecSync
mobjADC.FetchOptions = adcFetchUpFront
mobjADC.Refresh
```

If no records are found, then we close the window. Otherwise, we reset the <DIV> tags:

```
if mobjADC.Recordset.Recordcount = 0 then
   alert "No matches found."
   window.close
else
   mintPageNumber = 1    ' Initialize the page number.
   SetPageDisplay        ' Display the current page and page count.
                         ' Display the number of records found.
```

```
        divRecordCount.innerHTML = "<FONT class=DataLabelFont>Records Found: " & _
                            "</FONT><FONT class=DataFont>" & _
                            mobjADC.Recordset.Recordcount & "</FONT>"
        SetNavigationDisplay ' Show the appropriate navigational buttons.
        <%                   '--- Hide appropriate fields.
        for intField = 1 to CLng(Request("HiddenFieldCount"))
          strFieldName = RetrieveValue(CStr(Request("HiddenFields")), intField)
          response.write "divCol" & strFieldName & ".style.display = ""none""" & vbCr
          response.write "divDataCol" & strFieldName & _
                            ".style.display = ""none""" & vbCr
        next
        %>
    end if
  end sub
```

You'll see that we called the `SetPageDisplay` method here. This method simply displays the current page number and the total number of pages on the page into a `<DIV>` tag. The `SetNavigationDisplay` method is also called within the `window_onload` method. This method determines which buttons we need to display: the previous page button, the next page button, both or neither. Here's the code for those functions:

```
sub SetPageDisplay()
  '--- Display the current page and page count.
  divPaging.innerHTML = "<FONT class=DataFontLabel>Page </FONT>" & _
                "<FONT class=DataFont>" & mintPageNumber & _
                " </FONT><FONT class=DataFontLabel>of</FONT>" & _
                "<FONT class=DataFont>  " & PageCount & "</FONT>"
end sub
```

```
function PageCount()
  '--- The number of pages in the recordset based on the dataPageSize.
  PageCount = mobjADC.Recordset.PageCount
end function
```

```
Sub SetNavigationDisplay()
  '--- Show the appropriate navigational buttons.
  '--- Set display for Previous Button
  If mintPageNumber = 1 Then
    frmList.btnPreviousPage.style.display = "none"
  Else
    frmList.btnPreviousPage.style.display = ""
  End If
  '--- Set display for Next Button
  If mintPageNumber = PageCount Then
    frmList.btnNextPage.style.display = "none"
  Else
    frmList.btnNextPage.style.display = ""
  End If
End Sub
```

Next, to emulate the rollover effect for the table's rows, we define some event procedures for the table itself. These `mouseover` procedures simply highlight and unhighlight the rows in the table when the mouse moves over them. `tblList_onmouseover` highlights the row we are on with a selector bar:

```
sub tblList_onmouseover()
   DetermineLastRecordNumber()
   if mlngLastRecord > 0 then
      tblList.rows(mlngLastRecord).className = "Highlight"
   end if
end sub
```

`tblList_onmouseout` unhighlights the row we just left:

```
sub tblList_onmouseout()
   DetermineLastRecordNumber()
   if mlngLastRecord > 0 then
      tblList.rows(mlngLastRecord).className = "UnHighlight"
   end if
end sub
```

When the user clicks on a table row, we use `tblList_onclick` to gather the row's data and we return it to the calling page, delimited by the "|" character:

```
sub tblList_onclick()
   dim strRow    '--- The row of data that we return.
   dim lngCell   '--- The current cell, as we traverse them.
   dim lngRec    '--- The row we are on.

   lngCell = 0
   lngRec = CurrentRecord(window.event.srcElement.recordNumber)
   if lngRec > 0 then
      for lngCell = 0 to tblList.rows(lngRec).cells.length - 1
        strRow = strRow & tblList.rows(lngRec).cells(lngCell).innerText & "|"
      next
      window.returnValue = strRow
      window.close
   end if
end sub
```

`CurrentRecord` simply returns the current record number:

```
function CurrentRecord(lngRec)
   dim lngPageSize
   if lngRec <> 0 then
      lngPageSize = tblList.dataPageSize
      lngRec = lngRec - (lngPageSize * (mintPageNumber - 1))
   end if
   CurrentRecord = lngRec
end function
```

And `DetermineLastRecordNumber` determines which record the mouse was last over, and then sets the `lngLastRecord` variable appropriately:

```
Sub DetermineLastRecordNumber()
   Dim lngRecordNumber
   On Error Resume Next
   lngRecordNumber = Window.Event.SrcElement.RecordNumber
   If lngRecordNumber > 0 Then
      lngRecordNumber = (lngRecordNumber mod tblList.DataPageSize)
      If lngRecordNumber = 0 Then
```

```
        lngRecordNumber = tblList.DataPageSize      _
      end if
    End If
    mlngLastRecord = lngRecordNumber
  End Sub
```

To allow the user to select a row, we define the `onclick` event procedure for the `tblList` table. When the user selects a row from the table, this event procedure is fired and determines which row was selected by using the `CurrentRecord` function. This function determines the current row by factoring the page size, the current page and the record number that was selected. Finally, the `tblList_onclick` event procedure grabs the data from each cell of the table and puts it into a string, delimited by the pipe character. This string is then set to the `window.returnValue` and then the window is closed, thus returning control back to the `Caller.htm` page once again.

Odds and Ends

Let's take a quick look at the rest of the client-side script on this page. The `PageControl` method uses the `srcElement` property to determine which button was pressed, then it goes forward or backward one page:

```
sub PageControl()
  Dim objElement
  Set objElement = window.event.srcElement
  If objElement.id = "btnPreviousPage" Then
    tblList.PreviousPage
    mintPageNumber = mintPageNumber - 1
  Else
    tblList.NextPage
    mintPageNumber = mintPageNumber + 1
  End If
  SetNavigationDisplay
  SetPageDisplay
end sub
```

The `SortData` method is called when a user clicks on a column header in the table. It accepts the column to sort by and then determines which direction to sort. It does this by determining if the user clicked the same column twice in a row. If so, the sort order is reversed; otherwise the sort order is set to ascending (`True`). The `Reset` method is called to refresh the table's data, then the navigation buttons and page count displays are updated by calling the `SetNavigationDisplay` and `SetPageDisplay` methods:

```
sub SortData(strSearchColumn)
  dim booDir
  if mobjADC.SortColumn = CStr(strSearchColumn) then
    booDir = not CBool(mobjADC.SortDirection)
  else
    booDir = true
  end if
  mobjADC.SortDirection = booDir
  mobjADC.SortColumn = CStr(strSearchColumn)
  mobjADC.Reset
  mintPageNumber = 1
  SetNavigationDisplay
  SetPageDisplay
end sub
```

The remaining code contains a list of mouse control functions. Notice that we use the `Point` and `DontPoint` styles again when we move the mouse over the buttons. The `btnCancel_onclick` event is self-explanatory as it closes the window without making a selection. The `btnNextPage_onclick` event procedure and its corresponding `btnPreviousPage_onclick` event procedure both call the `PageControl` method. Here they all are, just for completeness:

```
sub btnCancel_onmouseover()
    frmList.btnCancel.className="Point"     ' Make the cursor a pointing hand
end sub

sub btnCancel_onmouseout()
    frmList.btnCancel.className="DontPoint" ' Make the cursor normal.
end sub

sub btnCancel_onclick()
    window.close
end sub

sub btnNextPage_onclick()
    PageControl      ' Go to the next page of data in the pick list.
end sub

sub btnNextPage_onmouseover()
    frmList.btnNextPage.className="Point"     ' Make the cursor a pointing hand.
end sub

sub btnNextPage_onmouseout()
    frmList.btnNextPage.className="DontPoint"     ' Make the cursor normal.
end sub

sub btnPreviousPage_onclick()
    PageControl      ' Go to the previous page of data in the pick list.
end sub

sub btnPreviousPage_onmouseover()
    frmList.btnPreviousPage.className="Point"     ' Make the cursor a pointing hand.
end sub

sub btnPreviousPage_onmouseout()
    frmList.btnPreviousPage.className="DontPoint" ' Make the cursor normal.
end sub
```

Wrapping Up

As you can see, there is quite a bit going on here; but the hard part is done for you. You may be able to grab the entire `Caller.htm` file and use it in your application, but you can use the `RetrieveValue`, `FillData` and `EncodeURL` functions verbatim. Also, don't forget that the `RDSPickList.asp` is completely generic and reusable, too.

The pick list is quite a useful tool that really reaps the benefits of RDS, DHTML and client-side scripting. I have used it in several situations – including the order entry scenario I described earlier in this section. Whenever I need my users to be able to choose from a list using a variety of criteria, I always use the RDS pick list. You could cut out the middle man here, too. If you do not need to search by several fields (as in our example), you could simply cut out the SearchCriteria.htm page and have the user enter the criteria on the Caller.htm page. Feel free to use it in your applications as you see fit and to distort and contort it as needed – that's what I do!

Summary

The RDS.DataControl object is a very flexible tool, and we can bind all kinds of data to many types of HTML tags and page elements, including various intrinsic HTML tags, such as <INPUT>, <TEXTAREA>, and <SELECT>. We talked about how to use the <DIV> and <SPAN> tags to display data without an editable HTML element. Further, we showed how to use the <A> and <IMG> tags on a page that uses DHTML to manage client-side datasets.

As you can tell, DHTML provides us with an arsenal of tools for managing client-side data access. When these data-aware HTML tags are combined with RDS, we can display data from practically any place and display it in practically any form. There are some very powerful pages we can create using these tools, as we saw when we created the repeated rows table with sorting and paging features. RDS is a tool that few developers use because of its lack of publicity. However, it is quickly becoming a favorite tool of Intranet, Extranet and LAN developers!

14

The Oracle Factor

Oracle is one of the most important players in database technology today. As much as Microsoft would like to make Oracle go away, they can't and they never will. Indeed while all of us to a greater or lesser extent consume Microsoft technologies, we know that these technologies would not exist and could not continue to get better unless Microsoft was challenged from the outside. The developer who knows how to use ADO against both SQL Server and Oracle is the developer who will know how to program to most of the data that exists in relational database models. The Oracle factor is large and in this chapter we will take an in-depth look at what it means to put ADO up against Oracle.

The overall approach in this chapter is from the standpoint of developers coming from a SQL Server or Access background, who are familiar with ADO (especially after reading this book!), and want to use ADO with Oracle. This and the following chapter, together with the Oracle quick reference appendix, should cover what a professional needs to get started with Oracle and ADO. We will cover the following topics:

- ❑ What is Oracle
- ❑ How does Oracle differ from SQL Server
- ❑ Oracle tricks and set-up
- ❑ ADO talks to Oracle
- ❑ ASP talks to Oracle
- ❑ Oracle pitfalls to avoid
- ❑ Setting up Oracle for MTS

What is Oracle?

In this section we will not go into great depth about all of Oracle – indeed we could not, as there is too much to cover. But what we will do is provide some information that will give you an easy transition from SQL Server to Oracle. (For those of you who are Oracle veterans, you can probably skip this overview and head on to the meaty pieces where ADO and Oracle come together). Oracle, like SQL server, is a relational database model, in fact it is the most widely used relational database model in the world.

> *On UNIX systems Oracle is the most dominant database server. On NT based systems the market share is somewhat tighter, however Oracle does lead. The exact numbers are hard to come by since both Microsoft and Oracle state their cases differently for market share. For example Oracle might use license revenue, while Microsoft is more inclined to use a price/transaction number. Suffice it to say that Oracle is the dominant player and that SQL Server strategy is to attack from the low end of the market.*

Oracle 8 is the latest version of the Oracle Server line of products, but a significant number of users are still using version 7.3 of Oracle server. Personal Oracle is a PC/Desktop version of the Oracle Database Server, with which you can work on a stand-alone or networked PC and write or test code against an Oracle database. The examples in this book are written against Personal Oracle. One of the tremendous strengths with Personal Oracle is that code written against a Personal Oracle database requires no change when you point the code at your enterprise's Oracle Server. Oracle Technology also allows you to export a group of tables from your main Oracle server and import them into Personal Oracle. 30 day trial software is available from Oracle's website www.oracle.com.

Important Oracle Terminology

While we can assume knowledge of views, triggers, indexes, and so on, there are some other fundamental terms that you should become familiar with when using Oracle after working with SQL Server.

Users

The first and most confusing difference when coming to Oracle from SQL Server is what I call the "missing database". When we look at SQL Server, we expect to see the data organized into databases:

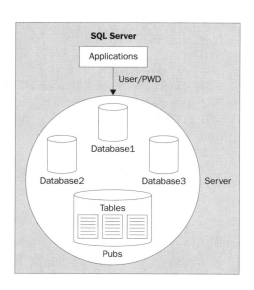

Indeed when we drill down on a SQL Server, this is exactly what we do see. Even in a connection string we see the database:

```
strConnect = "driver={SQL Server};" & _
    "server=MyServer;database=pubs;uid=sa;pwd=snake"
```

The concept of a database as a container of specific data is lost in Oracle. From the standpoint of a SQL Server user, there are no databases per se. Instead, data is grouped by users:

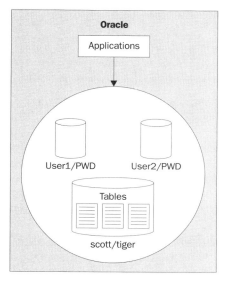

A user owns a packet of data and all the rights to that packet. For example, the Pubs database in SQL Server might become the Authors user in Oracle, where all the people and programs using the Authors data identify themselves to the system as Authors. The connection string might look like this:

```
strConnect = "driver={Microsoft ODBC For Oracle};" & _
    "server=MyOraServer;uid=Author;pwd=snake"
```

So in Oracle, the SQL Server concept of the database with tables and users is condensed into the user with tables. The following list describes some further Oracle terms with which we need to be familiar:

SGA

The SGA is the system global area or shared global area. This global area is the database-wide system memory. This area is sharable and all background processes and user processes can have access to all the data and control structures in this area.

Instance

An instance is the memory space (SGA and user processes) that Oracle has set aside for the database. For a programmer, an instance name is analogous to a SQL Server server name. In the connection string above the instance name is MyOraServer.

Schema

A schema is a logical grouping of database objects. To us the schema is synonymous with the User discussed above – which means that an Oracle schema is like a SQL Server database.

Roles

Roles are named groups of related privileges that are granted to users or other roles. Roles are used to supply dynamic levels of access to users and applications. For example you might allow all of your applications to connect to a set of tables through a user but then restrict permissions through roles:

```
objConn.ConnectionString = strConn
objConn.Open
if userType = SUPERVISOR then
      objConn.Execute set role super identified by superAccess
else
      objConn.Execute set role regular identified by regularAccess
end if
```

The role names are `super` and `regular` and the role passwords are `superAccess` and `regularAccess`.

Synonym

A synonym is an alias for a database object. In Oracle you can use synonyms to establish levels of abstraction between client and server objects. In cases where underlying objects are renamed or redefined, code that uses synonyms is safe because the synonyms on the server would just need to be redefined, but code that used the intrinsic object names would have to be fixed and recompiled.

SQL*Net

SQL*Net is network software that, when installed on a computer, allows for network connectivity between client applications and database services regardless of the network protocols available.

SQL*Plus

A data querying tool that is supplied to a client with an Oracle install. This tool is used in roughly the same way as SQL Server's Microsoft ISQL

PL/SQL

Procedure Language/Standard Query Language (PL/SQL) is the database programming language for Oracle.
PL/SQL resembles BASIC and is roughly analogous to TSQL.
For a while now with SQL Server we have all connected to databases through ODBC, at least those of us writing code to talk to enterprise level data servers. Now ADO gives us a chance to talk to data through OLEDB. The question that comes to mind is how does that differ from ODBC, both programmatically and practically.

Connecting to Oracle

We discussed using ODBC and/or OLEDB to connect to a data source in Chapter 1. There is no particular rule about whether to use ODBC or OLEDB to connect to Oracle, although you will get better performance if you can connect to your data through the OLEDB provider, as this does not go through an intermediary ODBC layer. We've tried to provide as much information as possible, so that you will be able to understand why your code works as it does.

Oracle and ODBC

When you connect to an Oracle database through ODBC you have two methods that you can follow, as with any ODBC connection. The first is to use a DSN that is registered on your machine. The second is to use the connection string directly in your code.

You will need a valid SQL*Net connection string. SQL Net Easy Configuration is a tool that allows you to create an alias that you can reference in an ODBC DSN to connect to your Oracle Server. It is added to your install group by the Oracle installer. We'll see how to set this SQL*Net connection string (under Adding an Instance Reference) when we cover Oracle client software a little further on.

Setting up a DSN

When setting up a DSN for the latest Microsoft Oracle driver you are prompted for a server. This is where you type in your instance name. If you are using your local instance in Personal Oracle you can use `"2:"`. If you are using an older Microsoft driver, a 3rd party driver, or an Oracle driver you may be prompted for a connection string. Once again, this is where you would enter your instance name.

Going "DSN-less"

With the most recent Microsoft drivers we can use the term `"server"`.

```
Call objRS.Open("select * from emp" _
        , "driver={Microsoft ODBC for Oracle};" & _
          "server=2:;uid=scott;pwd=tiger" _
        , adOpenForwardOnly)
```

Alternatively an earlier driver will require the term `"ConnectString"`.

```
Call objRS.Open("select * from emp" _
        , "driver={Microsoft ODBC Driver for Oracle};" & _
          "ConnectString=2:;uid=scott;pwd=tiger" _
        , adOpenForwardOnly)
```

Oracle and OLEDB

To connect to Oracle with OLEDB we again have two options: we can either set up a datalink file, or we can use a connection string.

Creating a Datalink File

A datalink file is analogous to the DSN that we saw above for connecting to Oracle with ODBC. Setting up a datalink file for Oracle is easy, and it is a good way to see the different OLEDB providers that are currently installed on your machine. Here are the necessary steps:

1. Right click in Explorer and select New | Microsoft Data Link

2. Give the new datalink file a meaningful name

3. Right click the file, and bring up the Properties screen

4. On the Provider tab, select the Oracle OLEDB Provider and then click Next

5. On the Connection tab, fill in the server name (your Oracle instance), the user ID (optional), and the password (also optional).

Here is a connection that uses the data link file:

```
Call objRS.Open("select * from emp" _
        , "file name=c:\OraADOTest.UDL" _
        , adOpenForwardOnly)
```

Going "Datalink-less"

Of course it's not essential to set up a data link file. If you choose not to then your connection string will look like this:

```
Call objRS.Open("select * from emp" _
        , "provider=MSDAORA;" & _
          "password=tiger;" & _
          "user id=scott;" & _
          "data source=2:" _
        , adOpenForwardOnly)
```

Oracle 8 Support with OLEDB and ODBC

A significant number of Oracle users are still using Oracle 7.x. Those who are using Oracle 8 will be pleased with many of the new features and extensions that Oracle has added. As of this time, the latest Microsoft OLEDB providers and ODBC Drivers do support Oracle 8. However, Microsoft makes some caveats in their support for Oracle 8. Oracle 8 has introduced several new data types, among them some that support unicode: NCHAR, NVARCHAR, and NCLOB. Oracle 8 also supports some multimedia data types: CLOB, BLOB, and BFILE. Neither the Microsoft OLEDB provider nor the Microsoft ODBC driver supports these data types in their current versions.

Setting Up Oracle and ADO

In this section we will start by looking at Oracle client software versions and ODBC driver versions, that are recommended for use with IIS and ASP. When we ensure that the correct drivers are used and that the appropriate patches from Oracle are installed we help create a stable platform for our applications. After this we will cover the other Oracle-specific software that is necessary to work with ADO.

Recommended Drivers and Software Versions

If you are connecting with ODBC then the recommended ODBC driver from Microsoft is the Microsoft ODBC for Oracle driver (Msorcl32.dll) version 2.573.2927 (or later). Don't be fooled by the version number. Many of us have the 2.7x.xx version of this driver on our machines, and while it may appear that 2.7x is later than 2.573., note that the second number (.7x and .573) is the revision number. Therefore, the .573 is the newer of the two.

For a list of third-party OLEDB suppliers see Appendix E.

The next chart shows the correct versions of the Oracle software that should be installed. For updates to this information check the Oracle website at www.oracle.com.

Oracle Server	7.3.3.0.0	7.3.4.0.0	8.0.3.0.0	8.0.4.0.0
Required Support Files	7.3.3.5.2	7.3.4.2.0	8.0.3.2.3	8.0.4.2.4
SQL*Net	2.3.3.0.4	2.3.4.0.4	N/A	N/A
Net8	N/A	N/A	8.0.3.0.4	8.0.4.0.3

Oracle support will supply you with patches and updates as needed and as your licensing agreement allows.

Client Access to Oracle

The following example is a step-by-step setup guide to installing the necessary software for client access to an Oracle database. This example will use SQL*Net version 2.3.3.0.0 with the required support files version 7.3.3.0.0 on a computer running Windows NT 4.0 Server.

> *Ideally the machine you are using should be running a clean and freshly-built with NT 4.0, the latest reliable option pack, the latest reliable service pack. We'll let you judge exactly what a "reliable" service pack actually means.*

First remember when installing the Microsoft Data Access Components 2.0 to choose the following:

❑ ODBC Components
❑ OLE DB Components
❑ ODBC Driver for Oracle Databases
❑ OLE DB Provider for Oracle Databases
❑ Microsoft ActiveX Data Objects

Installing the Oracle Support Files and SQL*Net

For ASP to communicate with Oracle through ADO you need to install Oracle's client software on your Web server. From your Oracle software compact disc or network drive (if your Oracle install is on the network), run Setup from the root directory.

❑ **Select Language**.
❑ **Select Installation Directory**. You will be prompted that the install directory path information needs to be added to the registry. The Oracle installer will automatically do this for you. At this point, Setup will exit and you will have to restart again. Repeat the above steps. This is annoying, but you shouldn't be nonplussed. Just start the install all over again. Think of the first attempt at an Oracle install as a "dry run". If you work with Oracle for any time at all, you will get used to its little idiosyncrasies.
❑ **Select Oracle7 Client Products.**
❑ **Select Application User**. When you are prompted to install the Oracle documentation either on your hard disk drive or to read it from the compact disc, choose the appropriate location. The Oracle documentation is not the best or the easiest to read in the world. The appropriate location for the documentation, especially on a web server, might be nowhere i.e. you could choose not to install it.

The Oracle client Setup will now copy the files and configure the client software.

Adding an Instance reference

An instance reference is an alias that you can reference in an ODBC DSN to connect to your Oracle Server. You can create it with the SQL*Net Easy Configuration tool, which should have been installed with the steps above. To run this tool, select Start | Programs | Oracle for Windows NT | SQL Net Easy Configuration. Next follow these steps:

- ❑ **Select Add Database Alias**. The database alias is the way that your machine will know where your Oracle instance is. Type in a name for the alias (for example, the instance name).
- ❑ **Select the protocol**. Most commonly this will be TCP/IP.
- ❑ **Specify the host machine** (usually the IP address) **and the database instance**. This is the name of the instance. (You can get this information from your database administrator).

You will now be able to connect to an Oracle instance though your ASP page. Let's move on to an example which will show how we do this.

An ASP Oracle example

This section will go over connecting and retrieving data from Oracle to an ASP page. The example is purposely simple and free from many advanced techniques to clearly illustrate the point at hand. However, we must realize that the example will not apply to every installation of Oracle client software.

For more detailed assistance, talk to your DBA or to Oracle.

In this example we will connect to the Scott schema in Personal Oracle and retrieve data from the Emp table. Once we get the data we will format it into a table. Before we go to the code let's take a look at the table structure. In an Oracle tool called SQL Worksheet (part of the Oracle Enterprise Tools) I typed the command describe emp. The command describe in Oracle displays the structure of a table. Here is the structure of the emp table:

```
SQLWKS> describe emp
Column Name                         Null?     Type
------------------------------- -------- ----
EMPNO                           NOT NULL NUMBER(4)
ENAME                                    VARCHAR2(10)
JOB                                      VARCHAR2(9)
MGR                                      NUMBER(4)
HIREDATE                                 DATE
SAL                                      NUMBER(7,2)
COMM                                     NUMBER(7,2)
DEPTNO                                   NUMBER(2)
```

Next we will set up a simple ASP file that will display all the records in this table. Like the pubs database in SQL Server, the Scott schema in Oracle is a small sample data collection. The Emp table has very few rows and is a good candidate for display in this way. Let's walk through the ASP script:

```
<%@ LANGUAGE="VBSCRIPT" %>

<HTML>
<HEAD>
<TITLE>Simple Connect To Oracle</TITLE>
```

```
</HEAD>
<BODY>
<%
Dim objRS 'an ado record set
Dim strEmpNo
Dim strEName
Dim strJob
Dim strMgr
Dim datHireDate
Dim curSal
Dim curComm
Dim strDeptNo
```

First we've declared all the variables on this page at the top. (This is a great boon both for you and for those that use this code after you). We'll be connecting to our Oracle instance through the Recordset object:

```
set objRS = createobject("ADODB.Recordset")
Call objRS.Open("select * from emp" _
        , "Provider=MSDAORA;" & _
            "Password=tiger;" & _
            "User ID=scott;" & _
            "data source=2:" _
        , adOpenForwardOnly)
```

Note that the connection string uses a full description of the connection mechanics; no Microsoft Data Link File is needed. We open the recordset forward-only for the best performance. Next we can see that each column gets its own variable. Believe it or not, this is the most efficient way of accessing the columns – especially if the same columns are going to be accessed again and again.

```
set strEmpNo = objRS ("empNo")
set strEName = objRS ("eName")
set strJob = objRS ("Job")
set strMgr = objRS("Mgr")
set datHireDate = objRS("HireDate")
set curSal = objRS("Sal")
set curComm = objRS("Comm")
set strDeptNo = objRS("DeptNo")
response.write "<TABLE BORDER=1 WIDTH='80%'>"
response.write "<THEAD>"
response.write "<TR>"
response.write "<TH>Employee Number</TH>"
response.write "<TH>Name</TH>"
response.write "<TH>Job Title</TH>"
response.write "<TH>Manager</TH>"
response.write "<TH>Hire Date</TH>"
response.write "<TH>Salary</TH>"
response.write "<TH>Comm</TH>"
response.write "<TH>Department</TH>"
response.write "</TR>"
response.write "<TBODY>"
Do While Not objRS.EOF
    response.write "<TR>"
        response.write "<TD>" & strEmpNo & "</TD>"
        response.write "<TD>" & strEName & "</TD>"
        response.write "<TD>" & strJob & "</TD>"
```

```
        response.write "<TD>" & strMgr & "</TD>"
        response.write "<TD>" & datHireDate & "</TD>"
        response.write "<TD>" & curSal & "</TD>"
        response.write "<TD>" & curComm & "</TD>"
        response.write "<TD>" & strDeptNo & "</TD>"
        response.write "</TR>"
        objRS.MoveNext
Loop
response.write "</TABLE>"

%>
</BODY>
</HTML>
```

After the rows are returned, we assign the columns to our column variable, once again stressing efficiency and code readability. The HTML Table then gives us a simple display of the data. When we call `objRS.MoveNext` all our column variables are automatically updated to point at the correct data.

So, now we know how to reach Oracle data from ASP, let's look at some of the problems you may encounter.

Oracle Pitfalls (and how to avoid them)

Oracle and ADO are a great match – and Oracle **is** a great way to store data. However, nothing is perfect, especially in emerging technology. One particular cause of problems is the driver you choose. Should you use the Microsoft ODBC driver for Oracle or the OLE DB provider when making a connection? I always start out using the OLE DB provider for Oracle, which most of the time gives me sufficient functionality. If I get unexpected results or run into some limitations, then I begin experimenting with the ODBC Drivers. For instance, on one occasion I needed to use the Microsoft ODBC Driver for Oracle Version 2.0 because of some unexpected interactions that I was having between ADO and Oracle Objects for OLE (OO4O).

In this section we will discuss some caveats that you should observe when using ADO against Oracle, particularly when using ODBC drivers. Some of these problems are reported to occur when you use the latest ODBC drivers from Microsoft, so they might not occur when you use other drivers.

Beware Stored Procedures with an Abundance of Parameters

Stored procedures are a great way to get and use data. Often we use stored procedures to return a lot of data. However, when using stored procedures with 10 or more parameters, and when using Microsoft's ODBC Driver you will receive the error:

```
Access Violation (0xC0000005) in ORA804.DLL @01B20002.
```

or:

```
    Microsoft OLE DB Provider for ODBC Drivers error '80040e14' [Microsoft][ODBC
driver for Oracle]Syntax error or access violation Spud.asp, line 777
```

The problem is not Bill's fault this time. Instead it is a bug in Oracle's 8.0.4.0.0 and 8.0.4.0.4 client files. The good news is that a fix is available by upgrading your Oracle Client software to version 8.0.4.2.0 or higher, by downloading these files from Oracle or requesting them from your Oracle contact person. The funny thing is that this problem was not evident in the 8.0.3.0.0 version.

A Problem with Record Set Based Updates

I've never been a big fan of recordset- or result set-based updating – especially through Oracle. One problem that you might run across with these kinds of updates is that only `forward-only` cursors will work without error. If you use another cursor type (`static`, `keyset`, or `dynamic`) with ADO, you may receive this error message:

```
Microsoft][ODBC driver for Oracle]Degree of derived table does not match
column list
Source Microsoft OLE DB Provider for ODBC Drivers
SQLState 21S02
NativeError 0
```

This is a bug within the Microsoft ODBC Driver. If this happens to you, you are probably using an out-of-date driver and should get the latest. I would suggest that you look into using action queries to update your data. Of course, using action queries puts the onus of concurrency on you. In other words you need to make sure that you do not overwrite other users' recent changes to the underlying data.

Oracle and transactions

One thing that you need to keep in mind when programming against an Oracle database is that it will not commit your changes unless you tell it to, or unless your program ends. Oracle works in an implied transaction state. Depending on how your Oracle server is tuned you may have to execute a `commit` command to enforce changes to the data immediately.

On one occasion when I was testing a program, I used SQL Worksheet (an Oracle query tool) to input some test data. Then I ran my program and the test data was not anywhere to be seen. Back to SQL Worksheet – the data was there; back to the code – no sign of the data. A few weeks with SQL Server had taken its toll. When I realized what was happening, I issued a commit to my SQL Worksheet window and my code was suddenly able to activate the data.

Be careful when testing with numeric fields

You may get stray `Type Mismatch` errors when performing functions with Oracle numeric data. Be careful when doing the following:

```
If OraRecordSet("Age") < 18 then ...
```

or:

```
GallonsRemaining = OraRecordset("ReserveTank") + 11.56
```

Instead use your conversion functions (and make sure to check for Null) to enforce the correct type. Microsoft reports that `CLng` is the most efficient of the conversion functions.

```
If CLng(OraRecordSet("Age")) < 18 then ...
```

or:

```
GallonsRemaining = CSng(OraRecordset("ReserveTank")) + 11.56
```

Oracle does not have an integer data type, only numeric. Numeric types have exact precision and scale must be converted to a specific type before being used. However, you should be able to be compare floating point numbers to integers (after all floating point numbers are approximate values).

Oracle's numeric data type can be interpreted differently by different drivers. For example an integer stored in a numeric field will be interpreted by some ODBC drivers (for example, Intersolv version 3.01) as a double-precision floating point (i.e. a VBScript VarType of 5), whereas the Microsoft ODBC for Oracle is more accurate and returns a VBScript VarType of 14 – which is numeric. The ADO `Type` property always returns type 131 (numeric).

Stored Procedures

When calling an Oracle Stored Procedure through ADO you must make sure that you set up the command object correctly. Failure to do so will result in degradation of performance by a factor of 10. The root cause is that the MS Oracle ODBC driver was modified in its later incarnations to allow for the use of Oracle Packages. The side-effect was that a call to the underlying ODBC API function, `SQLProcedureColumns`, breaks down performance by increasing the amount of SQL generated.

You may fall into this trap if you do not change the `CommandType` property of your `Command` object from the default, `adCmdUnknown`, to `adCmdStoredProc`. It is always a good idea to set the `CommandType` property to the correct value when you can. By setting it you allow ADO to optimize your command calls;however, if you set the `.CommandType` property incorrectly then you will encounter a run-time error when executing your command.

Be careful when using Oracle synonyms

Remember that a synonym is a pointer to or an alias of an Oracle object, (such as a table, view, snapshot, package, function, procedure, sequence, or another synonym). The most current ODBC drivers for Oracle do not support synonyms when calling stored procedures, but they will work when they point to other Oracle objects. This is a bug in the driver.

In-line Comments Are Parsed – Beware

When using in-line comments in your SQL statements, such as these –

```
select *
from emp
where
/* A is A */
ENAME = 'GAULT'
```

– you may get the error message:

```
"Syntax Error or Access Violation".
```

This may puzzle you if you used the 1.0 driver successfully with in-line comments. The good news is that the latest ODBC driver from Microsoft fixes this problem. If you are still getting this problem with in-line comments then you must install the latest driver from Microsoft.

> **Remember that you can send optimization directives to the Oracle database engine through in-line comments.**

Erroneous Access Violation On a Stored Procedure

When you grant access, revoke access, and then re-grant access to a table accessed by a stored procedure you will receive an erroneous error message:

```
Return:    SQL_ERROR=-1
szErrorMsg="[Microsoft][ODBC driver for Oracle]Wrong number of
parameters"
szErrorMsg="[Microsoft][ODBC driver for Oracle]Syntax error or access
violation"
```

The underlying cause of this is not the fault of the Microsoft ODBC driver but instead a bug in an Oracle function. The solution to this problem is to recompile all stored procedures after the grants to the tables that they access have been changed.

Table Aliases Don't Work with KeySet Cursors

When using the Microsoft ODBC Driver and keyset cursors, SELECT statements with table aliases will cause the following error:

```
[Microsoft][ODBC driver for Oracle]Cannot use Keyset-driven cursor on
    join, with union, intersect or minus or on read only result set"
```

The driver does not re-write the SQL statement to the Oracle server with the correct syntax. Internally the Oracle server raises the following error:

```
ORA-00964: table name not in FROM list
```

When using the less efficient cursor types such as keyset and dynamic, you should take a cold, hard look at what you are trying to accomplish. The error above can in most cases be avoided by using a forward-only or static cursor type.

Watch out for Stored Procedures with no Parameters

When you call a package procedure that does not take a parameter then the latest Microsoft ODBC for Oracle driver will generate the following error:

```
SYNTAX ERROR OR ACCESS VIOLATION
```

The workaround for this behavior is to create a stored procedure with a dummy parameter. Microsoft has acknowledged that this is a bug in their latest ODBC driver for Oracle.

Oracle Access Through IIS may be Hindered by Permission Problems

When we log into an Oracle database as a user, we are authenticated through SQL*Net Authentication services. This service works well for users entering through desktop applications and Oracle tools, such as SQLPlus, SQL Worksheet, Schema Manager, etc. However, when the user attempting the login is a service such as IIS, authentication fails reporting the following reason:

```
[Microsoft][ODBC driver for Oracle][Oracle]ORA-12641: TNS:authentication
    service failed to initialize
```

333

The reason for this behavior is a known limitation of SQL*Net Authentication. To get around this problem you'll need to edit your Sqlnet.ora file. The Sqlnet.ora file contains configuration information for your Oracle server and can be usually found in the Network/Admin directory under the Oracle home directory. When you find this file, open it in a text editor and add the following line:

```
SQLNET.AUTHENTICATION_SERVICES = (none)
```

Oracle and Transactional ASP Scripts

Often it is desirable to use transactions when working with data and databases, and ASP scripts can act 'transactionally' using MTS. By using transactional ASP scripts we have a relatively easy way to code transactions across COM components, perform transactions across differing database server types, and pool database connections. Accessing Oracle from a transactional ASP script can be done in the same way as accessing SQL; however we first have to configure Oracle to support MTS transactions.

> Remember that the Oracle literature uses the MTS acronym to refer to "Multi-Threaded Server" and not "Microsoft Transaction Server" and the two have nothing in common.

Setting-up Oracle to run against MTS

MTS only works with Oracle 7.3.3 and higher. The following software is required to access an Oracle database from MTS components.

Oracle 7.3

Component	Version
Oracle Server on Windows NT	7.3.3.5.2 or later
Oracle SQL*Net	2.3.3.0.4 or later
Oracle Ociw32.dll	1.0.0.5 or later
Oracle Sqllib18.dll	1.8.3.0.4 or later
Oracle Xa73.dll	7.3.3.5.2 or later

Oracle 8

Component	Version
Oracle Server on Windows NT	8.0.4.1.1c or later
Oracle Net*	
Oracle Ociw32.dll	8.0.4.0.0 or later
Oracle Sqllib18.dll	8.0.4.1.0 or later
Oracle Xa80.dll	8.0.4.1.0 or later

To prepare Oracle to work with the MTS, follow these steps (Oracle, MTS, and ADO are assumed to be installed):

1. If you are using the Oracle 7.3 Client software, you can skip this step. If you are using the Oracle 8 Client software, you must modify the values of two registry keys.

> **Changing the registry yourself is risky – a mistake can have dire consequences. Make sure you know what you're doing, and always run RDISK and create an emergency back-up disk before attempting registry edits.**

Under the following registry key are two string-named values that specify the names of the Oracle 7.3 Client software DLLs:

```
HKEY_LOCAL_MACHINE\SOFTWARE\ Microsoft\Transaction
Server\Local Computer\My Computer String-Named Values: OracleXaLib "xa73.dll"
OracleSqlLib "sqllib18.dll"
```

Change these values to specify the names of the Oracle 8 Client software .dlls:

```
OracleXaLib "xa80.dll" OracleSqlLib "sqllib80.dll"
```

2. If you are upgrading from the beta release of MTS 2.0 then you should delete the `Dtcxatm.log` file. However, after this upgrade you should never delete this log again, as it may contain valuable recovery information. This step is not needed if you never installed the beta release of MTS 2.0.

3. Perform the following steps to enable Oracle XA transaction support:

❑ The Oracle system administrator must create views known as V$XATRANS$. To do this, the administrator must run an Oracle- supplied script, named `Xaview.sql`. This file can be found in the directory: `<MainDrive>:\ORANT\RDBMS73\ADMIN`

❑ The Oracle system administrator must grant SELECT access to the public on these views. For example: `Grant Select on V$XATRANS$ to public`

❑ In the Oracle Instance Manager, from the View menu, click Advanced Mode and then select Initialization Parameters in the left pane. In the right pane, select Advanced Tuning and increase the `distributed_transactions` parameter, to allow more concurrent MTS transactions to update the database at a single time. You can consult your Oracle Server documentation for more information about configuring Oracle XA transaction support.

4. Integrated security allows your NT authentication to be passed through to your Oracle database. To use integrated security, you must configure Microsoft Distributed Transaction Coordinator to run under a login ID and password authorized to connect to your Oracle database. The MSDTC needs this information because it opens your Oracle database to tell it the outcome of in doubt transactions. Configure the login ID for the MSDTC as follows:

❑ Select Start | Settings | Control Panel | Services

❑ Double click MSDTC.

❑ Select Log On As and specify a login ID and password.

❑ Use the Oracle security administration tools to make sure that the login ID you specify is authorized to open your Oracle database.

5. Configure the Oracle "Multi-Threaded Server" feature if you want to open a database link to a remote Oracle database (see your Oracle documentation for directions). This is essential, because when using transaction support, if the Oracle "Multi-Threaded Server" feature is not configured properly, Oracle reports the following error:

```
ORA-24777: Cannot create migratable transaction
```

Summary

As we look back on this chapter, what have we seen? We've broken the silence between Oracle and ADO and then once again between Oracle and ASP. I think ADO makes it easy to talk to Oracle – and hopefully you saw that it was not that hard. We went over some problems that you may encounter going up against Oracle, many of which have workarounds. Finally, we looked at what it takes to run MTS against Oracle. In the next chapter, we will see ADO go up against stored procedures.

15

Supporting Oracle Stored Procedures

In this chapter we will take a look at calling Oracle stored procedures, packages, and functions from ADO. Great stuff! Stored procedures are fast, precompiled routines that reside on the server. We will cover the following areas:

- ❑   Stored Procedures and General Troubleshooting.
- ❑   Package Definition and Use.
- ❑   Calling a Stored Procedure.
- ❑   Oracle Function Use.

Stored Procedures

This chapter will open up some more ways for you to improve the performance of your code through stored procedures. Let's recap on why we would want to use stored procedures. Stored procedures are great for two reasons. The first is that they represent code that is used over and over again, and in your quest as a programmer your holy grail (or at least one of them) should be code re-use. The second is that they push functionality out of your code and down to the server. Stored procedures are faster than code in general, as they usually require less information to be sent from the client to the server (since you are only sending parameters rather then the entire SQL Query).

ODBC Call Syntax

I've used ODBC call syntax for calling stored procedures in the examples in this chapter, because it is concise, travels well from Oracle to SQL Server, and gets the object (ADO or RDO and RDS) to build my parameter list for me. ODBC syntax for calling stored procedures is characterized by the key word `call`, curly braces `{}`, and question marks `?`, which are used in place of parameters:

```
{ Call ProcName(?,?,?) }
```

or

```
{ ? = Call FuncName(?,?,?)}
```

When ADO sees the call syntax it will automatically generate the parameter collection. Each question mark gets a parameter in the collection. The parameters are enumerated from left to right (0 to 2 in the first example and 0 to 3 in the second example).

General Troubleshooting

Many developers report having trouble calling Oracle stored procedures. Here are several reasons why you might be having trouble calling your stored procedure.

- ❑ Security issues – Do you have permission? Remember that Oracle has tight security; so you may be logging in to the Oracle instance as the wrong user. Your login might not have the corrrect grants. The stored procedure that you are calling might be touching objects that your login does not have the rights to touch.
- ❑ Type issues – Are you using the correct data types from ADO? See the first example, where we return a composite (table) type.
- ❑ Packages – Are you calling a procedure in a package? When calling a procedure in a package you must use the package name in the call (`{ call package.procedure( ? [, ? . . .] ) }`).
- ❑ Bugs in the ODBC Driver or OLE DB Provider – Is it really your problem? You might be hitting a limitation of your transport mechanism. Look at a known issue list of the ODBC or OLE DB provider that you are using, and the *Oracle Pitfalls* section in the previous chapter.

As a final note, the first thing that I always do is practice calling the stored procedure from SQL Plus or Oracle SQL worksheet. When I can do that, it proves that there is nothing wrong with the stored procedure itself.

Getting a Recordset from an Oracle Package

A package is a container of related database objects. These objects can be procedures, functions, cursors, and so on. A package is most often made up of two parts, the package specification and the package body. If you are a C or C++ programmer then you might think of the package specification as a set of declarations, because that's exactly what it is. Having the specification separated from the body allows for the body to change without affecting other objects that use the package.

A Sample Package

For our sample package we'll use the same example Oracle table, emp, that we saw in the previous chapter. Let's take a close look at the package specification below.

The very first line is a directive to Oracle that handles redundant specifications. This will create a new, or replace an existing, package.

```
create or replace package OraResultSet as
```

Next we declare several data types as type table. The table type is a PL/SQL composite type. Each table type variable represents an array of data (all the data in one column). The %type notation specifies the exact type of each "array". This %type notation allows us to relate a variable in a script to the type of an underlying column, without explicitly stating the type. That way, if the column type changes, your script does not have to change.

```
type tbl_empno is table of emp.empno%type
    index by binary_integer;

type tbl_ename is table of emp.ename%type
    index by binary_integer;

type tbl_job is table of emp.job%type
    index by binary_integer;

type tbl_mgr is table of emp.mgr%type
    index by binary_integer;

type tbl_hiredate is table of emp.hiredate%type
    index by binary_integer;

type tbl_sal is table of emp.sal%type
    index by binary_integer;

type tbl_comm is table of emp.comm%type
    index by binary_integer;

type tbl_deptno is table of emp.deptno%type
    index by binary_integer;
```

After the types are declared, we signal our intention to use the types in the declaration of the empResultSet procedure. All the parameters of the empResultSet procedure are listed with the out keyword indicating that they are output parameters.

```
procedure empResultSet (o_empno out tbl_empno,
                        o_ename out tbl_ename,
                        o_job out tbl_job,
                        o_mgr out tbl_mgr,
                        o_hiredate out tbl_hiredate,
                        o_sal out tbl_sal,
                        o_comm out tbl_comm,
                        o_deptno out tbl_deptno);

procedure showResult ;
end OraResultSet;
```

After the empResultSet procedure we declare the showResult procedure. This procedure is included to show an example of debug output. The last line of the package specification is the End statement.

The listing below shows the package body. It is quite simple. In the body of empResultSet we open a cursor into the emp table. We will then loop through the cursor with the implicit declaration of emp_rec in the loop. This loops through the recordset and populates each of our output arrays. After they are populated, the procedure ends and the output parameters are available for the caller.

```
create or replace package body OraResultSet as

procedure empResultSet (o_empno out tbl_empno,
                        o_ename out tbl_ename,
                        o_job out tbl_job,
                        o_mgr out tbl_mgr,
                        o_hiredate out tbl_hiredate,
                        o_sal out tbl_sal,
                        o_comm out tbl_comm,
                        o_deptno out tbl_deptno)

is
cursor emp_cur is select * from emp;
cnt number default 1;
begin
for emp_rec in emp_cur
loop
    o_empno(cnt) := emp_rec.empno;
    o_ename(cnt) := emp_rec.ename;
    o_job(cnt) := emp_rec.job;
    o_mgr(cnt) := emp_rec.mgr;
    o_hiredate(cnt) := emp_rec.hiredate;
    o_sal(cnt) := emp_rec.sal;
    o_comm(cnt) := emp_rec.comm;
    o_deptno(cnt) := emp_rec.deptno;
    cnt := cnt + 1;
end loop;

end;
```

The showresult procedure is defined next. We will not be calling the showresult procedure from code, instead it is provided for debugging. The showresult procedure calls the EmpResultSet procedure that returns the output into the variables fldempno, fldname, etc. Remember that these are column arrays.

```
procedure showresult  is
fldempno tbl_empno;
fldename tbl_ename;
fldjob tbl_job;
fldmgr tbl_mgr;
fldhiredate tbl_hiredate;
fldsal tbl_sal;
fldcomm tbl_comm;
flddeptno tbl_deptno;
```

```
numofrows number;
cnt number;
cursor getCount is select count(*) from emp;
begin
open getCount;
fetch getCount into numofrows;
close getCount;
dbms_output.put_line('Num: '|| numofrows);
oraresultset.empresultset(fldempno,fldename,fldjob,fldmgr,fldhiredate,_
                          fldsal,fldcomm,flddeptno);
For loop_index in 1 .. numofrows
loop
dbms_output.put_line('Record: ' ||loop_index);
dbms_output.put_line('EmpNo: '||fldempno(loop_index));
dbms_output.put_line('Name: '||fldename(loop_index));
dbms_output.put_line('Job: ' || fldjob(loop_index));
dbms_output.put_line('Mgr: ' || fldmgr(loop_index));
dbms_output.put_line('HireDate: ' || fldhiredate(loop_index));
dbms_output.put_line('Sal: ' || fldsal(loop_index));
dbms_output.put_line('Comm: ' || fldcomm(loop_index));
dbms_output.put_line('DeptNo: ' || flddeptno(loop_index));
dbms_output.put_line('');
end loop;
end showresult;


end;
/
```

We loop through the arrays and use the call to `dbms_output.put_line`, a built-in Oracle function, to show the output.

The `dbms_output.put_line` *function is the same as* `Print` *in SQL Server.*

Testing Your Output

Now before we code, let's test our output by calling our package from an Oracle Worksheet window. We can see this in the adjacent screenshot, including the syntax for calling our package, `execute oraresultset.showresult`.

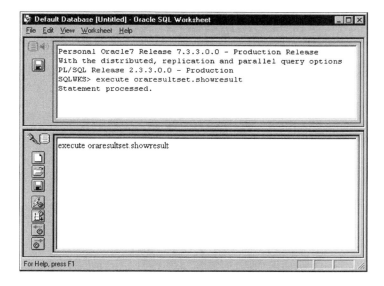

However, as you can see, when we execute `oraresultset.showresult` in a freshly opened Oracle SQL Worksheet window we get no output. We only get the message: Statement Processed. To see the output we need to execute the following line in our Oracle SQL Worksheet window:

```
set serveroutput on
```

When we do this, the output is displayed. The output is shown in the next screenshot:

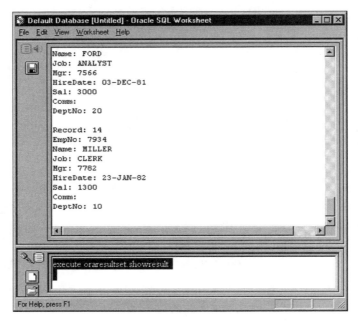

Next let's look at an ASP script that uses ADO to call a package.

Calling a Package with ASP

We'll look at an ASP script that uses a `Connection`, a `Command`, and a `Recordset` object to call the sample package we looked at earlier. The connection is opened using ODBC.

```
<%@ LANGUAGE="VBSCRIPT" %>

<HTML>
<HEAD>
<TITLE>Calling a Package</TITLE>
</HEAD>
<BODY>
<H1>Recordset from a Stored Procedure</H1>
<%
    dim objConn ' as ADO connection
    set objConn = CreateObject("ADODB.Connection")
    dim objComm 'as ADO command
    set objComm = CreateObject("ADODB.Command")
    dim objRS ' as ADO Recordset
```

```
set objRS = CreateObject("ADODB.Recordset")
dim strConnect 'as string
dim strSQL 'as string

'Initialize the string
strConnect = "driver={Microsoft ODBC for Oracle};SERVER=2:;
              uid=scott;pwd=tiger"
```

Remember that a schema is identified by a userid and a password, so here we are using the scott/tiger database schema.

The ODBC call statement has some new syntax. In addition to the usual call keyword, it now has an additional resultset keyword. After the resultset keyword comes the number of rows of data expected back. The call will fail if you use a number that is lower than the number of rows *actually* returned, but there is no penalty for *overestimating* the number of rows sent back. Also notice that the resultset keyword, the row estimate, and the parameter list, are all enclosed within another set of curly braces.

```
strSQL = "{call OraResultSet.empResultSet(" & _
    "{resultset " & _
    "20," & _
    "o_empno," & _
    "o_ename," & _
    "o_job," & _
    "o_mgr," & _
    "o_hiredate," & _
    "o_sal," & _
    "o_comm," & _
    "o_deptno})" & _
    "}"
'Connect to database
objConn.ConnectionString = strConnect
objConn.CursorLocation = 3 'adUseClient
objConn.Open

'Set up command object
set objComm.ActiveConnection = objConn
objComm.CommandText = strSQL
objComm.CommandType = 1 'adCmdText

'Set up recordset
objRS.CursorType = 3 'adOpenStatic
objRS.LockType = 1 'adLockReadOnly
set objRS.Source = objComm

'Now get the recordset from the stored procedure
objRS.Open

'View data
dim objField
Response.Write "<TABLE Border=1>"
Response.Write "<THEAD>"
Response.Write "<TR>"
for each objField in objRS.Fields
  Response.Write "<TH>" & objField.name & "</TH>"
next
```

```
   Response.Write "</TR>"
   Response.Write "<TBODY>"
   Do While Not objRS.EOF
      Response.Write "<TR>"
      for each objField in objRS.Fields
        Response.Write "<TD>" & objField.Value & "</TD>"
      next
      Response.Write "</TR>"
      objRS.MoveNext
   Loop
   Response.Write "</TABLE>"

%>

</BODY>
</HTML>
```

After we instantiate the recordset, we then set its `Source` property to our `Command` object. By calling the `Open` method on the recordset, we populate our recordset with data. The later part of the script displays the data in a table.

Getting Output Values from a Stored Procedure

While getting a recordset from a package may be cool (well at least I think it is), a maybe more common task is using regular stored procedures with input and output parameters. In our next example, we will access the `emp` table in the `scott/tiger` schema. Our stored procedure will take an employee ID and return the employee name. If the name is not found, we will return `NOTFOUND`.

Here is our stored procedure `GetData`:

```
create or replace procedure
GetData (EmployeeNum in Number, EmployeeName out varchar2) is

cursor Emp_cur (empnum emp.empno%type)

is select ename from emp where empno=empnum;

begin
   open emp_cur(EmployeeNum);
   fetch emp_cur into EmployeeName;
   if emp_cur%notfound then
      EmployeeName := 'NOTFOUND';
   end if;
   close emp_cur;
end GetData;
```

Note that in the `GetData` stored procedure, the parameters are marked with the `in` and `out` keywords. The `Emp_cur` is declared as a cursor type with the `empnum` parameter. In the body of the procedure, the procedure parameter, `EmployeeNum`, is passed in to the cursor. Afterwards we fetch on the cursor into `EmployeeName`. We either return `NOTFOUND`, or the result of the cursor fetch.

Here is our stored procedure in action in our ASP script, `GetData.asp`:

```
<%@ LANGUAGE="VBSCRIPT" %>

<HTML>
<HEAD>
<TITLE>Get The Employee Name</TITLE>
</HEAD>
<BODY>
<H1>Simple Stored Procedure From ASP and ADO</H1>
<FORM NAME="Stored Procedure" ACTION="GetData.asp" METHOD="POST">
<H2>Enter Employee ID</H2>
<INPUT NAME="empID" TYPE="text" VALUE="1234"><P>
<INPUT NAME="Get Data" TYPE="submit" VALUE="Fire!">

</FORM>
<% if request("empID") <> "" then %>
<%
    'Draw results
    Dim objConn 'As ADODB.Connection
    Dim objComm 'As ADODB.Command
    Set objConn = CreateObject("ADODB.Connection")
    Set objComm = CreateObject("ADODB.Command")

    objConn.Open _
            "driver={Microsoft ODBC for Oracle};server=2:;uid=scott;pwd=tiger;"
    Set objComm.ActiveConnection = objConn

    objComm.CommandType = 1 'adCmdText
    objC.CommandText = "{ call GetData(?,?) }"

    'We are passing parameters by ordinance position,
    'but you can also use named parameters
    objComm.Parameters(0).Value = cInt(request("empID"))
    objComm.Execute

    response.write "<H3>Employee Name is:</H3>"
    response.write objComm.Parameters(1).Value
  end if
%>

</BODY>
</HTML>
```

Of note in the script is the line where we set the `CommandText` property (in bold). When the `Command` object reads that line it automatically populates its `Parameters` collection based on the ? list.

I've preferred to use ODBC call syntax methods for code readability in this example, rather than adding parameters manually.

We only need to set the value of the input parameter and execute the command before we can write our answer. This screenshot shows the output of the script:

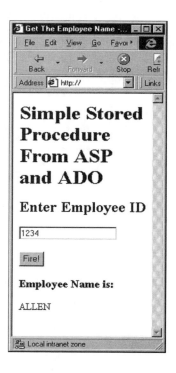

Using Functions

Functions are stored procedures that have return values. In this section we see a very simple example that illustrates what is needed to pull return values back from the Oracle database through ADO. First let's look at this simple function that takes two values and returns their sum:

```
create or replace function ExFunct (Num1 in number, Num2 in Number) return number
is
    temp number;
begin
    temp := Num1 + Num2;
    return temp;
end ExFunct;
```

Notice that our function definition uses the keywords return number (in bold) to indicate that the function returns a number. The numbers are added together and then sent back via the line return temp (also in bold).

In the next ASP script we see how to call a function through ADO. It is very similar to calling a stored procedure, with the exception of the structure of the ODBC call syntax, where the ? appears before the keyword call (in bold). Once again, the ADO connection can intelligently form the Parameters collection as soon as its CommandText property is set. As in the previous example, we are passing parameters by ordinance position, but you can also use named parameters.

```
<%@ LANGUAGE="VBSCRIPT" %>

<HTML>
<HEAD>
<TITLE>Hey Function</TITLE>
</HEAD>
<BODY>
<H1>Getting a Return Value</H1>
<FORM NAME="Stored Function" ACTION="Add2.asp" METHOD="POST">
<H2>Enter First Number</H2>
<INPUT NAME="Num1" TYPE="text" VALUE="1"><P>
<H2>Second Number</H2>
<INPUT NAME="Num2" TYPE="text" VALUE="2"><P>
<INPUT NAME="AddIt" TYPE="submit" VALUE="Add!">

</FORM>
<% if request("Num1") <> "" then %>
<%
    'Draw results
    Dim objConn 'As ADODB.Connection
    Dim objComm 'As ADODB.Command
    Set objConn = CreateObject("ADODB.Connection")
    Set objComm = CreateObject("ADODB.Command")

    objConn.Open _
          "driver={Microsoft ODBC for Oracle};server=2:;uid=scott;pwd=tiger;"
    Set objComm.ActiveConnection = objConn

    objComm.CommandType = 1 'adCmdText
    objComm.CommandText = "{ ? = call ExFunct(?,?) }"
    objComm.Parameters(1).Value = cInt(request("Num1"))
    objComm.Parameters(2).Value = cInt(request("Num2"))
    objComm.Execute

    response.write "<H3>Answer is:</H3>"
    response.write objComm.Parameters(1).Value & _
      " + " & _
      objComm.Parameters(2).Value & _
      " = " & _
      objComm.Parameters(0).Value
end if
%>
```

The figure below shows the output of our script:

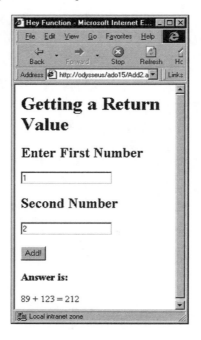

Summary

The quest for reusable code and efficient programming techniques goes on. What we saw in this chapter was some tools that will help you in that quest. The use of stored procedures, packages, and functions pushes much used and common routines down on to the database server, where we can take advantage of larger amounts of memory and processing power. The other thing that you should keep in mind as you go over this chapter is that all these samples do use the scott/tiger database schema. This is the sample data that ships with Oracle, so you can try all this code out yourself.

ADO 2.0 Reference

ADO provides a rich set of interfaces consisting of objects, collections, properties, methods and events with which we can interact with the ADO object model. These interfaces allow us to use ADO to access and manipulate data within our applications. In this section we will describe all the interfaces of the ADO 2.0 object model:

- ❑ Objects and Collections
- ❑ Properties
- ❑ Methods
- ❑ Events

This appendix is divided in two parts. It first looks at ADO's objects and collections defining each and providing a quick reference guide to their respective properties, methods and events. It then presents these in alphabetical order looking in more details at their use and syntax.

ADO Objects

The Command Object

A Command object is a definition of a specific command that you intend to execute against a data source. Use a Command object to query a database and return records in a Recordset object, to execute a bulk operation, to manipulate the structure of a database or to execute a stored procedure (or equivalent) against a data source. The Command object has the following properties, methods and collections:

Properties	ActiveConnection	CommandTimeout	Prepared
	CommandText	CommandType	
		Name	
Methods	Cancel	CreateParameter	Execute
Collections	Parameters	Properties	

The Connection Object

A Connection object represents a connection to a data source that you intend to execute queries against to retrieve or modify data. The Connection object has the following properties, methods, events and collections:

Properties	Attributes	DefaultDatabase	Provider
	CommandTimeOut	IsolationLevel	State
	ConnectionString	Mode	Version
	ConnectionTimeout		
	CursorLocation		
Methods	BeginTrans	CommitTrans	OpenSchema
	Cancel	Execute	RollbackTrans
	Close	Open	
Events	BeginTransComplete	InfoMessage	
	CommitTransComplete	RollbackTransComplete	
	ConnectComplete	WillConnect	
	Disconnect		
	ExecuteComplete		
Collections	Errors		
	Properties		

The Error Object

An Error object contains the details about an error that occurred on its corresponding connection. The Error object has the following properties:

Properties			
	Description	NativeError	SQLState
	HelpContext	Number	
	HelpFile	Source	

The Field Object

The Field object contains all attributes and information regarding a particular field in a Recordset object. The Field object has the following properties and methods:

Properties			
	ActualSize	Name	Precision
	Attributes	NumericScale	Type
	DataFormat	Optimize	UnderlyingValue
	DefinedSize	Originalvalue	Value
Methods	AppendChunk	GetChunk	

The Parameter Object

A Parameter object contains all information regarding a parameter of a Command object that will be used to execute a stored procedure or a parameterized query. The Parameter object has the following properties, method and collection:

Properties			
	Attributes	Name	Size
	Direction	NumericScale	Type
		Precision	Value
Methods	AppendChunk		
Collections	Properties		

The Property Object

A `Property` object is used to describe dynamic features of a `Recordset`, `Connection`, `Command` and `Field` objects that are not available to all types of recordsets. The `Property` object has the following properties:

Properties	Attributes	Name	Type	Value

The Recordset Object

The `Recordset` object is used to store all records of data retrieved from a data source, in rows and columns. A recordset always points to one, and only one, specific row of data within itself at any one time. The `ADOBD.Recordset ProgID` can be used to create a `Recordset` object. However, if you are only using this object you can create a recordset by using the `ADOR.Recordset ProgID`. This `ProgID` uses less resources as the `ADOR` library does not contain the overhead of the other objects such as the `Connection` or the `Command` objects. The `Recordset` object has the following properties, methods, events and collections:

Properties	Absolutepage	DataMember	PageCount
	AbsolutePosition	DataSource	PageSize
	ActiveCommand	EditMode	RecordCount
	Active_ Connection	EOF	Source
	BOF	Filter	Sort
	Bookmark	LockType	State
	CacheSize	MarshallOptions	Status
	CursorLocation	MaxRecords	StayInSync
	CursorType		
Methods	AddNew	Find	NextRecordset
	Cancel	GetRows	Open
	CancelBatch	GetString	Requery
	CancelUpdate	Move	Resync
	Clone	MoveFirst	Save
	Close	MoveLast	Supports
	CompareBookmarks	MoveNext	Update
	Delete	MovePrevious	UpdateBatch

Events	EndOfRecordset	MoveComplete	WillChangeRecord
	FetchComplete	RecordChange_ Complete	WillChange_ Recordset
	FetchProgress FieldChange_ Complete	Recordset_ ChangeComplete	WillMove
		WillChangeField	
Collections	Fields Properties		

ADO Collections

The Errors Collection

The Errors collection contains all of the Error objects that pertain to the collection's corresponding connection. The Errors collection has the following property and methods:

Properties	Count	
Methods	Clear	Item

The Fields Collection

The Fields collection contains all the Field objects that are contained within their corresponding Recordset object. The Fields collection has the following property and methods:

Properties	Count		
Methods	Append Delete	Item	Refresh

The Parameters Collection

The Parameter collection contains all the Parameter objects of their corresponding Command object. The Parameter collection has the following property and methods:

Properties	Count		
Methods	Append	Delete Item	Refresh

The Properties Collection

The `Properties` collection contains all `Property` objects that pertain to a `Recordset` object. The `Properties` collection has the following property and methods:

Properties	Count	
Methods	Item	Refresh

Properties

AbsolutePage (Recordset Object)

The `AbsolutePage` specifies the page where the current record resides.

```
Recordset.AbsolutePage = position
```

AbsolutePosition (Recordset Object)

The `AbsolutePosition` specifies the ordinal position of a `Recordset` object's current record. This signifies which record is current in the recordset. You can also set the current record by setting this property. You can set this property to any long integer value from 1 to the number of records or by specifying one of the following constants:

Constant	Value	Description
adPosEOF	-3	The current record is at the end of the file and the EOF property of the recordset is true.
adPosBOF	-2	The current record is at the beginning of the file and the BOF property of the recordset is true.
adPosUnkown	-1	The recordset is either empty or the data provider does not support this property.

It is not safe to assume that we can use this property to represent a record number. There is no guarantee that a record will have the same `AbsolutePosition` if the recordset is re-opened, re-queried or after deletes.

```
Recordset.AbsolutePosition = position
```

ActiveCommand (Command Object)

The `ActiveCommand` is a read-only property that represents the `Command` object that created the associated `Recordset` object. This property is most useful when you are only given the `Recordset` object that was created from a `Command` object. In this case, we can use the `ActiveCommand` property to retrieve a reference to the `Command` object.

```
Set object_variable = Recordset.ActiveCommand
```

ActiveConnection (Command Object, Recordset Object)

The `ActiveConnection` represents which `Connection` object the `Command` object or `Recordset` object is associated with. This property can be set to a `Connection` object or to a connection string. We can also set the `ActiveConnection` or a recordset to `nothing` when we want to disconnect that recordset.

```
Set Recordset.ActiveConnection = Connection
```
or
```
Set Command.ActiveConnection = Connection
```

ActualSize (Field Object)

The `ActualSize` represents the length of a field's data value. This is not the defined length of the field, but rather the actual length. For example, a field in SQL Server defined as `VARCHAR(100)` that contains the value "Johnny" has an `ActualSize` of 6 and a `DefinedSize` of 100.

```
size = Recordset.Fields(index).ActualSize
```

Attributes (Connection Object, Field Object, Parameter Object, Property Object)

The `Attributes` property indicates one or more characteristics of a `Connection`, `Parameter`, `Field`, or `Property` object.

```
attribute = Recordset.Fields(index).Attributes
```

BOF (Recordset Object)

The `BOF` property is read-only and indicates whether current record position is before the first record of the recordset. The value of this property is a boolean value and therefore is either true or false.

```
if Recordset.BOF then
```

Bookmark (Recordset Object)

The `Bookmark` property represents a unique value that points to a particular record in a recordset. This is a variant value that that can be retrieved from a recordset to remember the location of a specific record. This property can later be set to the remembered value to go back to the corresponding location in the recordset. However, bookmarks are not valid across different object instances (unless it is a recent clone) nor are they valid on the same recordset source after it has been closed and reopened or even required.

```
bookmark_variable = Recordset.Bookmark
```

CacheSize (Recordset Object)

The `CacheSize` property indicates how many records are stored in the local memory cache at a single time. By default, the `CacheSize` is set to 1 record, but it can be changed to any long integer value greater than 0. Changing the value of the `CacheSize` property to n before opening a recordset will make the data provider retrieve the first n amount of records into the local memory buffer which can dramatically improve performance.

```
Recordset.CacheSize = size
```

CommandText (Command Object)

The CommandText property contains the text of a Command object that we want to execute against a data provider. The command text, a string value, could be either the name of a table, the name of a stored procedure, a SQL statement or a provider specific command.

When setting the CommandText property to a string value, it is most efficient to also specify the CommandType property to the type of command text we plan on executing (i.e. adCmdTable, adCmdText, adCmdStoredProc). Otherwise, the default value of the CommandType property is adCmdUnknown, which means that ADO must figure out what type of command text we are using.

```
Command.CommandText = command_string
```

CommandTimeout (Command Object)

The CommandTimeout property indicates how many seconds to wait for a command to execute before terminating the attempt and returning an error. This property can be read or written to and, by default, is set to 30 seconds. Sometimes it is advantageous to set the CommandTimeout higher when we know a command will take more than 30 seconds to complete.

```
Command.CommandTimeout = number_of_seconds
```

CommandType (Command Object)

The CommandType property indicates the type of command text we plan on executing. The default value of the CommandType property is adCmdUnknown, which means that ADO must figure out what type of command text we are using. The CommandType can be any of the following values:

Constant	Description
adCmdText	The CommandText is a textual representation of a command such as a SQL statement.
adCmdTable	The CommandText is the name of a table whose columns are returned by an internally generated SQL query.
adCmdTableDirect	The CommandText is the name of a table whose columns are all returned.
adCmdStoredProc	The CommandText is the name of a stored procedure.
adCmdUnknown	The type of CommandText is not known.
adCmdFile	The CommandText is the name of a file from a persistent recordset.

```
Command.CommandType = CommandTypeEnum
```

ConnectionString (Connection Object)

The ConnectionString property contains the information required by the data provider to establish a connection to a data source. This value is a string value whose arguments differ depending on the provider.

```
Connection.ConnectionString = ConnectString
```

ConnectionTimeout (Connection Object)

The ConnectionTimeout property indicates how many seconds to wait for a connection to be established before terminating the attempt and returning an error. This property can be read or written to and, by default, is set to 15 seconds.

```
Connection.ConnectionTimeout = number_of_seconds
```

Count (Errors Collection, Fields Collection, Parameters Collection, Properties Collection)

The Count property is a read-only property that indicates the number of objects within a collection. All ADO collections' first elements have an index of 0.

```
counter_variable = Collection.Count
```

CursorLocation (Recordset Object, Connection Object)

The CursorLocation property indicates the location of the cursor engine as being server-side or client-side. The default value is adUseServer.

As a general rule, we use client-side cursors when we want to perform operations not supported by server-side cursors. Such cases are when we want to use the paging features or create disconnected recordsets. By default, the CursorLocation of the Connection object is propagated to any Recordset objects that use that Connection object.

Constant	Value	Description
adUseClient	3	The cursor is supplied by a local cursor library allowing many features that server-side cursors do not. This setting may use more resources than a server-side cursor.
adUseServer	2	The cursor is supplied by the data provider, and therefore is limited to operations supported by that data provider. This setting is usually more sensitive to data changes.

```
Recordset.CursorLocation = client_or_server_side_cursor
```

CursorType (Recordset object)

The CursorType property indicates the type of cursor used on a recordset. This property is read/write when the recordset is closed and read-only when the recordset is open. The CursorType must be one of the following values:

Constant	Description
adOpenForwardOnly	The default type and usually most efficient. This type only allows scrolling forward through the recordset.
adOpenKeyset	Deletions and modifications to data by other users is noticeable and all type of navigation through the recordset is allowed. Additions to the data by other users are not visible.

Table Continued on Following Page

Constant	Description
adOpenDynamic	Additions, deletions and modifications to data by other users is noticeable and any type of navigation through the recordset is allowed.
adOpenStatic	Additions, deletions and modifications to data by other users is not noticeable. However, any type of navigation through the recordset is allowed.

If the CursorType value that we set is not supported by the data provider, the provider will change the CursorType to a type that it does support. If the CursorLocation is adUseClient (client-side), the CursorType is set to adOpenStatic.

```
Recordset.CursorType = type_of_cursor
```

DataMember (Recordset Object)

The DataMember property indicates the data member to retrieve from the object referenced by the DataSource property when using data bound controls.

```
Recordset.DataMember = name_of_datamember
```

DataSource (Recordset Object)

The DataSource property indicates the Data Environment that contains a Recordset object, to be used with data bound controls.

```
Set Recordset.DataSource = name_of_data_environment
```

DefaultDatabase (Connection Object)

The DefaultDatabase property can be used to retrieve or set the current database to be used on a Connection object.

```
Connection.DefaultDatabase = database_name
```

DefinedSize (Field Object)

The DefinedSize represents the defined length of a field's data value. This is the defined length of the field and not the actual length. For example, a field in SQL Server defined as VARCHAR(100) that contains the value "Colleen" has an ActualSize of 7 and a DefinedSize of 100.

```
size = Recordset.Fields(index).DefinedSize
```

Description (Error Object)

An explanation of the error represented by an Error object. This property is read-only.

```
description_variable = Connection.Errors(index).Description
```

Direction (Parameter Object)

The `Direction` property indicates the type of `Parameter` object. Valid values are as follows:

Constant	Value	Description
adParamUnknown	0	Indicates the direction is unknown and that ADO must determine the direction.
adParamInput	1	Indicates an input parameter.
adParamOutput	2	Indicates an output parameter.
adParamInputOuput	3	Indicates a single parameter that represents an input and output
adParamReturnValue	4	Indicates a return value.

```
Command.Parameters(index).Direction = parameter_direction
```

EditMode (Recordset Object)

The `EditMode` property is a read-only property that indicates the editing status of the current record in a recordset.

Constant	Value	Description
adEditNone	0	Indicates that no editing operation is in progress.
adEditInProgress	1	Indicates that data in the current record has been altered, but not yet saved.
adEditAdd	2	Indicates that the `AddNew` method has been called and a new record is in the buffer, but has not yet been saved.
adEditDelete	4	Indicates that the current record has been deleted.

```
Recordset.EditMode = mode
```

EOF (Recordset Object)

The `EOF` property is read-only and indicates whether current record position is after the last record of the recordset. The value of this property is a boolean value and therefore is either true or false.

```
do while Recordset.EOF
```

Filter (Recordset Object)

The Filter property is used to limit the view of data in a recordset. The Filter can be a valid value from the following list:

❑ Criteria String: a string of one or more sets of criteria (similar to criteria in a SQL WHERE clause) concatenated with AND and OR operators.

❑ Bookmark Array: an array of bookmark values, that refer to unique records in the recordset.

❑ Filter Constant: a constant value from the table below:

Constant	Value	Description
adFilterNone	0	Removes the current filter and restores all records in a recordset.
adFilterPendingRecords	1	Limits the viewing of a recordset to records that have been changed but not sent to the server yet. (Only applicable in batch update mode.)
adFilterAffectedRecords	2	Limits the viewing of a recordset to records that have been affected by the last Delete, Resync, UpdateBatch or CancelBatch. (Only applicable in batch update mode.)
adFilterFetchedRecords	3	Limits the viewing of a recordset to records in the local cache.
adFilterConflictingRecords	5	Limits the viewing of a recordset to records that caused the failure of the last batch update attempt. (Only applicable in batch update mode.)

```
Recordset.Filter = filter_type
```

IsolationLevel (Connection Object)

The IsolationLevel property is used to set the isolation level of a Connection object. By default, we can not overwrite pending changes from more highly isolated transactions. So if we want to, we must set the IsolationLevel accordingly.

```
Connection.IsolationLevel = isolation_type
```

Constant	Description
adXactUnspecified	The provider is using a different IsolationLevel than is specified. However, the setting can not be determined.
adXactChaos	Indicates that you can not overwrite pending changes from more highly isolated transactions.
adXactBrowse	You can see changes made in other transactions even before they are committed
adXactReadUncommitted	You can see changes made in other transactions even before they are committed
adXactCursorStability	You can see changes made in other transactions only after they have been committed
adXactReadCommitted	You can see changes made in other transactions only after they have been committed
adXactRepeatableRead	You can not see changes made in other transactions
adXactIsolated	The transactions are executed in isolation of any other transactions
adXactSerializable	The transactions are executed in isolation of any other transactions

LockType (Recordset Object)

The LockType property is used to determine which type of locking to use on the records. The LockType must be a valid value from the following list:

Constant	Value	Description
adLockReadOnly	1	The data is read-only; it can not be edited. This is the default setting.
adLockPessimistic	2	The record is locked as soon as the record is first edited and is released when the changes are saved.
adLockOptimistic	3	The record is locked briefly while the changes are being saved.
adLockBatchOptimistic	4	This indicates that we are in batch update mode.

```
Recordset.LockType = locking_type
```

MarshallOptions (Recordset Object)

The `MarshallOptions` property is used to determine which type of marshalling of the records to use. The `MarshallOptions` must be a valid value from the following list:

Constant	Value	Description
adMarshallAll	0	All records are returned to the server. This is the default setting.
adMarshallModifiedOnly	1	Only records that were modified are returned to the server, thus saving resources.

When using client-side, disconnected recordsets, the records that are returned to the calling process are returned using a technique called marshalling. In some cases, we can drastically reduce overhead and increase performance by only marshalling modified records. This is extremely useful over the Internet.

```
Recordset.MarshallOptions = marshall_setting
```

MaxRecords (Recordset Object)

The `MaxRecords` property is used to specify the maximum amount of records to return from a query. The default setting is 0, which indicates that all records will be returned. This property is useful when we want to limit the number of records returned from a query.

```
Recordset.MaxRecords = maximum_number_of_records
```

Mode (Connection object)

The `Mode` property is used set permissions to modify data in a `Connection` object. The default value indicates that no permissions have been set (`adModeUnknown`). Other possible values are as follows:

Constant	Value	Description
adModeUnknown	0	Indicates that the permissions have not yet been set.
adModeRead	1	Indicates read-only permissions.
adModeWrite	2	Indicates write-only permissions.
adModeReadWrite	3	Indicates read/write permissions.
adModeShareDenyRead	4	Prevents others from opening connections with read permissions.
adModeShareDenyWrite	8	Prevents others from opening connections with write permissions.
adModeShareExclusive	12	Prevents others from opening connections.
adModeShareDenyNone	16	Prevents others from opening connections with any permissions.

```
Connection.Mode = connection_mode
```

Name (Command Object, Field Object, Parameter Object, Property Object)

The Name property is used to determine the name of its corresponding object.

```
field_name = Recordset.Fields(index).Name
```

NativeError (Error Object)

The NativeError property represents the data provider's specific error number.

```
error_number = Connection.Errors(index).NativeError
```

Number (Error Object)

The Number property represents the ADO error number.

```
error_number = Connection.Errors(index).Number
```

NumericScale (Field Object, Parameter Object)

The NumericScale property indicates the scale of a numeric value in a Field or Parameter object. This value indicates the number of decimal places to which numeric values will be resolved.

```
decimal_places = Recordset.Fields(index).NumericScale
```

Optimize (Field Object's Properties Collection)

The Optimize property indicates whether a client-side index exists on a Field object. (This property is actually an element of the Field object's Properties collection.) The index is internal to ADO and improves Sort and Find operations. To create an index on a Field object, set the Optimize property to True. To remove the index, set the property to False.
This dynamic property only exists if the CursorLocation is set to adUseClient.

```
Recordset.Fields(index).Properties("OPTIMIZE") = boolean_value
```

OriginalValue (Field Object)

The OriginalValue property indicates the data value contained within a Field object before any changes were made to it. When in immediate update mode (changes are written to the provider when you issue the Update method), the OriginalValue is the value before any changes since the last Update call. When in batch update mode (changes are not written until the UpdateBatch method is issued), the OriginalValue is the value before any changes since the last UpdateBatch call.

```
field_value = Recordset.Fields(index).OriginalValue
```

PageCount (Recordset Object)

The PageCount property indicates the number of pages of data the Recordset object contains.

```
number_of_page = Recordset.PageCount
```

PageSize (Recordset Object)

The PageSize property indicates the number of records that constitute a single page.

```
Recordset.PageSize = number_of_records
```

Precision (Field Object)

The `Precision` property indicates the degree of precision for numeric values in a numeric `Parameter` or `Field` object. This value indicates the total number of digits used to represent numeric values.

```
Recordset.Precision = total_number_of_digits
```

Prepared (Command Object)

The `Prepared` property indicates whether or not to create and save a compiled version of a `Command` before execution. Setting this property to `True` will create a compiled version of the query specified in the `CommandText` property before its `Command` object's first execution. This may slow the first execution of the command, but should speed up its performance in subsequent executions.

```
Command.Prepared = boolean_value
```

Provider (Connection Object)

The `Provider` property indicates the name of the provider for a `Connection` object. This value can be read or written to, and can also be set by specifying the provider argument in the `ConnectionString` property. This property is read-only when the connection is open.

```
Connection.Provider = provider_name
```

RecordCount (Recordset Object)

The `RecordCount` property is a read-only property that indicates number of records in the current recordset. This property returns -1 when ADO can not determine how many records exist in the recordset. The value will be the exact number of records if the `Recordset` object supports positioning or bookmarks, `Supports(adApproxPosition)` is `True` or `Supports(adBookmark)` is `True`.

```
number_of_records = Recordset.RecordCount
```

Size (Parameter Object)

The `Size` property indicates the maximum length of the `Value` property of a `Parameter` object. If the parameter's data type is character based or other variable length data, we must set its `Size` before appending it to the `Parameters` collection.

```
size = Command.Parameters(index).Size
```

Sort (Recordset Object)

The `Sort` property specifies the sort order of a `Recordset` object. The `Sort` property sorts a `Recordset` using a comma separated list of field names to sort by, where each field name is the valid name of a `Field` object in the recordset. `Sort` can also specify descending or ascending order on each field.

As soon as we set this property, an index is created on the recordset and it is re-sorted in the specified sort order. Sorting is only applicable if the `CursorLocation` is set to `adUseClient`.

```
Recordset.Sort = sort_order_string
```

Source (Error Object)

The `Source` property of the `Error` object indicates the object or application that caused the error.

```
source_of_error = Connection.Errors(index).Source
```

Source (Recordset Object)

The Source property of the Recordset object indicates the source of the data for the recordset. This source could be a Command object, a SQL statement, a table name or the name of a stored procedure.

```
Recordset.Source = source_for_recordset
```

SQLState (Error Object)

The SQLState property of the Error object indicates a five character string that represents an error as translated by ODBC. This is an ANSI standard error, as different providers may implement the same error with different error numbers.

```
error_value = Connection.Errors(index).SQLState
```

State (Connection Object, Recordset Object)

The State property indicates whether the object is open, closed or somewhere in between.

Constant	Value	Description
adStateClosed	0	Indicates that the object is closed.
adStateOpen	1	Indicates that the object is open.
adStateConnecting	2	Indicates that the Recordset object is connecting asynchronously.
adStateExecuting	4	Indicates that the Recordset object is executing a command asynchronously.
adStateFetching	8	Indicates that the Recordset object is retrieving its rows of data asynchronously

```
state_value = Recordset.State
```

Status (Recordset Object)

The Status property indicates the status of the recordset and its data modifications (if any).

```
status_value = Recordset.Status
```

StayInSync (Recordset Object)

The StayInSync property indicates that a hierarchical recordset should keep the parent rows in sync while the child rows are updated. If this property is set to True in a hierarchical recordset, any changes to child records will be reflected in the parent recordset.
This property only applies to hierarchical recordsets, which require the provider to be MSDataShape.

```
Recordset.StayInSync = True
```

Type (Field Object, Parameter Object, Property Object)

The Type property indicates the data type of a Parameter, Field or Property object.

```
datatype_value = Recordset.Fields(index).Type
```

UnderlyingValue (Field Object)

The UnderlyingValue property indicates a Field object's current value in the database. This value can change if other users change the field's data value.

```
field_value = Recordset.Fields(index).UnderLyingValue
```

Value (Field Object)

The Value property indicates the current data value contained within a Field object.

```
field_value = Recordset.Fields(index).Value
```

Version (Connection Object)

The Version property is a read-only property that indicates the version of the ADO implementation.

```
ADO_version= Connection.Version
```

Methods

AddNew (Recordset Object)

The AddNew method creates a new record in an updateable Recordset object. If the arguments are not supplied, a blank, new record is created. Then, code can be written to set the values of the fields before saving the record. If arguments are passed to the AddNew method, then the new record is created and saved: it is not left in an editable state.

```
Recordset.AddNew field_list, field_values
```

field_list	Optional. A single name or an array of names or ordinal positions of the fields in the new record.
field_values	Optional. A single value or an array of values for the fields in the new record. If field_list is an array, then field_values must be an array as well. The order of the values must correspond to the order of the fields in the field_list.

Example:
```
vntFields = Array("First_Name", "Last_Name", Age)
vntValues = Array("Colleen", "Papa", 25)
objRS.AddNew vntFields, vntValues
```

Append (Fields Collection, Parameters Collection)

Appends an object to a collection. If the collection is the Fields collection, the object appended is a Field object. If the collection is a Parameters collection, a Parameter object is appended.

```
Recordset.Fields.Append Name, Type, DefinedSize, Attrib
```

```
Command.Parameters.Append Parameter
```

Name	A string value that represents the unique name of the new `Field` object.
Type	A **DataTypeEnum**, whose default value is `adEmpty`. This is the data type of the new `Field` object.
DefinedSize	Optional. The defined size of the new `Field` object, in characters or bytes.
Attrib	Optional. A **FieldAttributeEnum**, whose default value is `adFldDefault`. This specifies attributes for the new field. If this argument is not specified, the attributes are derived from the `Type` argument.

or

Parameter	A valid `Parameter` object.

Example:

```
objRS.Fields.Append "LastName", adVarChar, 25
```
or
```
Set objParm = objCmd.CreateParameter("Percentage", adInteger, adParamInput)
objCmd.Parameters.Append objParm
```

AppendChunk (Field Object, Parameter Object)

Appends data to a large text or binary data `Field` or `Parameter` object.

```
Recordset.Fields(index).AppendChunk Data
```

Data	A variant value containing the data you want to append to the object.

Example:

```
objRS.Fields(0).AppendChunk vntData
```

BeginTrans (Connection Object)

Begins a new transaction on a `Connection` object.

```
Connection.BeginTrans
```

Example:

```
objConn.BeginTrans
```

Cancel (Command Object, Connection Object, Recordset Object)

Cancels execution of a pending, asynchronous `Execute` or `Open` method call. This method will cause an error if the action was not issued as asynchronous.

```
Command.Cancel
```

or

```
Connection.Cancel
```

or

```
Recordset.Cancel
```

Example:

```
objCmd.Cancel
```

CancelBatch (Recordset Object)

Cancels execution of a pending batch update.

```
Recordset.CancelBatch AffectRecords
```

AffectRecords	Optional. An **AffectEnum** value that determines how many records the CancelBatch method will affect. Can be one of the following constants:

Constant	Value	Description
adAffectCurrent	1	Cancel pending updates only for the current record.
adAffectGroup	2	Cancel pending updates for records that satisfy the current Filter property setting.
adAffectAll	3	Default. Cancel pending updates for all records in the Recordset object.

Example:

```
objRS.CancelBatch adAffectGroup
```

CancelUpdate (Recordset Object)

Cancels any changes made to the current record or to a new record prior to calling the Update method.

```
Recordset.CancelUpdate
```

Example:

```
objRS.CancelUpdate
```

Clear (Errors Collection)

Removes all Error objects from the Errors collection.

```
Connection.Errors.Clear
```

Example:

```
objConn.Errors.Clear
```

Clone (Recordset Object)

Creates a duplicate Recordset object from an existing Recordset object. Optionally, we can specify that the clone should be read-only.

```
Set RecordsetDuplicate = RecordsetOriginal.Clone(LockType)
```

LockType	Optional. A **LockTypeEnum** value that specifies the lock type of the original recordset or read-only. Can be one of the following constants:

Constant	Description
adLockUnspecified	Default. The clone is created with the same lock type as the original.
adLockReadOnly	The clone is created as read-only.
adLockOptimistic	The clone uses optimistic locking.
adLockBatchOptimistic	The clone uses optimistic locking and is intended for batch update mode.

Example:

```
set objRS = objRS.Clone(adLockReadOnly)
```

Close (Recordset Object, Connection Object)

Closes a Recordset or Connection object. This object must be open or an error will be generated.

```
Recordset.Close
```
or
```
Connection.Close
```

Example:
```
objRS.Close
```

CommitTrans (Connection Object)

Commits (saves) an existing transaction on a Connection object.

```
Connection.CommitTrans
```

Example:
```
objConn.CommitTrans
```

CompareBookmarks (Recordset Object)

Compares two bookmarks and returns an indication of their relative values. The return value must be one of the following constant values:

Constant	Value	Description
adCompareLessThan	0	The first bookmark is before the second.
adCompareEqual	1	The bookmarks are equal.
adCompareGreaterThan	2	The first bookmark is after the second.
adCompareNotEqual	3	The bookmarks are not equal and not ordered.
adCompareNotComparable	4	The bookmarks cannot be compared.

```
Recordset.CompareBookmarks(Bookmark1, Bookmark2)
```

Example:
```
Result = objRS.CompareBookmarks(vntBookmark1, vntBookmark2)
```

CreateParameter (Command Object)

Creates a new Parameter object with specified properties.

```
Set Parameter = Command.CreateParameter(Name, Type, Direction, Size, Value)
```

Name	A string value that represents the unique name of the Parameter object.
Type	Optional. This is the data type of the Parameter object. See the Type property for valid settings.
Direction	Optional. The type of Parameter object. See the Direction property for valid settings.
Size	Optional. Specifies the maximum length for the parameter value in characters or bytes.
Value	Optional. Specifies the value for the Parameter object.

Example:
```
Set objParm = objCmd.CreateParameter("percentage", adInteger, adParamInput, , 50)
```

Delete (Fields Collection)

Deletes an object from the Fields collection.

```
Fields.Delete Field
```

Field	A variant designating the Field object to delete from the Fields collection. This must be the name of the Field object and not the ordinal position.

Example:
```
objRS.Fields.Delete "LastName"
```

374

Delete (Parameters Collection)

Deletes an object from the Parameters collection.

```
Command.Parameters.Delete Index
```

Index	The index represents the name of the Parameter object to delete.

Example:
```
objCmd.Parameters.Delete "Percentage"
```

Delete (Recordset Object)

Deletes the current record (or group of records) from a recordset.

```
Recordset.Delete AffectRecords
```

AffectRecords	Optional. An **AffectEnum** value that determines how many records the Delete method will affect. Can be one of the following constants:

Constant	Value	Description
adAffectCurrent	1	Default. Delete only the current record.
adAffectGroup	2	Delete all records that satisfy the current Filter property setting.
adAffectAll	3	Deletes all records in the Recordset object.

Example:
```
objRS.Delete adAffectCurrent
```

Execute (Command Object)

Executes a query, SQL statement, or stored procedure specified in the CommandText property of the Command object. When used to return rows, this method returns a Recordset object.

```
Set Recordset = Command.Execute(RecordsAffected, Parameters, Options)
```

RecordsAffected	Optional. The provider returns the number of records affected by the operation.
Parameters	Optional. An array of parameter values passed with a SQL statement.
Options	Optional. Indicates how the provider should evaluate the CommandText property. Should be one of the following constant values:

Constant	Description
adCmdText	The CommandText is a textual representation of a command such as a SQL statement.
adCmdTable	The CommandText is the name of a table whose columns are returned by an internally generated SQL query.
adCmdTableDirect	The CommandText is the name of a table whose columns are all returned.
adCmdStoredProc	The CommandText is the name of a stored procedure.
adCmdUnknown	The type of CommandText is not known.
adExecuteAsync	Execute this command asynchrounously.
adFetchAsync	Fetch the command's data asynchronously.

Example:

```
set objRS = objCmd.Execute()
```

Execute (Connection Object)

Executes a specified query, SQL statement, or stored procedure.

```
Set Recordset = Connection.Execute(CommandText, RecordsAffected, Options)
```

CommandText	A SQL statement, table name, stored procedure or provider specific text to execute.
RecordsAffected	Optional. The provider returns the number of records affected by the operation.
Options	Optional. Indicates how the provider should evaluate the CommandText argument. Should be one of the following constant values:

Constant	Description
adCmdText	The CommandText is a textual representation of a command such as a SQL statement.
adCmdTable	The CommandText is the name of a table whose columns are returned by an internally generated SQL query.
adCmdTableDirect	The CommandText is the name of a table whose columns are all returned.
adCmdStoredProc	The CommandText is the name of a stored procedure.

Constant	Description
adCmdUnknown	The type of CommandText is not known.
adExecuteNoRecords	The command will not return any records. If rows are retrieved by the query, they will be discarded.
adExecuteAsync	Execute this command asynchronously
adFetchAsync	Fetch the command's data asynchronously

Example:
```
set objRS = objCmd.Execute()
```

Find (Recordset Object)

Searches a recordset for the record that satisfies the specified criteria. If the criteria is matched, the recordset position is set on the found record; otherwise, the position is set on the end of the recordset.

```
Recordset.Find Criteria , SkipRows ,SearchDirection ,Start
```

Criteria	A string containing a statement that specifies the column name, comparison operator, and value to use in the search.
SkipRows	Optional. The offset from the current row or Start bookmark to begin the search.
SearchDirection	Optional. **SearchDirectionEnum** value that specifies whether the search should begin on the current row or the next available row in the direction of the search. Its value can be adSearchForward or adSearchBackward.
Start	Optional. A bookmark to use as the starting position for the search.

Example:
```
objRS.Find "FirstName = 'Kadi' AND Age > 1"
```

GetChunk (Field Object)

Returns all or a portion of the contents of a large text or binary data Field object.

```
variable = Recordset.Fields(index).GetChunk(size)
```

Size	An expression equal to the number of bytes or characters you want to retrieve.

Example:
```
vntData = objRS.Fields(0).GetChunk(1024)
```

GetRows (Recordset Object)

Retrieves multiple records of a `Recordset` object into an array.

```
variable = Recordset.GetRows( Rows ,Start ,Fields)
```

Rows	Optional. The number of rows to retrieve from the recordset. The default value is `adGetRowsRest` (-1).
Start	Optional. The bookmark for the record from which the `GetRows` operation should begin. You can also use one of the following `BookmarkEnums`: `adBookmarkCurrent`, `adBookmarkFirst`, `adBookmarkLast`.
Fields	Optional. The single field name or ordinal position of an array of field names or ordinal positions.

Example:

```
vntData = objRS.GetRows(adGetRowsRest)
```

GetString (Recordset Object)

Returns a recordset in a string format delimited by specified columns and rows.

```
set variable = Recordset.GetString(StringFormat, NumRows, ColumnDelimiter,
RowDelimiter)
```

StringFormat	Specifies that the `recordset` should be converted to the following format: `adClipString`.
NumRows	Optional. The number of rows in the `recordset` to convert. If the `NumRows` is not specified or if it is greater than the total number of rows in the `recordset`, then all the rows in the `recordset` are converted.
ColumnDelimiter	Optional. The character to separate the columns in the string with. By default, the *Tab* is used.
RowDelimiter	Optional. The character to separate the rows in the string with. By default, the *Carriage Return* is used.

Example:

```
set vntData = objRS.GetString(adClipString, 100, ";")
```

Move (Recordset Object)

Moves the position of the current record in a recordset.

```
Recordset.Move NumRecords, Start
```

NumRecords	The number of records by which the current record position moves.
Start	Optional. The bookmark for the record from which the navigation should begin. You can also use one of the following BookmarkEnums: adBookmarkCurrent, adBookmarkFirst, adBookmarkLast.

Example:
```
objRS.Move 10, adBookmarkCurrent
```

MoveFirst (Recordset Object)

Moves the position of the current record to the first record in a recordset.

```
Recordset.MoveFirst
```

Example:
```
objRS.MoveFirst
```

MoveLast (Recordset Object)

Moves the position of the current record to the last record in a recordset.

```
Recordset.MoveLast
```

Example:
```
objRS.MoveLast
```

MoveNext (Recordset Object)

Moves the position of the current record to the next record in a recordset.

```
Recordset.MoveNext
```

Example:
```
objRS.MoveNext
```

MovePrevious (Recordset Object)

Moves the position of the current record to the previous record in a recordset.

```
Recordset.MovePrevious
```

Example:
```
objRS.MovePrevious
```

NextRecordset (Recordset Object)

Clears the current Recordset object and returns the next Recordset by advancing through a series of commands.

```
Set Recordset2 = Recordset1.NextRecordset(RecordsetAffected)
```

RecordsAffected	Optional. The provider returns the number of records affected by the operation.

Example:
```
Set objRS = objRS.NextRecordset
```

Open (Connection Object)

Opens a connection to a data source.

```
Connection.Open ConnectionString, UserID, Password, OpenOptions
```

ConnectionString	Optional. Contains the information required by the data provider to establish a connection to a data source. This value is a string value whose arguments differ depending on the provider.
UserID	Optional. The user name to use to establish the connection.
Password	Optional. The password to use to establish the connection.
OpenOptions	Optional. A ConnectOptionEnum value. If set to adConnectAsync, the connection will be opened asynchronously.

Example:
```
objConn.Open "Provider=SQLOLEDB.1;Initial Catalog=MyDatabaseName;Data
Source=MyComputerName"
```

Open (Recordset Object)

Opens a recordset cursor.

```
Recordset.Open Source, ActiveConnection, CursorType, LockType, Options
```

Source	Optional. A variant that evaluates to a valid Command object, SQL statement, table name, file name of a persisted recordset or stored procedure.
ActiveConnection	Optional. A valid Connection object or a Connection string (see ConnectionString property)
CursorType	Optional. A **CursorTypeEnum** value that determines the type of cursor (see CursorType property).
LockType	Optional. A **LockTypeEnum** value that determines what type of locking the provider should use when opening a recordset. (see LockType property)
Options	Optional. Indicates how the provider should evaluate the Source argument. Should be one of the following constant values:

Constant	Description
adCmdText	The CommandText is a textual representation of a command such as a SQL statement.
adCmdTable	The CommandText is the name of a table whose columns are returned by an internally generated SQL query.
adCmdTableDirect	The CommandText is the name of a table whose columns are all returned.
adCmdStoredProc	The CommandText is the name of a stored procedure.
adCmdUnknown	The type of CommandText is not known.
adCmdFile	Indicates that the persisted Recordset should be restored from the file named in the Source argument.

Example:

```
objConn.Open "Provider=SQLOLEDB.1;Initial Catalog=MyDatabaseName;Data
Source=MyComputerName"
objRS.Open "authors", objConn, adOpenStatic, adLockPessimistic, adCmdTable
```

OpenSchema (Connection Object)

Obtains database schema information from the provider in the form of a returned Recordset object. (see Appendix D for more details on this topic)

```
Set Recordset = Connection.OpenSchema(QueryType, Criteria, SchemaID)
```

QueryType	The type of schema query to run.
Criteria	Optional. Array of query constraints for each QueryType option, as listed below.
SchemaID	The GUID for a provider-schema query not defined by the OLE DB specification. This parameter is required if QueryType is set to adSchemaProviderSpecific; otherwise, it is not used.

Example:

```
Set objRS = objConn.OpenSchema(adSchemaTables)
```

Refresh (Parameters Collection, Fields Collection, Properties Collection)

Updates the objects in the collection to reflect objects available from and specific to the provider.

```
collection.Refresh
```

In the Fields collection, the Refresh method will retrieve the attributes of the given fields in the Fields collection from the data provider.

Example:

```
objRS.Fields.Refresh
```

In the Parameters collection, the Refresh method will retrieve the attributes of the given parameters for a command, such as a stored procedure, from the data provider.

Example:

```
objCmd.Parameters.Refresh
```

In the Properties collection, the Refresh method will retrieve the dynamic properties that the provider exposes.

Requery (Recordset Object)

Updates the data in a Recordset object by re-executing the query on which the Recordset object is based.

```
Recordset.Requery Options
```

Options	Optional. A bitmask indicating options affecting this operation. If this parameter is set to adExecuteAsync, this operation will execute asynchronously.

Example:

```
objRS.Requery
```

Resync (Recordset object)

Refreshes the data in the current Recordset object from the underlying database.

```
Recordset.Resync AffectRecords, ResyncValues
```

AffectRecords	Optional. An **AffectEnum** value that determines how many records the Resync method will affect. Can be one of the following constants:

Constant	Value	Description
adAffectCurrent	1	Refreshes only the current record.
adAffectGroup	2	Refreshes records that satisfy the current Filter property setting.
adAffectAll	3	Default. Refreshes all records in the Recordset object.

ResyncValues	Optional. A **ResyncEnum** value that specifies whether underlying values are overwritten. Can be one of the following constants:

Constant	Value	Description
adResyncAllValues	2	Default. Data is overwritten and pending updates are canceled.
adResyncUnderlyingValues	1	Data is not overwritten and pending updates are not canceled.

Example:
```
objRS.Resync adAffectGroup
```

RollbackTrans (Connection Object)

Cancels an existing transaction on a Connection object.

```
Connection.RollbackTrans
```

Example:
```
objConn.RollbackTrans
```

Save (Recordset Object)

Saves (persists) the recordset in a file.

```
Recordset.Save FileName, PersistFormat
```

FileName	Optional. Complete path name of the file where the Recordset object is to be saved.
PersistFormat	Optional. The format in which the recordset is to be saved. Currently in ADO 2.0, the default, and only valid value is adPersistADTG (an ADO proprietary format).

Example:

```
objRS.Save "c:\test.dat", adPersistADTG
```

If a Filter is engaged on the recordset, only those records will be persisted. The first time you save the recordset, specify the FileName. Subsequent times, omit the FileName, otherwise, you will overwrite the file each time.

For security reasons, this method can not be used from a script executed by Internet Explorer.

Supports (Recordset Object)

Determines whether a given Recordset object supports a particular type of functionality.

```
boolean_variable Recordset.Supports(CursorOptions)
```

CursorOptions	One or more of the following constants of the **CursorOptionEnum**:

Constant	Description
adAddNew	You can use the AddNew method to add new records.
adApproxPosition	You can read and set the AbsolutePosition and AbsolutePage properties.
adBookmark	You can use the Bookmark property.
adDelete	You can use the Delete method.

Constant	Description
adHoldRecords	You can retrieve more records or change the next retrieve position without committing all pending changes.
adMovePrevious	You can use the MoveFirst and MovePrevious methods.
adResync	You can update the cursor with the data visible in the underlying database, using the Resync method.
adUpdate	You can use the Update method to modify existing data.
adUpdateBatch	You can use batch updating.

Example:

```
if objRS.Supports(adAddNew) then
```

Update (Recordset Object)

Saves any changes you make to the current record of a Recordset object.

```
Recordset.Update Fields, Values
```

Fields	Optional. A variant representing a single name or a variant array representing names or ordinal positions of the field or fields you wish to modify.
Values	Optional. A single value or an array of values for the fields in the new record. If Fields is an array, then Values must be an array as well. The order of the values must correspond to the order of the fields in the Fields list.

Example:

```
objRS.Update "CompanyName", "BlueSand"
```

UpdateBatch (Recordset Object)

Saves any pending changes you make to the records of a Recordset object when you are in batch update mode. To get into batch update mode, set the LockType property to adLockBatchOptimistic (see LockType property for more details).

```
Recordset.UpdateBatch AffectRecords
```

AffectRecords	Optional. An **AffectEnum** value that determines how many records the UpdateBatch method will affect. Can be one of the following constants:

Constant	Value	Description
adAffectCurrent	1	Write pending changes only for the current record.
adAffectGroup	2	Write pending changes for records that satisfy the current Filter property.
adAffectAll	3	Default. Write pending changes for all records in the Recordset object.

Example:

```
objRS.UpdateBatch
```

You should only use UpdateBatch with a KeySet or Static type of cursor.

Events

BeginTransComplete (ConnectionEvent)

The BeginTransComplete event is fired after a successful BeginTrans method has been executed.

```
BeginTransComplete TransactionLevel, ErrorObject, EventStatus, ConnectionObject
```

TransactionLevel	An integer value containing the new transaction level of the BeginTrans that caused this event to fire.
ErrorObject	Describes the error that occurred if the EventStatus is adStatusErrorsOccurred.
EventStatus	An EventStatusEnum status value that specifies the status of this event.
ConnectionObject	The Connection object for which the event occurred.

Example:

```
Sub BeginTransComplete(TransactionLevel, ErrorObject, EventStatus,
ConnectionObject)

End Sub
```

CommitTransComplete (ConnectionEvent)

The CommitTransComplete event is fired after a successful CommitTrans method has been executed.

```
CommitTransComplete ErrorObject, EventStatus, ConnectionObject
```

ErrorObject	Describes the error that occurred if the EventStatus is adStatusErrorsOccurred.
EventStatus	An EventStatusEnum status value that specifies the status of this event.
ConnectionObject	The Connection object for which the event occurred.

Example:

```
Sub CommitTransComplete(ErrorObject, EventStatus, ConnectionObject)

End Sub
```

ConnectComplete (ConnectionEvent)

The ConnectComplete event is fired immediately after an attempt to open a connection on a Connection object.

```
ConnectComplete ErrorObject, EventStatus, ConnectionObject
```

ErrorObject	Describes the error that occurred if the EventStatus is adStatusErrorsOccurred.
EventStatus	An EventStatusEnum status value that specifies the status of this event.
ConnectionObject	The Connection object for which the event occurred.

Example:

```
Sub ConnectComplete(ErrorObject, EventStatus, ConnectionObject)

End Sub
```

Disconnect (ConnectionEvent)

The Disconnect event is fired immediately after a Connection object is closed.

```
Disconnect EventStatus, ConnectionObject
```

EventStatus	An EventStatusEnum status value that specifies the status of this event.
ConnectionObject	The Connection object for which the event occurred.

Example:

```
Sub Disconnect(EventStatus, ConnectionObject)

End Sub
```

EndOfRecordset (ConnectionEvent)

The EndOfRecordset event is fired when an attempt to move to a record past the end of a recordset is made.

```
EndOfRecordset MoreData, EventStatus, RecordsetObject
```

MoreData	A boolean value that, when set to True, can be used to indicate that we have just added a new record to the recordset; thus there is more data and we are not at the end of the recordset, yet. This parameter can be used because it is possible to append new records to the end of a recordset while in this event.
EventStatus	An EventStatusEnum status value that specifies the status of this event.
RecordsetObject	The Recordset object for which the event occurred.

Example:

```
Sub EndOfRecordset(MoreData, EventStatus, RecordsetObject)

End Sub
```

ExecuteComplete (ConnectionEvent)

The ExecuteComplete event is fired after a command has finished executing.

```
ExecuteComplete RecordsAffected, ErrorObject, EventStatus, CommandObject,
RecordsetObject, ConnectionObject
```

RecordsAffected	A long value representing the number of records affected by the command.
ErrorObject	Describes the error that occurred if the EventStatus is adStatusErrorsOccurred.
EventStatus	An EventStatusEnum status value that specifies the status of this event.
CommandObject	The Command object for which the event occurred, if applicable.
RecordsetObject	The Recordset object for which the event occurred, if applicable.
ConnectionObject	The Connection object for which the event occurred, if applicable.

Example:

```
Sub ExecuteComplete(RecordsAffected, ErrorObject, EventStatus, CommandObject,
RecordsetObject, ConnectionObject)

End Sub
```

FetchComplete (RecordsetEvent)

The FetchComplete event is fired after a recordset, executing asynchronously, has finished retrieving its data.

```
FetchComplete ErrorObject, EventStatus, RecordsetObject
```

ErrorObject	Describes the error that occurred if the EventStatus is adStatusErrorsOccurred.
EventStatus	An EventStatusEnum status value that specifies the status of this event.
RecordsetObject	The Recordset object for which the event occurred, if applicable.

Example:

```
Sub FetchComplete(ErrorObject, EventStatus, RecordsetObject)

End Sub
```

FetchProgress (RecordsetEvent)

The FetchProgress event is fired periodically during the execution of an asynchronous operation to report the status of the fetch.

```
FetchProgress Progress, MaxRecords, RecordsetObject
```

Progress	A long value representing the number of records currently retrieved.
MaxRecords	A long value representing the maximum number of records expected to be retrieved.
RecordsetObject	The Recordset object for which the event occurred, if applicable.

Example:

```
Sub FetchProgress(Progress, MaxRecords, RecordsetObject)

End Sub
```

FieldChangeComplete (ConnectionEvent)

The FieldChangeComplete event is fired after the value of one or more Field objects has changed.

```
FieldChangeComplete FieldCount, Fields, ErrorObject, EventStatus, RecordsetObject
```

FieldCount	A long value representing the number of Field objects in the Fields array parameter.
Fields	An array of variants that contains FieldCount amount of Field objects.
ErrorObject	Describes the error that occurred if the EventStatus is adStatusErrorsOccurred.
EvenStatus	An EventStatusEnum status value that specifies the status of this event.
RecordsetObject	The Recordset object for which the event occurred, if applicable.

Example:

```
Sub FieldChangeComplete(FieldCount, Fields, ErrorObject, EventStatus,
RecordsetObject)

End Sub
```

InfoMessage (ConnectionEvent)

The InfoMessage event is fired whenever a ConnectionEvent operation completes successfully and additional information is returned by a provider.

```
InfoMessage ErrorObject, EventStatus, ConnectionObject
```

ErrorObject	Describes the error that occurred if the EventStatus is adStatusErrorsOccurred.
EventStatus	An EventStatusEnum status value that specifies the status of this event.
ConnectionObject	The Connection object for which the event occurred.

Example:

```
Sub InfoMessage(ErrorObject, EventStatus, ConnectionObject)

End Sub
```

MoveComplete (ConnectionEvent)

The MoveComplete event is fired *before* a pending operation changes the current position in the recordset.

```
MoveComplete EventReason, ErrorObject, EventStatus, RecordsetObject
```

EventReason	An EventReasonEnum value that specifies the reason this event occurred. This value can be adRsnMoveFirst, adRsnMoveLast, adRsnMoveNext, adRsnMovePrevious, adRsnMove or adRsnRequery.
ErrorObject	Describes the error that occurred if the EventStatus is adStatusErrorsOccurred.
EventStatus	An EventStatusEnum status value that specifies the status of this event.
RecordsetObject	The Recordset object for which the event occurred, if applicable.

Example:

```
Sub MoveComplete(EventReason, ErrorObject, EventStatus, RecordsetObject)
End Sub
```

RecordChangeComplete (ConnectionEvent)

The RecordChangeComplete event is fired after one or more rows in a recordset have changed.

```
RecordChangeComplete EventReason, RecordsChanging, ErrorObject, EventStatus,
RecordsetObject
```

EventReason	An `EventReasonEnum` value that specifies the reason this event occurred. This value can be `adRsnAddNew`, `adRsnDelete`, `adRsnUpdate`, `adRsnUndoUpdate`, `adRsnUndoAddNew`, `adRsnUndoDelete` or `adRsnFirstChange`.
RecordsChanging	A long value representing the number of records that changed.
ErrorObject	Describes the error that occurred if the `EventStatus` is `adStatusErrorsOccurred`.
EventStatus	An `EventStatusEnum` status value that specifies the status of this event.
RecordsetObject	The `Recordset` object for which the event occurred, if applicable.

Example:

```
Sub RecordChangeComplete(EventReason, RecordsChanging, ErrorObject, EventStatus,
RecordsetObject)

End Sub
```

RecordsetChangeComplete (ConnectionEvent)

The `RecordChangeComplete` event is fired after a recordset has changed.

```
RecordChangeComplete EventReason, ErrorObject, EventStatus, RecordsetObject
```

EventReason	An `EventReasonEnum` value that specifies the reason this event occurred. This value can be `adRsnReQuery`, `adRsnReSynch`, `adRsnClose` or `adRsnOpen`.
ErrorObject	Describes the error that occurred if the `EventStatus` is `adStatusErrorsOccurred`.
EventStatus	An `EventStatusEnum` status value that specifies the status of this event.
RecordsetObject	The `Recordset` object for which the event occurred, if applicable.

Example:

```
Sub RecordChangeComplete(EventReason, ErrorObject, EventStatus, RecordsetObject)

End Sub
```

RollbackTransComplete (ConnectionEvent)

The `RollbackTransComplete` event is fired after a successful `RollbackTrans` method has been executed.

```
RollbackTransComplete ErrorObject, EventStatus, ConnectionObject
```

ErrorObject	Describes the error that occurred if the EventStatus is adStatusErrorsOccurred.
EventStatus	An EventStatusEnum status value that specifies the status of this event.
ConnectionObject	The Connection object for which the event occurred.

Example:

```
Sub RollbackTransComplete(ErrorObject, EventStatus, ConnectionObject)

End Sub
```

WillChangeField (ConnectionEvent)

The WillChangeField event is fired before a pending operation changes the value of one or more Field objects in the recordset.

```
WillChangeField FieldCount, Fields, EventStatus, RecordsetObject
```

FieldCount	A long value representing the number of Field objects in the Fields array parameter.
Fields	An array of variants that contains FieldCount amount of Field objects.
EventStatus	An EventStatusEnum status value that specifies the status of this event.
RecordsetObject	The Recordset object for which the event occurred, if applicable.

Example:

```
Sub WillChangeField(FieldCount, Fields, EventStatus, RecordsetObject)

End Sub
```

WillChangeRecord (ConnectionEvent)

The WillChangeRecord event is fired before one or more rows in a recordset have changed.

```
WillChangeRecord EventReason, RecordsChanging, EventStatus, RecordsetObject
```

EventReason	An EventReasonEnum value that specifies the reason this event occurred. This value can be adRsnAddNew, adRsnDelete, adRsnUpdate, adRsnUndoAddNew, adRsnUndoDelete or adRsnFirstChange.
RecordsChanging	A long value representing the number of records that changed.
EventStatus	An EventStatusEnum status value that specifies the status of this event.
RecordsetObject	The Recordset object for which the event occurred, if applicable.

Example:

```
Sub WillChangeRecord(EventReason, RecordsChanging, EventStatus, RecordsetObject)

End Sub
```

WillChangeRecordset (ConnectionEvent)

The `WillChangeRecordset` event is fired before a pending operation changes a recordset.

```
WillChangeRecordset EventReason, EventStatus, RecordsetObject
```

EventReason	An `EventReasonEnum` value that specifies the reason this event occurred. This value can be `adRsnReQuery`, `adRsnReSynch`, `adRsnClose` or `adRsnOpen`.
EventStatus	An `EventStatusEnum` status value that specifies the status of this event.
RecordsetObject	The `Recordset` object for which the event occurred, if applicable.

Example:

```
Sub WillChangeRecordset(EventReason, EventStatus, RecordsetObject)

End Sub
```

WillConnect (ConnectionEvent)

The `WillConnect` event is fired before a connection starts. The parameters to be used in the pending connection are supplied as input parameters and can be changed before the method returns. This method may return a request that the pending connection be canceled.

```
WillConnect ConnectionString, UserID, Password, Options, EventStatus,
ConnectionObject
```

ConnectionString	A string containing the connection information for the pending `Connection` object.
UserID	A string containing the User ID for the pending `Connection` object.
Password	A string containing the password for the pending `Connection` object.
Options	A Long value that indicates how the provider should evaluate the `ConnectionString` parameter.
EventStatus	An `EventStatusEnum` status value that specifies the status of this event.
ConnectionObject	The `Connection` object for which the event occurred.

Example:

```
Sub WillConnect(ConnectionString, UserID, Password, Options, EventStatus,
ConnectionObject)

End Sub
```

WillExecute (ConnectionEvent)

The WillExecute event is fired before a pending command executes on this connection and gives the user an opportunity to examine and modify the pending execution parameters. This method may return a request that the pending command be canceled.

```
WillExecute Source, CursorType, LockType, Options, EventStatus, CommandObject,
RecordsetObject, ConnectionObject
```

Source	A string containing the SQL name of a stored procedure, file or table.
CursorType	A CursorTypeEnum containing the type of cursor for the recordset that will be opened. This parameter cannot be changed if it is set to adOpenUnspecified when this event is fired.
LockType	A LockTypeEnum containing the lock type for the recordset that will be opened. This parameter cannot be changed if it is set to adLockUnspecified when this event is fired.
Options	A long value that can be used to execute the Command or open the recordset.
EventStatus	An EventStatusEnum status value that specifies the status of this event.
ConnectionObject	The Connection object for which the event occurred.

Example:
```
Sub WillExecute(Source, CursorType, LockType, Options, EventStatus, CommandObject,
RecordsetObject, ConnectionObject)

End Sub
```

WillMove (ConnectionEvent)

The WillMove event is fired *before* a pending operation changes the current position in the recordset.

```
WillMove EventReason, EventStatus, RecordsetObject
```

EventReason	An EventReasonEnum value that specifies the reason this event occurred. This value can be adRsnMoveFirst, adRsnMoveLast, adRsnMoveNext, adRsnMovePrevious, adRsnMove or adRsnRequery.
EventStatus	An EventStatusEnum status value that specifies the status of this event.
RecordsetObject	The Recordset object for which the event occurred, if applicable.

Example:
```
Sub WillMove(EventReason, EventStatus, RecordsetObject)

End Sub
```

RDS 2.0 Reference

RDS has a number of objects, properties, methods and events that we use to interact with the RDS object model, and which allow us to use RDS to access data remotely over the HTTP protocol. In this appendix we will look at the three objects of the RDS object model (DataControl, DataSpace and DataFactory) and their respective properties, methods and events organized in the following pages in alphabetical order.

Objects and Collections

RDS.DataControl Object

An RDS.DataControl object binds a data query recordset to one or more HTML controls to display the ADOR.Recordset data on a web page. Multiple RDS.DataControl objects can be used on a single web page to link several recordsets to several visual controls.

The class ID for the RDS.DataControl object is BD96C556-65A3-11D0-983A-00C04FC29E33.

For a basic scenario, at the very least you need to set the SQL, Connect, and Server properties of the RDS.DataControl object, which will automatically call the default business object, RDSServer.DataFactory. All the properties of the RDS.DataControl object are optional because custom business objects (created using the RDS.DataSpace) can replace their functionality.

```
<OBJECT CLASSID="clsid:BD96C556-65A3-11D0-983A-00C04FC29E33" ID="DataControl"
    <PARAM NAME="Connect" VALUE="DSN=DSNName;UID=user_id;PWD=password;">
    <PARAM NAME="Server" VALUE="http://the_web_server">
    <PARAM NAME="SQL" VALUE="QueryText">
</OBJECT>
```

The `RDS.DataControl` object has the following properties, methods and events:

	Connect	Handler	SortColumn
	ExecuteOptions	InternetTimeout	SortDirection
Properties	FetchOptions	ReadyState	SQL
	FilterColumn	Recordset	URL
	FilterCriterion	SourceRecordset	
	FilterValue	Server	
Methods	Cancel	MoveFirst	Refresh
	CancelUpdate	MoveLast	Reset
	ConvertToString	MoveNext	SubmitChanges
	CreateRecordset	MovePrevious	
Events	onError	onReadyChange	

RDS.DataSpace Object

The `RDS.DataSpace` object creates client-side proxies to custom business objects located on the middle tier. RDS needs business object proxies so that client-side components can communicate with business objects located on the middle tier. Proxies facilitate the packaging, un-packaging, and marshalling of the application's recordset data across process or machine boundaries, usually via HTTP.

`RDS.DataSpace` creates and uses the business object proxy on demand whenever an instance of its middle-tier business object counterpart is created. RDS supports the following protocols: HTTP, HTTPS (HTTP Secure Sockets), DCOM, and in-process (the client components and the business object reside on the same computer).

The `RDS.DataSpace` object is the ideal method to invoke business rules that exist in the middle tier, written in languages such as Visual Basic or C++.

The class ID for the `RDS.DataSpace` object is BD96C556-65A3-11D0-983A-00C04FC29E36 and can be declared as shown in the syntax below. However, the `RDS.DataSpace` can be declared using client-side scripting code, also shown below.

```
<OBJECT CLASSID="clsid:BD96C556-65A3-11D0-983A-00C04FC29E36" ID="DataSpace">
</OBJECT>
```

or

```
set MyDataSpace = CreateObject("RDS.DataSpace")
```

The `RDS.DataFactory` object has the following property and method:

Properties	InternetTimeout
Methods	CreateObject

RDSServer.DataFactory Object

This default server-side business object implements methods that provide read/write data access to specified data sources for client-side applications. The `RDSServer.DataFactory` object is designed as a server-side automation object that receives client requests. The `RDSServer.DataFactory` object provides read and write access to specified data sources, but doesn't contain any validation or business rules logic.

If you use a method that is available in both the `RDSServer.DataFactory` and `RDS.DataControl` objects, RDS uses the `RDS.DataControl` version by default.

You can create server-side business objects that call the `RDSServer.DataFactory` methods, such as `Query` and `CreateRecordset`. This is helpful if you want to add functionality to your business objects, but take advantage of existing RDS technologies.

If you want your web application to handle task-specific server-side processing, you can replace the `RDSServer.DataFactory` with a custom business object and refer to it using the `RDS.DataSpace`.

The class id for the `RDSServer.DataFactory` object is 9381D8F5-0288-11D0-9501-00AA00B911A5.

```
<OBJECT CLASSID="clsid:9381D8F5-0288-11D0-9501-00AA00B911A5" ID="DataFactory">
</OBJECT>
```

The `RDSServer.DataFactory` object has the following methods:

Methods	CreateRecordset	Query

Recordset Object

The `Recordset` object is used to store all records of data retrieved from a data source, in rows and columns. A `Recordset` object always points to one, and only one, specific row of data within itself at any one time. The `ADOR.Recordset ProgID` can be used to create a `Recordset` object in the client.

Properties

Connect (RDS.DataControl Object)

Sets or returns the database name from which the query and update operations are run. You can set the `Connect` property at design time in the `RDS.DataControl` object's `<OBJECT>` tags, or at run time in client-side scripting code.

Design-time syntax:
```
<PARAM NAME="Connect" VALUE="DSN=DSNName;UID=user_id;PWD=password;">
```
Run-time syntax:
```
DataControl.Connect = "DSN=DSNName;UID=user_id;PWD=password;"
```

399

The Connect property takes the following parameters:

DSNName	A string that specifies the system data source name that identifies a specific database.
User_id	A string that represents a valid user account on the server.
Password	A string that represents a valid password for the user account.
DataControl	An object variable that represents an RDS.DataControl object that should use the connection.

Design-time Example:
```
<PARAM NAME="Connect" VALUE="DSN=pubs;UID=sa;PWD=jazzy;">
```
Run-time Example:
```
objDataControl.Connect = "DSN=pubs;UID=sa;PWD=jazzy"
```

DataSpace (RDS.DataControl Object)

Sets or returns the RDS.DataSpace object reference for the RDS.DataControl object.
Run-time syntax:
```
Set objMyDataSpace = DataControl.DataSpace
```

Run-time Example:
```
Set objDS = objDC.DataSpace
```

ExecuteOptions (RDS.DataControl Object)

The ExecuteOptions property indicates whether or not asynchronous execution is enabled. The ExecuteOptions property can be either of the following values:

Constant	Value	Description
adcExecSync	1	Executes the next refresh of the recordset synchronously.
adcExecAsync	2	Default: Executes the next refresh of the recordset asynchronously.

If ExecuteOptions is set to adcExecAsync, then this asynchronously executes the next Refresh call on the RDS.DataControl object's recordset. If you try to call Reset, Refresh, SubmitChanges, CancelUpdate or Recordset methods while another asynchronous operation is executing that might change the RDS.DataControl object's recordset, and an error occurs. In other words, you should not make any changes to the data in a recordset while an asynchronous operation is executing.

If an error occurs during an asynchronous operation, the RDS.DataControl object's ReadyState value changes from adcReadyStateLoaded to adcReadyStateComplete, and the Recordset property value remains *Nothing*.

Design-time syntax:

```
<PARAM NAME="ExecuteOptions" VALUE="execute_options_value">
```

Run-time syntax:

```
DataControl.ExecuteOptions = execute_options_value
```

Design-time Example:

```
<PARAM NAME="ExecuteOptions" VALUE="2">
```

Run-time Example:

```
const adcExecAsync = 2
objDataControl.ExecuteOptions = adcExecAsync
```

FetchOptions (RDS.DataControl Object)

The FetchOptions property indicates whether or not asynchronous fetching is enabled. The FetchOptions property can be any of the following values:

Constant	Value	Description
adcFetchUpFront	1	All the records of the recordset are fetched before control is returned to the application. The complete recordset is fetched before the application is allowed to do anything with it.
adcFetchBackground	2	Control can return to the application as soon as the first batch of records has been fetched. A subsequent read of the recordset that attempts to access a record not fetched in the first batch, will be delayed until the sought record is actually fetched, at which time control returns to the application.
adcFetchAsync	3	Default. Control returns immediately to the application while records are fetched in the background. If the application attempts to read a record that hasn't yet been fetched, the closest record to the desired one will be read, then control will return immediately and will indicate that the end of the recordset has been reached.

Design-time syntax:

```
<PARAM NAME="FetchOptions" VALUE="fetch_options_value">
```

Run-time syntax:

```
DataControl.FetchOptions = fetch_options_value
```

Design-time Example:
```
<PARAM NAME="FetchOptions" VALUE="3">
```
Run-time Example:
```
const adcExecAsync = 3
objDataControl.FetchOptions = adcFetchAsync
```

FilterColumn (RDS.DataControl Object)

The FilterColumn property specifies the column on which to evaluate the filter criteria.
```
DataControl.FilterColumn = column_name
```

DataControl	An object variable that represents an RDS.DataControl object.
Column_name	A String value specifying the column on which to evaluate the filter criteria. The filter criteria are specified in the FilterCriterion property.

Example:
```
objDataControl.FilterColumn = "age"
```

FilterCriterion (RDS.DataControl Object)

The FilterCriterion property specifies the operator to use with the filter value. Calling the Reset method when both the Filter and Sort properties are set, results in the rowset being first filtered then sorted.
```
DataControl.FilterCriterion = "operator"
```

DataControl	An object variable that represents an RDS.DataControl object.
operator	A String value specifying the operator which determines how to evaluate the filter criteria. Can be any one of the following: <, <=, >, >=, =, or <>. Note that the != operator is invalid here – we need to use <> instead.

Example:
```
objDataControl.FilterCriterion = ">"
```

FilterValue (RDS.DataControl Object)

The FilterValue property indicates the value to filter the recordset on.
```
DataControl.FilterValue = "filter_value"
```

DataControl	An object variable that represents a RDS.DataControl object.
First_value	A String value that represents a data value with which to filter records.

Example:
```
objDataControl. FilterValue = 25
```

Handler (RDS.DataControl Object)

The Handler property sets or returns a string containing the name of a server-side customization program (*handler*) that extends the functionality of the RDSServer.DataFactory object. This string also contains any parameters used by the *handler,* all separated by commas (","). If a semicolon appears anywhere in the string this will result in unpredictable behavior.

The functionality this property supports is called customization. You can write your own handler, provided it supports the IDataFactoryHandler interface. The name of the default handler is MSDFMAP.Handler, and its default parameter is a customization file named MSDFMAP.INI. Use this property to invoke alternate customization files created by your server administrator. The alternative to setting the Handler property is to specify a handler and parameters in the ConnectionString property; that is, "Handler=*handlerName,parm1,parm2,...,*".

```
DataControl.Handler = string
```

DataControl	An object variable that represents an RDS.DataControl object.
String	A string value that contains the name of the *handler* and any parameters, all separated by commas.

InternetTimeout (RDS.DataControl Object, RDS.DataSpace Object)

The InternetTimeout property sets or gets the number of milliseconds before a request over the internet will time out. The default value is 300000 milliseconds or 300 seconds (5 minutes).

```
RDSObject.InternetTimeout = long_value
```

RDSObject	An object variable that represents an RDS.DataControl or an RDS.DataSpace object.
Long_value	A long value that represents the number of milliseconds.

Example:

```
objDataControl.InternetTimeout = 15000
```
or
```
objDataSpace.InternetTimeout = 15000
```

ReadyState (RDS.DataControl Object)

The ReadyState property returns a constant that indicates the progress of an RDS.DataControl object as it fetches data into its Recordset object.

If an error occurs during an asynchronous operation, the ReadyState property changes to adcReadyStateComplete, the State property changes from adStateExecuting to adStateClosed, and the Recordset object Value property remains *Nothing*.

The ReadyState property can be any one of the following constant values:

Constant	Value	Description
adcReadyStateLoaded	2	The current query is still executing and no rows have been fetched. The RDS.DataControl object's recordset is not available for use.
adcReadyStateInteractive	3	An initial set of rows retrieved by the current query have been stored in the RDS.DataControl object's recordset and are available for use. The remaining rows are still being fetched.
adcReadyStateComplete	4	All rows retrieved by the current query have been stored in the RDS.DataControl object's recordset and are available for use. This state will also exist if an operation aborted due to an error, or if the Recordset object is not initialized.

```
DataControl.ReadyState = ready_state_value
```

Example:
```
const adcReadyStateComplete = 4
if objDataControl.ReadyState = adcReadyStateComplete then
```

Recordset and SourceRecordset (RDS.DataControl Object)

The Recordset and SourceRecordset properties of the RDS.DataControl object represent the ADOR.Recordset object returned from a custom business object. You can set the SourceRecordset property or read the Recordset property at run time in client-side scripting code.

SourceRecordset is a write-only property, in contrast to the Recordset property, which is a read-only property. Ideally the SourceRecordset property should be set to a recordset returned from a custom business object.

```
DataControl.SourceRecordset = recordset
```
or
```
recordset = DataControl.Recordset
```

Example:
```
objRS = objDataControl.Recordset
```

Server (RDS.DataControl Object)

The Server property indicates the Internet Information Server name and communication protocol. You can set the Server property at design time in the RDS.DataControl object's OBJECT tags, or at run time in client-side scripting code.

Design-time syntax:
```
<PARAM NAME="Server" VALUE="server_address">
```
Run-time syntax:
```
DataControl.Server = "server_address"
```

server_address	A string that specifies the address of the web server.
DataControl	An object variable that represents an RDS.DataControl object.

Design-time Example:
```
<PARAM NAME="Server" VALUE="http://123.123.123.123">
```
Run-time Example:
```
objDataControl.Server = "http://123.123.123.123"
```

SortColumn (RDS.DataControl Object)

The SortColumn property indicates the column on which to apply the Sort method.

To sort on a recordset, you must first save any pending changes. If you are using the RDS.DataControl object, you can use the SubmitChanges method. For example, assuming the RDS.DataControl object is named ADC1, your code would be ADC1.SubmitChanges. When using an ADO recordset created with the CreateRecordset method, the recommended way to save pending changes is the use of the UpdateBatch method. For example, your code could be: myRS.UpdateBatch or ADC1.Recordset.UpdateBatch.
```
DataControl.SortColumn = column_name
```

DataControl	An object variable that represents an RDS.DataControl object.
Column_name	A string value specifying the column on which to apply the Sort method.

Example:
```
objDataControl.SortColumn = "age"
```

SortDirection (RDS.DataControl Object)

The SortDirection property specifies the direction in which the recordset is to be sorted (ascending or descending).
```
DataControl.SortDirection = value
```

DataControl	An object variable that represents an RDS.DataControl object.
value	A boolean value specifying the direction in which the recordset is to be sorted. True = Ascending, False = descending.

Example:
```
objDataControl.SortDirection = True
```

SQL (RDS.DataControl Object)

The SQL property represents the query string with which we retrieve records. You can set the SQL property at design time in the RDS.DataControl object's <OBJECT> tags, or at run time in client-side scripting code. In general, this is a SQL statement (using the dialect of the database server), such as SELECT * FROM NewTitles. To ensure that records are matched and updated accurately, an updatable query must contain a field other than a Long Binary field or a computed field.

Design-time syntax:
```
<PARAM NAME="SQL" VALUE="query_string">
```

Run-time syntax:
```
DataControl.SQL = " query_string "
```

query_string	A string that specifies the SQL statement to retrieve the data for the recordse.
DataControl	An object variable that represents an RDS.DataControl object.

Design-time Example:
```
<PARAM NAME="SQL" VALUE="SELECT au_lname, au_fname FROM authors">
```

Run-time Example:
```
objDataControl.SQL = " SELECT au_lname, au_fname FROM authors"
```

Methods

Cancel (RDS.DataControl Object)

Issuing the Cancel method cancels the currently running asynchronous execution or fetch. When you call Cancel, ReadyState is automatically set to adcReadyStateLoaded, and the recordset will be emptied.
```
DataControl.Cancel
```

Example:
```
objDataControl.Cancel
```

CancelUpdate (RDS.DataControl Object)

Issuing the CancelUpdate method discards all the pending changes associated with the specified Recordset object, restoring the values since the last Refresh method call.

```
DataControl.CancelUpdate
```

Example:
```
objDataControl.CancelUpdate
```

ConvertToString (RDS.DataFactory Object)

Issuing the ConvertToString method converts a recordset to a MIME compliant string that represents the recordset data.

With .asp files, use ConvertToString to embed the recordset on a server-generated HTML page to transport it to a client computer. ConvertToString first loads the recordset into Client Cursor Engine tables, and then generates a stream in MIME format.

On the client, RDS can convert the MIME string back into a fully functioning recordset. It works well for handling fewer than 400 rows of data with no more than 1024 bytes per row.

If you are using ASP to embed the resulting MIME string in a client HTML page, be aware that versions of VBScript earlier than version 2.0 limit the string size to 32K. If this limit is exceeded, an "Out of string space" error is returned. Keep the query scope relatively small when using MIME embedding via .asp files. To fix this, download the latest version of VBScript from http://www.microsoft.com/vbscript.

```
DataControl.ConvertToString(recordset)
```

DataControl	An object variable that represents an RDS.DataControl object.
Recordset	An object variable that represents a Recordset object.

Example:
```
objDataControl.ConvertToString(objRS)
```

CreateObject (RDS.DataSpace Object)

The CreateObject method creates a proxy for the target business object and returns a pointer to it. The proxy packages and marshals data to the server-side stub for communications with the business object to send requests and data over the Internet.

HTTP Syntax:
```
set object = DataSpace.CreateObject("ProgID", "http://webServer")
```

HTTPS Syntax:
```
set object = DataSpace.CreateObject("ProgID", "https://webServer")
```

DCOM Syntax:
```
set object = DataSpace.CreateObject("ProgID", "machine_name")
```

HTTP Example:
```
set objMyObject = objDataSpace.CreateObject("MyBusinessRules.MyBusinessObject",
"http://www.bluesand.com")
```

HTTPS Example:
```
set objMyObject = objDataSpace.CreateObject("MyBusinessRules.MyBusinessObject",
"https://www.bluesand.com")
```

DCOM Example:
```
set objMyObject = objDataSpace.CreateObject("MyBusinessRules.MyBusinessObject",
"BlueSand")
```

CreateRecordset (RDS.DataControl Object, RDSServer.DataFactory Object)

The CreateRecordset method creates an empty disconnected recordset (see Chapter 8). The server-side business object can populate the resulting ADOR.Recordset with data from a non-OLE DB data provider, such as an operating system file containing stock quotes.

```
object.CreateRecordset(columns_info)
```

Object	An object variable that represents an RDSServer.DataFactory or RDS.DataControl object.
Columns_info	A variant array of arrays defining each column in the recordset being created. Each column definition contains an array of four required attributes, as described below:

Attribute	Description
Name	Name of the column header.
Type	Integer of data type.
Size	Integer of width in characters, regardless of data type.
Nullability	Boolean value.

MoveFirst (RDS.DataControl Object's Recordset Object)

Moves the position of the cursor to make the current record the first record in a recordset.

```
DataControl.Recordset.MoveFirst
```

Example:

```
objDataControl.Recordset.MoveFirst
```

MoveLast (RDS.DataControl Object's Recordset Object)

Moves the position of the cursor to make the current record the last record in a recordset.

```
DataControl.Recordset.MoveLast
```

Example:

```
objDataControl.Recordset.MoveLast
```

MoveNext (RDS.DataControl Object's Recordset Object)

Moves the position of the cursor to make the current record the next record in a recordset.

```
DataControl.Recordset.MoveNext
```

Example:
```
objDataControl.Recordset.MoveNext
```

MovePrevious (RDS.DataControl Object's Recordset Object)

Moves the position of the cursor to make the current record the previous record in a recordset.
```
DataControl.Recordset.MovePrevious
```

Example:
```
objDataControl.Recordset.MovePrevious
```

Query (RDSServer.DataFactory Object)

The Query method uses a valid SQL query string to return a recordset. The query should use the SQL dialect of the database server. If an error occurs during the execution of the query, a result status is returned.
```
set recordset = DataFactory.Query(Connection, Query)
```

Recordset	An object variable that represents a recordset.
DataFactory	An object variable that represents an RDSServer.DataFactory object.
Connection	A string containing the server connection information. This is similar to the Connect property.
Query	A string containing the SQL query.

Example:
```
set objRS = objDataFactory.Query("dsn=pubs;UID=sa;PWD=jazzy;", "SELECT *
FROM authors")
```

Refresh (RDS.DataControl Object)

Re-queries the ODBC data source specified in the Connect property and updates the query results.

Set the Connect, Server, and SQL properties before you use the Refresh method. All data-bound controls associated with an RDS.DataControl object will reflect the new set of records. Any pre-existing Recordset object is released, and any unsaved changes are discarded.
```
DataControl.Refresh
```

Example:
```
objDataControl.Refresh
```

Reset (RDS.DataControl Object)

The Reset method executes the sort or filter on a client-side recordset based on the specified sort and filter properties.

If there are changes to the original data that haven't yet been submitted, the Reset method will fail. First, use the SubmitChanges method to save any changes in a read/write recordset, and then use the Reset method to sort or filter the records

```
DataControl.Reset(value)
```

Value	A boolean value that specifies whether you want to filter on the existing filter.

Example:

```
objDataControl.Reset
```

SubmitChanges (RDS.DataControl Object)

The SubmitChanges method submits pending changes of the locally cached updatable recordset to the ODBC data source specified in the Connect property. The Connect, Server and SQL properties must be set before you can use the SubmitChanges method with the RDS.DataControl object.

```
DataControl.SubmitChanges
```

or:

```
DataFactory.SubmitChanges Connection, Recordset
```

Connection	A string value that represents the connection created with the RDS.DataControl object's Connect property.
Recordset	An object variable that represents a Recordset object.

Example:

```
objDataControl.SubmitChanges
```

Events

OnError (RDS.DataControl Object)

The onError event is fired when an error occurs during an operation on the RDS.DataControl. The parameters StatusCode, Description and Source can be read and used to determine which action should be taken. The CancelDisplay parameter can be set to prevent the error from being displayed in a dialog box.

```
OnError StatusCode, Description, Source, CancelDisplay
```

StatusCode	An integer value containing the status code of the error that occurred.
Description	A string value that represents the description of the error that occurred.
Source	A string value that that contains the name of the query or command that caused the error.
Canceldisplay	A boolean value that the programmer can set to prevent the error from being displayed in a dialog box.

Example:

```
Sub onError(StatusCode, Description, Source, CancelDisplay)

End Sub
```

OnReadyStateChange (RDS.DataControl Object)

The onReadyStateChange event is fired when the value of the ReadyState property changes. The ReadyState property reflects the progress of an RDS.DataControl object as it asynchronously fetches data into its Recordset object.

```
onReadyStateChange
```

Example:

```
Sub onReadyStateChange()

End Sub
```

Detailed Properties Collection

This appendix lists the OLE DB Connection, Recordset and Field properties and provides for each its full name, its data type, and a short reference explanation (including its read/write status).

These properties are dynamic – as they are contained within a collection – and it's important to remember that different OLE DB providers support different subsets and combinations of these properties. This means that the combinations available to you are based on which OLE DB provider you use and the types of cursor locations you choose.

You must refer to these properties using the collection syntax by specifying the collection's key value (the name of the property). For example, to refer to the OPTIMIZE property of a field object's Properties collection, do the following:

```
BooGetTheValue = objMyRecordset.Fields("MyField").Properties("OPTIMIZE"). Value
```

The last section of this appendix describes the correct usage of these properties.

Connection Properties

Below is a table of the dynamic Connection properties. Not all of these are supported by every OLE DB provider.

Name	Description	Data Type
Accessible Procedures	Identifies accessible procedures. **Read-only**.	Boolean
Accessible Tables	Identifies accessible tables. **Read-only**.	Boolean

Table Continued on Following Page

Name	Description	Data Type
Active Sessions	Indicates the maximum possible number of concurrently active sessions. Value=0 means no limit. **Read-only**.	Long
Active Statements	Indicates the maximum possible number of concurrently active statements. **Read-only**.	Long
Application Name	Identifies the client application name. **Read/Write**.	String
Asynchable Abort	Indicates whether transactions can be aborted asynchronously. **Read-only**.	Boolean
Asynchable Commit	Indicates whether transactions can be committed asynchronously. **Read-only**.	Boolean
Asynchronous Processing	Specifies the asynchronous processing performed on the rowset. **Read/Write**.	DBPROPVAL_ASYNCH
Auto Translate	Indicates whether OEM/ANSI character conversion is used. **Read/Write**.	Boolean
Autocommit Isolation Level	When in autocommit mode, indicates the transaction isolation level. **Read/Write**.	DBPROPVAL_OS
Cache Authentication	Indicates whether the data source object can cache passwords or other sensitive authentication information. **Read/Write**.	Boolean
Catalog Location	Indicates the position of the catalog name in a text command's table name. Returns 1 (DBPROPVAL_CL_START) if the catalog is at the start of the name or 2 (DBPROPVAL_CL_END) if the catalog is at the end of the name. **Read/Write**.	DBPROPVAL_CL

Name	Description	Data Type
Catalog Term	Specifies the name of the data source used for a catalog, such as 'catalog' or 'database'. **Read/Write**.	String
Catalog Usage	Specifies how catalog names can be used in text commands in the form of zero or more DBPROPVAL_CU constants. **Read/Write**.	DBPROPVAL_CU
Column Definition	Defines the valid clauses for the definition of a column. **Read/Write**.	DBPROPVAL_CD
Connect Timeout	Specifies the amount of time, in seconds, to wait for the initialization to complete. **Read/Write**.	Long
Connection Status	Indicates the status of the current connection. **Read-only**.	DBPROPVAL_CS
Current Catalog	Indicates the name of the current catalog. **Read/Write**.	String
Current Language	Identifies the language used for system messages selection and formatting. The language must be installed on the SQL Server or initialization of the data source fails. **Read/Write**.	String
Data Source	Specifies the name of the target database. **Read/Write**.	String
Data Source Name	Indicates the name of the data source. **Read-only**.	String
Data Source Object Threading Model	Specifies the threading models supported by the data source object. **Read-only**.	DBPROPVAL_RT
DBMS Name	Indicates the name of the product accessed by the provider. **Read-only**.	String

Table Continued on Following Page

Name	Description	Data Type
DBMS Version	Indicates the version of the product accessed by the provider. **Read-only**.	String
Driver Name	Identifies the ODBC Driver name. **Read-only**.	String
Driver ODBC Version	Identifies the ODBC Driver version. **Read-only**.	String
Driver Version	Identifies the Driver ODBC version. **Read-only**.	String
Encrypt Password	Specifies whether the client program requires passwords to be sent to the data source encrypted. **Read/Write**.	Boolean
Extended Properties	Gives provider-specific extended connection information. **Read/Write**.	String
File Usage	Identifies the usage count of the ODBC driver. **Read-only**.	Long
GROUP BY Support	Indicates the relationship between the columns in a GROUP BY clause and the non-aggregated columns in the select list. **Read-only**.	DBPROPVAL_BG
Heterogeneous Table Support	Specifies whether the provider can join tables from different catalogs or providers. **Read-only**.	DBPROPVAL_HT
Identifier Case Sensitivity	Specifies how identifiers treat case sensitivity. **Read-only**.	DBPROPVAL_IC
Initial Catalog	The name of the initial, or default, catalog to use when connecting to the data source. If the provider supports changing the catalog for an initialized data source, a different catalog name can be specified in the **Current Catalog** property. **Read/Write**.	String

Name	Description	Data Type
Integrated Security	Indicates the authentication service name used by the server to identify the user. **Read/Write**.	String
Integrity Enhancement Facility	Indicates whether the data source supports the optional Integrity Enhancement Facility. **Read-only**.	Boolean
Isolation Levels	Identifies the supported transaction isolation levels. **Read-only**.	DBPROPVAL_TI
Isolation Retention	Identifies the supported transaction isolation retention levels. **Read-only**.	DBPROPVAL_TR
Jet OLEDB:Database Password	Indicates the database password. **Read/Write**.	String
Jet OLEDB:Global Partial Bulk Ops	Specifies whether bulk operations are allowed with partial values. **Read/Write**.	Boolean
Jet OLEDB:Registry Path	Identifies the registry key that contains values for the Jet database engine. **Read/Write**.	String
Jet OLEDB:System database	Identifies the path and file name for the workgroup file. **Read/Write**.	String
Like Escape Clause	Identifies the LIKE escape clause. **Read-only**.	String
Locale Identifier	Identifies the client's preferred locale ID. **Read/Write**.	Long
Location	Specifies the location of the target data source (usually the server name). **Read/Write**.	String
Log Text and Image Writes	Specifies whether writes to text and images fields are logged in the transaction log. **Read/Write**.	Boolean

Table Continued on Following Page

Name	Description	Data Type
Mask Password	Specifies whether the client requires that the password be sent to the data source in masked form. **Read/Write**.	Boolean
Max Columns in Group By	Identifies the maximum allowable number of columns in a GROUP BY clause. **Read-only**.	Long
Max Columns in Index	Identifies the maximum allowable number of columns in an index. **Read-only**.	Long
Max Columns in Order By	Identifies the maximum allowable number of columns in an ORDER BY clause. **Read-only**.	Long
Max Columns in Select	Identifies the maximum allowable number of columns in a SELECT statement. **Read-only**.	Long
Max Columns in Table	Identifies the maximum allowable number of columns in a table. **Read-only**.	Long
Maximum BLOB Length	Identifies the maximum allowable size of a BLOB field. **Read-only**.	Long
Maximum Index Size	Specifies the maximum number of bytes allowed in the combined columns of an index. Value=0 if the limit is unknown or unspecified. **Read-only**.	Long
Maximum Open Chapters	Specifies the maximum number of chapters that can be open at any one time. Value=1 if a chapter must be released before a new chapter can be opened. Value=0 if the provider does not support chapters. **Read-only**.	Long

Name	Description	Data Type
Maximum OR Conditions	Specifies the maximum number of disjunct conditions supportable in a view filter. Multiple conditions of a view filter are joined in a logical OR. Returns a value=1 if the provider does not support joining multiple conditions. Returns value=0 if the provider does not support view filters. **Read-only**.	Long
Maximum Row Size	Specifies the maximum possible length of a single row in a table. Value=0 if the limit is unknown or unspecified. **Read-only**.	Long
Maximum Row Size Includes BLOB	Specifies whether the Maximum Row Size property includes the length for BLOB data. **Read-only**.	Boolean
Maximum Sort Columns	Specifies the maximum number of columns that can be supported in a View Sort. Value=0 if the limit is unknown or unspecified. **Read-only**.	Long
Maximum Tables in SELECT	Specifies the maximum number of tables allowed in the FROM clause of a SELECT statement. Value=0 if the limit is unknown or unspecified. **Read-only**.	Long
Mode	Specifies the access permissions. **Read/Write**.	DB_MODE
Multi-Table Update	Identifies whether the provider can update rowsets derived from multiple tables. **Read-only**.	Boolean
Multiple Connections	Identifies whether the provider silently creates additional connections to support concurrent Command, Connection, or Recordset objects. This only applies to providers that must spawn multiple connections, and not to providers that support multiple connections natively. **Read/Write**.	Boolean

Table Continued on Following Page

419

Name	Description	Data Type
Multiple Parameter Sets	Identifies whether the provider supports multiple parameter sets. **Read-only**.	Boolean
Multiple Results	Identifies whether the provider supports multiple results objects and what restrictions it places on those objects. **Read-only**.	DBPROPVAL_MR
Multiple Storage Objects	Identifies whether the provider supports multiple, open storage objects at the same time. **Read-only**.	Boolean
Network Address	Identifies the network address of the SQL Server. **Read/Write**.	String
Network Library	Identifies the name of the Net-Library (DLL) used to communicate with the SQL Server. **Read/Write**.	String
NULL Collation Order	Identifies where NULLs are sorted in a list. **Read-only**.	DBPROPVAL_NC
NULL Concatenation Behavior	Specifies how the data source handles concatenation of NULL-valued character data type columns with non-NULL valued character data type columns. **Read-only**.	DBPROPVAL_CB
Numeric Functions	Identifies the numeric functions supported by the ODBC driver and data source. **Read-only**.	SQL_FN_NUM
OLE DB Services	Specifies which OLE DB services to enable. **Read/Write**.	DBPROPVAL_OS
OLE DB Version	Specifies the version of OLE DB supported by the provider. **Read-only**.	String
OLE Object Support	Specifies the way in which the provider supports access to BLOBs and OLE objects stored in columns. **Read-only**.	DBPROPVAL_OO

Name	Description	Data Type
ORDER BY Columns in Select List	Identifies whether columns in an ORDER BY clause must be in the SELECT list. **Read-only**.	Boolean
Outer Join Capabilities	Identifies the outer join capabilities of the ODBC data source. **Read-only**.	SQL_OJ
Outer Joins	Indicates whether outer joins are supported or not. **Read-only**.	Boolean
Output Parameter Availability	Identifies the time at which output parameter values become available. **Read-only**.	DBPROPVAL_OA
Packet Size	Specifies the network packet size in bytes. Value must be between 512 and 32767. The default is 4096. **Read/Write**.	Long
Pass By Ref Accessors	Indicates whether the provider supports the DBACCESSOR_PASSBYREF flag. **Read-only**.	Boolean
Password	Specifies the password to be used to connect to the data source. **Read/Write**.	String
Persist Encrypted	Whether or not the consumer requires that the data source object persist sensitive authentication information, such as a password, in encrypted form. **Read/Write**.	Boolean
Persist Security Info	Indicates whether the data source object is allowed to persist sensitive authentication information, such as a password, along with other authentication information. **Read/Write**.	Boolean
Persistent ID Type	Specifies the type of DB ID that the provider uses when persisting DB IDs for tables, indexes and columns. **Read-only**.	DBPROPVAL_PT

Table Continued on Following Page

421

Name	Description	Data Type
Prepare Abort Behavior	Identifies how aborting a transaction affects prepared commands. **Read-only**.	DBPROPVAL_CB
Prepare Commit Behavior	Identifies how committing a transaction affects prepared commands. **Read-only**.	DBPROPVAL_CB
Procedure Term	Specifies the data source provider's name for a procedure, eg, 'database procedure', 'stored procedure'. **Read-only**.	String
Prompt	Specifies whether to prompt the user during initialization. **Read/Write**.	DBPROMPT
Protection Level	Specifies the level of protection of data sent between client and server. Applies only to network connections other than RPC. **Read/Write**.	DB_PROT_LEVEL
Provider Friendly Name	Identifies the friendly name of the provider. **Read-only**.	String
Provider Name	Identifies the filename of the provider. **Read-only**.	String
Provider Version	Identifies the version of the provider. **Read-only**.	String
Quoted Identifier Sensitivity	Identifies how quoted identifiers treat case. **Read-only**.	DBPROPVAL_IC
Data Source	Indicates whether or not the data source is **Read-only**.	Boolean
Reset Datasource	Specifies the data source state to reset. **Write only**.	DBPROPVAL_RD
Rowset Conversions on Command	Indicates whether callers can enquire about a command and the conversions supported by the command. **Read-only**.	Boolean
Schema Term	Identifies the name the data source uses for a schema, eg, 'schema' or 'owner'. **Read-only**.	String

Name	Description	Data Type
Schema Usage	Specifies how schema names can be used in commands. **Read-only**.	DBPROPVAL_SU
Server Name	Identifies the name of the server. **Read-only**.	String
Sort on Index	Indicates whether the provider supports setting a sort order only for columns contained in an index. **Read-only**.	Boolean
Special Characters	Identifies the data store's special characters. **Read-only**.	String
SQL Grammar Support	Identifies the SQL grammar level supported by the ODBC driver. Value=0 means no conformance, value=1 means Level 1 conformance, and value=2 means Level 2 conformance. **Read-only**.	Long
SQL Support	Identifies the level of support for SQL. **Read-only**.	DBPROPVAL_SQL
SQLOLE Execute a SET TEXTLENGTH	Identifies whether SQLOLE executes a SET TEXTLENGTH before accessing BLOB fields. **Read-only**.	Boolean
Stored Procedures	Indicates whether stored procedures are available. **Read-only**.	Boolean
String Functions	Identifies the string functions supported by the ODBC driver and data source. **Read-only**.	SQL_FN_STR
Structured Storage	Identifies which interfaces the rowset supports on storage objects. **Read-only**.	DBPROPVAL_SS
Subquery Support	Identifies the predicates in text commands that support sub-queries. **Read-only**.	DBPROPVAL_SQ
System Functions	Identifies the system functions supported by the ODBC Driver and data source. **Read-only**.	SQL_FN_SYS

Table Continued on Following Page

Name	Description	Data Type
Table Term	Specifies the name used by the data source for a table, eg, 'table' or 'file'. **Read-only**.	String
Time/Date Functions	Identifies the time/date functions supported by the ODBC Driver and data source. **Read-only**.	SQL_SDF_CURRENT
Transaction DDL	Indicates whether Data Definition Language (DDL) statements are supported in transactions. **Read-only**.	DBPROPVAL_TC
Use Procedure for Prepare	Indicates whether SQL Server is to use temporary stored procedures for prepared statements. **Read/Write**.	SSPROPVAL_USEPROC FORPREP
User Authentication Mode	Indicates whether Windows NT Authentication is used to access SQL Server. **Read/Write**.	Boolean
User ID	Specifies the User ID to be used when connecting to the data source. **Read/Write**.	String
User Name	Specifies the User Name used in a particular database. **Read-only**.	String
Window Handle	Identifies the window handle to be used if the data source object needs to prompt for additional information. **Read/Write**.	Long
Workstation ID	Identifies the workstation. **Read/Write**.	String

Recordset Properties

Listed below are the dynamic properties of the ADO Recordset. Like all the other dynamic properties some may not be supported by your OLEDB provider.

Name	Description	Data Type
Access Order	Indicates the order in which columns must be accessed in a rowset. **Read/Write**.	DBPROPVAL_AO

Name	Description	Data Type
Append Only Rowset	A rowset opened with this property will initially contain no rows. **Read/Write**.	Boolean
Asynchronous Rowset Processing	Identifies the asynchronous processing performed on the rowset. **Read/Write**.	DBPROPVAL_ASYNCH
Auto Recalc	For chaptered recordsets using COMPUTE, automatically recalculate the summary if the detail lines change. **Read/Write**.	Integer
Batch Size	The number of rows in a batch. **Read/Write**.	Integer
Background Thread Priority	The priority of the background thread for asynchronous actions. **Read/Write**.	Integer
BLOB Accessibility on Forward-Only Cursor	Indicates whether or not BLOB columns can be accessed irrespective of their position in the column list. If True then the BLOB column can be accessed even if it is not the last column. If False then the BLOB column can only be accessed if it is the last column, and any non-BLOB columns after this will not be accessible. **Read/Write**.	Boolean
Blocking Storage Objects	Indicates whether storage objects might prevent use of other rowset methods. **Read/Write**.	Boolean
Bookmark Information	Identifies additional information about bookmarks over the rowset. **Read-only**.	DBPROPVAL_BI
Bookmark Type	Identifies the bookmark type supported by the rowset. **Read/Write**.	DBPROPVAL_BMK
Bookmarkable	Indicates whether the rowset supports bookmarks. **Read-only**.	Boolean
Bookmarks Ordered	Indicates whether the relative position of bookmarks can be compared. **Read/Write**.	Boolean

Table Continued on Following Page

Name	Description	Data Type
Bulk Operations	Reveals the optimizations that a provider may employ for updating the rowset. **Read-only**.	DBPROPVAL_BO
Cache Child Rows	Indicates whether child rows in a chaptered recordset are cached. **Read/Write**.	Boolean
Cache Deferred Columns	Indicates whether the provider caches the value of a deferred column when the client first gets a value from that column. **Read/Write**.	Boolean
Change Inserted Rows	Indicates whether the client can delete or update newly inserted rows. An inserted row is assumed to be one that has been transmitted to the data source, as opposed to a pending insert row. **Read/Write**.	Boolean
Column Privileges	Reveals whether access rights are restricted on a column-by-column basis. **Read-only**.	Boolean
Column Set Notification	Indicates whether column changes can be cancelled. **Read-only**.	DBPROPVAL_NP
Column Writable	Indicates whether a particular column is writable. **Read/Write**.	Boolean
Command Timeout	The number of seconds to wait before a command times out. Value=0 indicates an infinite time-out. **Read/Write**.	Long
Concurrency Control Method	Identifies the method used for concurrency control when using server based cursors. **Read/Write**.	SSPROPVAL_CONCUR
Cursor Engine Version	Exposes the version of the cursor engine. **Read-only**.	String
Defer Column	Indicates if the data in a column is fetched only when specifically requested. **Read/Write**.	Boolean

Name	Description	Data Type
Delay Storage Object Updates	Indicates whether in delay update mode, storage objects are also used in delayed update mode. **Read/Write**.	Boolean
Fetch Backward	Indicates whether a rowset can fetch data backwards. **Read/Write**.	Boolean
Filter Operations	Identifies which comparison operations are supported when using Filter on a particular column. **Read-only**.	DBPROPVAL_CO
Find Operations	Identifies which comparison operations are supported when using Find on a particular column. **Read-only**.	DBPROPVAL_CO
FOR BROWSE Versioning Columns	Indicates whether the rowset contains a primary key or a time-stamp. It is only applicable with rowsets created with the SQL FOR BROWSE statement. **Read/Write**.	Boolean
Force No Command Preparation When Executing a Parameterized Command	Identifies whether or not a temporary stored procedure is created for parameterized commands. **Read/Write**.	Boolean
Force No Command Reexecution when Failure to Satisfy all Required Properties	Identifies whether or not the command is re-executed if the command properties are invalid. **Read/Write**.	Boolean
Force No Parameter Rebinding when Executing a Command	Identifies whether or not command parameters are rebound every time the command is executed. **Read/Write**.	Boolean
Force SQL Server Firehose Mode Cursor	Identifies whether or not a forward-only, read-only cursor is always created. **Read/Write**.	Boolean

Table Continued on Following Page

Name	Description	Data Type
Generate a Rowset that Can Be Marshalled	Identifies whether or not the rowset that is to be created can be transported across process boundaries. **Read/Write**.	Boolean
Hold Rows	Indicates whether the rowset allows the consumer to retrieve more rows or change the next fetch position whilst holding previously fetched rows with pending changes. **Read/Write**.	Boolean
Immobile Rows	Indicates whether the rowset will reorder inserted or updated rows. **Read/Write**.	Boolean
Include SQL_FLOAT, SQL_DOUBLE, and SQL_REAL in QBU WHERE clauses	When using a query-based update, setting this to True will include REAL, FLOAT and DOUBLE numeric types in the WHERE clause, otherwise they will be omitted. **Read/Write**.	Boolean
Initial Fetch Size	Identifies the initial size of the cache into which records are fetched. **Read/Write**.	Long
Jet OLEDB:ODBC Pass-Through Statement	Identifies the statement used for a SQL Pass-through statement. **Read/Write**.	String
Jet OLEDB:Partial Bulk Ops	Indicates whether or not bulk operations will complete if some of the values fail. **Read-only**.	Boolean
Jet OLEDB:Pass Through Query Connect String	Identifies the Connect string for an ODBC pass through query. **Read/Write**.	String
Literal Bookmarks	Indicates whether bookmarks can be compared as a series of bytes. **Read/Write**.	Boolean
Literal Row Identity	Indicates whether the client can perform a binary comparison of two row handles to determine whether they point to the same row. **Read-only**.	Boolean

Name	Description	Data Type
Lock Mode	Sets or gets the level of locking performed by the rowset. **Read/Write**.	DBPROPVAL_LM
Maximum BLOB Length	Identifies the maximum length of a BLOB field. **Read-only**.	Long
Maximum Open Rows	Specifies the maximum number of rows that can be active at the same time. **Read/Write**.	Long
Maximum Pending Rows	Specifies the maximum number of rows that can have pending changes at the same time. **Read/Write**.	Long
Maximum Rows	Specifies the maximum number of rows that can be returned in the rowset. Value= 0 if there is no limit. **Read/Write**.	Long
Memory Usage	Gets or sets the amount of memory that can be used by the rowset. Value=0 the amount is unlimited. If between 1 and 99 it specifies a percentage of the available virtual memory. If 100 or greater it specifies a number of kilobytes. **Read/Write**.	Long
Notification Granularity	Identifies when the consumer is notified for methods that operate on multiple rows. **Read/Write**.	DBPROPVAL_NT
Notification Phases	Identifies the notification phases supported by the provider. **Read-only**.	DBPROPVAL_NP
Objects Transacted	Indicates whether any object created on the specified column is transacted. **Read/Write**.	Boolean
ODBC Concurrency Type	Identifies the ODBC concurrency type. **Read-only**.	Integer
ODBC Cursor Type	Identifies the ODBC cursor type. **Read-only**.	Integer

Table Continued on Following Page

429

Name	Description	Data Type
Others' Changes Visible	Specifies whether the rowset is able to see updates to or deletions from the underlying data performed by other clients. **Read/Write**.	Boolean
Others' Inserts Visible	Specifies whether the rowset is able to see inserts into the underlying data by other clients. **Read/Write**.	Boolean
Own Changes Visible	Specifies whether the rowset can see its own updates to and deletions from the underlying data. **Read/Write**.	Boolean
Own Inserts Visible	Specifies whether the rowset can see its own inserts into the underlying data. **Read/Write**.	Boolean
Position On the Last Row After Insert	Identifies whether the cursor is placed on the last row after an insert. **Read-only**.	Boolean
Preserve on Abort	Indicates whether, after aborting a transaction, the rowset remains active. **Read/Write**.	Boolean
Preserve on Commit	Indicates whether the rowset remains active after committing a transaction. **Read/Write**.	Boolean
Query Based Updates/Deletes /Inserts	Identifies whether queries can be used for updates, deletes, and inserts. **Read/Write**.	Boolean
Quick Restart	Indicates whether RestartPosition is relatively quick to execute. **Read/Write**.	Boolean
Reentrant Events	Indicates whether the provider supports reentrancy during callbacks. **Read-only**.	Boolean
Remove Deleted Rows	Indicates whether the provider removes rows it detects as having been deleted from the rowset. **Read/Write**.	Boolean

Name	Description	Data Type
Report Multiple Changes	Indicates whether an update or delete can affect multiple rows and whether the provider can detect that multiple rows have been updated or deleted. **Read-only**.	Boolean
Return Pending Inserts	Indicates whether methods that fetch rows can return pending insert. **Read-only**.	Boolean
Row Delete Notification	Indicates whether deleting a row is cancellable. **Read-only**.	DBPROPVAL_NP
Row First Change Notification	Indicates whether changes to the first row are cancellable. **Read-only**.	DBPROPVAL_NP
Row Insert Notification	Indicates whether inserting a new row is cancellable. **Read-only**.	DBPROPVAL_NP
Row Privileges	Indicates whether access rights are restricted on a row-by-row basis. **Read-only**.	Boolean
Row Resynchronization Notification	Indicates whether re-synchronizing a row is cancellable. **Read-only**.	DBPROPVAL_NP
Row Threading Model	Identifies the threading model supported by the rowset. **Read/Write**.	DBPROPVAL_RT
Row Undo Change Notification	Indicates whether undoing a change is cancellable. **Read-only**.	DBPROPVAL_NP
Row Undo Delete Notification	Indicates whether undoing a delete is cancellable. **Read-only**.	DBPROPVAL_NP
Row Undo Insert Notification	Indicates whether undoing an insert is cancellable. **Read-only**.	DBPROPVAL_NP
Row Update Notification	Indicates whether updating a row is cancellable. **Read-only**.	DBPROPVAL_NP
Rowset Fetch Position Change Notification	Indicates whether changing the fetch position is cancellable. **Read-only**.	DBPROPVAL_NP
Rowset Release Notification	Indicates whether releasing a rowset is cancellable. **Read-only**.	DBPROPVAL_NP

Table Continued on Following Page

Name	Description	Data Type
Scroll Backward	Specifies whether the rowset has bi-directional scrolling. **Read/Write**.	Boolean
Server Cursor	Indicates whether the cursor underlying the rowset (if any) must be created on the server. **Read/Write**.	Boolean
Server Data on Insert	Indicates whether, at the time an insert is transmitted to the server, the provider retrieves data from the server to update the local data cache. **Read/Write**.	Boolean
Skip Deleted Bookmarks	Indicates whether the rowset allows positioning to continue if a bookmarked row was deleted. **Read/Write**.	Boolean
Strong Row Identity	Indicates whether the handles of newly inserted rows can be compared. **Read-only**.	Boolean
Unique Rows	Indicates whether each row is uniquely identified by its column values. **Read/Write**.	Boolean
Updatability	Identifies the supported methods for updating a rowset. **Read/Write**.	DBPROPVAL_UP
Update Criteria	Identifies the criteria used when performing a requery on chaptered recordsets. **Read/Write**.	String
Update Operation	Identifies the operation to be performed with a requery on chaptered recordsets. **Read/Write**.	String
Use Bookmarks	Indicates whether the rowset supports bookmarks. **Read/Write**.	Boolean

Field Properties

The Field properties names are different from the other properties because they are less 'readable' and appear more like the schema column names.

Name	Description	Data Type
BASECATALOGNAME	The name of the catalog. **Read-only**.	String
BASECOLUMNNAME	The name of the column. **Read-only**.	String
BASESCHEMANAME	The name of the schema. **Read-only**.	String
BASETABLENAME	The name of the table. **Read-only**.	String
CALCULATIONINFO	Accesses the calculations for summary and grouped recordsets (client-side cursors only). **Read-only**	Binary
DATETIMEPRECISION	The number of digits in the fraction seconds portion in a date/time field. **Read-only**.	Long
ISAUTOINCREMENT	Identifies whether the column is an auto increment type, such as an Access Autonumber or a SQL Server IDENTITY column. **Read-only**.	Boolean
ISCASESENSITIVE	Identifies whether the contents of a field are case sensitive. Useful when searching. **Read-only**.	Boolean
ISSEARCHABLE	Identifies whether a field is searchable. **Read-only**.	DB_SEARCHABLE
KEYCOLUMN	Identifies whether the value of the field is used to uniquely identify the column. **Read-only**.	Boolean
OCTETLENGTH	The maximum column length in bytes. Used for character or binary data columns. **Read-only**.	Long

Table Continued on Following Page

Name	Description	Data Type
OPTIMIZE	Identifies whether the column is indexed locally. This is only available for client-side cursors. **Read/Write**.	Boolean
RELATIONCONDITIONS	Returns the conditions for the relationships between chaptered recordsets. This is only available for client cursors.	Binary

Property Usage

Using the properties is quite simple, despite the fact that there are so many of them. You simply use the property name to index into the `Properties` collection. For example, to find out the name the provider gives to procedures you could do this:

```
Print oConn.Properties("Procedure Term")
```

For SQL Server this returns `stored procedure` and for Access this returns `STORED QUERY`.

You can enumerate all of the properties very simply:

```
For Each oProp In oConn.Properties
   Print oProp.Name
   Print oProp.Value
Next
```

This will print out the property name and value.

For those properties that return custom types, you need to identify whether these return a bitmask or a simple value. In its simplest forms, these properties will just return a single value. For example, to find out whether your provider supports output parameters on stored procedures you can query the `Output Parameter Availability` property. This is defined as returning values of type `DBPROPVAL_OA`, which are as follows:

Constant	Value
DBPROPVAL_OA_ATEXECUTE	2
DBPROPVAL_OA_ATROWRELEASE	4
DBPROPVAL_OA_NOTSUPPORTED	1

Examining this property when connected to SQL Server gives you a value of 4, indicating that output parameters are available when the recordset is closed. Access, on the other hand, returns a value of 1, indicating that output parameters are not supported.

For those properties that return bitmask, you'll need to use boolean logic to identify which values are set. For example, to query the provider and examine what features of SQL are supported, you would use the SQL Support property. For Access this returns 512, which corresponds to DBPROPVAL_SQL_SUBMINIMUM, indicating that not even the ANSI SQL92 Entry level SQL facilities are provided. SQL Server on the other hand, returns 283, but there isn't a single value for this, so it must be a combination of values. This in fact corresponds to:

Constant	Value
DBPROPVAL_SQL_ESCAPECLAUSES	256
DBPROPVAL_SQL_ANSI92_ENTRY	16
DBPROPVAL_SQL_ANDI89_IEF	8
DBPROPVAL_SQL_CORE	2
DBPROPVAL_SQL_MINIMUM	1

You can check to see whether a specific value is set by ANDing that value with one of the constants above. For example:

```
lngSQLSupport = oConn.Properties("SQL Support")
If (lngSQLSupport AND DBPROPVAL_SQL_CORE) = DBPROPVAL_SQL_CORE Then
   core facilities are supported
End If
```

Database Schemas

This appendix details the schema objects that can be accessed using the OpenSchema method of the Connection object. The first table lists the type of queries that can be passed as a parameter of this method, giving for each a concise description and identifying the main providers that support them. The second table lists for each schema object the values of the criteria or restrictions on which the search can be based, together with their data type and a short description. Finally the last part of this section summarizes how to use schemas.

There are two terms that are important when dealing with schemas:

❑ A **Catalog** may be compared to a normal paper catalog, but in this case contains a list of schemas. It will always contain an INFORMATION_SCHEMA, which gives information about the list of schema objects it contains. When using SQL Server or Access, a catalog is referred to as a database.

❑ A **Schema** is a collection of database objects that are owned, or have been created by a particular user. Microsoft Access does not support schemas and all database objects are contained in a single schema.

Schemas

These are passed as arguments to an OpenSchema method call when you need to query information for a particular Connection object.

Schema	Description	Drivers Supported
adSchemaAsserts	Identifies the assertions defined in the catalog	SQL, ODBC Jet, ODBC SQL
adSchemaCatalogs	Defines the physical attributes of the catalog of a database. When using SQL Server the catalogs are the databases within the Server, and for Access, the catalog contains the current database.	
adSchemaCharacterSets	Identifies the character sets supported by the catalog.	
adSchemaCheckConstraints	Identifies the valid values allowed for columns that are available in the catalog.	
adSchemaCollations	Identifies how the catalog sorts data.	
adSchemaColumnDomainUsage	Identifies the columns that use domains for integrity checking.	
adSchemaColumnPrivileges	Identifies the privileges on table columns for a given user.	SQL, ODBC SQL
adSchemaColumns	Identifies the columns of tables.	SQL, ODBC Jet, ODBC SQL
adSchemaConstraintsColumn _Usage	Identifies the columns used for referential integrity constraints, unique constraints, check constraints and assertions.	
adSchemaConstraintsTable _Usage	Identifies the tables used for referential integrity constraints, unique constraints, check constraints and assertions.	

Schema	Description	Drivers Supported
adSchemaForeignKeys	Identifies the foreign key column, as used in referential integrity checks.	ODBC SQL
adSchemaIndexes	Identifies the list of indexes in the catalog.	SQL, ODBC Jet, ODBC SQL
adSchemaKeyColumnUsage	Identifies the key columns and table names in the catalog.	
adSchemaPrimaryKeys	Identifies the primary keys and table names in the catalog.	SQL, ODBC SQL
adSchemaProcedureColumns	Identifies the columns used in procedures.	ODBC Jet
adSchemaProcedureParameters	Identifies the parameters of stored procedures.	SQL, ODBC Jet, ODBC SQL
adSchemaProcedures	Identifies stored procedures or queries.	SQL, ODBC Jet, ODBC SQL
adSchemaProviderSpecific	Returns provider dependent settings.	
adSchemaProviderTypes	Identifies the data types supported by the provider.	SQL, ODBC Jet, ODBC SQL
adSchemaReferentialConstraints	Identifies the referential integrity constraints of the catalog.	
adSchemaSchemata	Identifies the schemas that are owned by a particular user.	SQL, ODBC SQL
adSchemaSQLLanguages	Identifies the conformance levels and other options supported by the catalog.	
adSchemaStatistics	Identifies the catalog statistics.	SQL

Table Continued on Following Page

Schema	Description	Drivers Supported
adSchemaTableConstraints	Identifies the referential table constraints.	
adSchemaTablePrivileges	Identifies the user privileges of tables.	SQL
adSchemaTables	Identifies the tables in a catalog.	SQL, ODBC Jet, ODBC SQL
adSchemaTranslations	Identifies character translations that the catalog supports.	
adSchemaUsagePrivileges	Identifies the usage privileges that are available to a user.	
adSchemaViewColumnUsage	Identifies the columns used in views.	
adSchemaViewTableUsage	Identifies the tables used in views.	
adSchemaViews	Identifies the views in the catalog.	

Restrictions

Calling the OpenSchema method of the Connection object returns a Recordset object containing the given schema information. Each query type returns a particular table. Listed below for each query type are the column headers. These can be passed as restriction arguments in the OpenSchema method call to filter the query.

Schema	Column Headers	Data Type	Description
adSchema _Asserts	CONSTRAINT_CATALOG	String	Catalog name, or Null if the provider does not support catalogs.
	CONSTRAINT_SCHEMA	String	Schema name, or Null if the provider does not support schemas.
	CONSTRAINT_NAME	String	Constraint name.
	IS_DEFERRABLE	Boolean	**True** if the assertion is deferrable, **False** otherwise.
	INITIALLY_DEFERRED	Boolean	**True** if the assertion is initially deferred, **False** otherwise.

Schema	Column Headers	Data Type	Description
	DESCRIPTION	String	Description of the assertion.
adSchema _Catalogs	CATALOG_NAME	String	Catalog name.
	DESCRIPTION	String	Catalog description.
adSchema _CharacterSets	CHARACTER_SET _CATALOG	String	Catalog name, or Null if the provider does not support catalogs.
	CHARACTER_SET _SCHEMA	String	Schema name, or Null if the provider does not support schemas.
	CHARACTER_SET _NAME	String	Character set name.
	FORM_OF_USE	String	Name of form-of-use of the character set.
	NUMBER_OF _CHARACTERS	Big Integer	Number of characters in the character repertoire.
	DEFAULT_COLLATE _CATALOG	String	Catalog name containing the default collation, or Null if the provider does not support catalogs or different collations.
	DEFAULT_COLLATE _SCHEMA	String	Schema name containing the default collation, or Null if the provider does not support schemas or different collations.
	DEFAULT_COLLATE _NAME	String	Default collation name, or Null if the provider does not support different collations.
adSchemaCheck _Constraints	CONSTRAINT _CATALOG	String	Catalog name, or Null if the provider does not support catalogs.
	CONSTRAINT_SCHEMA	String	Schema name, or Null if the provider does not support schemas.
	CONSTRAINT_NAME	String	Constraint name.

Table Continued on Following Page

441

Schema	Column Headers	Data Type	Description
	CHECK_CLAUSE	String	The WHERE clause specified in the CHECK constraint.
	DESCRIPTION	String	Check constraint description.
adSchema _Collations	COLLATION _CATALOG	String	Catalog name, or Null if the provider does not support catalogs.
	COLLATION _SCHEMA	String	Schema name, or Null if the provider does not support schemas.
	COLLATION_NAME	String	Collation name.
	CHARACTER_SET _CATALOG	String	Catalog name containing the character set on which the collation is defined, or Null if the provider does not support catalogs or different character sets.
	CHARACTER_SET _SCHEMA	String	Schema name containing the character set on which the collation is defined, or Null if the provider does not support schema or different character sets.
	CHARACTER_SET _NAME	String	Character set name on which the collation is defined, or Null if the provider does not support different character sets.
	PAD_ATTRIBUTE	String	'NO PAD' if the collation being described has the NO PAD attribute, 'PAD SPACE' if the collation being described has the PAD SPACE attribute. This identifies whether variable length character columns are padded with spaces.
adSchema _ColumnDomain _Usage	DOMAIN_CATALOG	String	Catalog name, or Null if the provider does not support catalogs.

Schema	Column Headers	Data Type	Description
	DOMAIN_SCHEMA	String	Schema name, or Null if the provider does not support schemas.
	DOMAIN_NAME	String	View name.
	TABLE_CATALOG	String	Catalog name in which the table is defined, or Null if the provider does not support catalogs.
	TABLE_SCHEMA	String	Unqualified schema name in which the table is defined, or Null if the provider does not support schemas.
	TABLE_NAME	String	Table name.
	COLUMN_NAME	String	Column name. This column, together with the COLUMN_GUID and COLUMN_PROPID columns, forms the column ID. One or more of these columns will be Null depending on which elements of the DBID structure the provider uses.
	COLUMN_GUID	GUID	Column GUID.
	COLUMN_PROPID	Long	Column property ID.
adSchemaColumn _Privileges	GRANTOR	String	User who granted the privileges on the table in TABLE_NAME.
	GRANTEE	String	User name (or "PUBLIC") to whom the privilege has been granted.
	TABLE_CATALOG	String	Catalog name in which the table is defined, or Null if the provider does not support catalogs.

Table Continued on Following Page

Schema	Column Headers	Data Type	Description
	TABLE_SCHEMA	String	Schema name in which the table is defined, or Null if the provider does not support schemas.
	TABLE_NAME	String	Table name.
	COLUMN_NAME	String	Column name.
	COLUMN_GUID	GUID	Column GUID.
	COLUMN_PROPID	Long	Column property ID.
	PRIVILEGE_TYPE	String	Privilege type. One of the following: SELECT, DELETE, INSERT, UPDATE, REFERENCES.
	IS_GRANTABLE	Boolean	**True** if the privilege being described was granted with the WITH GRANT OPTION clause, **False** if the privilege being described was not granted with the WITH GRANT OPTION clause.
adSchema _Columns	TABLE_CATALOG	String	Catalog name, or Null if the provider does not support catalogs.
	TABLE_SCHEMA	Long	Schema name, or Null if the provider does not support schemas.
	TABLE_NAME	String	Table name. This column cannot contain a Null.
	COLUMN_NAME	String	The name of the column, or Null if this cannot be determined.
	COLUMN_GUID	GUID	Column GUID, or Null for providers that do not use GUIDs to identify columns.

Schema	Column Headers	Data Type	Description
	COLUMN_PROPID	Long	Column property ID, or Null for providers that do not associate PROPIDs with columns.
	ORDINAL_POSITION	Long	The ordinal of the column, or Null if there is no stable ordinal value for the column. Columns are numbered starting from one.
	COLUMN_HASDEFAULT	Boolean	**True** if column has a default value, **False** if the column does not have a default value or it is unknown whether the column has a default value.
	COLUMN_DEFAULT	String	Default value of the column.
	COLUMN_FLAGS	Long	A bitmask that describes column characteristics. The DBCOLUMNFLAGS enumerated type specifies the bits in the bitmask. The values for DBCOLUMNFLAGS can be found in Appendix I. This column cannot contain a Null value.
	IS_NULLABLE	Boolean	**True** if the column might be nullable, **False** if the column is known not to be nullable.
	DATA_TYPE	Integer	The column's data type. If the data type of the column varies from row to row, this must be a **Variant**. This column cannot contain Null. For a list of valid Types, see DataTypeEnum in Appendix G.

Table Continued on Following Page

Schema	Column Headers	Data Type	Description
	TYPE_GUID	GUID	The GUID of the column's data type. Providers that do not use GUIDs to identify data types should return Null in this column.
	CHARACTER_MAXIMUM_ LENGTH	Long	The maximum possible length of a value in the column. (see note 1 at the end of the table)
	CHARACTER_OCTET_ LENGTH	Long	Maximum length in octets (bytes) of the column, if the type of the column is character or binary. A value of zero means the column has no maximum length. Null for all other types of columns.
	NUMERIC_PRECISION	Integer	If the column's data type is numeric, this is the maximum precision of the column. The precision of columns with a data type of **Decimal** or **Numeric** depends on the definition of the column. If the column's data type is not numeric, this is Null.
	NUMERIC_SCALE	Integer	If the column's type is **Decimal** or **Numeric**, this is the number of digits to the right of the decimal point. Otherwise, this is Null.
	DATETIME_PRECISION	Long	Datetime precision (number of digits in the fractional seconds portion) of the column if the column is a datetime or interval type. If the column's data type is not datetime, this is Null.

Schema	Column Headers	Data Type	Description
	CHARACTER_SET_CATALOG	String	Catalog name in which the character set is defined, or Null if the provider does not support catalogs or different character sets.
	CHARACTER_SET_SCHEMA	String	Schema name in which the character set is defined, or Null if the provider does not support schemas or different character sets.
	CHARACTER_SET_NAME	String	Character set name, or Null if the provider does not support different character sets.
	COLLATION_CATALOG	String	Catalog name in which the collation is defined, or Null if the provider does not support catalogs or different collations.
	COLLATION_SCHEMA	String	Schema name in which the collation is defined, or Null if the provider does not support schemas or different collations.
	COLLATION_NAME	String	Collation name, or Null if the provider does not support different collations.
	DOMAIN_CATALOG	String	Catalog name in which the domain is defined, or Null if the provider does not support catalogs or domains.
	DOMAIN_SCHEMA	String	Unqualified schema name in which the domain is defined, or Null if the provider does not support schemas or domains.
	DOMAIN_NAME	String	Domain name, or Null if the provider does not support domains.

Table Continued on Following Page

Schema	Column Headers	Data Type	Description
	DESCRIPTION	String	Description of the column, or Null if there is no description associated with the column.
adSchema _Constraints _ColumnUsage	TABLE_CATALOG	String	Catalog name in which the table is defined, or Null if the provider does not support catalogs.
	TABLE_SCHEMA	String	Schema name in which the table is defined, or Null if the provider does not support schemas.
	TABLE_NAME	String	Table name.
	COLUMN_NAME	String	Column name.
	COLUMN_GUID	GUID	Column GUID.
	COLUMN_PROPID	Long	Column property ID.
	CONSTRAINT_CATALOG	String	Catalog name, or Null if the provider does not support catalogs.
	CONSTRAINT_SCHEMA	String	Schema name, or Null if the provider does not support schemas.
	CONSTRAINT_NAME	String	Constraint name.
adSchema _Constraints _TableUsage	TABLE_CATALOG	String	Catalog name in which the table is defined, or Null if the provider does not support catalogs.
	TABLE_SCHEMA	String	Schema name in which the table is defined, or Null if the provider does not support schemas.
	TABLE_NAME	String	Table name.
	CONSTRAINT_CATALOG	String	Catalog name, or Null if the provider does not support catalogs.

Schema	Column Headers	Data Type	Description
	CONSTRAINT_SCHEMA	String	Schema name, or Null if the provider does not support schemas.
	CONSTRAINT_NAME	String	Constraint name.
adSchemaForeign _Keys	PK_TABLE_CATALOG	String	Catalog name in which the primary key table is defined, or Null if the provider does not support catalogs.
	PK_TABLE_SCHEMA	String	Schema name in which the primary key table is defined, or Null if the provider does not support schemas.
	PK_TABLE_NAME	String	Primary key table name.
	PK_COLUMN_NAME	String	Primary key column name.
	PK_COLUMN_GUID	GUID	Primary key column GUID.
	PK_COLUMN_PROPID	Long	Primary key column property ID.
	FK_TABLE_CATALOG	String	Catalog name in which the foreign key table is defined, or Null if the provider does not support catalogs.
	FK_TABLE_SCHEMA	String	Schema name in which the foreign key table is defined, or Null if the provider does not support schemas.
	FK_TABLE_NAME	String	Foreign key table name.
	FK_COLUMN_NAME	String	Foreign key column name.
	FK_COLUMN_GUID	GUID	Foreign key column GUID.
	FK_COLUMN_PROPID	Long	Foreign key column property ID.

Table Continued on Following Page

449

Schema	Column Headers	Data Type	Description
	ORDINAL	Long	The order of the column in the key. For example, a table might contain several foreign key references to another table. The ordinal starts over for each reference; for example, two references to a three-column key would return 1, 2, 3, 1, 2, 3.
	UPDATE_RULE	String	The action if an UPDATE rule was specified. This will be Null only if the provider cannot determine the UPDATE_RULE. In most cases, this implies a default of NO ACTION. (see note 2 at the end of the table).
	DELETE_RULE	String	The action if a DELETE rule was specified. This will be Null if the provider cannot determine the DELETE_RULE. In most cases, this implies a default of NO ACTION. (see note 2 at the end of the table).
	FK_NAME	String	Foreign key name, or Null if the provider does not support named foreign key constraints.
	PK_NAME	String	Primary key name, or Null if the provider does not support named primary key constraints.
	DEFERRABILITY	Integer	Deferrability of the foreign key. Value is one of the following DBPROPVAL_DF types, as shown in Appendix I.
adSchema _Indexes	TABLE_CATALOG	String	Catalog name, or Null if the provider does not support catalogs.

Schema	Column Headers	Data Type	Description
	TABLE_SCHEMA	String	Unqualified schema name, or Null if the provider does not support schemas.
	TABLE_NAME	String	Table name.
	INDEX_CATALOG	String	Catalog name, or Null if the provider does not support catalogs.
	INDEX_SCHEMA	String	Schema name, or Null if the provider does not support schemas.
	INDEX_NAME	String	Index name.
	PRIMARY_KEY	Boolean	Whether the index represents the primary key on the table, or Null if this is not known.
	UNIQUE	Boolean	Whether index keys must be unique. This will be **True** if the index keys must be unique, and **False** if duplicate keys are allowed.
	CLUSTERED	Boolean	Whether an index is clustered.
	INTEGRATED	Boolean	Whether the index is integrated (all base table columns are available from the index). This will be **True** if the index is integrated, and **False** if the index is not integrated. For clustered indexes, this value must always be **True**.
	TYPE	Integer	The type of the index. One of the DBPROPVAL_IT constants as shown in Appendix I

Table Continued on Following Page

Schema	Column Headers	Data Type	Description
	FILL_FACTOR	Long	For a B+-tree index, this property represents the storage utilization factor of page nodes during the creation of the index.
	INITIAL_SIZE	Long	The total amount of bytes allocated to this structure at creation time.
	NULLS	Long	Whether null keys are allowed This will be one of the DBPROPVAL_IN constants as shown in Appendix I.
	SORT_BOOKMARKS	Boolean	How the index treats repeated keys. This will be **True** if the index sorts repeated keys by bookmark, and **False** if it doesn't.
	AUTO_UPDATE	Boolean	Whether the index is maintained automatically when changes are made to the corresponding base table. This will be **True** if the index is automatically maintained, and **False** if it isn't.
	NULL_COLLATION	Long	How Nulls are collated in the index. This will be one of the DBPROPVAL_NC constants as shown in Appendix I.
	ORDINAL_POSITION	Long	Ordinal position of the column in the index, starting with 1.
	COLUMN_NAME	String	Column name.
	COLUMN_GUID	GUID	Column GUID.
	COLUMN_PROPID	Long	Column property ID.

Schema	Column Headers	Data Type	Description
	COLLATION	Integer	Identifies the sort order, and will be one of the DB_COLLATION constants as shown in Appendix I.
	CARDINALITY	Unsigned Big Integer	Number of unique values in the index.
	PAGES	Long	Number of pages used to store the index.
	FILTER_CONDITION	String	The WHERE clause identifying the filtering restriction.
	INTEGRATED	Boolean	Whether the index is integrated, that is, all base table columns are available from the index. This will be **True** if the index is integrated, and **False** if it isn't. Clustered indexes always set this value to **True**.
adSchemaKey _ColumnUsage	CONSTRAINT_CATALOG	String	Catalog name, or Null if the provider does not support catalogs.
	CONSTRAINT_SCHEMA	String	Schema name, or Null if the provider does not support schemas.
	CONSTRAINT_NAME	String	Constraint name.
	TABLE_CATALOG	String	Catalog name in which the table containing the key column is defined, or Null if the provider does not support catalogs.
	TABLE_SCHEMA	String	Schema name in which the table containing the key column is defined, or Null if the provider does not support schemas.

Table Continued on Following Page

Schema	Column Headers	Data Type	Description
	TABLE_NAME	String	Table name containing the key column.
	COLUMN_NAME	String	Name of the column participating in the unique, primary, or foreign key.
	COLUMN_GUID	GUID	Column GUID.
	COLUMN_PROPID	Long	Column property ID.
	ORDINAL_POSITION	Long	Ordinal position of the column in the constraint being described.
adSchema _PrimaryKeys	PK_NAME	String	Primary key name, or Null if the provider does not support primary key constraints.
	TABLE_CATALOG	String	Catalog name in which the table is defined, or Null if the provider does not support catalogs.
	TABLE_SCHEMA	String	Schema name in which the table is defined, or Null if the provider does not support schemas.
	TABLE_NAME	String	Table name.
	COLUMN_NAME	String	Primary key column name.
	COLUMN_GUID	GUID	Primary key column GUID.
	COLUMN_PROPID	Long	Primary key column property ID.
	ORDINAL	Long	The order of the column names (and GUIDs and property IDs) in the key.
adSchema _Procedure _Columns	PROCEDURE_CATALOG	String	Catalog name, or Null if the provider does not support catalogs.
	PROCEDURE_SCHEMA	String	Schema name, or Null if the provider does not support schemas.

Schema	Column Headers	Data Type	Description
	PROCEDURE_NAME	String	Table name.
	COLUMN_NAME	String	The name of the column, or Null if this cannot be determined. This might not be unique.
	COLUMN_GUID	GUID	Column GUID.
	COLUMN_PROPID	Long	Column property ID.
	ROWSET_NUMBER	Long	Number of the rowset containing the column. This is greater than one only if the procedure returns multiple rowsets.
	ORDINAL_POSITION	Long	The ordinal of the column. Columns are numbered starting from 1, or Null if there is no stable ordinal value for the column.
	IS_NULLABLE	Boolean	Will be **True** if the column might be nullable, or **False** if the column is known not to be nullable.
	DATA_TYPE	Integer	The indicator of the column's data type. For a list of valid types, see DataTypeEnum in Appendix G.
	TYPE_GUID	GUID	The GUID of the column's data type.
	CHARACTER_MAXIMUM_LENGTH	Long	The maximum possible length of a value in the column. (see note 1 at the end of the table).
	CHARACTER_OCTET_LENGTH	Long	Maximum length in octets (bytes) of the column, if the type of the column is character or binary. A value of zero means the column has no maximum length. Null for all other types of columns.

Table Continued on Following Page

Schema	Column Headers	Data Type	Description
	NUMERIC_PRECISION	Integer	If the column's data type is numeric, this is the maximum precision of the column. If the column's data type is not numeric, this is Null.
	NUMERIC_SCALE	Integer	If the column's type is DBTYPE_DECIMAL or DBTYPE_NUMERIC, this is the number of digits to the right of the decimal point. Otherwise, this is Null.
	DESCRIPTION	String	Column description
adSchema _Procedure _Parameters	PROCEDURE_CATALOG	String	Catalog name, or Null if the provider does not support catalogs.
	PROCEDURE_SCHEMA	String	Schema name, or Null if the provider does not support catalogs.
	PROCEDURE_NAME	String	Procedure name.
	PARAMETER_NAME	String	Parameter name, or Null if the parameter is not named.
	ORDINAL_POSITION	Integer	If the parameter is an input, input/output, or output parameter, this is the one-based ordinal position of the parameter in the procedure call. If the parameter is the return value, this is zero.
	PARAMETER_TYPE	Integer	The type (direction) of the parameter, which will be one of the DBPARAM_TYPE constants, as shown in Appendix I. If the provider cannot determine the parameter type, this is Null.

Schema	Column Headers	Data Type	Description
	PARAMETER_HASDEFAULT	Boolean	**True** if the parameter has a default value, or **False** if it doesn't or the provider doesn't know whether it has a default value.
	PARAMETER_DEFAULT	String	Default value of parameter. A default value of Null is a valid default.
	IS_NULLABLE	Boolean	**True** if the parameter might be nullable, or **False** if the parameter is not nullable.
	DATA_TYPE	Integer	The indicator of the parameter's data type. For a list of valid types, see DataTypeEnum in Appendix G.
	CHARACTER_MAXIMUM _LENGTH	Long	The maximum possible length of a value in the parameter. (see note 1 at end of table).
	CHARACTER_OCTET _LENGTH	Long	Maximum length in octets (bytes) of the parameter, if the type of the parameter is character or binary. A value of zero means the parameter has no maximum length. Null for all other types of parameters.
	NUMERIC_PRECISION	Integer	If the column's data type is numeric, this is the maximum precision of the column. If the column's data type is not numeric, this is Null.
	NUMERIC_SCALE	Integer	If the column's type is DBTYPE_DECIMAL or DBTYPE_NUMERIC, this is the number of digits to the right of the decimal point. Otherwise, this is Null.
	DESCRIPTION	String	Parameter description

Table Continued on Following Page

Schema	Column Headers	Data Type	Description
	TYPE_NAME	String	Provider-specific data type name.
	LOCAL_TYPE_NAME	String	Localized version of TYPE_NAME, or Null if the data provider does not support a localized name.
adSchema _Procedures	PROCEDURE_CATALOG	String	Catalog name, or Null if the provider does not support catalogs.
	PROCEDURE_SCHEMA	String	Schema name, or Null if the provider does not support schemas.
	PROCEDURE_NAME	String	Procedure name.
	PROCEDURE_TYPE	Integer	Identifies whether there will be a return value or not, and will be one of the DB_PT constants as defined in Appendix I.
	PROCEDURE_DEFINITION	String	Procedure definition.
	DESCRIPTION	String	Procedure description.
	DATE_CREATED	Date/Time	Date when the procedure was created or Null if the provider does not have this information.
	DATE_MODIFIED	Date/Time	Date when the procedure definition was last modified or Null if the provider does not have this information.
adSchema _Provider _Specific	None		
adSchema _Provider _Types	TYPE_NAME	String	Provider-specific data type name.
	DATA_TYPE	Integer	The indicator of the data type.

Schema	Column Headers	Data Type	Description
	COLUMN_SIZE	Long	The length of a non-numeric column or parameter refers to either the maximum or the defined length for this type by the provider. For character data, this is the maximum or defined length in characters. For datetime data types, this is the length of the String representation (assuming the maximum allowed precision of the fractional seconds component).
			If the data type is numeric, this is the upper bound on the maximum precision of the data type.
	LITERAL_PREFIX	String	Character or characters used to prefix a literal of this type in a text command.
	LITERAL_SUFFIX	String	Character or characters used to suffix a literal of this type in a text command.
	CREATE_PARAMS	String	The creation parameters are specified by the consumer when creating a column of this data type. For example, the SQL data type DECIMAL needs a precision and a scale. In this case, the creation parameters might be the String "precision, scale". In a text command to create a DECIMAL column with a precision of 10 and a scale of 2, the value of the TYPE_NAME column might be DECIMAL() and the complete type specification would be DECIMAL(10,2).
	IS_NULLABLE	Boolean	**True** if the data type is nullable, **False** if the data type is not nullable, and Null if it is not known whether the data type is nullable.
	CASE_SENSITIVE	Boolean	**True** if the data type is a character type and is case sensitive, or **False** if the data type is not a character type or is not case sensitive.

Table Continued on Following Page

Schema	Column Headers	Data Type	Description
	SEARCHABLE	Long	Identifies whether the column can be used in WHERE clauses, and will be one of the DB_SEARCHABLE constants as shown in Appendix I.
	UNSIGNED_ATTRIBUTE	Boolean	**True** if the data type is unsigned, **False** if the data type is signed, or Null if not applicable to data type.
	FIXED_PREC_SCALE	Boolean	**True** if the data type has a fixed precision and scale, or **False** if the data type does not have a fixed precision and scale.
	AUTO_UNIQUE_VALUE	Boolean	True if values of this type can be autoincrementing, or False if values of this type cannot be autoincrementing.
	LOCAL_TYPE_NAME	String	Localized version of TYPE_NAME, or Null if a localized name is not supported by the data provider.
	MINIMUM_SCALE	Integer	The minimum number of digits allowed to the right of the decimal point, for decimal and numeric data types. Otherwise, this is Null.
	MAXIMUM_SCALE	Integer	The maximum number of digits allowed to the right of the decimal point, for decimal and numeric data types. Otherwise, this is Null.
	GUID	GUID	The GUID of the type. All types supported by a provider are described in a type library, so each type has a corresponding GUID.
	TYPELIB	String	The type library containing the description of this type.
	VERSION	String	The version of the type definition. Providers may wish to version type definitions. Different providers may use different version schemes, such as a timestamp or number (integer or float), or Null if not supported.

Schema	Column Headers	Data Type	Description
	IS_LONG	Boolean	**True** if the data type is a BLOB that contains very long data; the definition of very long data is provider-specific, or **False** if the data type is a BLOB that does not contain very long data or is not a BLOB.
	BEST_MATCH	Boolean	**True** if the data type is the best match between all data types in the data source and the OLEDB data type indicated by the value in the DATA_TYPE column, or **False** if the data type is not the best match.
	IS_FIXEDLENGTH	Boolean	**True** if columns of this type created by the DDL will be of fixed length or **False** if columns of this type created by the DDL will be of variable length.
			If the field is Null, it is not known whether the provider will map this field with a fixed or variable length.
adSchema _Referential Constraints	CONSTRAINT_CATALOG	String	Catalog name, or Null if the provider does not support catalogs.
	CONSTRAINT_SCHEMA	String	Schema name, or Null if the provider does not support schemas.
	CONSTRAINT_NAME	String	Constraint name.
	UNIQUE_CONSTRAINT _CATALOG	String	Catalog name in which the unique or primary key constraint is defined, or Null if the provider does not support catalogs.

Table Continued on Following Page

Schema	Column Headers	Data Type	Description
	UNIQUE_CONSTRAINT _SCHEMA	String	Unqualified schema name in which the unique or primary key constraint is defined, or Null if the provider does not support schemas.
	UNIQUE_CONSTRAINT _NAME	String	Unique or primary key constraint name.
	MATCH_OPTION	String	The type of match that was specified. (see note 3 at end of table).
	UPDATE_RULE	String	The action if an UPDATE rule was specified. This will be Null only if the provider cannot determine the UPDATE_RULE. In most cases, this implies a default of NO ACTION. (see note 2 at end of table).
	DELETE_RULE	String	The action if a DELETE rule was specified. This will be Null if the provider cannot determine the DELETE_RULE. In most cases, this implies a default of NO ACTION. (see note 2 at end of table).
	DESCRIPTION	String	Human-readable description of the constraint.
adSchemaSchemata	CATALOG_NAME	String	Catalog name, or Null if the provider does not support catalogs.
	SCHEMA_NAME	String	Unqualified schema name.
	SCHEMA_OWNER	String	User that owns the schemas.

Schema	Column Headers	Data Type	Description
	DEFAULT_CHARACTER _SET_CATALOG	String	Catalog name of the default character set for columns and domains in the schemas, or Null if the provider does not support catalogs or different character sets.
	DEFAULT_CHARACTER _SET_SCHEMA	String	Unqualified schema name of the default character set for columns and domains in the schemas, or Null if the provider does not support different character sets.
	DEFAULT_CHARACTER _SET_NAME	String	Default character set name, or Null if the provider does not support different character sets.
adSchemaSQL _Languages	SQL_LANGUAGE _SOURCE	String	Should be "ISO 9075" for standard SQL.
	SQL_LANGUAGE_YEAR	String	Should be "1992" for ANSI SQL92-compliant SQL.
	SQL_LANGUAGE _CONFORMANCE	String	The language conformance level. (see note 4 at end of table).
	SQL_LANGUAGE _INTEGRITY	String	This will be **Yes** if optional integrity feature is supported, or **No** if optional integrity feature is not supported.
	SQL_LANGUAGE _IMPLEMENTATION	String	Null for "ISO 9075" implementation.
	SQL_LANGUAGE _BINDING_STYLE	String	"DIRECT" for C/C++ callable direct execution of SQL.

Table Continued on Following Page

Schema	Column Headers	Data Type	Description
	SQL_LANGUAGE _PROGRAMMING _LANGUAGE	String	Null.
adSchemaStatistics	TABLE_CATALOG	String	Catalog name, or Null if the provider does not support catalogs.
	TABLE_SCHEMA	String	Schema name, or Null if the provider does not support schemas.
	TABLE_NAME	String	Table name.
	CARDINALITY	Unsigned Big Integer	Cardinality (number of rows) of the table.
adSchemaTable _Constraints	CONSTRAINT _CATALOG	String	Catalog name, or Null if the provider does not support catalogs.
	CONSTRAINT_SCHEMA	String	Schema name, or Null if the provider does not support schemas.
	CONSTRAINT_NAME	String	Constraint name.
	TABLE_CATALOG	String	Catalog name in which the table is defined, or Null if the provider does not support catalogs.
	TABLE_SCHEMA	String	Unqualified schema name in which the table is defined, or Null if the provider does not support schemas.
	TABLE_NAME	String	Table name.
	CONSTRAINT_TYPE	String	The constraint type. (see note 5 at end of table).
	IS_DEFERRABLE	Boolean	**True** if the table constraint is , or **False** if the table constraint is not, deferrable.

Schema	Column Headers	Data Type	Description
	INITIALLY_DEFERRED	Boolean	**True** if the table constraint is initially deferred, or **False** if the table constraint is initially immediate.
	DESCRIPTION	String	Column description
adSchemaTable _Privileges	GRANTOR	String	User who granted the privileges on the table in TABLE_NAME.
	GRANTEE	String	User name (or "PUBLIC") to whom the privilege has been granted.
	TABLE_CATALOG	String	Catalog name in which the table is defined, or Null if the provider does not support catalogs.
	TABLE_SCHEMA	String	Unqualified schema name in which the table is defined, or Null if the provider does not support schemas.
	TABLE_NAME	String	Table name.
	PRIVILEGE_TYPE	String	Privilege type. Can be one of the following values: SELECT, DELETE, INSERT, UPDATE, REFERENCE.
	IS_GRANTABLE	Boolean	**False** if the privilege being described was granted with the WITH GRANT OPTION clause, or **True** if the privilege being described was not granted with the WITH GRANT OPTION clause.
adSchemaTables	TABLE_CATALOG	String	Catalog name, or Null if the provider does not support catalogs.

Table Continued on Following Page

465

Schema	Column Headers	Data Type	Description
	TABLE_SCHEMA	String	Schema name, or Null if the provider does not support schemas.
	TABLE_NAME	String	Table name. This column cannot contain a Null.
	TABLE_TYPE	String	Table type. This column cannot contain a Null. (see note 6 at end of table).
	TABLE_GUID	GUID	GUID that uniquely identifies the table. Providers that do not use GUIDs to identify tables should return Null in this column.
	DESCRIPTION	String	Human-readable description of the table, or Null if there is no description associated with the column.
	TABLE_PROPID	Long	Property ID of the table. Providers which do not use PROPIDs to identify columns should return Null in this column.
	DATE_CREATED	Date/Time	Date when the table was created or Null if the provider does not have this information.
	DATE_MODIFIED	Date/Time	Date when the table definition was last modified or Null if the provider does not have this information.
adSchema _Translations	TRANSLATION _CATALOG	String	Catalog name, or Null if the provider does not support catalogs.
	TRANSLATION _SCHEMA	String	Schema name, or Null if the provider does not support schemas.
	TRANSLATION_NAME	String	Translation name.

Schema	Column Headers	Data Type	Description
	SOURCE_CHARACTER _SET_CATALOG	String	Catalog name containing the source character set on which the translation is defined, or Null if the provider does not support catalogs.
	SOURCE_CHARACTER _SET_SCHEMA	String	Unqualified schema name containing the source character set on which the translation is defined, or Null if the provider does not support schemas.
	SOURCE_CHARACTER _SET_NAME	String	Source character set name on which the translation is defined.
	TARGET_CHARACTER _SET_CATALOG	String	Catalog name containing the target character set on which the translation is defined, or Null if the provider does not support catalogs.
	TARGET_CHARACTER _SET_SCHEMA	String	Unqualified schema name containing the target character set on which the translation is defined, or Null if the provider does not support schemas.
	TARGET_CHARACTER _SET_NAME	String	Target character set name on which the translation is defined.
adSchemaUsage _Privileges	GRANTOR	String	User who granted the privileges on the object in OBJECT_NAME.
	GRANTEE	String	User name (or "PUBLIC") to whom the privilege has been granted.
	OBJECT_CATALOG	String	Catalog name in which the object is defined, or Null if the provider does not support catalogs.

Table Continued on Following Page

Schema	Column Headers	Data Type	Description
	OBJECT_SCHEMA	String	Unqualified schema name in which the object is defined, or Null if the provider does not support schemas.
	OBJECT_NAME	String	Object name.
	OBJECT_TYPE	String	Object type. (see note 7 at end of table).
	PRIVILEGE_TYPE	String	Privilege type.
	IS_GRANTABLE	Boolean	**True** if the privilege being described was granted with the WITH GRANT OPTION clause, or **False** if the privilege being described was not granted with the WITH GRANT OPTION clause.
adSchemaView _ColumnUsage	VIEW_CATALOG	String	Catalog name, or Null if the provider does not support catalogs.
	VIEW_SCHEMA	String	Schema name, or Null if the provider does not support schemas.
	VIEW_NAME	String	View name.
	TABLE_CATALOG	String	Catalog name in which the table is defined, or Null if the provider does not support catalogs.
	TABLE_SCHEMA	String	Schema name in which the table is defined, or Null if the provider does not support schemas.
	TABLE_NAME	String	Table name.
	COLUMN_NAME	String	Column name.
	COLUMN_GUID	GUID	Column GUID.
	COLUMN_PROPID	Long	Column property ID.
adSchemaView _TableUsage	VIEW_CATALOG	String	Catalog name, or Null if the provider does not support catalogs.

Schema	Column Headers	Data Type	Description
	VIEW_SCHEMA	String	Schema name, or Null if the provider does not support schemas.
	VIEW_NAME	String	View name.
	TABLE_CATALOG	String	Catalog name in which the table is defined, or Null if the provider does not support catalogs.
	TABLE_SCHEMA	String	Schema name in which the table is defined, or Null if the provider does not support schemas.
	TABLE_NAME	String	Table name.
adSchemaViews	TABLE_CATALOG	String	Catalog name, or Null if the provider does not support catalogs.
	TABLE_SCHEMA	String	Schema name, or Null if the provider does not support schemas.
	TABLE_NAME	String	View name.
	VIEW_DEFINITION	String	View definition. This is a query expression.
	CHECK_OPTION	Boolean	**True** if local update checking only, or **False** for cascaded update checking (same as no CHECK OPTION specified on view definition).
	IS_UPDATABLE	Boolean	**True** if the view is updateable, or **False** if the view is not updateable.
	DESCRIPTION	String	View description
	DATE_CREATED	Date/Time	Date when the view was created or Null if the provider does not have this information.
	DATE_MODIFIED	Date/Time	Date when the view definition was last modified or Null if the provider does not have this information.

Notes:

1. CHARACTER_MAXIMUM_LENGTH will vary depending upon the data type of the column: for character, binary or bit columns, this is one of the following:

    ❑ The maximum length of the column in characters, bytes or bits respectively, if one is defined. For example, a CHAR(5) column in a SQL table has a maximum length of five (5).

    ❑ The maximum length of the data type in characters, bytes or bits respectively, if the column does not have a defined length.

    ❑ Zero (0) if neither the column nor the data type has a defined maximum length.

It will be Null for all other types of columns.

2. For UPDATE_RULE and DELETE_RULE, the values will be one of the following: CASCADE, SET NULL, SET DEFAULT, NO ACTION.

3. For MATCH_OPTION, the values will be one of the following: NONE (no match), PARTIAL, FULL.

4. SQL_LANGUAGE_CONFORMANCE will be one of the following values: ENTRY, INTERMEDIATE, FULL.

5. CONSTRAINT_TYPE will be one of the following values: UNIQUE, PRIMARY KEY, FOREIGN KEY, CHECK.

6. TABLE_TYPE will be one of the following values: ALIAS, TABLE, SYNONYM, SYSTEM TABLE, VIEW, GLOBAL TEMPORARY, LOCAL TEMPORARY.

7. OBJECT_TYPE will be one of the following values: DOMAIN, CHARACTER SET, COLLATION, TRANSLATION.

Schema Usage

Schemas are mainly used to obtain catalog or database information from the provider. All that is needed is the use of the OpenSchema method of the Connecton object. Calling this method returns a Recordset object containing the required information. For example to list all the tables in a particular connection:

```
Set objRec=objConn.OpenSchema (adSchemaTables)
While Not objRec.EOF
    Print objRec("TABLE_NAME")
    ObjRec.MoveNext
Wend
```

This simply opens a recordset on the tables schema and loops through it printing each table name. You could use the TABLE_TYPE column to check for system tables:

```
Set objRec=objConn.OpenSchema (adSchemaTables)
While Not objRec.EOF
            If objRec("TABLE_TYPE")<>"SYSTEM_TABLE" Then
        Print objRec("TABLE_NAME")

            End if
        ObjRec.MoveNext
Wend
```

The OpenSchema may take a Restrictions argument that will limit the returned values to the required rows. This can be done through an array that matches the column names. For example, to find only the system tables:

```
Set objRec=objConn.OpenSchema (adSchemaTables, Array(Empty, Empty,_
Empty, "SYSTEM_TABLES"))
```

Since the type is the fourth column of the recordset, you need to specify empty values for the columns you wish to skip.

When connecting to Microsoft Access you should be aware of a few things. First if you wish to view the queries you might have to use both the adSchemaProcedures and adSchemaViews depending upon the query type: normal Select queries appear as views, whereas action queries (UPDATE, DELETE,etc...) and CrossTab queries appear as procedures. This is only for the native Jet provider. For the ODBC provider, Select and Crosstab queries appear as tables with a table type of VIEW.

OLE DB Providers

This appendix will help you find and connect to the most common Microsoft OLE DB providers on your machine. The appendix also provides information about companies that make OLE DB providers for various types of data types and platforms. Several of the company web sites listed below contain product demos and offer product evaluation downloads.

How do I know what OLE DB Providers are on my machine?

To find out what OLE DB Providers are on your machine:

1. Open your Windows or NT Explorer (not IE).

2. Right click in the file list frame.

3. Select New | Microsoft Data Link.

4. Enter a name for the data link (you can leave the default).

5. Right click the data link and select Properties from the popup menu.

6. After the Data Link file's property dialog box appears, click on the Provider Tab (see the screenshot below). This will list the providers available on your machine.

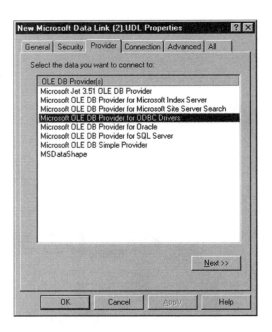

Common Microsoft OLE DB Providers

Listed below are some example connection strings for the common Microsoft OLE DB providers available at the time of going to press. In addition, here are some websites you can check for provider updates and providers for new software releases:

❑   http://www.microsoft.com/data/reference/ado2/mdaprv01_99m7.htm
❑   http://www.microsoft.com/data/reference/oledb2/sdkprovidersoverview_5yk7.htm
❑   http://premium.microsoft.com/msdn/library/sdkdoc/dasdk/ado/mdrefadoprovinfo.htm

Microsoft Jet 3.51 OLE DB Provider

A sample connection string is:

```
Provider = Microsoft.Jet.OLEDB.3.51;
         Data Source=C:\Program Files\DevStudio\VB\Nwind.mdb
```

Microsoft OLE DB Provider for Microsoft Index Server

A sample connection string is:

```
Provider = MSIDXS;Data Source=web;Locale Identifier=1033
```

Microsoft OLE DB Provider for ODBC Drivers

A sample connection string with a DSN is:

```
Provider = MSDASQL.1;User ID=scott;Data Source=OraTest
```

A sample DSN-less connection string is:

```
Provider=MSDASQL.1;Extended Properties="driver={SQL Server};
        server=Odysseus;database=pubs;uid=sa; "
```

Microsoft OLE DB Provider for Oracle

A sample connection string is:

```
Provider=MSDAORA.1; Password=tiger;User ID=scott;Data Source=2:
```

Microsoft OLE DB Provider for SQL Server

A sample connection string is:

```
Provider=SQLOLEDB.1;Password=foo;User ID=sa;Initial Catalog=pubs;
        Data Source=ODYSSEUS
```

Microsoft OLE DB Provider for Microsoft Active Directory Service

For this provider the `Provider` property of the connection string needs to be set to `ADSDSOObject`.

Third Party Offerings

Here are some third party OLE DB providers. You can find a complete and current list on the Microsoft web site at http://www.microsoft.com/data/oledb/products/prod640.htm

Company Name and Web Address	Product	Description
Applied Information Sciences, Inc. *http://www.uniaccess.com/products*	AIS UniAccess for OS 2200	Supports access to a variety of Unisys OS 2200 mainframe information sources, including relational and non-relational data.
ASNA *http://www.asna.com/*	Acceler8-DB and DataGate/400	Acceler8DB for Windows and AS/400 systems follows the DB2/400 model used on AS/400s to store and present data via physical and logical files. DataGate/400 for Windows lets you access DB2/400 databases through an AS/400 server.

Table Continued on Following Page

475

Company Name and Web Address	Product	Description
Blue Angel Technologies *http://www.blueangeltech.com*	MetaDoor Provider	MetaDoor Provider supplies a Z39.50-compliant OLE DB Service Provider. Z39.50 enables uniform access to diverse information sources..
IBM *http://www.as400.ibm.com/clientaccess/oledb/*	Client Access for Windows 95/NT SDK	DB2/400 and AS/400
Intersolv *http://www.microfocus.com/products/data.htm*	DataDirect Connect OLE DB and DataDirect SequeLink OLE DB Edition	DataDirect Connect OLE DB provides access to non-SQL or MAP-based data stores. The product allows any ADO or OLE DB-enabled application to access and combine data from multiple sources through a single standard interface. Supported server platforms include Windows NT and Unix. DataDirect SequeLink OLE DB Edition provides access to relational databases. Supported platforms include Windows 95/98/NT, AS/400, Digital UNIX, DG Aviion, HP-UX, IBM-AIX, OS/390, Sinix, and Sun Solaris.
ISG *http://www.isgsoft.com*	ISG Navigator	ISG Navigator is supported across multiple platforms. ISG Navigator-based solutions work with relational database management systems, indexed sequential files, and hierarchical databases. They also interact with flat files, spreadsheets, mail folders, and many other data sources.
MetaWise *http://www.metawise.com*	MetaWise DP	A component of MetaWise DAO, that can access AS/400 and VSAM files through a Windows NT or Windows 95 client.
Sequiter *http://www.sequiter.com/products/oledb-info.htm*	CodeBase OLE DB Data Provider (currently in beta testing; available Spring 1999)	The CodeBase OLE DB Data Provider is xBASE-compatible and runs on a variety of platforms.

Oracle Tables and Functions

This appendix has been compiled with a developer in mind, and contains some useful common information for programming against Oracle. The purpose of ADO is to abstract the database from the code as much as possible; however, when we sit down to write code we also need to look at the data. This appendix provides two types of information that I have found useful in this context:

- ❑   Common Data Dictionary Tables
- ❑   Common Functions

The Data Dictionary tables are extremely useful when you need metadata (that is, data about your data), and while that might seem obscure, there will come a time when you'll really need to know this information. The listing here of the Data Dictionary objects is not exhaustive, it only includes the ones that you may need the most. The same applies to the functions.

> *In fact I excluded the string functions, simply because VBScript and VB do so much already for you, that I cannot see much need for server-side string functions. Just know that they exist.*

For more information on Oracle I recommend *Essential Oracle* by Tom Luers, published by Sams. (It's currently out of print but if you can find a copy it's a great concise book.) There is also a forthcoming book from Wrox on VB and Oracle (ISBN 1861001789).

Selections From the Data Dictionary

The Data Dictionary is your way to access much of the metadata in Oracle. The tables depicted here are all DBA views, but many are available to non-DBA users. Not all of the Data Dictionary tables are included, only the ones that might be the most helpful to the developer. Remember, if anyone asks you to do too much with the data, remind them that you're a developer, not a DBA! The ones available to all users are prefixed with USER_ or ALL_.

Storage Tables

The tables in this section are used to query database storage and available space.

DBA_TABLESPACES

Description of all tablespaces in the database.

Structure

Column Name	Type
TABLESPACE_NAME	VARCHAR2(30)
INITIAL_EXTENT	NUMBER
NEXT_EXTENT	NUMBER
MIN_EXTENTS	NUMBER
MAX_EXTENTS	NUMBER
PCT_INCREASE	NUMBER
STATUS	VARCHAR2(9)
CONTENTS	VARCHAR2(9)

Usage

```
select * from USER_TABLESPACES
```
or
```
select * from DBA_TABLESPACES
```

DBA_FREE_SPACE

Free extents in all tablespaces. The values returned depend on the user's permissions.

Structure

Column Name	Type
TABLESPACE_NAME	VARCHAR2(30)
FILE_ID	NUMBER
BLOCK_ID	NUMBER
BYTES	NUMBER
BLOCKS	NUMBER

Usage

```
    select * from USER_FREE_SPACE
or
    select * from DBA_FREE_SPACE
```

DBA_ROLLBACK_SEGS

Exposes the rollback segment information.

Structure

Column Name	Type
SEGMENT_NAME	VARCHAR2(30)
OWNER	VARCHAR2(6)
TABLESPACE_NAME	VARCHAR2(30)
SEGMENT_ID	NUMBER
FILE_ID	NUMBER
BLOCK_ID	NUMBER
INITIAL_EXTENT	NUMBER
NEXT_EXTENT	NUMBER
MIN_EXTENTS	NUMBER
MAX_EXTENTS	NUMBER
PCT_INCREASE	NUMBER
STATUS	VARCHAR2(16)
INSTANCE_NUM	VARCHAR2(40)

Usage

```
    select * from DBA_ROLLBACK_SEGS
```

DBA_TS_QUOTAS

Exposes tablespace quotas for all users.

Structure

Column Name	Type
TABLESPACE_NAME	VARCHAR2(30)
USERNAME	VARCHAR2(30)
BYTES	NUMBER
MAX_BYTES	NUMBER
BLOCK	NUMBER
MAX_BLOCKS	NUMBER

Usage

```
select * from USER_TS_QUOTAS
```

or

```
select * from DBA_TS_QUOTAS
```

DBA_SEGMENTS

Provides information about storage allocation for all database segments.

Structure

Column Name	Type
OWNER	VARCHAR2(30)
SEGMENT_NAME	VARCHAR2(81)
SEGMENT_TYPE	VARCHAR2(17)
TABLESPACE_NAME	VARCHAR2(30)
HEADER_FILE	NUMBER
HEADER_BLOCK	NUMBER
BYTES	NUMBER
BLOCKS	NUMBER
EXTENTS	NUMBER
INITIAL_EXTENT	NUMBER
NEXT_EXTENT	NUMBER

Column Name	Type
MIN_EXTENTS	NUMBER
MAX_EXTENTS	NUMBER
PCT_INCREASE	NUMBER
FREELISTS	NUMBER
FREELIST_GROUPS	NUMBER

Usage

```
select * from USER_SEGMENTS
```

or

```
select * from DBA_SEGMENTS
```

DBA_EXTENTS

Shows you the extents of all the segments in the database.

Structure

Column Name	Type
OWNER	VARCHAR2(30)
SEGMENT_NAME	VARCHAR2(81)
SEGMENT_TYPE	VARCHAR2(17)
TABLESPACE_NAME	VARCHAR2(30)
EXTENT_ID	NUMBER
FILE_ID	NUMBER
BLOCK_ID	NUMBER
BYTES	NUMBER
BLOCKS	NUMBER

Usage

```
select * from USER_EXTENTS
```

or

```
select * from DBA_EXTENTS
```

DBA_DATA_FILES

This table exposes information about database files.

Structure

Column Name	Type
FILE_NAME	VARCHAR2(257)
FILE_ID	NUMBER
TABLESPACE_NAME	VARCHAR2(30)
BYTES	NUMBER
BLOCKS	NUMBER
STATUS	VARCHAR2(9)

Usage

```
select * from DBA_DATA_FILES
```

Security Tables

These tables supply metadata on database security.

DBA_USERS

This table exposes information for all the users of the database. Note that the user might not have access rights to some of the tables.

Structure

Column Name	Type
USERNAME	VARCHAR2(30)
USER_ID	NUMBER
PASSWORD	VARCHAR2(30)
DEFAULT_TABLESPACE	VARCHAR2(30)
TEMPORARY_TABLESPACE	VARCHAR2(30)
CREATED	DATE
PROFILE	VARCHAR2(30)

Usage

```
select * from USER_USERS
```

or

```
select * from DBA_USERS
```

DBA_TAB_PRIVS

Displays all the grants on the database objects.

Structure

Column Name	Type
GRANTEE	VARCHAR2(30)
OWNER	VARCHAR2(30)
TABLE_NAME	VARCHAR2(30)
GRANTOR	VARCHAR2(30)
PRIVILEGE	VARCHAR2(40)
GRANTABLE	VARCHAR2(3)

Usage

```
select * from USER_TAB_PRIVS
```

or

```
select * from DBA_TAB_PRIVS
```

DBA_SYS_PRIVS

Displays the description of system access granted to users and to roles.

Structure

Column Name	Type
GRANTEE	VARCHAR2(30)
PRIVILEGE	VARCHAR2(40)
ADMIN_OPTION	VARCHAR2(3)

Usage

```
select * from USER_SYS_PRIVS
```

or

```
select * from DBA_SYS_PRIVS
```

DBA_PROFILES

This table shows the resource limits for each profile.

Structure

Column Name	Type
PROFILE	VARCHAR2(30)
RESOURCE_NAME	VARCHAR2(32)
LIMIT	VARCHAR2(40)

Usage

```
select * from DBA_PROFILES
```

DBA_ROLES

Exposes all roles that are in the database.

Structure

Column Name	Type
ROLE	VARCHAR2(30)
PASSWORD_REQUIRED	VARCHAR2(8)

Usage

```
select * from DBA_ROLES
```

DBA_ROLE_PRIVS

Exposes a list of users and their roles (and roles that have role grants).

Structure

Column Name	Type
GRANTEE	VARCHAR2(30)
GRANTED_ROLE	VARCHAR2(30)
ADMIN_OPTION	VARCHAR2(3)
DEFAULT_ROLE	VARCHAR2(3)

Usage

```
select * from USER_ROLE_PRIVS
```

or

```
select * from DBA_ROLE_PRIVS
```

Procedure and Trigger Tables

One-stop shopping for procedure and trigger information.

DBA_TRIGGERS

Exposes trigger descriptions across the entire database or user.

Structure

Column Name	Type
OWNER	VARCHAR2(30)
TRIGGER_NAME	VARCHAR2(30)
TRIGGER_TYPE	VARCHAR2(16)
TRIGGERING_EVENT	VARCHAR2(26)
TABLE_OWNER	VARCHAR2(30)
TABLE_NAME	VARCHAR2(30)
REFERENCING_NAMES	VARCHAR2(87)
WHEN_CLAUSE	VARCHAR2(2000)
STATUS	VARCHAR2(8)
DESCRIPTION	VARCHAR2(2000)
TRIGGER_BODY	LONG

Usage

```
   select * from USER_TRIGGERS
or
   select * from DBA_TRIGGERS
```

DBA_OBJECT_SIZE

Exposes all PL/SQL objects (i.e. indexes, packages, tables, views, etc.) defined in the database or user.

Structure

Column Name	Type
OWNER	VARCHAR2(30)
NAME	VARCHAR2(30)
TYPE	VARCHAR2(12)

Table Continued on Following Page

Column Name	Type
SOURCE_SIZE	NUMBER
PARSED_SIZE	NUMBER
CODE_SIZE	NUMBER
ERROR_SIZE	NUMBER

Usage

```
select * from USER_OBJECT_SIZE
```
or
```
select * from DBA_OBJECT_SIZE
```

DBA_TRIGGER_COLS

Displays what columns in the database are touched by triggers.

Structure

Column Name	Type
TRIGGER_OWNER	VARCHAR2(30)
TRIGGER_NAME	VARCHAR2(30)
TABLE_OWNER	VARCHAR2(30)
TABLE_NAME	VARCHAR2(30)
COLUMN_NAME	VARCHAR2(30)
COLUMN_LIST	VARCHAR2(3)
COLUMN_USAGE	VARCHAR2(17)

Usage

```
select * from USER_TRIGGER_COLS
```
or
```
select * from DBA_TRIGGER_COLS
```

DBA_SOURCE

Source location of all stored objects (packages, stored procedures, etc.) in the database.

Structure

Column Name	Type
OWNER	VARCHAR2(30)
NAME	VARCHAR2(30)
TYPE	VARCHAR2(12)
LINE	NUMBER
TEXT	VARCHAR2(2000)

Usage

```
select * from USER_SOURCE
```

or

```
select * from DBA_SOURCE
```

DBA_ERRORS

Displays a list of current errors in all stored objects on the database.

Structure

Column Name	Type
OWNER	VARCHAR2(30)
NAME	VARCHAR2(30)
TYPE	VARCHAR2(12)
SEQUENCE	NUMBER
LINE	NUMBER
POSITION	NUMBER
TEXT	VARCHAR2(2000)

Usage

```
select * from USER_ERRORS
```

or

```
select * from DBA_ERRORS
```

DBA_DEPENDENCIES

Exposes the dependencies of all objects in the database.

Structure

Column Name	Type
OWNER	VARCHAR2(30)
NAME	VARCHAR2(30)
TYPE	VARCHAR2(12)
REFERENCED_OWNER	VARCHAR2(30)
REFERENCED_NAME	VARCHAR2(30)
REFERENCED_TYPE	VARCHAR2(12)
REFERENCED_LINK_NAME	VARCHAR2(128)

Usage

```
select * from USER_DEPENDENCIES
```
or
```
select * from DBA_DEPENDENCIES
```

Object Tables

The tables that hold metadata on all the database tables, sequences, view, and other objects.

DBA_CATALOG

Displays a catalog of all tables, views, synonyms, and sequences.

Structure

Column Name	Type
TABLE_NAME	VARCHAR2(30)
TABLE_TYPE	VARCHAR2(11)

Usage

```
select * from USER_CATALOG
```
or
```
select * from DBA_CATALOG
```

DBA_OBJECTS

Displays all clusters, views, tables, synonyms, sequences, database links, packages, package bodies, and indexes for the database or for the user.

Structure

Column Name	Type
OWNER	VARCHAR2(30)
OBJECT_NAME	VARCHAR2(128)
OBJECT_ID	NUMBER
OBJECT_TYPE	VARCHAR2(13)
CREATED	DATE
LAST_DDL_TIME	DATE
TIMESTAMP	VARCHAR2(75)
STATUS	VARCHAR2(7)

Usage

```
    select * from USER_OBJECTS
```
or
```
    select * from DBA_OBJECTS
```

Column Tables

These supply metadata for columns of all tables.

DBA_COL_PRIVS

Shows grant information on all the columns of the database.

Structure

Column Name	Type
GRANTEE	VARCHAR2(30)
OWNER	VARCHAR2(30)
TABLE_NAME	VARCHAR2(30)
COLUMN_NAME	VARCHAR2(30)
GRANTOR	VARCHAR2(30)
PRIVILEGE	VARCHAR2(40)
GRANTABLE	VARCHAR2(3)

Usage

```
    select * from USER_COL_PRIVS
```
or
```
    select * from DBA_COL_PRIVS
```

DBA_CONSTRAINTS

Exposes all constraints placed on all the tables in the database or for the user.

Structure

Column Name	Type
OWNER	VARCHAR2(30)
CONSTRAINT_NAME	VARCHAR2(30)
CONSTRAINT_TYPE	VARCHAR2(1)
TABLE_NAME	VARCHAR2(30)
SEARCH_CONDITION	LONG
R_OWNER	VARCHAR2(30)
R_CONSTRAINT_NAME	VARCHAR2(30)
DELETE_RULE	VARCHAR2(9)
STATUS	VARCHAR2(8)

Usage

```
select * from USER_CONSTRAINTS
```

or

```
select * from DBA_CONSTRAINTS
```

DBA_TAB_COLUMNS

Exposes the column definitions for all tables, views, and clusters.

Structure

Column Name	Type
OWNER	VARCHAR2(30)
TABLE_NAME	VARCHAR2(30)
COLUMN_NAME	VARCHAR2(30)
DATA_TYPE	VARCHAR2(9)
DATA_LENGTH	NUMBER
DATA_PRECISION	NUMBER
DATA_SCALE	NUMBER
NULLABLE	VARCHAR2(1)

Column Name	Type
COLUMN_ID	NUMBER
DEFAULT_LENGTH	NUMBER
DATA_DEFAULT	LONG
NUM_DISTINCT	NUMBER
LOW_VALUE	RAW(32)
HIGH_VALUE	RAW(32)
DENSITY	NUMBER
NUM_NULLS	NUMBER
NUM_BUCKETS	NUMBER
LAST_ANALYZED	DATE
SAMPLE_SIZE	NUMBER

Usage

```
select * from USER_TAB_COLUMNS
```

or

```
select * from DBA_TAB_COLUMNS
```

Table Tables

Information about tables is at your code's fingertips.

DBA_TAB_COMMENTS

Provides extra information about all the tables in the database.

Structure

Column Name	Type
OWNER	VARCHAR2(30)
TABLE_NAME	VARCHAR2(30)
TABLE_TYPE	VARCHAR2(11)
COMMENTS	VARCHAR2(2000)

Usage

```
select * from USER_TAB_COMMENTS
```

or

```
select * from DBA_TAB_COMMENTS
```

DBA_TABLES

Exposes information on all the tables in the database.

Structure

Column Name	Type
OWNER	VARCHAR2(30)
TABLE_NAME	VARCHAR2(30)
TABLESPACE_NAME	VARCHAR2(30)
CLUSTER_NAME	VARCHAR2(30)
PCT_FREE	NUMBER
PCT_USED	NUMBER
INI_TRANS	NUMBER
MAX_TRANS	NUMBER
INITIAL_EXTENT	NUMBER
NEXT_EXTENT	NUMBER
MIN_EXTENTS	NUMBER
MAX_EXTENTS	NUMBER
PCT_INCREASE	NUMBER
FREELISTS	NUMBER
FREELIST_GROUPS	NUMBER
BACKED_UP	VARCHAR2(1)
NUM_ROWS	NUMBER
BLOCKS	NUMBER
EMPTY_BLOCKS	NUMBER
AVG_SPACE	NUMBER
CHAIN_CNT	NUMBER
AVG_ROW_LEN	NUMBER
DEGREE	VARCHAR2(10)
INSTANCES	VARCHAR2(10)
CACHE	VARCHAR2(5)
TABLE_LOCK	VARCHAR2(8)

Usage

```
    select * from USER_TABLES
```
or
```
    select * from DBA_TABLES
```

Synonym, View, and Sequence Tables

These are *very* helpful when you are trying to get into the data and you need to see what you have out there.

DBA_SYNONYMS

Displays all synonyms in the database or defined for the user.

Structure

Column Name	Type
OWNER	VARCHAR2(30)
SYNONYM_NAME	VARCHAR2(30)
TABLE_OWNER	VARCHAR2(30)
TABLE_NAME	VARCHAR2(30)
DB_LINK	VARCHAR2(128)

Usage

```
    select * from USER_SYNONYMS
```
or
```
    select * from DBA_SYNONYMS
```

DBA_VIEWS

Provides you with a detailed listing of views in the database or for the user.

Structure

Column Name	Type
OWNER	VARCHAR2(30)
VIEW_NAME	VARCHAR2(30)
TEXT_LENGTH	NUMBER
TEXT	LONG

Usage

```
    select * from USER_VIEWS
```
or
```
    select * from DBA_VIEWS
```

DBA_SEQUENCES

Displays information about all the sequences tables in the database or for a user.

Structure

Column Name	Type
SEQUENCE_OWNER	VARCHAR2(30)
SEQUENCE_NAME	VARCHAR2(30)
MIN_VALUE	NUMBER
MAX_VALUE	NUMBER
INCREMENT_BY	NUMBER
CYCLE_FLAG	VARCHAR2(1)
ORDER_FLAG	VARCHAR2(1)
CACHE_SIZE	NUMBER
LAST_NUMBER	NUMBER

Usage

```
select * from USER_SEQUENCES
```
or
```
select * from DBA_SEQUENCES
```

Common Functions

These sections point out some common functions that are available to you when programming with Oracle.

Conversion Functions

When programming against Oracle the conversion functions come into play quite often. For instance, Oracle is not as forgiving as some databases on dates, so I always use the to_date function when saving dates.

Function	Usage and Description	Example

TO_CHAR	`TO_CHAR(input[,format])`
	
	Converts a number or a date into a character.
		`select to_char(786,'999.99') from dual`
		
		Result:
		
		`TO_CHAR`
		
		`-------`
		
		` 786.00`

TO_DATE	`TO_DATE(string[,format])`
	
	Always use this when programmatically saving a date.
		`Update MyTable`
		
		`set lastUpdated = to_date('12/16/1998 06:18:13 PM','MM/DD/YYYY HH:MI:SS AM')`
		
		`where MyKey = 'ABCD'`

TO_NUMBER	`TO_NUMBER(char[,format])`
	
	Converts a string to a number
		`select to_number('1700') from dual`
		
		Result:
		
		`TO_NUMBER`
		
		`----------`
		
		`      1700`

Group Functions

Group functions are useful when you need to know composite information about a table or tables.

Function	Usage and Description	Example

AVG	`AVG(COLUMN NAME)`
	
	Returns the average value of the matching expression.
		`select avg(sal) from emp`
		
		Result:
		
		`AVG(SAL)`
		
		`----------`
		
		`2073.21429`

Function	Usage and Description	Example

COUNT	COUNT(Expression)
	
	Returns the number of matching the expression.
		`select count(*) from emp`
		
		Result:
		
		`COUNT(*)`
		`----------`
		`        14`

DISTINCT	DISTINCT(Expression)
	
	Returns the count of unique rows matching the expression
		`select distinct(JOB) from emp`
		
		Result:
		
		`JOB`
		`---------`
		`ANALYST`
		`CLERK`
		`MANAGER`
		`PRESIDENT`
		`SALESMAN`

MAX	MAX(EXPRESSION)
	
	Returns the maximum value of an expression.
		`select MAX(SAL) from emp`
		
		Result:
		
		`MAX(SAL)`
		`----------`
		`      5000`

MIN	MIN(EXPRESSION)
	
	Returns the minimum of the evaluated expression.
		`select MIN(SAL) from emp`
		
		Result:
		
		`MIN(SAL)`
		`----------`
		`       800`

SUM	SUM(EXPRESSION)
	
	Returns the sum of the expression.
		`select SUM(SAL) Payroll from emp`
		
		Result:
		
		`PAYROLL`
		`----------`
		`     29025`

Date Functions

These date functions are great to know about – they can save you a lot of client-side coding.

Function	Usage and Description	Example

ADD_MONTHS	`ADD_MONTHS(Date, Number of Months)`
	
	Returns a date given an initial date and the number of months to add.
		`select add_months (sysdate,2) from dual`
		
		Result:
		
		`ADD_MONTH`
		`---------`
		`16-FEB-99`

LAST_DAY	`LAST_DAY(DATE)`
	
	Calculates the last day of the month specified.
		`select last_day('1-FEB-00') from dual`
		
		Result:
		
		`LAST_DAY`
		`---------`
		`28-FEB-00`

MONTHS_BETWEEN	`MONTHS_BETWEEN (DATE1,DATE2)`
	
	Calculate the months between two dates.
		`select months_between('1-FEB-99','1-DEC-98') from dual`
		
		Result:
		
		`MONTHS_BET`
		`----------`
		`        2`

SYSDATE	`SYSDATE`
	
	Returns the current date.
		`select add_months (sysdate,2) from dual`
		
		Result:
		
		`ADD_MONTH`
		`---------`
		`16-FEB-99`

Number Functions

These number functions are pretty common to all languages.

Function	Usage and Description	Example
| ABS | `ABS(number)`<br><br>Calculates the absolute value. | ```
select abs(-4) from dual
```<br><br>Result:<br><br>```
ABS(-4)
----------
         4
``` |
| POWER | `Power(Number,Exponent)`<br><br>Raises a number to a power | ```
select power(2,37) from dual
```<br><br>Result:<br><br>```
POWER(2,37)
----------
1.3744E+11
``` |
| ROUND | `Round(Number,Precision)`<br><br>Rounds a number | ```
select Round(56.7893,2) from dual
```<br><br>Result:<br><br>```
ROUND(56.7)
----------
     56.79
``` |
| TRUNC | `Trunc(Number,Precision)`<br><br><br>Truncates a number to the desired number of decimal places | ```
select TRUNC(56.7893,2) from dual
```<br><br>Result:<br><br>```
TRUNC(56.7)
----------
     56.78
``` |

ADO 2.0 and RDS 2.0 Enumerators

ADO 2.0 Enumerators

ADO enumerators provide a consistent interface for developers to set properties and to pass and evaluate arguments of methods or events. A side effect of the enumerators is that they make your code more readable and thus more maintainable. For example, it doesn't take a brain surgeon to figure out that if the `CursorLocation` property of a recordset is set to `adUseClient` that we have a client side cursor. However, if we see 3 as its setting, we have to remember that 3 = client side. That is just tracking one setting. Imagine trying to remember all of the settings of all of the properties! You get the point. So with that said, we've included all of the enumerators included in ADO 2.0 in this section as a quick reference table.

Class	Constant	Value
AffectEnum	adAffectAllChapters	4
	adAffectCurrent	1
	adAffectGroup	2
BookMarkEnum	adBookMarkCurrent	0
	adBookMarkFirst	1
	adBookMarkLast	2

Table Continued on Following Page

Class	Constant	Value
CommandTypeEnum	adCmdFile	256
	adCmdStoredProc	4
	adCmdTable	2
	adCmdTableDirect	512
	adCmdText	1
	adCmdUnknown	8
CompareEnum	adCompareEqual	1
	adCompareGreaterThan	2
	adCompareLessThan	0
	adCompareNotComparable	4
	adCompareNotEqual	3
ConnectModeEnum	adModeRead	1
	adModeReadWrite	3
	adModeShareDenyNone	16
	adModeShareDenyRead	4
	adModeShareDenyWrite	8
	adModeShareExclusive	12
	adModeUnknown	0
	adModeWrite	2
ConnectOptionEnum	adAsyncConnect	16
ConnectPromptEnum	adPromptAlways	1
	adPromptComplete	2
	adPromptCompleteRequired	3
	adPromptNever	4
CursorLocationEnum	adUseClient	3
	adUseServer	2

Class	Constant	Value
CursorOptionEnum	adAddNew	16778240
	adApproxPosition	16384
	adBookmark	8192
	adDelete	16779264
	adFind	524288
	adHoldRecords	256
	adMovePrevious	512
	adNotify	262144
	adResync	131072
	adUpdate	16809984
	adUpdateBatch	65536
CursorTypeEnum	adOpenDynamic	2
	AdOpenForwardOnly	0
	adOpenKeyset	1
	adOpenStatic	3
DataTypeEnum	adBigInt	20
	adBinary	128
	adBoolean	11
	adBSTR	8
	adChapter	136
	adChar	129
	adCurrency	6
	adDate	7
	adDBDate	133
	adDBFileTime	137
	adDBTime	134

Table Continued on Following Page

Class	Constant	Value
	adDBTimeStamp	135
	adDecimal	14
	adDouble	5
	adEmpty	0
	adError	10
	adFileTime	64
	adGUID	72
	adIDispatch	9
	adInteger	3
	adIUnknown	13
	adLongVarBinary	205
	adLongVarChar	201
	adLongVarWChar	203
	adNumeric	131
	adPropVariant	138
	adSingle	4
	adSmallInt	2
	adTinyInt	16
	adUnsignedBigInt	21
	adUnsignedInt	19
	adUnsignedSmallInt	18
	adUnsignedTinyInt	17
	adUserDefined	132
	adVarBinary	204
	adVarChar	200
	adVariant	12
	adVarNumeric	139

Class	Constant	Value
	adVarWChar	202
	adWChar	130
EditModeEnum	adEditAdd	2
	adEditDelete	4
	adEditInProgress	1
	adEditNone	0
ErrorValueEnum	adErrBoundToCommand	3707
	adErrDataConversion	3421
	adErrFeatureNotAvailable	3251
	adErrIllegalOperation	3219
	adErrInTransaction	3246
	adErrInvalidArgument	3001
	adErrInvalidConnection	3709
	adErrInvalidParamInfo	3708
	adErrItemNotFound	3265
	adErrNoCurrentRecord	3021
	adErrNotExecuting	3715
	adErrNotReentrant	3710
	adErrObjectClosed	3704
	adErrObjectInCollection	3367
	adErrObjectNotSet	3420
	adErrObjectOpen	3705
	adErrOperationCancelled	3712
	adErrProviderNotFound	3706
	adErrStillConnecting	3713
	adErrStillExecuting	3711
	adErrUnsafeOperation	3716

Table Continued on Following Page

Class	Constant	Value
EventReasonEnum	adRsnAddNew	1
	adRsnClose	9
	adRsnDelete	2
	adRsnFirstChange	11
	adRsnMove	10
	adRsnMoveFirst	12
	adRsnMoveLast	15
	adRsnMoveNext	13
	adRsnMovePrevious	14
	adRsnRequery	7
	adRsnResynch	8
	adRsnUndoAddNew	5
	adRsnUndoDelete	6
	adRsnUndoUpdate	4
	adRsnUpdate	3
EventStatusEnum	adStatusCancel	4
	adStatusCantDeny	3
	adStatusErrorsOccurred	2
	adStatusOK	1
	adStatusUnwantedEvent	5
ExecuteOptionEnum	adAsyncExecute	16
	adAsyncFetch	32
	adAsyncFetchNonBlocking	64
	adExecuteNoRecords	128
	adRunAsync	256

Class	Constant	Value
FieldAttributeEnum	adFldCacheDeferred	4096
	adFldFixed	16
	adFldIsNullable	32
	adFldKeyColumn	32768
	adFldLong	128
	adFldMayBeNull	64
	adFldMayDefer	2
	adFldNegativeScale	16384
	adFldRowID	256
	adFldRowVersion	512
	adFldUnknownUpdatable	8
	adFldUpdatable	4
FilterGroupEnum	adFilterAffectedRecords	2
	adFilterConflictingRecords	5
	adFilterFetchedRecords	3
	adFilterNone	0
	adFilterPendingRecords	1
GetRowsOptionEnum	adGetRowsRest	-1
IsolationLevelEnum	adXactBrowse	256
	adXactChaos	16
	adXactCursorStability	4096
	adXactIsolated	1048576
	adXactReadCommitted	4096
	adXactReadUncommitted	256
	adXactRepeatableRead	65536
	adXactSerializable	1048576
	adXactUnspecified	-1

Table Continued on Following Page

Class	Constant	Value
LockTypeEnum	adLockBatchOptimistic	4
	adLockOptimistic	3
	adLockPessimistic	2
	adLockReadOnly	1
MarshallOptionsEnum	adMarshallAll	0
	adMarshallModifiedOnly	1
ObjectStateEnum	adStateClosed	0
	adStateConnecting	2
	adStateExecuting	4
	adStateFetching	8
	adStateOpen	1
ParameterAttributesEnum	adParamLong	128
	adParamNullable	64
	adParamSigned	16
ParameterDirectionEnum	adParamInput	1
	adParamInputOutput	3
	adParamOutput	2
	adParamReturnValue	4
	adParamUnknown	0
PersistFormatEnum	adPersistADTG	0
PositionEnum	adPosBOF	-2
	adPosEOF	-3
	adPosUnknown	-1
PropertyAttributesEnum	adPropNotSupported	0
	adPropOptional	2
	adPropRead	512
	adPropRequired	1
	adPropWrite	1024

Class	Constant	Value
RecordStatusEnum	adRecCanceled	256
	adRecCantRelease	1024
	adRecConcurrencyViolation	2048
	adRecDBDeleted	262144
	adRecDeleted	4
	adRecIntegrityViolation	4096
	adRecInvalid	16
	adRecMaxChangesExceeded	8192
	adRecModified	2
	adRecMultipleChanges	64
	adRecNew	1
	adRecObjectOpen	16384
	adRecOK	0
	adRecOutOfMemory	32768
	adRecPendingChanges	128
	adRecPermissionDenied	65536
	adRecSchemaViolation	131072
	adRecUnmodified	8
ResyncEnum	adResyncAllValues	2
	adResyncUnderlyingValues	1
SchemaEnum	adSchemaAsserts	0
	adSchemaCatalogs	1
	adSchemaCharacterSets	2
	adSchemaCheckConstraints	5
	adSchemaCollations	3
	adSchemaColumnPrivileges	13
	adSchemaColumns	4

Table Continued on Following Page

Class	Constant	Value
	adSchemaColumnsDomainUsage	11
	adSchemaConstraintColumnUsage	6
	adSchemaConstraintTableUsage	7
	adSchemaCubes	32
	adSchemaDBInfoKeywords	30
	adSchemaDBInfoLiterals	31
	adSchemaDimensions	33
	adSchemaForeignKeys	27
	adSchemaHierarchies	34
	adSchemaIndexes	12
	adSchemaKeyColumnUsage	8
	adSchemaLevels	35
	adSchemaMeasures	36
	adSchemaMembers	38
	adSchemaPrimaryKeys	28
	adSchemaProcedureColumns	29
	adSchemaProcedureParameters	26
	adSchemaProcedures	16
	adSchemaProperties	37
	adSchemaProviderSpecific	-1
	adSchemaProviderTypes	22
	adSchemaReferentialContraints	9
	adSchemaSchemata	17
	adSchemaSQLLanguages	18
	adSchemaStatistics	19
	adSchemaTableConstraints	10
	adSchemaTablePrivileges	14
	adSchemaTables	20

Class	Constant	Value
	adSchemaTranslations	21
	adSchemaUsagePrivileges	15
	adSchemaViewColumnUsage	24
	adSchemaViews	23
	adSchemaViewTableUsage	25
SearchDirectionEnum	adSearchBackward	-1
	adSearchForward	1
StringFormatEnum	adClipString	2
XactAttributeEnum	adXactAbortRetaining	262144
	adXactCommitRetaining	131072

RDS 2.0 Enumerators

RDS enumerators provide a consistent interface for developers, as with ADO 2.0, to set properties and to pass and evaluate arguments of methods or events. In this section, we've listed all of the enumerators included in RDS 2.0 in a quick reference table.

Class	Constant	Value
ADCExecuteOptionEnum	adcExecAsync	2
	adcExecSync	1
ADCFetchOptionEnum	adcFetchAsync	3
	adcFetchBackground	2
	adcFetchUpFront	1
ADCReadyStateEnum	adcReadyStateComplete	4
	adcReadyStateInteractive	3
	adcReadyStateLoaded	2

ADO/RDS Hints and Troubleshooting

As with any development tool, in ADO and RDS there are glitches, pitfalls, tips, tricks, undocumented issues, or problems that are just plain difficult to tackle. Throughout my experiences I have run into several of these issues, all of which caused me some grief. So I've tried to compile these issues and their solutions into this appendix. I know it won't be the solution to all of the pitfalls you cross, but hopefully it will solve a good portion of them. Here is a list of the topics I'll cover in this appendix:

- ❑ MSADC Permissions
- ❑ RDS Custom Business Object Registry Settings
- ❑ Marking Components Safe for Scripting
- ❑ Creating Registry Files
- ❑ Declare RDS Objects without the Object Tag
- ❑ Referencing a Child Recordset of a Hierarchical Cursor
- ❑ Try a Client-Side Cursor
- ❑ Setting the RDS Server Parameter
- ❑ Making IE RDS-Friendly
- ❑ Listing of Properties by Provider

MSADC Permissions

If you receive the error Internet Server Error, you most likely have an access violation. So what do you do? It probably means that you have not set up the proper permissions to some of the MSADC folders. Try making sure that the `C:\Program Files\Common Files\system\MSADC` folder is a valid virtual directory with read and execute (including script) permissions. Also, make sure that the IIS Anonymous user has read and execute (including script) permissions for the `C:\Program Files\Common Files\System` directory and all sub directories.

To check if the `C:\Program Files\Common Files\system\MSADC` folder is a virtual directory on your web site, start by opening the IIS Manager utility from within the Microsoft Management Console (MMC). Then, open your web site and check to see if the MSADC virtual directory exists. The next screenshot shows the MSADC virtual directory after it has been set up.

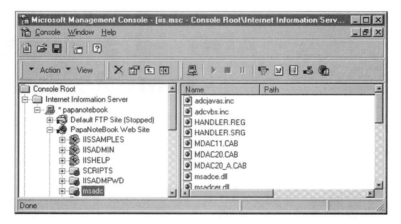

If your MSADC folder is not set up as a virtual directory on your web site, then follow these steps. Right click on the web site in the MMC and select New then Virtual Directory from the popup menus. Then, in the dialog box, enter the name of the virtual directory (MSADC), as shown in the next screenshot. Then click the Next button.

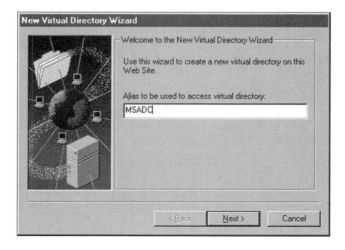

Enter the physical path to the MSADC directory, shown below. Then click the Next button.

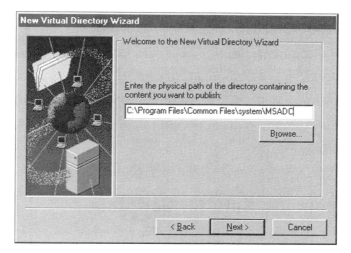

Specify that the MSADC virtual directory should have read, write and execute permissions, as shown in the next screenshot. Then click the Finish button.

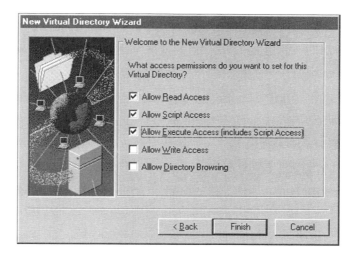

But wait, there is one more step. You've just created the virtual directory, but by default it is created as an application in the web site. You really do not need it to be an application, so you should remove that setting. To do this, right click the MSADC virtual directory and choose Properties from the popup menu. Then, click the Remove button on the Virtual Directory tab and voila! You've done it!

I have seen this occur on several Web servers that I have been called in to tune. Hopefully this will save you some time in your efforts.

RDS Custom Business Object Registry Settings

To successfully launch a custom business object component through a web server, the business object's ProgID must be entered into the registry. This protects the security of your web server by running only valid components. If you receive an error when trying to run your components, make sure you have correctly entered these settings in the server's registry.

To register a custom business object, open the Start menu and select Run from the menu. Then, type RegEdit in the textbox and click OK to open the Registry Editor. Navigate to the HKEY_LOCAL_MACHINE\System\CurrentControlSet\Services\W3SVC\Parameters\ADCL aunch registry key and select the ADCLaunch key. Then, from the Edit menu, point to New and click Key. Finally, type the ProgID (i.e. MyRules.ClassName) of your custom business object and click the Enter key (you can leave the Value entry blank).

Marking Components Safe for Scripting

You can mark your business objects as safe for scripting by the browser, so that your users don't get an IE message box. If you're using VB5.0 or VB6.0 you can use the Setup Wizard or Deployment Wizard respectively. If necessary, you can also edit the registry directly, although it's a good idea to back up your registry files first. To mark the component in the registry as safe for scripting, create the following registry keys:

❑ HKEY_CLASSES_ROOT\CLSID\<MyActiveXGUID>\Implemented
   Categories\{7DD95801-9882-11CF-9FA9-00AA006C42C4}
❑ HKEY_CLASSES_ROOT\CLSID\<MyActiveXGUID>\Implemented
   Categories\{7DD95802-9882-11CF-9FA9-00AA006C42C4}

Just replace the <MyActiveXGUID> with the CLSID of your component.

Creating Registry Files

If you are looking for a simpler way to make multiple registry entries, try using a .REG file that you can create in a text editor such as Notepad. In the registry file, you simply put the REGEDIT4 command at the top of a text file and follow that up with the registry entries. Shown below is a sample of a registry file that creates the entry to allow RDS to create the object in IE and to mark the objects as safe for scripting.

```
REGEDIT4

[HKEY_LOCAL_MACHINE\SYSTEM\CurrentControlSet\Services\W3SVC\Parameters\ADCLaunch\M
yRules.MyFirstClass]
[HKEY_CLASSES_ROOT\CLSID\{AAAA563C-4673-11D2-9B8F-00104B6036A9}\Implemented
Categories\{7DD95801-9882-11CF-9FA9-00AA006C42C4}]
[HKEY_CLASSES_ROOT\CLSID\{AAAA563C-4673-11D2-9B8F-00104B6036A9}\Implemented
Categories\{7DD95802-9882-11CF-9FA9-00AA006C42C4}]

[HKEY_LOCAL_MACHINE\SYSTEM\CurrentControlSet\Services\W3SVC\Parameters\ADCLaunch\
MyRules.MySecondClass]
[HKEY_CLASSES_ROOT\CLSID\{BBBC3A3D-6393-11D2-9BED-00104B6036A9}\Implemented
Categories\{7DD95801-9882-11CF-9FA9-00AA006C42C4}]
[HKEY_CLASSES_ROOT\CLSID\{BBBC3A3D-6393-11D2-9BED-00104B6036A9}\Implemented
Categories\{7DD95802-9882-11CF-9FA9-00AA006C42C4}]
```

Declare RDS Objects without the Object Tag

This isn't a major achievement, but I thought it was worth noting. You normally create an RDS object using the `<OBJECT>` tag. However, we can create the `RDS.DataSpace` object from VBScript as well. So here are your two options:

```
<!-- RDS.DataSpace -->
<OBJECT ID="objDS" HEIGHT="0" CLASSID="CLSID:BD96C556-65A3-11D0-983A-
00C04FC29E36"></OBJECT>
```

or

```
dim objDS
set objDS = CreateObject("RDS.DataSpace")
```

I don't know about you, but the latter method is a lot easier to remember to me!

Referencing a Child Recordset of a Hierarchical Cursor

Referencing a Child Recordset of a Hierarchical Cursor really is not that hard. The only thing that you should keep in here is that you must specify the `Value` property of the `Field` object (in fact Microsoft encourage you to do this for any `Field` object). What I mean is that ADO and AS seem to get confused when you do not specify this property, and assume that they will interpret the default property (which is `Value`). It is an understandable mistake - I made it. If this is confusing, let me show you what not to do and then what to do.

Wrong Way

```
set objChildRS = objParentRS.Fields("MyChapter")
```

Right Way

```
set objChildRS = objParentRS.Fields("MyChapter").Value
```

It is a slight difference that really shouldn't matter, but it will. If you forget, don't worry because ASP will remind you. This is an easy pitfall to avoid, once you have run across it.

Try a Client-Side Cursor

This is not a cure-all, but sometimes when you are getting an error in ADO code you might want to try a client-side cursor (`CursorLocation = adUseClient`). For example, sorting, indexing and disconnected recordsets only work with this type of cursor location. So it is an easy thing to try, but most likely is not the solution for all of your problems. Be careful not to use client-side cursors everywhere as they can be much more resource intensive that server-side cursors.

Setting the RDS Server Parameter

When using the `RDS.DataSpace` object we have to specify the `server` parameter. The `server` parameter indicates the Web server that houses the custom business object that RDS will refer to. Take a look at the code below:

```
set mobjDS = CreateObject("RDS.DataSpace")
strServer = "http://1.2.3.4"
set objMyObject = mobjDS.CreateObject("MyRules.MyObject", strServer)
```

This code creates the `RDS.DataSpace` object and then creates the business object using the IP of the Web server. What IP do you use? Well, you can use the IP of the Web site, ideally. But you have to make sure that your web site has set up the virtual directory to point to the MSADC folder. (Refer back to the section in this Appendix called *MSADC Permissions*)

If you neglect to do this, you will probably get the infamous `Internet Server Error` message. It is such a useful message, don't you think? Well, it means that the IP you gave it either does not exist or does not have the permissions set up for this virtual directory. (Actually, you could use any IP on the machine as long as it has these permissions set up.) This one caused me hours of fun one night. I hope it helps you out of your jam before it begins.

Making IE RDS-Friendly

As we mentioned earlier in the book, the one catch with RDS is that your users' IE browsers must allow for RDS to pass its information to and from their browsers, without violating any security settings. In other words, you could have everything set up correctly on the server and still find RDS won't work! One way to fix this is to lower the settings for the applicable web site from within the client's browser. (I usually distribute a document with these settings and instructions to my clients. Feel free to do the same.) Here is an explanation of the steps to add a web site to your local Intranet zone, and configure the security for this site so that you will have the proper security to access its features.

1. Open Internet Explorer 4.01.

2. Select View | Internet Options from the main menu. You should now be looking at the Internet Options dialog window.

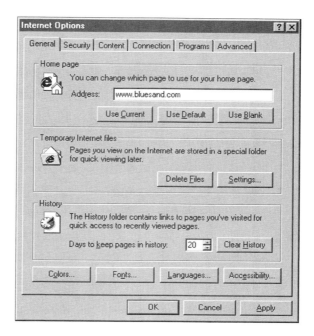

3. Click on the Security tab of the Internet Options dialog window.

4. In the Zone combo box, select the Local Intranet Zone. Here we will add your web site to the protected area of you local Intranet, to relax its security. (Basically this means that we trust this site.)

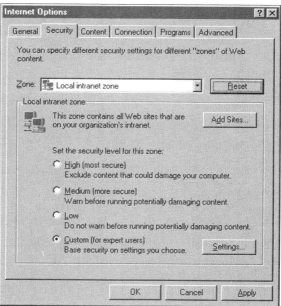

5. Click the Add Sites button to add the web site to your local Intranet. You should be presented with the following dialog box:

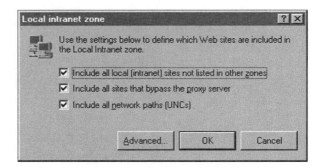

> **Make sure you check all of the boxes on this dialog window, as shown in the screenshot.**

6. Click the Advanced button and type the name of the web site in the space provided. Make sure you precede the site name with http://)

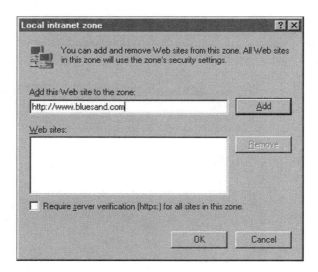

7. Click the Add button to add this web site to your local Intranet zone. Then click the OK button once, and on the next dialog, click the OK button again.

8. Now, back on the Security tab of the Internet Options dialog (shown in step 6 above), choose the Custom security level option and click the Settings button. You will be presented with the Security Settings dialog window.

9. Enable the following options:

   ❑ Download unsigned ActiveX controls
   ❑ Script ActiveX controls marked safe for scripting
   ❑ Initialize and script ActiveX controls not marked safe for scripting
   ❑ Download signed ActiveX controls
   ❑ Run ActiveX controls and plug-ins

10. Click the OK button to save your changes.

11. Then, on the Internet Options dialog window, click the OK button again, and close Internet Explorer.

The next time you use Internet Explorer to browse to that web site, you will have the proper security to access it.

Listing of Properties by Provider

The idea for this section was sparked by David Sussman's and Alex Homer's ADO 2.0 Programmer's Reference, by Wrox. (Thanks guys!) The information they gathered specifies the type of cursor you actually get depending upon the data provider, the CursorLocation, the CursorType and the LockType. Keep in mind that even though you might have asked for a dynamic cursor type, you might get a static cursor. ADO will automatically switch the types on for you, instead of raising an error. However, since this book covers Oracle usage from ADO, I added the information for the OLE DB Provider for Oracle as well.

OLE DB Provider for SQL Server

CursorLocation = adUseServer

Lock Type	Forward-Only cursor requested	Keyset cursor requested	Dynamic cursor requested	Static cursor requested
Read-Only	Forward-Only	Dynamic	Dynamic	Static

Lock Type	Forward-Only cursor requested	Keyset cursor requested	Dynamic cursor requested	Static cursor requested
Pessimistic	Forward-Only	Dynamic	Dynamic	Dynamic
Optimistic	Forward-Only	Dynamic	Dynamic	Dynamic
Batch Optimistic	Forward-Only	Dynamic	Dynamic	Dynamic

CursorLocation = adUseClient

Returned cursor is Static, independent of requested cursor type or lock type.

OLE DB Provider for Jet

CursorLocation = adUseServer

Lock Type	Forward-Only cursor requested	Keyset cursor requested	Dynamic cursor requested	Static cursor requested
Read-Only	Forward-Only	Keyset	Static	Static
Pessimistic	Keyset	Keyset	Keyset	Keyset
Optimistic	Keyset	Keyset	Keyset	Keyset
BatchOptimistic	Keyset	Keyset	Keyset	Keyset

CursorLocation = adUseClient

Returned cursor is Static, independent of requested cursor type or lock type.

OLE DB Provider for Oracle

CursorLocation = adUseServer

Returned cursor is Forward-Only, independent of requested cursor type or lock type.

CursorLocation = adUseClient

Returned cursor is Static, independent of requested cursor type or lock type.

OLE DB Provider for ODBC with SQL Server

CursorLocation = adUseServer

Lock Type	Forward-Only cursor requested	Keyset cursor requested	Dynamic cursor requested	Static cursor requested
Read-Only	Forward-Only	Static	Dynamic	Static
Pessimistic	Forward-Only	Static	Dynamic	Static

Lock Type	Forward-Only cursor requested	Keyset cursor requested	Dynamic cursor requested	Static cursor requested
Optimistic	Forward-Only	Static	Dynamic	Static
Batch Optimistic	Forward-Only	Static	Dynamic	Static

CursorLocation = adUseClient

Returned cursor is Static, independent of requested cursor type or lock type.

OLE DB Provider for ODBC with Access

CursorLocation = adUseServer

Lock Type	Forward-Only cursor requested	Keyset cursor requested	Dynamic cursor requested	Static cursor requested
Read-Only	Forward-Only	Keyset	Keyset	Static
Pessimistic	Forward-Only	Keyset	Keyset	Keyset
Optimistic	Forward-Only	Keyset	Keyset	Keyset
BatchOptimistic	Forward-Only	Keyset	Keyset	Keyset

CursorLocation = adUseClient

Returned cursor is Static, independent of requested cursor type or lock type.

OLE DB Provider for ODBC with Oracle

CursorLocation = adUseServer

Lock Type	Forward-Only cursor requested	Keyset cursor requested	Dynamic cursor requested	Static cursor requested
Read-Only	Forward-Only	Keyset	Keyset	Static
Pessimistic	Forward-Only	Keyset	Keyset	Keyset
Optimistic	Forward-Only	Keyset	Keyset	Keyset
BatchOptimistic	Forward-Only	Keyset	Keyset	Keyset

CursorLocation = adUseClient

Returned cursor is Static, independent of requested cursor type or lock type.

Don't Cache Connections Anymore

With the advent of connection pooling, caching database connections quickly became obsolete. The major reason we ever thought we had to cache a connection was because it was faster than repeatedly opening and closing a connection. Well, connection pooling blows that concept out of the water. In fact, opening and closing a connection each time you need one is actually preferable now that connection pooling brokers them for us.

But don't use it just because I say so, use it because it is a better solution. Consider the problems we can now circumvent because we are no longer caching connections. If you cache a connection and the connection is lost for any reason, when you go to use the connection again, you will receive an error. You could, of course, write some code that checks the connection each time before you use it to see if it is valid, but why bother? Let connection pooling handle this for us! Also, consider a Web application with 10,000 users hitting your site. Without connection pooling, you would have to cache 10,000 connections at a time! Yuk!

So how do we use connection pooling? That's simple – we open a connection right before we need one and we close it as soon as we are done with it. It is that easy! If I left you wanting more, check out the details in Chapter 3, The Connection Object.

DB Schema Constants

Miscellaneous Constants

These values are not included in the standard `adovbs.inc` include file (and are not automatically supplied when using Visual Basic), but can be found in `adocon.inc` (for ASP) and `adocon.bas` (for Visual Basic) from the supporting web site.

Many of these may not be necessary to you as an ADO programmer, but they are included here for completeness. In particular they are useful as bitmask values for entries in the `Properties` collection.

ADCPROP_UPDATECRITERIA_ENUM

Name	Value	Description
adCriteriaAllCols	1	Collisions should be detected if there is a change to any column.
adCriteriaKey	0	Collisions should be detected if there is a change to the key column.
adCriteriaTimeStamp	3	Collisions should be detected if a row has been accessed.
adCriteriaUpdCols	2	Collisions should be detected if there is a change to columns being updated.

DB_COLLATION

Name	Value	Description
DB_COLLATION_ASC	1	The sort sequence for the column is ascending.
DB_COLLATION_DESC	2	The sort sequence for the column is descending.

DB_IMP_LEVEL

Name	Value	Description
DB_IMP_LEVEL_ANONYMOUS	0	The client is anonymous to the server, and the server process cannot obtain identification information about the client and cannot impersonate the client.
DB_IMP_LEVEL_DELEGATE	3	The process can impersonate the client's security context while acting on behalf of the client. The server process can also make outgoing calls to other servers while acting on behalf of the client.
DB_IMP_LEVEL_IDENTIFY	1	The server can obtain the client's identity, and can impersonate the client for ACL checking, but cannot access system objects as the client.
DB_IMP_LEVEL_IMPERSONATE	2	The server process can impersonate the client's security context whilst acting on behalf of the client. This information is obtained upon connection and not on every call.

DB_MODE

Name	Value	Description
DB_MODE_READ	1	Read only.
DB_MODE_READWRITE	3	Read/Write (DB_MODE_READ + DB_MODE_WRITE).
DB_MODE_SHARE_DENY_NONE	16	Neither read nor write access can be denied to others.
DB_MODE_SHARE_DENY_READ	4	Prevents others from opening in read mode.
DB_MODE_SHARE_DENY_WRITE	8	Prevents others from opening in write mode.
DB_MODE_SHARE_EXCLUSIVE	12	Prevents others from opening in read/write mode (DB_MODE_SHARE_DENY_READ + DB_MODE_SHARE_DENY_WRITE).
DB_MODE_WRITE	2	Write only.

DB_PROT_LEVEL

Name	Value	Description
DB_PROT_LEVEL_CALL	2	Authenticates the source of the data at the beginning of each request from the client to the server.
DB_PROT_LEVEL_CONNECT	1	Authenticates only when the client establishes the connection with the server.
DB_PROT_LEVEL_NONE	0	Performs no authentication of data sent to the server.
DB_PROT_LEVEL_PKT	3	Authenticates that all data received is from the client.
DB_PROT_LEVEL_PKT_INTEGRITY	4	Authenticates that all data received is from the client and that it has not been changed in transit.
DB_PROT_LEVEL_PKT_PRIVACY	5	Authenticates that all data received is from the client, that it has not been changed in transit, and protects the privacy of the data by encrypting it.

DB_PT

Name	Value	Description
DB_PT_FUNCTION	3	Function; there is a returned value.
DB_PT_PROCEDURE	2	Procedure; there is no returned value.
DB_PT_UNKNOWN	1	It is not known whether there is a returned value.

DB_SEARCHABLE

Name	Value	Description
DB_ALL_EXCEPT_LIKE	3	The data type can be used in a WHERE clause with all comparison operators except LIKE.
DB_LIKE_ONLY	2	The data type can be used in a WHERE clause only with the LIKE predicate.
DB_SEARCHABLE	4	The data type can be used in a WHERE clause with any comparison operator.
DB_UNSEARCHABLE	1	The data type cannot be used in a WHERE clause.

DBCOLUMNDESCFLAG

Name	Value	Description
DBCOLUMNDESCFLAG_CLSID	8	The CLSID portion of the column description can be changed when altering the column.
DBCOLUMNDESCFLAG_COLSIZE	16	The column size portion of the column description can be changed when altering the column.
DBCOLUMNDESCFLAG_DBCID	32	The DBCID portion of the column description can be changed when altering the column.
DBCOLUMNDESCFLAG_ITYPEINFO	2	The type information portion of the column description can be changed when altering the column.
DBCOLUMNDESCFLAG_PRECISION	128	The precision portion of the column description can be changed when altering the column.
DBCOLUMNDESCFLAG_PROPERTIES	4	The property sets portion of the column description can be changed when altering the column.
DBCOLUMNDESCFLAG_SCALE	256	The numeric scale portion of the column description can be changed when altering the column.
DBCOLUMNDESCFLAG_TYPENAME	1	The type name portion of the column description can be changed when altering the column.
DBCOLUMNDESCFLAG_WTYPE	64	The data type portion of the column description can be changed when altering the column.

DBCOLUMNFLAGS

Name	Value	Description
DBCOLUMNFLAGS_CACHEDEFERRED	4096	Indicates that the value of a deferred column is cached when it is first read.
DBCOLUMNFLAGS_ISCHAPTER	8192	The column contains a Chapter value.
DBCOLUMNFLAGS_ISFIXEDLENGTH	16	All of the data in the column is of a fixed length.
DBCOLUMNFLAGS_ISLONG	128	The column contains a BLOB value that contains long data.

Name	Value	Description
DBCOLUMNFLAGS_ISNULLABLE	32	The column can be set to NULL, or the provider cannot determine whether the column can be set to NULL.
DBCOLUMNFLAGS_ISROWID	256	The column contains a persistent row identifier.
DBCOLUMNFLAGS_ISROWVER	512	The column contains a timestamp or other row versioning data type.
DBCOLUMNFLAGS_MAYBENULL	64	NULLs can be got from the column.
DBCOLUMNFLAGS_MAYDEFER	2	The column is deferred.
DBCOLUMNFLAGS_WRITE	4	The column may be updated.
DBCOLUMNFLAGS_WRITEUNKNOWN	8	It is not known if the column can be updated.

DBPARAMTYPE

Name	Value	Description
DBPARAMTYPE_INPUT	1	The parameter is an input parameter.
DBPARAMTYPE_INPUTOUTPUT	2	The parameter is both an input and an output parameter.
DBPARAMTYPE_OUTPUT	3	The parameter is an output parameter.
DBPARAMTYPE_RETURNVALUE	4	The parameter is a return value.

DBPROMPT

Name	Value	Description
DBPROMPT_COMPLETE	2	Prompt the user only if more information is needed.
DBPROMPT_COMPLETEREQUIRED	3	Prompt the user only if more information is required. Do not allow the user to enter optional information.
DBPROMPT_NOPROMPT	4	Do not prompt the user.
DBPROMPT_PROMPT	1	Always prompt the user for initialization information.

533

DBPROPVAL_AO

Name	Value	Description
DBPROPVAL_AO_RANDOM	2	Columns can be accessed in any order.
DBPROPVAL_AO_SEQUENTIAL	0	All columns must be accessed in sequential order determined by the column ordinal.
DBPROPVAL_AO_SEQUENTIALSTORAGEOBJECTS	1	Columns bound as storage objects can only be accessed in sequential order as determined by the column ordinal.

DBPROPVAL_ASYNCH

Name	Value	Description
DBPROPVAL_ASYNCH_BACKGROUNDPOPULATION	8	The rowset is populated asynchronously in the background.
DBPROPVAL_ASYNCH_INITIALIZE	1	Initialization is performed asynchronously.
DBPROPVAL_ASYNCH_POPULATEONDEMAND	32	The consumer prefers to optimize for getting each individual request for data returned as quickly as possible.
DBPROPVAL_ASYNCH_PREPOPULATE	16	The consumer prefers to optimize for retrieving all data when the row set is materialized.
DBPROPVAL_ASYNCH_RANDOMPOPULATION	4	Rowset population is performed asynchronously in a random manner.
DBPROPVAL_ASYNCH_SEQUENTIALPOPULATION	2	Rowset population is performed asynchronously in a sequential manner.

DBPROPVAL_BG

Name	Value	Description
DBPROPVAL_GB_COLLATE	16	A COLLATE clause can be specified at the end of each grouping column.
DBPROPVAL_GB_CONTAINS_SELECT	4	The GROUP BY clause must contain all non-aggregated columns in the select list. It can contain columns that are not in the select list.
DBPROPVAL_GB_EQUALS_SELECT	2	The GROUP BY clause must contain all non-aggregated columns in the select list. It cannot contain any other columns.
DBPROPVAL_GB_NO_RELATION	8	The columns in the GROUP BY clause and the select list are not related. The meaning on non-grouped, non-aggregated columns in the select list is data source dependent.
DBPROPVAL_GB_NOT_SUPPORTED	1	GROUP BY clauses are not supported.

DBPROPVAL_BI

Name	Value	Description
DBPROPVAL_BI_CROSSROWSET	1	Bookmark values are valid across all rowsets generated on this table.

DBPROPVAL_BMK

Name	Value	Description
DBPROPVAL_BMK_KEY	2	The bookmark type is key.
DBPROPVAL_BMK_NUMERIC	1	The bookmark type is numeric.

DBPROPVAL_BO

Name	Value	Description
DBPROPVAL_BO_NOINDEXUPDATE	1	The provider is not required to update indexes based on inserts or changes to the rowset. Any indexes need to be re-created following changes made through the rowset.
DBPROPVAL_BO_NOLOG	0	The provider is not required to log inserts or changes to the rowset.
DBPROPVAL_BO_REFINTEGRITY	2	Referential integrity constraints do not need to be checked or enforced for changes made through the rowset.

DBPROPVAL_CB

Name	Value	Description
DBPROPVAL_CB_NON_NULL	2	The result is the concatenation of the non-NULL valued column or columns.
DBPROPVAL_CB_NULL	1	The result is NULL valued.

DBPROPVAL_CB

Name	Value	Description
DBPROPVAL_CB_DELETE	1	Aborting a transaction deletes prepared commands.
DBPROPVAL_CB_PRESERVE	2	Aborting a transaction preserves prepared commands.

DBPROPVAL_CD

Name	Value	Description
DBPROPVAL_CD_NOTNULL	1	Columns can be created non-nullable.

DBPROPVAL_CL

Name	Value	Description
DBPROPVAL_CL_END	2	The catalog name appears at the end of the fully qualified name.
DBPROPVAL_CL_START	1	The catalog name appears at the start of the fully qualified name.

DBPROPVAL_CO

Name	Value	Description
DBPROPVAL_CO_BEGINSWITH	32	Provider supports the BEGINSWITH and NOTBEGINSWITH operators.
DBPROPVAL_CO_CASEINSENSITIVE	8	Provider supports the CASEINSENSITIVE operator.
DBPROPVAL_CO_CASESENSITIVE	4	Provider supports the CASESENSITIVE operator.
DBPROPVAL_CO_CONTAINS	16	Provider supports the CONTAINS and NOTCONTAINS operators.
DBPROPVAL_CO_EQUALITY	1	Provider supports the following operators: LT, LE, EQ, GE, GT, NE.
DBPROPVAL_CO_STRING	2	Provider supports the BEGINSWITH operator.

DBPROPVAL_CS

Name	Value	Description
DBPROPVAL_CS_COMMUNICATIONFAILURE	c	The DSO is unable to communicate with the data store.
DBPROPVAL_CS_INITIALIZED	1	The DSO is in an initialized state and able to communicate with the data store.
DBPROPVAL_CS_UNINITIALIZED	0	The DSO is in an uninitialized state.

DBPROPVAL_CU

Name	Value	Description
DBPROPVAL_CU_DML_STATEMENTS	1	Catalog names are supported in all Data Manipulation Language statements.
DBPROPVAL_CU_INDEX_DEFINITION	4	Catalog names are supported in all index definition statements.
DBPROPVAL_CU_PRIVILEGE_DEFINITION	8	Catalog names are supported in all privilege definition statements.
DBPROPVAL_CU_TABLE_DEFINITION	2	Catalog names are supported in all table definition statements.

DBPROPVAL_DF

Name	Value	Description
DBPROPVAL_DF_INITIALLY_DEFERRED	1	The foreign key is initially deferred.
DBPROPVAL_DF_INITIALLY_IMMEDIATE	2	The foreign key is initially immediate.
DBPROPVAL_DF_NOT_DEFERRABLE	3	The foreign key is not deferrable.

DBPROPVAL_DST

Name	Value	Description
DBPROPVAL_DST_MDP	2	The provider is a multidimensional provider.
DBPROPVAL_DST_TDP	1	The provider is a tabular data provider.
DBPROPVAL_DST_TDPANDMDP	3	The provider is both a TDP and a MD provider.

DBPROPVAL_HT

Name	Value	Description
DBPROPVAL_HT_DIFFERENT_CATALOGS	1	The provider supports heterogeneous joins between catalogs.
DBPROPVAL_HT_DIFFERENT_PROVIDERS	2	The provider supports heterogeneous joins between providers.

DBPROPVAL_IC

Name	Value	Description
DBPROPVAL_IC_LOWER	2	Identifiers in SQL are case insensitive and are stored in lower case in system catalog.
DBPROPVAL_IC_MIXED	8	Identifiers in SQL are case insensitive and are stored in mixed case in system catalog.
DBPROPVAL_IC_SENSITIVE	4	Identifiers in SQL are case sensitive and are stored in mixed case in system catalog.
DBPROPVAL_IC_UPPER	1	Identifiers in SQL are case insensitive and are stored in upper case in system catalog.

DBPROPVAL_IN

Name	Value	Description
DBPROPVAL_IN_DISALLOWNULL	1	The index does not allow entries where the key columns are NULL. An error will be generated if the consumer attempts to insert a NULL value into a key column.
DBPROPVAL_IN_IGNOREANYNULL	4	The index does not insert entries containing NULL keys.
DBPROPVAL_IN_IGNORENULL	2	The index does not insert entries where some column key has a NULL value.

DBPROPVAL_IT

Name	Value	Description
DBPROPVAL_IT_BTREE	1	The index is a B+ tree.
DBPROPVAL_IT_CONTENT	3	The index is a content index.
DBPROPVAL_IT_HASH	2	The index is a hash file using linear or extensible hashing.
DBPROPVAL_IT_OTHER	4	The index is some other type of index.

DBPROPVAL_LM

Name	Value	Description
DBPROPVAL_LM_INTENT	4	The provider uses the maximum level of locking to ensure that changes will not fail due to a concurrency violation.
DBPROPVAL_LM_NONE	1	The provider is not required to lock rows at any time to ensure successful updates.
DBPROPVAL_LM_READ	2	The provider uses the minimum level of locking to ensure that changes will not fail due to a concurrency violation.
DBPROPVAL_LM_RITE	8	
DBPROPVAL_LM_SINGLEROW	2	The provider uses the minimum level of locking to ensure that changes will not fail due to a concurrency violation.

DBPROPVAL_MR

Name	Value	Description
DBPROPVAL_MR_CONCURRENT	2	More than one rowset created by the same multiple results object can exist concurrently.
DBPROPVAL_MR_NOTSUPPORTED	0	Multiple results objects are not supported.
DBPROPVAL_MR_SUPPORTED	1	The provider supports multiple results objects.

DBPROPVAL_NC

Name	Value	Description
DBPROPVAL_NC_END	1	NULLs are sorted at the end of the list, regardless of the sort order.
DBPROPVAL_NC_HIGH	2	NULLs are sorted at the high end of the list.
DBPROPVAL_NC_LOW	4	NULLs are sorted at the low end of the list.
DBPROPVAL_NC_START	8	NULLs are sorted at the start of the list, regardless of the sort order.

DBPROPVAL_NP

Name	Value	Description
DBPROPVAL_NP_ABOUTTODO	2	The consumer will be notified before an action (ie the Will event).
DBPROPVAL_NP_DIDEVENT	16	The consumer will be notified after an action (ie the Complete event).
DBPROPVAL_NP_FAILEDTODO	8	The consumer will be notified if an action failed (ie a Will or Complete event).
DBPROPVAL_NP_OKTODO	1	The consumer will be notified of events.
DBPROPVAL_NP_SYNCHAFTER	4	The consumer will be notified when the rowset is resynchronized.

DBPROPVAL_NT

Name	Value	Description
DBPROPVAL_NT_MULTIPLEROWS	2	For methods that operate on multiple rows, and generate multiphased notifications (events), then the provider calls OnRowChange once for all rows that succeed and once for all rows that fail.
DBPROPVAL_NT_SINGLEROW	1	For methods that operate on multiple rows, and generate multiphased notifications (events), then the provider calls OnRowChange separately for each phase for each row.

DBPROPVAL_OA

Name	Value	Description
DBPROPVAL_OA_ATEXECUTE	2	Output parameter data is available immediately after the Command.Execute returns.
DBPROPVAL_OA_ATROWRELEASE	4	Output parameter data is available when the rowset is released. For a single rowset operation this is when the rowset is completely released (closed) and for a multiple rowset operation this is when the next rowset if fetched. The consumer's bound memory is in an indeterminate state before the parameter data becomes available.
DBPROPVAL_OA_NOTSUPPORTED	1	Output parameters are not supported.

DBPROPVAL_OO

Name	Value	Description
DBPROPVAL_OO_BLOB	1	The provider supports access to BLOBs as structured storage objects.
DBPROPVAL_OO_IPERSIST	2	The provider supports access to OLE objects through OLE.

DBPROPVAL_OS

Name	Value	Description
DBPROPVAL_OS_ENABLEALL	-1	All services should be invoked. This is the default.
DBPROPVAL_OS_RESOURCEPOOLING	1	Resources should be pooled.
DBPROPVAL_OS_TXNENLISTMENT	2	Sessions in an MTS environment should automatically be enlisted in a global transaction where required.

DBPROPVAL_PT

Name	Value	Description
DBPROPVAL_PT_GUID	8	The GUID is used as the persistent ID type.
DBPROPVAL_PT_GUID_NAME	1	The GUID Name is used as the persistent ID type.
DBPROPVAL_PT_GUID_PROPID	2	The GUID Property ID is used as the persistent ID type.
DBPROPVAL_PT_NAME	4	The Name is used as the persistent ID type.
DBPROPVAL_PT_PGUID_NAME	32	The Property GUID name is used as the persistent ID type.
DBPROPVAL_PT_PGUID_PROPID	64	The Property GUID Property ID is used as the persistent ID type.
DBPROPVAL_PT_PROPID	16	The Property ID is used as the persistent ID type.

DBPROPVAL_RD

Name	Value	Description
DBPROPVAL_RD_RESETALL	-1	The provider should reset all state associated with the data source, with the exception that any open object is not released.

DBPROPVAL_RT

Name	Value	Description
DBPROPVAL_RT_APTMTTHREAD	2	The DSO is apartment threaded.
DBPROPVAL_RT_FREETHREAD	1	The DSO is free threaded.
DBPROPVAL_RT_SINGLETHREAD	4	The DSO is single threaded.

DBPROPVAL_SQ

Name	Value	Description
DBPROPVAL_SQ_COMPARISON	2	All predicates that support subqueries support comparison subqueries.
DBPROPVAL_SQ_CORRELATEDSUBQUERIES	1	All predicates that support subqueries support correlated subqueries.
DBPROPVAL_SQ_EXISTS	4	All predicates that support subqueries support EXISTS subqueries.
DBPROPVAL_SQ_IN	8	All predicates that support subqueries support IN subqueries.
DBPROPVAL_SQ_QUANTIFIED	16	All predicates that support subqueries support quantified subqueries.

DBPROPVAL_SQL

Name	Value	Description
DBPROPVAL_SQL_ANDI89_IEF	8	The provider supports the ANSI SQL89 IEF level.
DBPROPVAL_SQL_ANSI92_ENTRY	16	The provider supports the ANSI SQL92 Entry level.
DBPROPVAL_SQL_ANSI92_FULL	128	The provider supports the ANSI SQL92 Full level.
DBPROPVAL_SQL_ANSI92_INTERMEDIATE	64	The provider supports the ANSI SQL92 Intermediate level.
DBPROPVAL_SQL_CORE	2	The provider supports the ODBC 2.5 Core SQL level.
DBPROPVAL_SQL_ESCAPECLAUSES	256	The provider supports the ODBC escape clauses syntax.
DBPROPVAL_SQL_EXTENDED	4	The provider supports the ODBC 2.5 EXTENDED SQL level.
DBPROPVAL_SQL_FIPS_TRANSITIONAL	32	The provider supports the ANSI SQL92 Transitional level.
DBPROPVAL_SQL_MINIMUM	1	The provider supports the ODBC 2.5 EXTENDED SQL level.
DBPROPVAL_SQL_NONE	0	SQL is not supported.
DBPROPVAL_SQL_ODBC_CORE	2	The provider supports the ODBC 2.5 Core SQL level.
DBPROPVAL_SQL_ODBC_EXTENDED	4	The provider supports the ODBC 2.5 EXTENDED SQL level.
DBPROPVAL_SQL_ODBC_MINIMUM	1	The provider supports the ODBC 2.5 EXTENDED SQL level.
DBPROPVAL_SQL_SUBMINIMUM	512	The provider supports the DBGUID_SQL dialect and parses the command text according to SQL rules, but does not support either the minimum ODBC level or the ANSI SQL92 Entry level.

DBPROPVAL_SS

Name	Value	Description
DBPROPVAL_SS_ILOCKBYTES	8	The provider supports IlockBytes.
DBPROPVAL_SS_ISEQUENTIALSTREAM	1	The provider supports IsequentialStream.
DBPROPVAL_SS_ISTORAGE	4	The provider supports Istorage.
DBPROPVAL_SS_ISTREAM	2	The provider supports IStream.

DBPROPVAL_SU

Name	Value	Description
DBPROPVAL_SU_DML_STATEMENTS	1	Schema names are supported in all Data Manipulation Language statements.
DBPROPVAL_SU_INDEX_DEFINITION	4	Schema names are supported in all index definition statements.
DBPROPVAL_SU_PRIVILEGE_DEFINITION	8	Schema names are supported in all privilege definition statements.
DBPROPVAL_SU_TABLE_DEFINITION	2	Schema names are supported in all table definition statements.

DBPROPVAL_TC

Name	Value	Description
DBPROPVAL_TC_ALL	8	Transactions can contain DDL and DML statements in any order.
DBPROPVAL_TC_DDL_COMMIT	2	Transactions can contain DML statements. DDL statements within a transaction cause the transaction to be committed.
DBPROPVAL_TC_DDL_IGNORE	4	Transactions can only contain DML statements. DDL statements within a transaction are ignored.
DBPROPVAL_TC_DML	1	Transactions can only contain Data Manipulation (DML) statements. DDL statements within a transaction cause an error.
DBPROPVAL_TC_NONE	0	Transactions are not supported.

DBPROPVAL_TI

Name	Value	Description
DBPROPVAL_TI_BROWSE	256	Changes made by other transactions are visible before they are committed.
DBPROPVAL_TI_CHAOS	16	Transactions cannot overwrite pending changes from more highly isolated transactions. This is the default.
DBPROPVAL_TI_CURSORSTABILITY	4096	Changes made by other transactions are not visible until those transactions are committed.
DBPROPVAL_TI_ISOLATED	1048576	All concurrent transactions will interact only in ways that produce the same effect as if each transaction were entirely executed one after the other.
DBPROPVAL_TI_READCOMMITTED	4096	Changes made by other transactions are not visible until those transactions are committed.
DBPROPVAL_TI_READUNCOMMITTED	256	Changes made by other transactions are visible before they are committed.
DBPROPVAL_TI_REPEATABLEREAD	65536	Changes made by other transactions are not visible.
DBPROPVAL_TI_SERIALIZABLE	1048576	All concurrent transactions will interact only in ways that produce the same effect as if each transaction were entirely executed one after the other.

DBPROPVAL_TR

Name	Value	Description
DBPROPVAL_TR_ABORT	16	The transaction preserves its isolation context (ie, it preserves its locks if that is how isolation is implemented) across the retaining abort.
DBPROPVAL_TR_ABORT_DC	8	The transaction may either preserve or dispose of isolation context across a retaining abort.
DBPROPVAL_TR_ABORT_NO	32	The transaction is explicitly not to preserve its isolation across a retaining abort.
DBPROPVAL_TR_BOTH	128	Isolation is preserved across both a retaining commit and a retaining abort.
DBPROPVAL_TR_COMMIT	2	The transaction preserves its isolation context (ie, it preserves its locks if that is how isolation is implemented) across the retaining commit.

Name	Value	Description
DBPROPVAL_TR_COMMIT_DC	1	The transaction may either preserve or dispose of isolation context across a retaining commit.
DBPROPVAL_TR_COMMIT_NO	4	The transaction is explicitly not to preserve its isolation across a retaining commit.
DBPROPVAL_TR_DONTCARE	64	The transaction may either preserve or dispose of isolation context across a retaining commit or abort. This is the default.
DBPROPVAL_TR_NONE	256	Isolation is explicitly not to be retained across either a retaining commit or abort.
DBPROPVAL_TR_OPTIMISTIC	512	Optimistic concurrency control is to be used.

DBPROPVAL_UP

Name	Value	Description
DBPROPVAL_UP_CHANGE	1	Indicates that SetData is supported.
DBPROPVAL_UP_DELETE	2	Indicates that DeleteRows is supported.
DBPROPVAL_UP_INSERT	4	Indicates that InsertRow is supported.

MD_DIMTYPE

Name	Value	Description
MD_DIMTYPE_MEASURE	2	A measure dimension.
MD_DIMTYPE_OTHER	3	The dimension is neither a time nor a measure dimension.
MD_DIMTYPE_TIME	1	A time dimension.
MD_DIMTYPE_UNKNOWN	0	The provider is unable to classify the dimension.

SQL_FN_NUM

Name	Value	Description
SQL_FN_NUM_ABS	1	The ABS function is supported by the data source.
SQL_FN_NUM_ACOS	2	The ACOS function is supported by the data source.
SQL_FN_NUM_ASIN	4	The ASIN function is supported by the data source.
SQL_FN_NUM_ATAN	8	The ATAN function is supported by the data source.
SQL_FN_NUM_ATAN2	16	The ATAN2 function is supported by the data source.
SQL_FN_NUM_CEILING	32	The CEILING function is supported by the data source.
SQL_FN_NUM_COS	64	The COS function is supported by the data source.
SQL_FN_NUM_COT	128	The COT function is supported by the data source.
SQL_FN_NUM_DEGREES	262144	The DEGREES function is supported by the data source.
SQL_FN_NUM_EXP	256	The EXP function is supported by the data source.
SQL_FN_NUM_FLOOR	512	The FLOOR function is supported by the data source.
SQL_FN_NUM_LOG	1024	The LOG function is supported by the data source.
SQL_FN_NUM_LOG10	524288	The LOG10 function is supported by the data source.
SQL_FN_NUM_MOD	2048	The MOD function is supported by the data source.
SQL_FN_NUM_PI	65536	The PI function is supported by the data source.
SQL_FN_NUM_POWER	1048576	The POWER function is supported by the data source.
SQL_FN_NUM_RADIANS	2097152	The RADIANS function is supported by the data source.
SQL_FN_NUM_RAND	131072	The RAND function is supported by the data source.
SQL_FN_NUM_ROUND	4194304	The ROUND function is supported by the data source.
SQL_FN_NUM_SIGN	4096	The SIGN function is supported by the data source.
SQL_FN_NUM_SIN	8192	The SIN function is supported by the data source.
SQL_FN_NUM_SQRT	10384	The SQRT function is supported by the data source.
SQL_FN_NUM_TAN	32768	The TAN function is supported by the data source.
SQL_FN_NUM_TRUNCATE	8388608	The TRUNCATE function is supported by the data source.

SQL_FN_STR

Name	Value	Description
SQL_FN_STR_ASCII	8192	The ASCII function is supported by the data source.
SQL_FN_STR_BIT_LENGTH	524288	The BIT_LENGTH function is supported by the data source.
SQL_FN_STR_CHAR	16384	The CHAR function is supported by the data source.
SQL_FN_STR_CHAR_LENGTH	1048576	The CHAR_LENGTH function is supported by the data source.
SQL_FN_STR_CHARACTER _LENGTH	2097152	The CHARACTER_LENGTH function is supported by the data source.
SQL_FN_STR_CONCAT	1	The CONCAT function is supported by the data source.
SQL_FN_STR_DIFFERENCE	32768	The DIFFERENCE function is supported by the data source.
SQL_FN_STR_INSERT	2	The INSERT function is supported by the data source.
SQL_FN_STR_LCASE	64	The LCASE function is supported by the data source.
SQL_FN_STR_LEFT	4	The LEFT function is supported by the data source.
SQL_FN_STR_LENGTH	16	The LENGTH function is supported by the data source.
SQL_FN_STR_LOCATE	32	The LOCATE function is supported by the data source.
SQL_FN_STR_LOCATE_2	65536	The LOCATE_2 function is supported by the data source.
SQL_FN_STR_LTRIM	8	The LTRIM function is supported by the data source.
SQL_FN_STR_OCTET_LENGTH	4194304	The OCTET_LENGTH function is supported by the data source.

Name	Value	Description
SQL_FN_STR_POSITION	8388608	The POSITION function is supported by the data source.
SQL_FN_STR_REPEAT	128	The REPEAT function is supported by the data source.
SQL_FN_STR_REPLACE	256	The REPLACE function is supported by the data source.
SQL_FN_STR_RIGHT	512	The RIGHT function is supported by the data source.
SQL_FN_STR_RTRIM	1024	The RTRIM function is supported by the data source.
SQL_FN_STR_SOUNDEX	131072	The SOUNDEX function is supported by the data source.
SQL_FN_STR_SPACE	262144	The SPACE function is supported by the data source.
SQL_FN_STR_SUBSTRING	2048	The SUBSTRING function is supported by the data source.
SQL_FN_STR_UCASE	4096	The UCASE function is supported by the data source.

SQL_FN_SYS

Name	Value	Description
SQL_FN_SYS_DBNAME	2	The DBNAME system function is supported.
SQL_FN_SYS_IFNULL	4	The IFNULL system function is supported.
SQL_FN_SYS_USERNAME	1	The USERNAME system function is supported.

SQL_OJ

Name	Value	Description
SQL_OJ_ALL_COMPARISON_OPS	64	The comparison operator in the ON clause can be any of the ODBC comparison operators. If this is not set, only the equals (=) comparison operator can be used in an outer join.
SQL_OJ_FULL	4	Full outer joins are supported.

Name	Value	Description
SQL_OJ_INNER	32	The inner table (the right table in a left outer join or the left table in a right outer join) can also be used in an inner join. This does not apply to full out joins, which do not have an inner table.
SQL_OJ_LEFT	1	Left outer joins are supported.
SQL_OJ_NESTED	8	Nested outer joins are supported.
SQL_OJ_NOT_ORDERED	16	The column names in the ON clause of the outer join do not have to be in the same order as their respective table names in the OUTER JOIN clause.
SQL_OJ_RIGHT	2	Right outer joins are supported.

SQL_SDF_CURRENT

Name	Value	Description
SQL_SDF_CURRENT_DATE	1	The CURRENT_DATE system function is supported.
SQL_SDF_CURRENT_TIME	2	The CURRENT_TIME system function is supported.
SQL_SDF_CURRENT_TIMESTAMP	4	The CURRENT_TIMESTAMP system function is supported.

SSPROP_CONCUR

Name	Value	Description
SSPROP_CONCUR_LOCK	4	Use row locking to prevent concurrent access.
SSPROP_CONCUR_READ_ONLY	8	The rowset is read-only. Full concurrency is supported.
SSPROP_CONCUR_ROWVER	1	Use row versioning to determining concurrent access violations. The SQL Table or tables must contain a timestamp column.
SSPROP_CONCUR_VALUES	2	Use the values of columns in the rowset row.

SSPROPVAL_USEPROCFORPREP

Name	Value	Description
SSPROPVAL_USEPROCFORPREP_OFF	0	A temporary stored procedure is not created when a command is prepared.
SSPROPVAL_USEPROCFORPREP_ON	1	A temporary stored procedure is created when a command is prepared. Temporary stored procedures are dropped when the session is released.
SSPROPVAL_USEPROCFORPREP_ON_DROP	2	A temporary stored procedure is created when a command is prepared. The procedure is dropped when the command is unprepared, or a new command text is set, or when all application references to the command are released.

Support and Errata

One of the most irritating things about any programming book can be when you find that bit of code you've just spent an hour typing in simply doesn't work. You check it a hundred times to see if you've set it up correctly and then you notice the spelling mistake in the variable name on the book page. Grrr! Of course, you can blame the authors for not taking enough care and testing the code, the editors for not doing their job properly, or the proofreaders for not being eagle-eyed enough, but this doesn't get around the fact that mistakes do happen.

We try hard to ensure no mistakes sneak out into the real world, but we can't promise that this book is 100% error free. What we can do is offer the next best thing by providing you with immediate support and feedback from experts who have worked on the book and try to ensure that future editions eliminate these gremlins. The following section will take you step by step through the process of posting errata to our web site to get that help. The sections that follow, therefore, are:

- ❑ Wrox Developers Membership
- ❑ Finding a list of existing errata on the web site
- ❑ Adding your own errata to the existing list
- ❑ What happens to your errata once you've posted it (why doesn't it appear immediately?)

There is also a section covering how to e-mail a question for technical support. This comprises:

- ❑ What your e-mail should include
- ❑ What happens to your e-mail once it has been received by us

So that you only need view information relevant to yourself, we ask that you register as a Wrox Developer Member. This is a quick and easy process, that will save you time in the long-run. If you are already a member, just update your membership to include this book.

Wrox Developer's Membership

To get your FREE Wrox Developer's Membership click on Membership in the navigation bar of our home site http://www.wrox.com.

This is shown in the following screen shot:

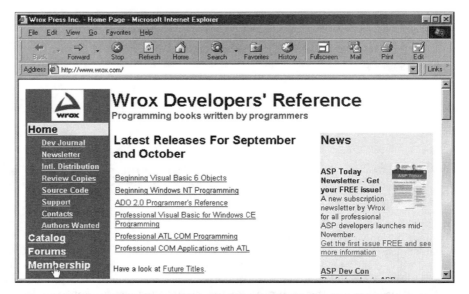

Then, on the next screen (not shown), click on **New User**. This will display a form. Fill in the details on the form and submit the details using the **Submit** button at the bottom. Before you can say 'The best read books come in Wrox Red' you will get this screen:

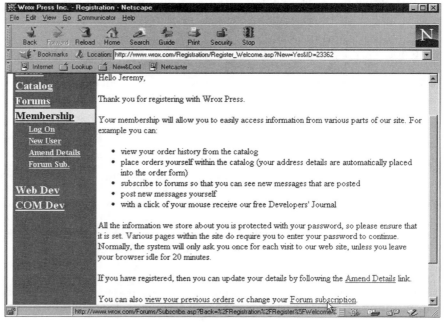

Finding an Errata on the Web Site.

Before you send in a query, you might be able to save time by finding the answer to your problem on our web site: http:\\www.wrox.com.

Each book we publish has its own page and its own errata sheet. You can get to any book's page by clicking on Support from the left hand side navigation bar.

From this page you can locate any books errata page on our site. Select your book from the pop-up menu and click on it.

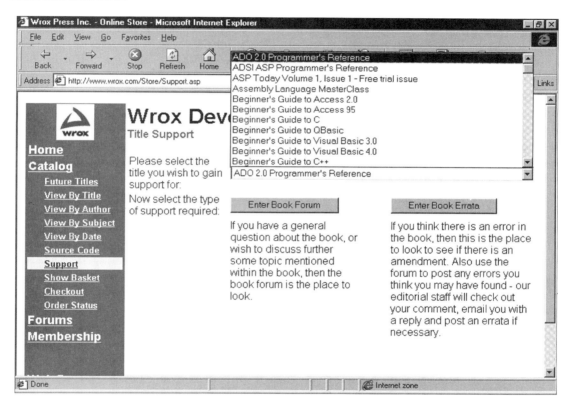

Then click on Enter Book Errata. This will take you to the errata page for the book. Select the criteria by which you want to view the errata, and click the Apply criteria button. This will provide you with links to specific errata. For an initial search, you are advised to view the errata by page numbers. If you have looked for an error previously, then you may wish to limit your search using dates. We update these pages daily to ensure that you have the latest information on bugs and errors.

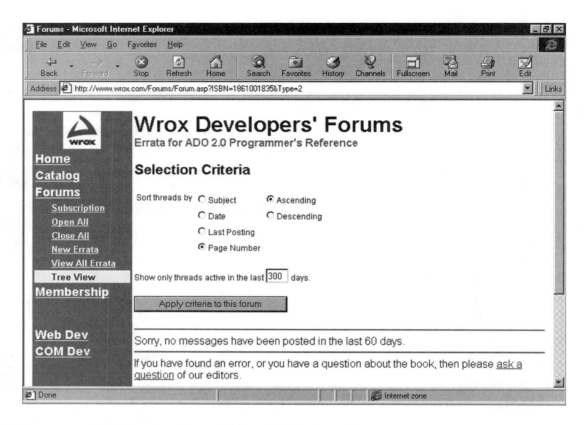

Adding an Errata to the Sheet Yourself

It's always possible that you may find that your error is not listed, in which case you can enter details of the fault yourself. It might be anything from a spelling mistake to a faulty piece of code in the book. Sometimes you'll find useful hints that aren't really errors on the listing. By entering errata you may save another reader hours of frustration, and of course, you will be helping us provide even higher quality information. We're very grateful for this sort of advice and feedback. You can enter errata using the 'ask a question' of our editors link at the bottom of the errata page. Click on this link and you will get a form on which to post your message.

Fill in the subject box, and then type your message in the space provided on the form. Once you have done this, click on the Post Now button at the bottom of the page. The message will be forwarded to our editors. They'll then test your submission and check that the error exists, and that the suggestions you make are valid. Then your submission, together with a solution, is posted on the site for public consumption. Obviously this stage of the process can take a day or two, but we will endeavor to get a fix up sooner than that.

E-mail Support

If you wish to directly query a problem in the book with an expert who knows the book in detail then e-mail support@wrox.com, with the title of the book and the last four numbers of the ISBN in the subject field of the e-mail. Your e-mail **MUST** include the title of the book the problem relates to, otherwise we won't be able to help you. The diagram below shows what else your e-mail should include:

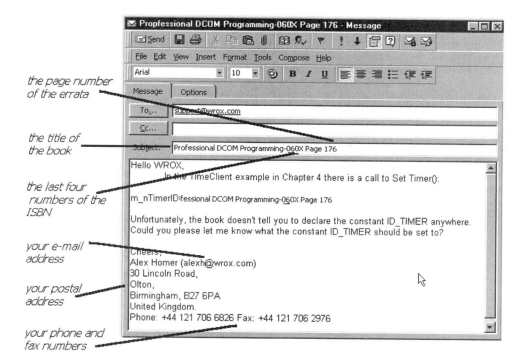

We won't send you junk mail. We need the details to save your time and ours. If we need to replace a disk or CD we'll be able to get it to you straight away. When you send an e-mail it will go through the following chain of support:

Customer Support

Your message is delivered to one of our customer support staff who are the first people to read it. They have files on most frequently asked questions and will answer anything general immediately. They answer general questions about the book and the web site.

Editorial

Deeper queries are forwarded to the technical editor responsible for that book. They have experience with the programming language or particular product and are able to answer detailed technical questions on the subject. Once an issue has been resolved, the editor can post the errata to the web site.

The Authors

Finally, in the unlikely event that the editor can't answer your problem, s/he will forward the request to the author. We try to protect the author from any distractions from writing. However, we are quite happy to forward specific requests to them. All Wrox authors help with the support on their books. They'll mail the customer and the editor with their response, and again all readers should benefit.

What we can't answer

Obviously with an ever growing range of books and an ever-changing technology base, there is an increasing volume of data requiring support. While we endeavor to answer all questions about the book, we can't answer bugs in your own programs that you've adapted from our code. So, while you might have loved the help desk systems in our Active Server Pages book, don't expect too much sympathy if you cripple your company with a live adaptation you customized from Chapter 12. But do tell us if you're especially pleased with the routine you developed with our help.

How to tell us exactly what you think.

We understand that errors can destroy the enjoyment of a book and can cause many wasted and frustrated hours, so we seek to minimize the distress that they can cause.

You might just wish to tell us how much you liked or loathed the book in question. Or you might have ideas about how this whole process could be improved. In which case you should e-mail feedback@wrox.com. You'll always find a sympathetic ear, no matter what the problem is. Above all you should remember that we do care about what you have to say and we will do our utmost to act upon it.

Index

Index

B

C

Index

P

Index

XML Applications

Authors: Various
ISBN: 1861001525
Price: $49.99 C$74.95 £45.99

If there were a chart of buzzwords surrounding the Internet, XML would currently be the top of the hit parade. XML was designed as a simplified form of SGML for use on the Web. As such it is an extremely powerful language for marking up documents. However, it is now being used in other areas and is rapidly gaining popularity as a data storage and transfer format.

By allowing authors to create their own tags, XML permits the use of tags that actually describe their content. You need never wish for a new tag again. Furthermore, presentation rules are kept separately meaning that the data marked up using XML can be used in a myriad of ways across different platforms and in different applications. This book pieces together the various parts of the XML jigsaw, teaching you how to create XML applications for the Web. After learning how to write documents using XML, we will show you many different ways in which data marked up in XML can be used and re-used, from displaying it in Web pages, to creating compound documents from multiple data sources.

Instant UML

Authors: Pierre-Alain Muller
ISBN: 1861000871
Price: $34.95 C$48.95 £32.49

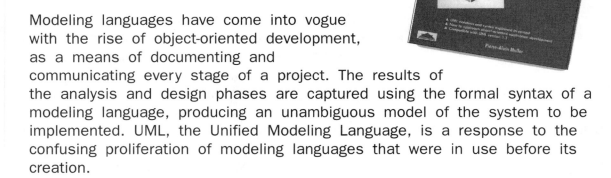

Modeling languages have come into vogue
with the rise of object-oriented development,
as a means of documenting and
communicating every stage of a project. The results of
the analysis and design phases are captured using the formal syntax of a
modeling language, producing an unambiguous model of the system to be
implemented. UML, the Unified Modeling Language, is a response to the
confusing proliferation of modeling languages that were in use before its
creation.

This book is much more than just a list of the UML syntax. It comprises a
description of object-oriented analysis, design and programming, a thorough
explanation of the UML notation and its use, discussion about a process
for modeling a project with UML, and a case study demonstrating this in
practice.

ASP Today

www.asptoday.com

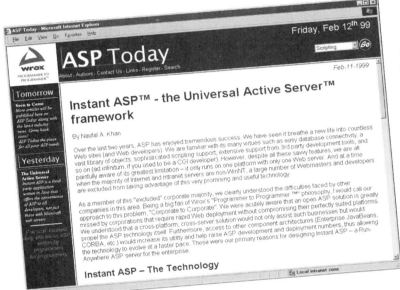

It's not easy keeping up to date with what's hot and what's not in the ever-changing world of internet development. Even if you stick to one narrow topic like ASP, trawling through the mailing lists each day and finding new and better code is still a twenty-four-seven job. Which is where we come in.

You already know Wrox Press from its series of titles on ASP and its associated technologies. We realise that we can't bring out a book everyday to keep you all up to date, so from March 1, we're starting a brand new website at www.asptoday.com which will do all the hard work for you. Every week you'll find new tips, tricks and techniques for you to try out and test in your development, covering ASP components, ADO, RDS, ADSI, CDO, Security, Site Design, BackOffice, XML and more. Look out also for bug alerts when they're found and fixes when they're available.

We hope that you won't be shy in telling us what you think of the site and the content we put on it either. If you like what you'll see, we'll carry on as we are, but if you think we're missing something, then we'll address it accordingly. If you've got something to write, then do so and we'll include it. We're hoping our site will become a global effort by and for the entire ASP community.

In anticipation,
Dan Maharry, ASPToday.com

Instant SQL Programmimng

Authors: Joe Celko
ISBN: 1874416508
Price: $29.95 C$41.95 £27.99

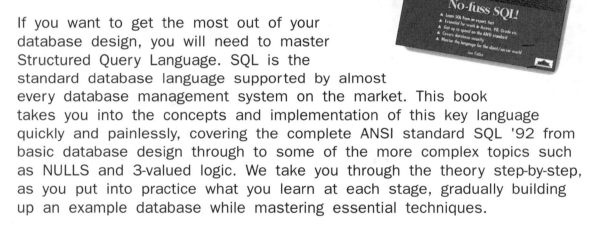

If you want to get the most out of your database design, you will need to master Structured Query Language. SQL is the standard database language supported by almost every database management system on the market. This book takes you into the concepts and implementation of this key language quickly and painlessly, covering the complete ANSI standard SQL '92 from basic database design through to some of the more complex topics such as NULLS and 3-valued logic. We take you through the theory step-by-step, as you put into practice what you learn at each stage, gradually building up an example database while mastering essential techniques.

Written by an expert in the SQL world, the book covers security issues and complex querying in a plain and fast style. Separate appendices focus on the different dialects of SQL, as produced by the likes of Sybase and Oracle. By the end of the book you will have created a full and useful application and will be well on the way to SQL excellence.

wrox

Wrox writes books for you. Any suggestions, or ideas about how you want information given in your ideal book will be studied by our team. Your comments are always valued at Wrox.

Free phone in USA 800-USE-WROX
Fax (773) 397 8990

UK Tel. (0121) 687 4100   Fax   (0121) 687 4101

Professional ADO RDS Programming with ASP

Name _____

Address _____

_____

_____

_____

City_____ State/Region _____

Country_____ Postcode/Zip _____

E-mail _____

Occupation _____

How did you hear about this book?_____

☐ Book review (name) _____

☐ Advertisement (name) _____

☐ Recommendation _____

☐ Catalog _____

☐ Other _____

Where did you buy this book?_____

☐ Bookstore (name)_____ City _____

☐ Computer Store (name)_____

☐ Mail Order_____

☐ Other_____

What influenced you in the purchase of this book?

☐ Cover Design

☐ Contents

☐ Other (please specify) _____

_____

What did you find most useful about this book? _____

_____

What did you find least useful about this book? _____

_____

Please add any additional comments. _____

_____

What other subjects will you buy a computer book on soon? _____

_____

What is the best computer book you have used this year?

_____

How did you rate the overall contents of this book?

☐ Excellent   ☐ Good

☐ Average   ☐ Poor

Note: This information will only be used to keep you updated about new Wrox Press titles and will not be used for any other purpose or passed to any other third party.

wrox

NB. If you post the bounce back card below in the UK, please send it to:

Wrox Press Ltd., Arden House, 1102 Warwick Road,
Acocks Green, Birmingham. B27 9BH. UK.

Computer Book Publishers